ENGLISH LITERATURE

OF THE

TWENTIETH CENTURY

With a Postscript on the Nineteen-Fifties

COMPANION VOLUME

———

By R. C. Churchill, M.A.

ENGLISH LITERATURE
OF THE EIGHTEENTH
CENTURY

———

UNIVERSITY TUTORIAL PRESS

ENGLISH LITERATURE

OF THE

TWENTIETH CENTURY

BY

A. S. COLLINS, Ph.D., M.A.

LATE SENIOR LECTURER IN ENGLISH IN THE UNIVERSITY OF LEICESTER
EDITOR OF "TREASURY OF MODERN POETRY"

*With a Postscript on the Nineteen-Fifties
by* FRANK WHITEHEAD, M.A., *Senior Lecturer in
Education, University of Sheffield Institute of
Education*

UNIVERSITY TUTORIAL PRESS LTD

9-10 GREAT SUTTON STREET, LONDON, E.C.1

Published 1951
Second Edition 1954
Third Edition 1956
Fourth Edition 1960
Reprinted 1962, 1965, 1969

SBN: 7231 0030 6 (Paperback)
7231 0031 4 (Full Bound)

PRINTED IN GREAT BRITAIN BY UNIVERSITY TUTORIAL PRESS LTD
FOXTON, NEAR CAMBRIDGE

PREFACE

ALL of us who snatch our reading in the intervals of active living have, I believe, a sensible need of such an introductory guide to the major writers and the main tendencies of our century as I have here ventured to attempt; a survey not too detailed or too opinionated, but, I hope, readable enough and full enough to encourage and enable the reader to find his way.

The present seems an unusually favourable moment at which to make such an attempt—not from any peculiar happiness in the current circumstances of ourselves or of literature or of publishing, but because this century has, in this one matter, been exceptionally kind. Rarely has a half-century evolved so clear a pattern in the sphere of literature. With the passing of the Victorian era, it began with the Indian summer of the old civilisation; the years of the First War had their own character; the twenties, however complex, had a general consistency in their disillusionment above and their modified traditions below; the thirties faced a dark future with growing competence; then in the forties, though during the Second War poetry was amazingly vital, creative power seemed largely to ebb away. At mid-century there is a lull, the landscape of literature is a level one, the giants are gone, the major figures are not young men. Very likely the lull is deceptive, but it gives the chance to look back and see at least the first forty years in a perspective that looks like truth.

I have not tried to please every kind of reader but have tried rather to communicate my own pleasure and appreciation than to be academically critical or historically informative. I trust, nevertheless, that there is adequate introductory criticism and sufficient information.

The concluding *List for Further Reading* is no more than it claims to be.   It shares the aim of the text to be in the nature of an introductory guide.   There the reader can find critical works which will lead him deep into many of the writers, particularly the more "difficult" writers such as Yeats, T. S. Eliot, and James Joyce.   There too he can find comprehensive and detailed books on special aspects of literature. To some of the books listed I am surely indebted for light shed in the years of my reading, but my conscious and unconscious debts to others are, and must be in the very nature of the task, too many to number or to remember.   I should, however, like to express my grateful thanks to Professor Geoffrey Bullough for many helpful criticisms and suggestions.

A. S. COLLINS.

NOTE TO THE FOURTH EDITION

THE present edition contains a Postscript on the Nineteen-Fifties by Frank Whitehead, M.A., Senior Lecturer in Education at the University of Sheffield Institute of Education, who has also made minor alterations and additions elsewhere.

CONTENTS

ENGLISH LITERATURE OF THE TWENTIETH CENTURY

CHAPTER I

HALF A CENTURY

Rarely can any half-century have held such complexity and contradiction, such progress and such retrogression, such marvels and such futility, as the first half of the twentieth century holds for the student of life and letters. The tide of human fortune has swept along with incomparable force, its passage often unpredictable, now forwards, now backwards, breaking up old boundaries, obliterating ancient landmarks, opening up new champaigns, sometimes only to destroy them again. New ideas and new inventions, both for good and for ill, have transformed mankind. In fifty years a whole new world, intellectual and physical, moral and aesthetic, political, social, and economic, has emerged. Yet the common man of the great English-speaking world has kept his head most remarkably amid all these changes. The fundamental truths that in all ages apply to human kind have never been forgotten by most, but, however changed in the manner of their expression, their apprehension has continued to testify to man's basic ideals and unquenchable hopes. Our literature in these years, even if sometimes obscurely, has been faithful to the agelong quest for the good life.

Life never falls truly into neat periods of years, and yet in this half-century each decade seems to offer a not unsatisfactory division, whereby the course of these far-reaching changes can be usefully plotted. In the first decade is the Indian summer of the old world ; in the second, comes the great storm ; in the third, a new world very unsteadily, but hopefully emerges ; in the fourth, disillusion and decay prepare the way for the outbreak of the storm renewed with even more devastating violence ; in the fifth, when the storm is abated, again a new world seeks to arise with a determination more cautious, but even more dauntless.

The first decade, seen from mid-century, can easily appear, especially to those old enough to remember it, a serene and golden time, and to the upper and middle classes in many ways it was so. Below, there was a poverty which the succeeding decades have largely eliminated, but poverty was not then, any more than it generally is, a theme with which creative writers much dealt. Aristocracy still meant a good deal, enough to draw the vehement attack of Lloyd George upon dukes in the course of his crusade for social democracy. But it was chiefly the comfortable middle classes who gave this decade its broad characteristics of material prosperity, a continuing faith in progress, and a rather self-satisfied philistine culture. The established way of life seemed secure ; the tempo of life, though increasing, was still leisurely ; work was agreeably broken by unclouded holidays ; there was time, and the inclination, to laugh and relax. The roads were not crowded ; only birds or balloons occupied the air ; on the high seas the might of Britain's navy inspired the nation with a proud confidence. Field-Marshal Lord Roberts failed in his efforts to warn his countrymen of the impending danger from Germany.

In this first decade, the vitality of our literature was considerable. After the interlude of the "nineties" with their note of lassitude and decadence, a new spirit found various expression. The Boer War had shaken the complacency of the nation. On one hand there was the proud imperial realism of Kipling, preaching active responsibility and fidelity to the agelong spirit of England enshrined in the tales told to the children in *Puck of Pook's Hill*. On another was Bernard Shaw's vision of Fabian Socialism, and H. G. Wells was fascinated by the possibilities of social progress opened up by the wonders of science. G. K. Chesterton, however, equally concerned to implement the coming of a better world, looked back to Merry England and the Middle Ages, as with his wit and fancy he pleaded for a simpler life, lived religiously, communally and heartily. E. M. Forster made war on the conventions of middle-class suburbia, teaching as the good life awareness of personal values and responsibilities. In poetry Masefield followed Kipling in singing of men of action, and not for him the ruler but "the ranker, the tramp of the road".

And yet what represents most truly this first decade in which the sands of the Golden Age were running out ? Signs of the impending storm, of a changing society, of disintegration and rebuilding, were to be seen by the prescient, but prescience is not a quality of the multitude. How that decade was felt by the many who enjoyed it is to be found rather in the novels of Arnold Bennett and Galsworthy. Bennett wrote of the Five Towns, the Potteries, proud of their material prosperity developed with such energy and skill in the previous century that now every corner of the world used their products. Galsworthy, with understanding, if not with approval, depicted the Forsyte way of life, prosperous, stable, and cultured, holding on to the rights and amenities of property. It is the world which the younger novelists, Hugh Walpole and Compton Mackenzie, drew in their earlier novels just as it was approaching its end. The children of that world were to see it no more after their childhood, but we can still feel its value as its children felt them if we read Kenneth Grahame's *Golden Age* or share with Dan and Una the meadows of that pre-machine age where Puck called up the visions of Old England. It was the country England tenaciously loved by Robert Bridges and later elegiacally celebrated by Sir Osbert Sitwell, the background of the great industrial cities of Britain's commercial climax, from which it was still easy to escape—even as it was easy enough to ignore the considerable poverty of the slums, for neither most writers nor those who did not live in them were yet slum-conscious.

Before the storm broke in 1914 tremors shook the industrial and political surface of Britain. A national rail strike in 1911 was followed by a great coal strike in 1912 ; the reign of George V had opened with sharp political strife, and in 1914 the German war broke across the threat of civil war in Ireland. Abroad, these years saw war upon war in the Balkans, and the menacing might of Germany. The sky darkened, but ordinary life still basked in the last golden rays, and young and old in hundreds of thousands greeted the war in Rupert Brooke's spirit of honour renewed and valour refreshed. By Christmas the Allies would celebrate victory in Berlin. It proved far otherwise. Yet for two years of bloody trench warfare and heavy loss of merchant shipping the morale of the nation stood unchanged. Nor did it weaken even in the dark days of March 1918 before the last great German onslaught. But the cruel loss and maiming of kin, and the unlifting strain of the battle-line brought with them disillusionment, doubt, and bitterness. When the strain was at length lifted, victory went to the heads of people and leaders alike. The war to end all wars had been fought and won. Heroism was to be rewarded with a world fit for heroes to live in. For a while recovery seemed to be swift. Many even hoped to pick up the ways of the old life before the war. But, amid the hopes of a new world, the nation realised fully neither the disintegrating forces that had been released nor the extent of the vast loss of spiritual power by exhaustion and death. The flower of a generation had perished.

In literature as in life optimism prevailed in the opening years of this second decade. Masefield courted violence and searched reality, but he loved beauty with a passionate and undimmed faith, and could still, without a hint of impending disaster, bid men "laugh and be proud to belong to the old proud pageant of man". Only the eternal mystery of human life wove the darker threads in the joyous lyrics of W. H. Davies and the haunting beauty of De la Mare. The younger poets who joined together in the Georgian group felt it was a world ready for new poets to sing of natural things in a natural way : they escaped from the towns and were glad. In the novel, H. G. Wells, enjoying the comedy of his little men, and with a mind full of hopeful ideas, taught with almost boisterous confidence that, given the expansive power of science, only planning was needed for an immense advance in civilised living. Arnold Bennett saw no change yet in the secure material path of success. D. H. Lawrence, with his childhood in a mining village not many years behind him, revealed a frightening intensity of passion in his characters, but his early novels, like those of Hugh Walpole and Compton Mackenzie, held no clear portent of the end of an age. In the drama, little change in kind occurred between the beginning of the century and 1914. Bernard Shaw continued his provokingly witty exploration of ideas, and Galsworthy his analysis of social problems. There were plays that satirised the middle classes. There was Barrie with his fantasy and pathos and stagecraft. So in poetry and the novel and the drama the old world remained intact. It is easy to be a prophet after the event, and to find in this pre-war world and its literature signs of the changes to come. When we look back now at T. S. Eliot's *Love Song of J. Alfred Prufrock*, we cannot but read into it an awareness of a dying world. But the truth remains that in that world as a whole there was no such recognition.

When the war came in August 1914, the poets greeted it as patriots sure of their cause. How high the initial enthusiasm ran in many can be read in C. E. Montague's impression of the early months among the new army in *Disenchantment*. Rupert Brooke voiced this feeling at its highest when he declared, "Now, God be thanked Who matched us with His hour", but John Freeman too wrote "Happy is England now", and even old Thomas Hardy said, "Press we to the field ungrieving". From H. G. Wells came *Mr Britling Sees it Through*. It was some two years before the poets felt the futilities of war more than its possibilities of glory and noble sacrifice. Siegfried Sassoon then with satiric anger dealt with the money-makers at home who gloried cheaply in the sacrifices of those at the front. The pathos of slaughtered youth and of survivors shattered in mind and body became a burden he could hardly endure. In hospital Wilfred Owen caught poetic inspiration from him. Edmund Blunden applied his pastoral observation and his feeling imagination to the bloody fields of France. When the war ended, Osbert Sitwell mocked with bitter irony at the whole business of war, battened on by the civilians entrenched in England and convention. In 1917 appeared Norman Douglas's *South Wind*, ironically detached from the contemporary scene—its time was not yet, but in a few years its unsettling wit and intelligence were to harmonise with the post-war atmosphere. As the war ended, H. G. Wells in *Joan and Peter* resumed his pleading for an efficient, progressive, planned civilisation. He had an urgent sense of "the generations rushing to waste like rapids". Something must be done. But he kept his humour alongside his visions.

It is still very difficult to see the twenties in perspective. This decade can easily appear a welter of contraries—of hope and despair, of the will to peace and an uprush of violence, of energy and exhaustion, of revived faith and growing scepticism, of high responsibilities recognised and irresponsibility rampant. It can also be over-simplified by looking at it through the work of outstanding writers. T. S. Eliot's *Waste Land* appeared as early as 1922, and a vision of the twenties was created in the light of that poem which was rather a myth than the truth. The young men and women of Aldous Huxley's early novels also suggested that the young had lost their morals, their faith, and their hope, and that their elders were little better. Michael Arlen's best-selling novel, *The Green Hat*, was quoted to over-emphasise the craze for living too fast to last. The dangerous General Strike of 1926 and the mounting unemployment can loom too large for a true picture.

Perhaps the truth may be that as a whole the nation had lost in many spheres its sense of security, and, further bewildered by new ideas and changed values, had no clear vision before it. It certainly did not lack vitality and hope. Its hope, indeed, was so large as to outrun reality, not so much transmuting the grim experience of the war into wisdom as forgetting it. Its vitality found expression in the idealism of the League of Nations Union, in considerable social advance despite great unemployment, and indeed in all the fields of work and sport. To see this decade as a Waste Land is like seeing the England of the days of Charles the Second through the lives and writings of its lax and cynical Court and ignoring the England that was at the same time the England of Bunyan and Wren and Isaac Newton, and of hundreds of thousands whom the disease and follies of the royal Court never touched. So the England of this decade is not to be seen through the satires of Noel Coward and Aldous Huxley, nor through the hopeless sensitivity of T. S. Eliot (who had yet to achieve the penitence of Ash Wednesday), nor through any glass that magnifies admitted ills of the decade.

This decade must be seen, moreover, with a recognition of its various strata : as, for example, those too young to have known battle, many of whom grew up restlessly to feel cheated of an experience ; the returned soldiers who had seen too much to resume life as it had been, or enough to make them nurse their remaining possibilities with anxious quietude or throw them away in reckless despair ; the multitude who had lost their nearest and dearest ; those who had weathered the storm as civilians, as against the soldiers; the women to whom the war had brought greater emancipation, of which the parliamentary vote was no insignificant part. The existence of these and many other broad and varying strata did not make for national unity. Nor should other factors be ignored, such as the influx into the universities of ex-service students, the development of broadcasting, the rising standard of living resulting in part from the growing acceleration in the mass production of goods, and the drawing together of town and country by improved transport and other services. Demarcation between social classes became much less distinct. But the young became, perhaps more than ever, further away from the old in their ideas, though their elders made great efforts to keep pace with them, for the emphasis fell very strongly on youth in those years when so many of the generation that would have been in the maturity of their middle years had gone. Indeed, all things considered, it is no wonder that the twenties were heady and distracted and full of contrarieties.

The literature of this third decade well represented all its complexity. H. G. Wells still led the vanguard of progressive thought, sure that the World State must come in due time as a blessing to men, and putting an undiminished confidence in a planned economy as the means to realising the finest aspirations of the human race—still sufficiently unaware of the Waste Land to indulge in the high spirits of *Bealby*. That the old order was passing, not without hope of a better, was more quietly expressed in the later Forsyte tales of Galsworthy or in such novels as Hugh Walpole's *Wintersmoon* and *Young Enchanted*. Aldous Huxley made all the newest ideas the incidental topics of novels which displayed the post-war a-morality, disillusion, and cynicism, and encouraged the young to adopt them as at least a pose. D. H. Lawrence had developed almost an idolatry, mystically apprehended, of violence and sexual passion. The new psychological knowledge, particularly of the subconscious mind and the theories of Freud and Jung, had an ever-deepening effect on literature, and very notably influenced the work of James Joyce and Virginia Woolf. There was much that was typical of the new generation in *The Flax of Dream* of Henry Williamson, in which he traced the life of his hero through the psychology of childhood and youth to his retreat, after service in France, from the fever of post-war gaiety to a cottage in Devon, where his now pacifist idealism was inspired by the nature-worship of Richard Jefferies and in part by Christ. E. M. Forster, however, nearly twenty years older than Williamson, though he too seemed to wish for a faith, could in his final novel, *A Passage to India*, see less hope than before of solving the problems of human division. The general public, one may note, supplied no demand for novels of the great war until some ten years after its close.

From some of the foremost poets came the darkest views of the twenties. Thomas Hardy, now over eighty, in his preface to a volume of his lyrics in 1922 declared sombrely that "men's minds appear . . . to be moving backwards rather than on". Yeats in *The Second Coming* saw anarchy rising in bloody violence to inaugurate a new and bestial age. Edith Sitwell, after startling the conventional and the impercipient with her new imagery and her technical experiments, during years when she created abundant beauty while acutely conscious of the materialism of the age in many ways, came in 1929 to her *Gold Coast Customs*, a symbolic poem of dark intensity, of which she wrote later: "it was written with anguish and I would not willingly re-live that birth". T. S. Eliot saw his vision of the Waste Land and the Hollow Men, seeking in cold despair a personal salvation through the culture of the ages, until he abandoned that for penitential renunciation to refresh his spirit.

But there were others less sensitive to the slowly impending doom. Elder poets like Binyon and Alfred Noyes celebrated the wonder of the machine age with caution but with no haunting fear. W. H. Davies and De la Mare changed little in their song, and neither did Masefield or the Georgians until their movement died away. Victoria Sackville-West sang pastorally in *The Land* with her eyes still truly fixed in the old fashion on the everlasting importance of agriculture and the imperturbable recurrence of the seasons. Edmund Blunden, as his memories of Flanders gradually found their proper place in the new context, chose the middle way where things human and natural, sanctified and confirmed by time, could bring their relative reassurance. From South Africa a young poet, Roy Campbell, in 1924 had put a Byronic energy into his *Flaming Terrapin*, and no doubt there were many young Englishmen capable of sharing its vitality. But it must be admitted that in those years the *Last Poems* of A. E. Housman, bringing back with them *A Shropshire Lad* of nearly a quarter of a century earlier, won from the rising generation an immediate response to their bitter and classical perfection.

The thirties, turbulent enough, seem however an easier theme for generalisation. The nation, having largely failed in the preceding decade to come to grips with its inherent destiny, appeared to ride forward almost without control to its second deadly testing. Among the younger, pacific idealism culminated in the lofty but ineffectual reactions through the League of Nations Union to the Italian rape of Abyssinia. Idealism of the Left with true insight appreciated the crucial nature of the Spanish Civil War, and yet in Britain the Labour party on the very brink of the European war opposed conscription. A great Conservative majority had been the nation's answer to the economic crisis of 1931, but on the Right there was no clearer vision in the sphere of economics than in the matter of international politics. Though among the younger people, especially those of the Left, the dangers to existing civilisation were ominously apparent, and in spite of Winston Churchill's warnings (to which might be added Rudyard Kipling's stern prophecy in his *Storm Cone* of 1932), the nation as a whole seemed determined to the last to believe that somehow good would be the final goal of ill. There were those who saw what Churchill saw, but they were few ; many felt that the state of things was rotten and called for a radical cure ; most lived, with or without ideals, as happily as might be from day to day under the ever lowering skies. At length all that lay in Munich and its rapid aftermath moulded the nation's mind and set it for the storm to beat upon.

For a while H. G. Wells had still looked for the fulfilment of his hopes, but, as the years passed, not the triumph but the death of humankind in self-induced disaster loomed before his vision. Aldous Huxley, who had never loved mankind, began to consider some way of saving its soul, as *Eyeless in Gaza* showed. E. M. Forster, vocal only in essays, confessed that he would have embraced the communist ideal had he had fewer years and so a younger courage, but he must remain in the liberal humanism from which T. S. Eliot had moved away to denounce the non-Christian approach with the mournful ardour of a minor prophet, half-possessed of the vision of a philosophic mystic. Religion of one kind or another was indeed much preached in those days, as in the erotic biological mysticism of John Cowper Powys.

But it was the group of young poets headed by Auden which made the most coherent and significant literary contribution to this fourth decade. When they began to write a little before 1930, they felt isolated from their audience, but within a few years they established contact. A much wider reading public was coming into existence, young, eager, and serious, partly contemporary in origin with these new poets and partly brought into existence by them. Plays like the Auden-Isherwood *Dog Beneath the Skin* and *The Ascent of F6* brought in more followers to join those who already by 1934 were in sympathy with the spirit expressed by Day Lewis in his *A Hope for Poetry*. These young poets believed in the Waste Land, but instead of despairing proposed to cure it. Auden led the way, and their poetry emulated left-wing propaganda both successfully and to its own confusion. They had vision and high talents, but, as MacNeice confessed in *Autumn Journal* in 1938 and as Auden showed by his withdrawal to America, their vision, though keen, was too partial. Neither party politics nor partisan poetry, however vital the latter, could win a national victory. Still younger poets, like Dylan Thomas and George Barker, equally impressed by the darkness and disease of their environment, with less presumption wrote rather to cure and please themselves alone. In that, though less intelligible even to a section of the nation, they were perhaps nearer the general way the nation lived while Hitler, not quite inexcusably, misjudged it.

The last decade of this half-century is too familiar to recount and too close to see clearly. Its literary output seems the least remarkable of the whole period of fifty years. First, the prosecution of the war took the greater part of men's energies ; then, the conditions in which the peace had to be won were so stringent that the creative spirit apparently failed to find an outlet. The paper shortage, which made even the English classics for a time unobtainable, denied to publishers and periodicals any considerable chance of encouraging new writers ; at least no new writers of outstanding promise have so far emerged.

One has the impression that particularly after the war ended the output of informative writing predominated over that of the higher creative literature. The prelude to the war and its course in all the many fields of operation were examined and told. The public demanded and received book after book, large and small, to give it facts and views about the innumerable problems, international and domestic, which cried out for solution and on which men's minds were divided. The cloud of economic testimony overshadowed nearly everything that was written. Naturally, however, for sheer relief the output of fiction was large, but even on the shelves of the circulating libraries, among the closely packed novels of entertainment in romance and detection, were many attempts to give through imaginary narratives knowledge of the contemporary and recent world, and even forecasts of the future like George Orwell's *Nineteen-Eighty-Four*. Moreover, popular informative literature abounded on every topic from psychology to archaeology, and surely at no period was it better or more attractively written. Broadcasting had no doubt prepared a large public, and equally it would seem to have taught the specialists the art of winning the mind as well as the ears of the largest audiences.

Yet this fifth decade was not without its notable, and even great literature. Great poetry had not died with Yeats in 1939. During the war Edith Sitwell, from whom no poetry had come in the thirties, produced poems unsurpassable for the depth of their humanity and the perfection of their craftsmanship. In the same years T. S. Eliot crowned his achievement with his *Quartets*. Poetry indeed seemed a remarkable contribution in our war effort; it came from so many poets, and from so many new young poets, to the great credit of publishers for producing it. On the whole perhaps it showed more talent and vitality than full achievement, but much was good, and some no doubt will last. Names are so numerous that it is probably invidious to select any, but there were Alun Lewis, Sidney Keyes, John Pudney, Anne Ridler, Laurence Whistler, to pick but a few. Nor were elder poets like De la Mare and Robert Graves and Herbert Read silent. The work, however, of those who had promised so much in the thirties, Auden, Day Lewis, Stephen Spender, and MacNeice, hardly fulfilled that promise. Day Lewis grew most in poetic stature; Auden had found no new strength or insight in America. Of other poets of the thirties, Dylan Thomas and George Barker justified their earlier admirers. But looking at the poetic scene as a whole it seems as though, with the ending of hostilities, the tide of poetic inspiration ebbed away from a hopeful flood to a mere trickle.

The English tongue had been used with all the force and fire of genius by Winston Churchill in his speeches in time of war, and when it was won his account of *The Second World War* joined his earlier volumes on *The World Crisis* in the roll of great histories. But it might be claimed that the greatest achievement in this decade in the realm of pure artistry in creative prose was the autobiographical volumes of Sir Osbert Sitwell, re-creating the old world, and especially the remarkable figure of his father; this exciting retrospection and the welcome it had from the reading public spoke of a widespread nostalgia in the austere post-war days when the future was being persistently planned, but showed a marked reluctance to emerge as ideally as was hoped.

As for the novel, its practitioners reached a high average level, but few of them really stood out by the force of individual vision and interpretation of life. Graham Greene, indeed, could not be mistaken as he continued to analyse the problem of evil and make his sinners bear their crosses to their crucifixion. Elizabeth Bowen, little behind Jane Austen in her satiric appreciation of the social comedy, not infrequently penetrated below the surface with her pitiful irony. But no novelists stood out in those years as Wells, Conrad, Bennett, and Galsworthy had done thirty years before, nor as Lawrence and Huxley and Virginia Woolf, or Walpole and Compton Mackenzie and Sheila Kaye Smith and the Powys brothers— and the list could go on. Now the roll of novelists seemed less distinguished, though it is impossible to deny distinction to such novelists as Evelyn Waugh and Charles Morgan and Alex Comfort. And among literary critics there was considerable re-examination of the values of literature, as by such academic scholars as Tillyard and Willey. But they again were of an older generation. How far, while power lay dormant, this decade was a great germinal period for literature remains to be seen.

CHAPTER II

YEATS

We may well approach the poetry of this half-century through Yeats, because not only did his long life, begun in 1865, stretch to 1939, but his poetry mirrored much of the changing spirit of the years. Rarely has even a great poet been so responsive to change, and shown himself as an old man so able to understand the thoughts of the young. In fifty years he evolved from a dreamer to a realist, and from a realist to a passionate metaphysical seer. Thought and passion drove him all his life. He was a poet all the time, and a great poet.

Yeats was born in Ireland, son of a pre-Raphaelite painter ; his brother, Jack Butler Yeats, was a notable artist too, and Yeats himself as a young man studied art for three years. Though as a boy he moved to London, his holidays were in the wild country of Sligo in Western Ireland, and there his soul was fashioned. There peasant and squire alike lived in an old world rich in folklore and folksong. The boy's imagination entered fairyland, and he was bewitched for life into a longing for magic. From the very soil of ancient Eire he drank the "dream of the noble and the beggarman", and for ever after the modern world seemed to him vulgar, and not real in any essential way. As a poet he grew up the last of the romantics, and the last of the aristocrats, unweariedly seeking the eternal reality behind the shows of time, even with the aid of clairvoyants and astrologists, and of his wife's automatic writing.

Yeats complained that as a young man he had been "deprived by Huxley and Tyndall, whom [he] detested, of the simpleminded religion of [his] childhood". This had driven him to make a new religion out of old Irish myth and poetry. Reacting from the modern scientific outlook, he consistently scorned science : facts in themselves meant nothing

in the spiritual universe of elemental forces which he perceived. He fell early under the influence of the French symbolist poets, finding in them "the only movement . . . saying
new things", yet it had not much that was new to teach one
who was already steeped in the highly symbolical poetry of
Ireland, and he had his own symbols. Again as a young man
Pater reinforced his belief in passion and sensation, and in the
pursuit of the finest artistic expression, but the pride of the
artist was already in his blood. He scorned the "new com-
monness" of democratic equality, and he had no faith in
"progress" as it was understood : instead he adopted a theory
of history revolving in cycles of two thousand years. Life was
a reservoir of racial memories, from which the poet could draw
by the magic of symbolic evocation.

Yeats never turned aside from this attitude, but the practical side of life in due time won upon him. With his deep
imaginative feeling for Ireland he could not fail to be brought,
for a time at least, into the political movement for a national
Ireland. The revival of the Irish drama saw him not only in
the rôle of poet-dramatist but taking a practical part in the
managing of the Abbey Theatre. Indeed the public and practical side of Yeats's life must not be underestimated : the
Senator of the Irish Free State parliament is an integral part
of the man. And the tension between the dreamer and the
man of affairs, between the poetic and the practical life, was
a dynamic force in his poetic creation. To the end he was
never quite sure which was the true path : to enjoy life to
the full, rejoicing in every note of the sensual music, even "if
it be life to pitch Into the frog spawn of a blind man's ditch",
or to pursue the eternal, to control life by the magic of art
and symbolism, to compel his soul "to study in a learned
school" until he was gathered up "into the artifice of eternity".

As the years passed, Yeats developed a striking, enigmatic
personality. It was a riddle not easy to read, this strange
compound of opposites, but impossible to ignore, for this
great prophetic artist was also a great showman, and riding
his personality with more and more spirit he delighted to
parade his sensibilities and prejudices in naked pride. He

who had followed "the old high way of love" made no com-
promises with the new world. "There is not a fool can call
me friend." In *A Prayer for my Daughter* he would have her
"live like some green laurel, Rooted in one dear perpetual
place", where "the soul recovers radical innocence, And
learns at last that it is self-delighting"; let "her bridegroom
bring her to a house, Where all's accustomed, ceremonious".
So the old poet in his lonely tower on the remote Irish shore
spoke always with passionate assurance, his eyes upon the
ancient Japanese sword of exquisite workmanship on his table,
and his tower no symbol of retreat but of one who still felt the
urgent drive to assert his values, torn by the struggle between
his dying body and the undying fire in his heart and brain.
But still,

> "only an aching heart
> Conceives a changeless work of art".

The earlier poetry of Yeats kept to one general manner for
some fifteen years, from the middle eighties to the end of
the century. The influence of the Pre-Raphaelites, followed by that of the French symbolists and of Walter
Pater, and by his association with Arthur Symons and the
Yellow Book group, brought him very close to the poets
who embraced the theory of Art for Art's sake. "Grey truth
is now her painted toy", he said of the modern world,
and he would have none of it, holding that "words
alone are certain good", the beauty of poetry the
only lasting truth. From the current day and the present
place he sought refuge in singing of fairyland and "of old
Eire, and the ancient ways". In several poems he used the
Rose as a symbol, noting later that "the quality symbolised
as the Rose differs from the Intellectual Beauty of Shelley
and Spenser in that I have imagined it as suffering with man,
and not as something pursued and seen from afar". Suffering, indeed, is the sad tone of most of these early poems.
The Sad Shepherd tells of a "man whom Sorrow named his
friend". The poet will "make the cloak of Sorrow"; he
imagines himself dreaming as he lies "buried under the sleepy
ground", or he speaks through an old man who has come to feel

that the Junes were warmer, the waves gayer, the herring more plentiful, the girls prettier "when I was a boy with never a crack in my heart". It is "the hour of the waning of love", and where love holds the world is no place for it, but "I would that we were, my beloved, white birds on the foam of the sea". To greyhaired Cuchulain in his bitter grief for his slaying of his own son whom he had not known death comes as a boon. As for "this tragic Eire", it is "that country where a man can be so crossed . . . that he's a loveless man".

All this sadness brimmed with languorous beauty of sound and rhythm and word and image, until *The Wind Among the Reeds* of 1899 was the last and the best volume of this kind. There he mourns for the change that has come upon him and his beloved, and he longs for the end of the world. Perfect beauty ever lures and is ever unattainable as in *The Song of Wandering Aengus* sung by a man now old with seeking the "glimmering girl with the apple blossom in her hair", whom in her first form as a little silver trout he had caught with his hazel wand as his rod and a berry for his bait. Now as Yeats sought perfect beauty he felt that "the wrong of unshapely things is a wrong too great to be told", and out of the realisation of the "wrong of unshapely things" a new strength was soon to come into his poetry.

As late as 1899 Yeats still believed that the true course was to "liberate the arts from 'their age' and from life". "I believe", he wrote, "that all men will more and more reject the opinion that poetry is a 'criticism of life' and be more and more convinced that it is a revelation of a hidden life". But with the new century a change soon came in his ideas and his poetry. In 1906 he wrote that "surely the idea of culture expressed by Pater can only create feminine souls". He was influenced by his friendship with the poet and dramatist Synge, who in 1908 expressed his view of poetry thus in the preface to his poems : "The poetry of exaltation will be always the highest ; but when men lose their poetic feeling for ordinary life, and cannot write poetry of ordinary things, their exalted poetry is likely to lose its strength of exaltation . . . In these days poetry is usually a flower of evil or good ;

but it is the timber of poetry that wears most surely, and there is no timber that has not strong roots among the clay and worms . . . It may almost be said that before verse can be human again it must learn to be brutal". No doubt Yeats's association with the nationalist movement in Irish politics also helped to change his ideas.

He did not publish much poetry in the first decade, giving himself mainly to the drama. When the *Green Helmet* volume appeared in 1910, he was well on the way to being a different poet, now acknowledging "the moral element in poetry" and the need for the arts to be "accepted into the social order and become a part of life". Inwardly he was distressed in a deeper way than before, having found bitterness and disillusion both in love and in politics, which for him had been an inseparable experience, for she whom he had loved in "the old high way of love", Maud Gonne, had led him into those tortured politics. He still pursued the old, high and hard path of art, but with a spirit distracted by "the seeming needs of my fool-driven land", and a heart vexed by the fickle, wilful and ignorant audiences of the Abbey Theatre, and chilled by "the timid breath" of commercialism to contempt of the approaching time when "all things at one common level lie". For a while he was denied that exaltation of the imagination from which alone comes poetic energy. The apparent decline of modern Ireland had blotted out the glamour of ancient Eire. One poem, *No Second Troy*, for the first time spoke with the fulness of new assurance, its rhetoric a weapon cold and strong, forged in the banked fires of feeling. But on the whole he was only working out his new manner, and it was somewhat flat, as he tried what was direct and austere, and forswore the old fashion when he sang as if "he had a sword upstairs". Now he says, "I may wither into the truth", and he would be "colder and dumber and deafer than a fish". He was also beginning that pruning of his earlier poetry that has taken some of the dreaminess and languor from it in the text we read to-day.

Responsibilities of 1914 was something of a resting place. Yeats, now nearly fifty, had stepped into his new world, and that world in Ireland as in Europe was still at peace, and so, with reservations, was Yeats. The volume bore a motto : "In dreams begins responsibility". Dreams are not abjured, but are seen as the starting place and no longer the goal of truth. His old manner, the "coat covered with embroideries out of old mythologies", is with quiet scorn thrown away : now for Yeats "there's more enterprise in walking naked".

His philosophical poem *The Dolls* through its allegory of the indignation of the dolls when the dollmaker's wife had a baby expressed the two poles from the one to the other of which Yeats continued to be drawn—the ideal of the unbreakable serenity of artifice and the fact of the crude warmth of life. But now he seemed to move more towards life. At any rate, he had left fairyland. Bitterly he lamented in September 1913 that "Romantic Ireland's dead and gone" : was it for this petty and malicious generation, for those who hated Synge's *Playboy of the Western World*, that Edward Fitzgerald and Robert Emmet and Wolfe Tone had died—for this, "all that delirium of the brave" ? With ironical joy he noted of the proud wayward squirrel that "no government appointed him". There is a thread of bitterness in the volume, but it goes with wisdom, strength and health, and carries a generous hatred of malice and meanness. He who has known the fool's triumph, and "love lost as soon as won", and "the best labourer dead and all the sheaves to bind" can with the pity of fore-knowledge ask in his faultless lyric *To a Child Dancing in the Wind* what need she, being young, has "to dread the monstrous crying of wind", and accept for himself and for us all the sad implicit answer. This lyric and its partner, *Two Years Later*, are as bare as rock, as cold and clear as a spring, and their voice is that of wind and water.

The Wild Swans at Coole in its title poem evokes a clear image of "those brilliant creatures . . . unwearied still . . . mysterious, beautiful", ever to delight men's eyes. But it is 1919, and his "heart is sore" ; this volume came three years after the Easter Rising. The unleashing of violence made a deep impression on Yeats. He had not expected it from the

dull faces as he had seen them. He was fascinated. Of a
sudden all seemed "changed utterly : a terrible beauty is
born". In the following years many notable poems arose
from his brooding upon the bloody violence of the civil war.
Yeats seemed to feel that in this violence lay creative power
as well as destruction, and that cyclic destiny itself had called
it forth: Louis MacNeice indeed later deduced "the fact that
Yeats had a budding fascist inside himself". Certainly his
imagination grew exalted again, as he saw evil gathering head.

In *The Second Coming* the power of the seer came upon
him, and he prophesied the dawn of an evil age. The horror of
these "dragon-ridden" days weighed upon, but did not
depress him, though against their anarchy the philosophers
who had "planned to bring the world under a rule" seemed
"but weasels fighting in a hole". Instead he acclaimed with
all the more passion the strength of the solitary soul, as
though he drank in energy from the high-charged atmosphere
of the times. In his remote tower, raging against his own
oncoming old age, he felt that he had never possessed imagination "more excited, passionate, fantastical . . . no, not in
boyhood". Poetically writing his will, he chose "upstanding
men that climb the streams" to inherit his pride,

> "The pride of people that were
> Bound neither to Cause nor to State".

In his later volumes, of which *The Tower* of 1928 and *The
Winding Stair* of 1933 probably contain his very finest achievement, all is proud, but all is not violent. It was in 1919 that
he summed up the qualities he would wish for his daughter—
radical innocence, housed in custom and ceremony, and free
from hatred. The proud magnificence of *Byzantium* and
Sailing to Byzantium seems to declare that he has finally
rejected the sensual music for the artifice of eternity. In
Among School Children as "a sixty-year-old smiling public
man" his "heart is driven wild" when the image of her whom
he had loved so long ago swims vividly into his mind, but his
complex feelings issue in the eternal question, "How can we
know the dancer from the dance ?"—how know the soul

apart from the body without which we have never known it, or even know which is soul and which is body. Philosophical questions tease his ever-questing mind : there is a war of opposites within us—is the artist driven to seek his opposite, Dante driven to build, in his worship of Beatrice, a Dante quite other than he whom his friends knew ? But in other moods not all the perfection of art, neither philosophy nor knowledge, could command Yeats : he "would be . . . ignorant and wanton as the dawn", he would "mock Plotinus' thought and cry in Plato's teeth", he held

> "Wisdom is the property of the dead,
>   A something incompatible with life ; and power,
>   Like everything that has the stain of blood,
>   A property of the living".

So in his *Prayer for Old Age* he prays to be guarded "from those thoughts men think in the mind alone". To the end his shall be the joint force of mind and senses. In his late "Crazy Jane" poems the salty realism of the madwoman proclaims how sensual truth is, and Tom the lunatic lives and dies in the faith that it is the vigour of the blood that gives to every form of life its individual value in the eye of God. Yet to the end the enigma of his great personality spoke in the words he wrote in 1938 for his epitaph in Drumcliffe churchyard :—

> "Cast a cold eye
>   On life, on death.
>   Horseman, pass by !"

The words of the great rhetorican ring out : in all his work, more perhaps than any other great poet, he used words not for the eye, not even for the ear, but to compel the lips.

CHAPTER III

POETRY UP TO 1914

What confidence and what joy mark much of the poetry of the first fourteen years of the century! Unrest of soul and introspection had little place, whether the poet was young or old. Poets sang and told stories as if that were the purpose of poetry. There was high seriousness, but it often went with high spirits. England and her heritage was something to rejoice in with pride. Beauty abounded undefiled. *Honour* was a word that had not lost its value, and poets could unashamedly declare their happiness. Bridges and Watson, Kipling and Chesterton and Belloc, W. H. Davies and De la Mare, Binyon and Alfred Noyes, Rupert Brooke and Flecker —such were the poets, whose work leaves us with this impression.

Some of the poets of these years were already well known in the preceding century. Hardy, then sixty but only then beginning to publish and to write most of his poetry, to our eyes overtops them all except Yeats as a writer. Yeats was in 1900 coming to the end of his first poetic period. Francis Thompson, to die in 1907, belongs rather to the years before. Bridges had some thirty years of poetic achievement behind him. William Watson had found the even tenor of his way, and so had Alice Meynell. It was Kipling whom all the English-speaking world at the turn of the century acclaimed as the greatest living poet. Binyon had already made a quiet entry, and Belloc stepped briskly in. Those who began to come before the public in the first years of the century included Masefield, W. H. Davies, De la Mare, Alfred Noyes, Chesterton, Wilfrid Gibson, and Gordon Bottomley. There was also Stephen Phillips, whose peculiar blend of the decadence of the eighteen-nineties with that of the Jacobeans seems to wear the least well among the work of all these poets. Then in the years just before the war a new generation of poets appeared, notably Rupert Brooke and Flecker, J. C. Squire and others of the Georgian group, and D. H. Lawrence. It makes fourteen years in which poetry showed a varied and vital abundance.

The two elder poets, Hardy and Bridges, were complete contrasts to one another in almost every way. In the poetry of Bridges his full Christian faith shone with sustaining power through all he wrote. Lacking that faith, Hardy had nothing so positive to offer, neither strength nor joy. Bridges, setting before himself love, beauty and honour, by no means failed to see the worst, but Hardy felt so compelled to take a full look at the worst that he was seldom in the mood to imagine the noblest. So it may be said that they represented the old world and the new—Bridges the passing age when men believed in God and in the need for men to follow the law of Christ in all hope and humility, Hardy bringing in the new century, with its declining faith and growing fear. Seen in that way Hardy's work may well possess the greater significance in the study of this half-century, for his view of life was more in harmony with its development, and as the years passed he became prophetically aware of the growing illness of civilisation. Indeed Hardy had in his earlier years as a novelist diagnosed the modern disease inherent in the dying of one faith without a new one to fill its place. But the consistent tragic vision with which he imagined the world of his novels may well have been for some time rather due to his temperament than to a truly prophetic insight. Nor, if Hardy's view has proved more in harmony with the major trends in life and literature, must it be ignored that the faith of Bridges, if not always with the full strength of his assurance, has never ceased to play an integral and supporting part in the national life.

Some have claimed for Hardy's poetry the greatness acknowledged in his novels. *The Dynasts* indeed, which was his major publication in the first decade, is a great work, but much of it is prose. His poetry is mainly lyric, and it makes a large volume, published between 1898 (though some was written earlier) and 1922, but changing little in essentials. It differs little from his novels either in its themes or in the purpose and view of life behind it. *Wessex Poems* and *Time's Laughingstocks* are true titles. It is largely of Wessex he writes, and of characters in that elder Wessex of the last century, where the impact of modern thought was beginning to be felt, but where the way of life was still hardly affected. The poet sees man as the sport of circumstances ; the power behind the universe takes no personal interest in him, and in producing beauty "has other aims than [man's] delight". He tells tales of tragic irony, of frustrated love, of passion followed by disillusion, misery and deceit, of a teasing woman who provokes tragedy, of lost faith. At times, despite the unpromising evidence, he yearns to be hopeful, and often a pity and tenderness for all creatures warms his writing. *The Dynasts*, which is both epic and drama, narrative and lyric, and tells the story of Europe between the battles of Trafalgar and Waterloo, has the massive strength of a high and complex theme shaped by a powerful mind. The epic machinery of the Choruses of Spirits gives Hardy the fullest scope to express his view of men as driven to their destinies by the unfeeling abstract forces of the universe.

In his verse Hardy was his own master : the Dorset dialect poet, William Barnes, alone had any influence upon him. Rejecting the musical poetry of Tennyson and his other contemporaries, he early found his own manner, often harsh, bare and hard, not seldom clumsy and prosaic, but achieving much in its total effect and capable of spontaneity and beauty. His thought and feeling were more important to Hardy than his technique, and so again he offers another contrast to the very conscious prosodic craftsmanship of Bridges.

Robert Bridges could not compete with Hardy in public notice. His contemplative poetry possessed no great popular appeal, and with an aristocratic self-possession he was indifferent to fame. When at the age of sixty-nine he was appointed Poet-Laureate in 1913, he was comparatively unknown, and for some years his small output excited satiric comment. Indeed, it was by his anthology, *The Spirit of Man* in 1917, that he first won general notice, and it was his great age and the crusted splendour of *The Testament of Beauty* in 1929

that gained him fame at the end. In this first decade, his production fell away, after many volumes of lyric, and sonnet,
and narrative poetry had shown the few who cared what a
fine artistry, serenely informed by a noble spirit, could achieve
in poetry. The love of the poetic art was his high stimulus,
and content to abide its exacting discipline he expressed his
sense of beauty in love and landscape, and his joy in all things,
and not least in the devout pursuit of duty. In his own life
he had found a deep personal happiness, and it gave a sweet
resonance and a pure integrity to his song of normal and even
commonplace things. However, in the first decade his poetry
fell below its best, and his experiments in classical prosody
were experiments rather than satisfying poems. But in 1913
he found a new strength, as *Noel: Christmas Eve 1913* testifies. It was a metrical triumph in a new rhythm, which
wedded natural speech rhythm to poetic tradition, for it was
consciously evolved from his study of Milton's prosody. At
peace in the comfort of Christ, the old poet

"on the hill
Heark'ning in the aspect
of th'eternal silence"

to the "constellated sounds" of the bells pealing from the
village churches in the valley below fully justified his choice
as the new Laureate.

Laurence Binyon, twenty-five years younger than Bridges,
brought a similar poetic quality into the new century, though
his muse also was too restrained and sought to continue and
renew the traditions of English poetry in too unspectacular
a way to attract the many. Yet Kipling himself, who had
made poetry popular again in the nineties, became in these
years a quieter and deeper poet. It is as though this last
golden age before the storm gave to most poets serenity and
balance, strength and assurance to sing of the lasting things.
Kipling had come to startle with his new theme of the common
soldier. After *Barrack Room Ballads*, his knowledge of hard
facts, his gifts of the telling word and the rich vocabulary,
his vital rhythms and metrical inventions, his story-telling
power, his emotional appeal, his conviction of our imperial

destiny, had all been applied to command the widest response to his songs and ballads. But after the Boer war he turned away from *Boots* and *Danny Deever*, from *McAndrew's Hymn* and *The Ballad of East and West*, even somewhat from the stern monitory pride of *Recessional*.

It was not that Kipling changed his views. He believed no less in "The White Man's Burden"; he feared no less that the dykes our fathers made might burst from neglect and sloth; he scorned no less the little men who looked down on the work of the great proconsuls. He still relished what he had relished before. To the end he remained in spirit closer to the Old Testament than to the New, with his fearful half-pagan worship of the Lord God of Hosts, whose secular deputies were "the Gods of the Copybook Headings". What he believed in his heart, whether indeed his courage masked an ultimate scepticism, will always be hard to decide, for in spite of his seemingly open qualities, which won his public, he had an essential reticence. But in this period between the end of the Boer war and the outbreak of the 1914 war we see the happiest Kipling, least given to grim warnings or bitter ironies, and the quietest Kipling.

In 1902 Kipling settled in Sussex. He had visited South Africa, and having actually seen war for the first time he was less warlike. His Sussex home was his first real English home, and he fell in love with Sussex, and lived as far as possible in the retirement he always preferred to publicity. Here he wrote *Puck of Pook's Hill* and *Rewards and Fairies*, and it is the poems attached to these stories that are his most significant poetry in these years. *Sussex* shows him giving his heart to this "one spot . . . beloved over all", "till the sure magic strike" when he and the soil shall be one. The magic did strike, and begot in him that visionary power which, extending beyond Sussex, brought old pagan Britain, and Roman Britain, and all England's following centuries, a land and peoples far removed and yet still living, into his vivid, brooding imagination. This England was "not any common Earth . . . but Merlin's Isle of Gramerye", whose days had been

rich with knowledge both for joy and tears ages before Domes-
day Book was made. The old gods and the fairies live again,
and the dark woods breathe their mysteries. The magic has
struck into his verses the power of quiet incantation, till we
know that a handful of English earth can "make whole . . . the
festered soul", and a posy of her flowers "cleanse and purify
webbed and inward-turning eye". But in his timeless vision
he knows that Cities and Thrones and Powers are born but
to a brief life, and that still "Iron—Cold Iron—is master of
men all!"

It was 1911 before Masefield made his name with *The
Everlasting Mercy*, but his first volume, *Salt Water Ballads*,
published in 1902 when he was twenty-four, had declared the
coming of a considerable new poet. From the time when,
after a childhood in Herefordshire, he was apprenticed to a
merchant ship as a boy of fourteen, he had seen a good deal
of life. He had not only served on the high seas, but he had
tramped the roads and worked on the farms of America, and
earned a hard living as odd-job man in a New York hotel.
So when he sang of ships and sailors and the open road, he
sang with knowledge, and for him, as for Kipling, to whose
example he was indebted, the common man speaking his
mother tongue was the theme of his first poems. His further
songs and ballads and his plays, *The Tragedy of Nan* and
Pompey the Great, steadily built up his reputation until his
succession of narrative poems, together with the sonnet
sequence and *Lollingdon Downs* of 1917, made a notable
volume of *Collected Poems* in 1923, which was the first such
volume for several years to sell to a wide popular public.
In his case, as far as his poetry is concerned, the war made
little check or change in his production, and without stopping
at *Dauber* and *The Daffodil Fields*, both of 1913, we can see
his work as a whole up to 1923 as an expression of the pre-
1914 world. Moreover, that his *Collected Poems* had such a
wide audience is a good indication of the fact that, below the
new world of the early twenties, a great part of the nation was
still loyal to its old tastes, and found Masefield sufficiently
modern.

Masefield had certainly seemed to some critics only too "modern", when in *The Everlasting Mercy*, telling the story of a drunken bruiser converted by a Quaker lady, he did not shrink from giving the coarse reality of his "hero" either in character or speech. But the poem ended with pure beauty, and this combined vision of sordidness and beauty was characteristic of Masefield. He had something of the universality of Shakespeare, a broad humanity, which could be felt by those who did not normally read poetry. He could tell a story in verse with unflagging zest, unafraid of melodrama or of a lavish pictorialism. In narrative he took Chaucer as his master, as *Reynard the Fox* particularly shows, and as storyteller he rivalled Chaucer and the best of the other English narrative poets, even Crabbe and Scott and Byron. Indeed his stature as a poet is shown by the fitness of such comparisons. He was not among the greatest, but he was, like Dryden, among the great all-round poets and men of letters, possessed of breadth and variety. He was not one of the concentrated artists, but his work is to be judged on its total effect, when it will be found that the true spirit of poetry is steadily pervasive. As one critic happily said, his was the "way of giving the root, stalk and leaves of poetry as well as the flower".

Masefield was essentially English—in the sense that Chaucer, and Dryden and Fielding were thoroughly English. He can conjure up the passage of the Magellan Straits, or the plains of the Argentine, or the galleys and prisons of the pirate Moors, but his characters never forget their native land. Masefield was as English as his themes—as the hunt in *Reynard the Fox*, the circus in *King Cole*, the race-course in *Right Royal*. "England" and "English" were favourite words with him : "Beautiful England's hands had fashioned them", he says of a pair of lovers, and of Robin Dawe the huntsman that what lay behind his face "was English character and mind", and of Tom Dansey the whip that "he loved the English countryside". To Masefield the English character was born of the English countryside, and he valued it the more for the national heritage and the local colour that set it apart from that of other nations. Soon poets and public were to be oppressed by awareness of the international and the cosmopolitan, and such English assurance as Masefield's was to seem out-of-date. Soon the consciousness of England's industrialisation was to put the country second to the towns in men's thoughts, but Masefield no more than any other poet of his day had yet lost the sense that rural England was the heart of England. Soon the English were to reproach themselves that the intellect had not been properly acknowledged in England, but Masefield seemed rather to hold with his Saul Kane that "the trained mind outs the upright soul". Soon happiness was to be suspect, but Masefield held that "the days that make us happy make us wise".

Dauber in many ways expressed Masefield's conception of life. The lad who would be a great painter had first to learn life the hard way, to realise the heroic in "so much of man's toil, compassed in naked manhood", and then, having shared man's tragic toil, to "paint it true". That the lad should die before he could put into practice the truth he had learned was less a matter for sorrow than the moulding of his character and the winning of his vision were cause for rejoicing. "It will go on", said Dauber dying; and Masefield ends his tale with the ship making her berth in stately beauty like a queen, rung cheerly in by peals of bells. His poems did not shun the dark mystery of life—his sonnets brood upon it—or the evil of passion or the agony of suffering, but his was the large view of Shakespeare and Scott, in which the tragic makes only its right proportion in the sum of life. It was "a radiant perception" that Masefield required of the best poetry—"a radiant perception of the life of the universe, of its persons, its powers, and its laws, as they exist eternally". He had no little success in giving it.

Yet another poet of those years who found life good, and wrote of it joyously was Alfred Noyes. He was twenty-two when his first book of poems appeared in 1902, and every year up to 1914 he published at least one fresh volume, among them being the twelve-book epic *Drake*. In 1920 his *Collected Poems* reached a third volume, and his output continued

to be copious, including his mature and thoughtful poetic
appraisal of the history and achievement of science, *The
Torchbearers*, 1922-1930. His reputation as a poet fell in the
different atmosphere of the twenties, and perhaps he had
written too much and sometimes too easily, but his poetry
before 1914 was popular in the best sense that it was possessed
of those qualities of spirit and technique which both won the
admiration of judges like Meredith and Alice Meynell and fulfilled the idea of the contemporary public as to what good
poetry was. He had not the rare mind of a Yeats which grows
younger as the man grows older, and so his poetry even more
than Masefield's remained of the older poetic kind, but some
of his lyrics at least will surely last.

Noyes was a Christian by faith, and, as his prose *The
Unknown God* shows, by intellectual conviction too. In joyous verse he sang, "The Lord of Life is risen again ; and
Love is Lord of all". To his assurance of the soul's immortality he added his faith in the wisdom of courage and the
rightness of joy. He had no doubt of the immortality of
poetry, for "where's the death can touch a song ?" The
beauty of nature inspired much of his verse—

> "Give me the sunlight and the sea,
> And who shall take my heaven from me ?"

Much too arose from his love of England, and perhaps his
best-known poem was *A Song of England* (1904), with its line
"There is a song of England that none shall ever sing"—
because to sing of a love so intimately felt would be always
beyond the power of words. He delighted to recreate the
brave Elizabethan world, not only thinking the day was
not too late for a regular epic on

> "The wild adventures and heroic deeds
> Of England's epic age",

but calling up Marlowe and Raleigh and others in his *Tales
of the Mermaid Tavern*. He had the pageant-master's view
of history. Of Robin Hood he made a poetic play.

In all, the muse of Alfred Noyes was at once serious with
high purpose and alive with high spirits and humour, robust

and delicate, real and fantastic. Ears that later learnt other and less tuneful music turned against his varied and catching melodies, just as his love of colour and of adjectives and his often carefree spontaneity later pained a more austere taste. It came to be regarded also as a defect that some of his ballads and poems had the quality that demands their reciting, but before 1914, as not seldom in the natural recurrence of taste, the virtue of what one might call public poetry was widely acknowledged. If he did not often write of the darker things, his prophetic denunciation of the horrors of war in *Lucifer's Feast* written about 1909 suggests it was not because he was unaware of them, but because there was so much else that compelled happy song.

Similarly Belloc and Chesterton, both true poets though they found their fullest expression in prose, belonged in spirit to this period before 1914. They lived many years after, fighting with pugnacious energy, Belloc for his views of history, Chesterton for his modern version of Merry England, and both for many other causes too. In the apparent stability of the first decade the gusto with which they laid about them, almost as though with friendly buffets they would knock some cheerful sense into men's heads, brought a response. They seemed leaders, robust in their faith. But after the 1914 war, though their swords were still keen to deal battle and bright to flash, their brave medievalism had only a pathetic charm. They could not but continue to delight and astonish, but the sweep of time had stranded them, though Belloc had been a prophet in the first decade when he foresaw the threat of the developing Servile State. The poetry of both was characterised by its love of God and its love of earth, by romantic idealism and an ironic laughter at contemporary follies, by the praise of wine and by the understanding of children. Chesterton indeed had something of the wild-eyed wonder of an oldfashioned child. In retrospect they seem great-hearted giants of an earlier age, singing from a full heart, Belloc, half French, in love with Europe and also with Sussex, Chesterton in love with the rolling roads of England,

thundering out his battle poem of *Lepanto* or his scorn of the
false rhetoric of F. E. Smith.

But if Belloc and Chesterton date, there was something
timeless in the poetry of W. H. Davies and De la Mare,
especially in that of the latter. The early years of the century
perhaps gave Davies the best background he could have had,
but his poetry, with its unsophisticated and wise joy, depends
no more upon time than does that of the early nineteenth
century John Clare. It became increasingly difficult to find
the leisure "to stand and stare" with him, but the rivers he
loved in South Wales still flowed as before, the birds of his
delight still sang and preened their beauty while the lambs
skipped and the flowers opened, and the moon he delighted
in was still undimmed. Certainly his poems as they continued
to appear in the twenties still found a wide public—the more
so no doubt because those days were becoming so conscious
of the expanding urban scene, which Davies left unnoted, that
he was all the more refreshing. Yet it would be a great error
to think of Davies as though he always sang a sweet and
simple song of country things in naïve happiness marvelling
"how men find time to hate" and to waste their lives on
serious follies. He who gave the story of his early life in
The Autobiography of a Super-Tramp knew the reverse side
of life, and his delight was balanced by a rage that would
sometimes break out as he thought of poverty and pain and
evil passions. Like De la Mare he could convey too the
mystery of things, as, amid all the joy of nature, he was
aware of the wind

> "Dragging the corn by her golden hair
> Into a dark and lonely wood".

The poetry of De la Mare must always remain unique,
for it comes even more than that of any similar poet from a
self-communing of the poet with himself. De la Mare spoke
of the intimate self-revelation of poets as resembling the chat-
tering of a child to himself on the brink of sleep : "that being
so, then it is only to a similar inward self, to a secret sharer
in others, that what the poets have written has any hope of
going home". This secret sharer must, like De la Mare, still

have alive within him the imagination of childhood, whose
world, the poet declared, "old as Eden and remote as the
stars, lies, like the fabric of a vision, bathed in an unearthly
atmosphere". It is an intangible dream world, and the poet
gives no more than hints, to be picked up only by a
most sensitive response to the personal idiosyncracy of
the poet's imagery, of the interpretation of life which lurks
elusively in and behind the beauty of the poems. In this
private world, full of the acutely realised sensations of our
real world, De la Mare speculates fearfully about that other
world which can be entered fully only through the gate of
Death. Fairies, phantoms and mysterious presences haunt
his poems. Silence has a tongue, and beauty can be sinister.
There are unseen listeners in the very corridors of the mind.
Life is a pilgrimage, amid the strangest hazards, to that unknown country wherefrom no traveller returns, at least as
flesh and blood. So fear often thrills, and sadness whispers
through his verses : there is shadow or mist, and a chill in the
air. And yet at other times there is radiance of light and joy,
just as it is sometimes the real world, not the other world,
that is in focus—though his usual vision is a fusion of both
worlds. All the time we are conscious that the psychological
insight of the poet is of the subtlest, and that a fine intellect
partners the imagination of childhood. Yet, as for thinking
in itself, perhaps his poem *Vain Questioning* most clearly
speaks his own view of how far it can lead the spirit foolishly
away from its true home

"Where all things transient to the changeless win".

By its strangeness of vision it might be thought that De
la Mare's poetry would have found only a small audience, but
it had a supreme power to accommodate its strangeness to many
more than could share his inner vision with any intimacy—
the power of perfect music. In that sphere it is hardly extravagant to claim that no poet of this half-century could rival
his continuous and varied lyric mastery. Another drawing
power in the earlier decades lay no doubt in his imagery,
which, however personal its use, was from sources then in the

common knowledge of most, being especially the Bible, and
fairy tales and *Pilgrim's Progress*. How rich a store of other
reading could fill De la Mare's mind with suggestions can
be judged from the several anthologies of genius which he
created.

Both W. H. Davies and De la Mare were among the first
contributors to *Georgian Poetry*, but the typical Georgians
were Drinkwater, Shanks, Freeman and J. C. Squire. The
Georgian group came together in 1911, when Edward Marsh
took up a suggestion of Rupert Brooke's, with the result that
the first volume of *Georgian Poetry* appeared in 1912, its aim
being to make the public conscious of a new generation of
poets, much as twenty years later Michael Roberts introduced
the poets of *New Signatures*. The first volume met with considerable success, and four more volumes followed, the last
in 1922, by which time Squire had become their acknowledged
leader, and Blunden a notable contributor. In the early
twenties the Georgians appeared outmoded, on the whole
with justice. Osbert Sitwell made merry at their expense in
The Jolly Old Squire, or Way down in Georgia, and the young
South African, Roy Campbell, ridiculed them, and much else,
in *The Georgiad*.

From the beginning the Georgians had hardly set the
Thames on fire. The very favourable reception in 1912 of
their limited and rather flat poetry was, indeed, a significant
comment on the poetic taste and general outlook of the poetry-
readers of that day. Poetry, the contemporary public clearly
held, should keep to a neat highway : let new poets renew
and modify the best traditions, without any excess, without
startling, without disturbing the comfortable surface of life.
The Georgians had, of course, a positive aim : it was to treat
natural things in a clear, natural and beautiful way, neither
too modern, nor too like Tennyson. In fact, they were a
little too conscious that in their work, as Marsh wrote in his
prefatory note of 1912, "English poetry [was] now once
again putting on a new strength and beauty", though the
reaction of the next generation was rather to be that they were

merely writing nice poetry for nice people, and that they were too inclined to indulge in mutual praise.

The Georgians felt the contrast between town and country, but without any real sense of the new industrial world and the advance of the machine age. The countryside was beautiful: there, as often as possible, one took a quiet pleasure, and when in town one longed for it and was soothed by the voice of a blackbird or by the fragrance and colour of a window-box. Distant lands had their fascination. Love was lovely, and childhood was innocence. History had its lessons. Indeed one is tempted to be unfair to them, because, thinking and feeling so unexceptionably, they now seem to have been so unaware of the hour about to strike, too insulated from outside forces. They did not know the tension of mind and spirit so soon to be characteristic of the modern world. Nothing seemed to them complex. Nearly all they wrote came only from the conscious levels of their well-regulated minds. But it is useless to blame them for limitations that were characteristic of their age. Within these limits they produced much that was pleasing.

Rupert Brooke himself was too true a poet to be labelled a Georgian, and Flecker also too individual. A typical Georgian was John Drinkwater, whose *Collected Poems* written over the years without any appreciable change impress more by their volume than by their distinction. Again and again he celebrated the English countryside, its streams and pools and woods, its birds and cattle and flowers, its shepherds and gypsies, with a cultured pastoral fancy untroubled by any urgencies. In *The Midlands* he surveyed from a Cotswold hill "these most beloved of English lands", with their white roads, and comely manors planned of old by men "who somehow moved in comely thought". *A Town Window* contrasted a drab inglorious Birmingham street with the beauty of Warwickshire woods. Even when, rather exceptionally, he lamented in *A Prayer* that now that men had the knowledge they lacked the will, his appeal to God lacked intensity. On the whole his poems by their colour and their easy rhythms evoke an agreeable impression of country scenes, but they never sting our senses: the awareness of a competent man of letters intervenes, and we are merely invited, not compelled, to enter the world of imagination. His most effective work was done as manager of the Birmingham Repertory Theatre, which he helped to found, and as a dramatist.

Drinkwater sustained the Georgian mood into and through the war, and much typical Georgian poetry came after 1914. The mood was a relief from the strain of war, and it harmonised with the nostalgic love of the peaceful English countryside felt in the trenches. In the later volumes came the poems of the closely associated J. C. Squire, Edward Shanks and John Freeman. Squire had first become known as a parodist, especially of Masefield. There was no strong impulse behind his other poetry, which is mostly reflective and descriptive: *The Lily of Malud* is among his best poems, but despite its beauty something lumbering in its verse and consciously literary in its manner denies it the effect of strangeness and mystery sought by the poet. Shanks was another lover of the countryside, especially in the silence of evening, and in the moonlight that floods so much Georgian poetry. His *Fête Galante: The Triumph of Love*, a pictorial ode on the psychological varieties of love, might well be taken to represent Georgian poetry at its best: the idea of Aristonöe gathering the young girls round her to teach them "all the alphabet, grammar and syntax of love" is fanciful, but the scene is a very English garden, and the girls are natural English girls, and the whole has a healthy beauty, and is conveyed in the vocabulary of good normal speech. In this poem Shanks is a more natural Tennyson. Freeman too wrote of nature and love, finding often a sad pleasure in both, and again we see earth's beauty

"in the silvery shine
Of the round, lovely, thoughtful moon".

Freeman was the most meditative of them all in a Wordsworthian way, but neither he nor his fellow poets had any of the great poet's depth of view and experience.

Rupert Brooke was only seven years younger than Freeman, while five and three years were all that separated him from Drinkwater and Squire, but his poetry flamed with a youth that contrasts strikingly with the mannered, middle-aged quality of their work. From Brooke poetry forced its way, whereas from the others it was rather coaxed, though it then came easily enough, indeed sometimes too easily. His *Collected Poems* are dated from his nineteenth year, and about half of his poetry had been written before *Georgian Poetry* was thought of.

The varying estimates of Brooke as a poet make an ironic commentary on literary taste and judgment. To his friends it was clear how true and fine a poet he was, and by the time of his death in the Aegean in 1915 his famous sonnets occasioned by the outbreak of the war had ensured his public fame. But those who were children in the war grew up in an intellectual climate antipathetic to the very idea of a romantic young poet acclaiming the virtues of war, and from the middle twenties it was impossible for many years to find Rupert Brooke valued with any justice by most of those who took literature seriously. Yet the poems mainly responsible for this antipathy and neglect were but the last fraction of a poetic output in which, moreover, there were points of contact with the post-war world. No doubt his portrait, showing him handsome with the combined radiance and melancholy of youth, helped with some to keep his poems a closed volume.

Brooke poured "the red sweet wine of youth" in his earlier poems. His poetry flamed with youth—flame indeed was then a favourite word and image of his. Now all was joy and radiance, and now melancholy engulfed him with the normal rapid alternation of youth. It was no melancholy cultivated for its own sake, or bred of a sense of the evil years, though certainly he anticipated the twenties in his love of the Jacobeans and their brooding on Death, and he did write of "the sullen years and the mark of pain". Probably as the years passed he became more conscious of the "world grown old and cold and weary", a world of "sick hearts", of which his last sonnets spoke, but his was personal poetry, and he did not relate his joys and griefs to the wider contemporary scene. We may

well suspect that a deeper prescience was in part responsible
for the restlessness and occasional bitterness of his spirit, but
the ecstasies and anguishes of love and his rich awareness of
"this tumultuous body" are explanation enough of much of
his poetry. He loved so intensely and felt such "infinite
hungers" that the real again and again fell short of his ideali-
sation, and the passing even of the glories of a single day
awoke anguished pangs that joy and beauty should be so
transient. "Each kiss lasts but the kissing." Love—"love
that was sweet lies at most"—gave him joyous satisfaction,
but never for long : and what of the passing of love into
habit ? the idea revolted him. He was very conscious of the
ultimate loneliness of every individual, of the sudden bleak-
ness when

> "our unwalled loves thin out in vacuous air",

So, though he rivalled Keats in the power of conveying the
very touch and taste and smell of things enjoyed, and though
there was often laughter in his heart, there was in all his
poetry a sense of pain and unease, a constant yearning for
"the ecstasy of . . . quietude", and his famous sonnets give
an impression of an almost overflowing personal release into
a finer world away from shame and "all the little emptiness
of love" to where "Nobleness walks in our ways again" in
time of war.

Flecker, after hard work in the consular service in the
Middle East, died in 1915 of tuberculosis when he had just
entered his thirties and like Brooke, whose friend he was, left
the impression of a poet of high promise only in part fulfilled. His imagination was in tune with the orientalism of
Constantinople and Smyrna and Damascus, and to his love
of the exotic he added a real knowledge, just as his luxuriant
fancy was curbed by a disciplined craftsmanship. His union
of strength and beauty in theme and feeling, rhythm and
diction, gave a proud perfection to his best work, which
marked him out from the other Georgians. There is a
splendour in the rich-coloured fabrics of his imaginings and
pictures of past and present : let him lie in the bare hospital

where he enumerates

> "The mat, the jug, the cupboard and the chair"

yet

> "the grey square of wall should fade away,
> And glow again, and open, and disclose
> The shimmering lake in which the planets swim,
> And all that lake a dewdrop on a rose".

None of the poets so far mentioned in this chapter, except Bridges, was notable for prosodic theory or experiment. Kipling and Masefield had both brought to poetry something of the common touch. The Georgians had their conception of what new poetry should be. But in none was there apparent any real sign of dissatisfaction with the state of English poetry. There were, however, around 1912 some who were conscious of the need for a new outlook and a new poetic expression. Notable among these was T. E. Hulme, who was killed in France in 1917 at the age of thirty-four. Hulme was a great conversationalist, with a mind that ranged brilliantly and originally through philosophy and aesthetics. He had many contacts, among them Epstein, Ezra Pound, Middleton Murry and C. R. W. Nevinson. Rupert Brooke he met, but he and Brooke were too different to harmonise. Hulme was anti-romantic, opposed especially to the vague romanticism which was sentimental about the soul and which thought beautiful poetry a substitute for religion. He did not believe in romantic individualism and inevitable human progress, but saw mankind as in need of discipline and submission to an authoritative ethical order. Indeed he anticipated T. S. Eliot in turning away from the humanism of the Renaissance in search of a revived classical tradition in life and letters. Eliot, however, first became acquainted with his ideas on the posthumous publication of his *Speculations* in 1924.

Hulme's attitude to poetry was expressed in a lecture on poetry in 1912. His main theme was that it was the discovery of a new verse form that gave new poetic life, and, as a corollary, that each age, because of its changed outlook, required a new verse form to express it. Until a new form was discovered, there could be only progressive decay and imitation.

He had been impressed by the freedom and the new life given to poetry in France in the eighties of the last century by the discovery of *vers libre*, and he felt that this harmonised with the new age whose philosophy was that truth was not absolute but relative. There was now a "tentative and half shy manner of looking at things"; poetry was introspective and was concerned with communicating vague and momentary phases of the poet's mind; and poetry was now to be read silently rather than aloud. In this new world *vers libre* was apt: here was the appropriate rhythm. But a new rhythm was not enough: it should be accompanied by new analogies —fresh metaphor must startle the reader out of the doze of habit. Here the classical cast of Hulme's mind dictated that the images must be clear, concise and accurate—they must call up a well-defined picture to the mind's eye.

This new kind of poetry as conceived and practised by Hulme was called Imagism, and Hulme has been called the Father of Imagism. His friend Ezra Pound shared his views, and there arose a movement both in England and America devoted to it. Hulme himself left only a very few poems, as brief as the ideals demanded: one, of four lines, merely depicts the moon seen through a ship's rigging, and the new image that catches the reader's attention is the comparison of the moon to "a child's balloon, forgotten after play". A perfect instance of the Imagist poem was Pound's:

> "The apparition of these faces in the crowd:
> Petals on a wet, black bough".

The last joint volume of Imagist poetry appeared in 1917, but the new technique made a notable contribution to later poetry, and one of the original Imagists, H. D., developed the manner into some of her best poetry, which appeared in the forties, as in *The Walls Do Not Fall* of 1944. The significance of the movement was that it provided evidence that there were poets more sensitive to at least some aspects of the changing atmosphere than were the Georgians. Ezra Pound preached the need of refreshing poetic inspiration by turning away from Keats and Tennyson to the study of world poetry, past and present. Imagism was but a beginning, but it was a beginning fraught with possibilities. Given the new rhythms and the new imagery, poetry might have had a rebirth without the unleashing of the various new forces in the wake of the war. The limitation of Imagism was that it concentrated too exclusively on a new technique, holding that the subject was relatively unimportant. But in the meantime the cult of direct, concise, clear treatment in a new rhythm worked for good.

CHAPTER IV

POETRY 1914 TO 1919

There were in August 1914 many poets, old and young, to write of the coming of war, and in the following years to tell at home and in the trenches of its progress, of the strain and the carnage, the nobleness and the futility. Yet there emerged only one great poet of the war, Wilfred Owen, though next to him stood the true poet who had inspired him, Siegfried Sassoon, while another, Edward Thomas, who had in 1914 at the age of thirty-six just found his vocation of poetry, produced in the three years left before death came to him in France some imperishable poetry touched only here and there by the fact of war. At home, the old poets, Hardy and Bridges and Alice Meynell were moved to write of the war, Kipling became a public voice again, and Binyon often made the war his theme. In the fighting services and on the battlefields, not only Rupert Brooke, Owen and Sassoon, but Robert Nichols, Robert Graves, Charles Sorley, Julian Grenfell, and Edmund Blunden were among many who made poetry out of war. Sorley and Grenfell were among those who fell. Two major poets stood outside the war : Yeats, whose poetry was affected not by the European war but by the Easter Rising in Ireland in 1916, and T. S. Eliot in whose volume of 1917 there was abundant evidence that the poet looked out upon the decay of western civilisation but no mention of the war. As the war ended, Osbert Sitwell, who had fought at Loos, wrote *The Next War*, a satiric poem bitterly prophetic.

In the autumn of 1914 there was a common expression of confident patriotism from the poets. There came Hardy's *Men Who March Away*, a "song of the soldiers" with "faith and fire within" them, believing in their "heart of hearts . . . victory crowns the just"—though the equally well-known poem of 1915, *In Time of 'The Breaking of Nations'*, thrust war's annals firmly into the background behind the eternal

figures of the man and horse harrowing clods and the maid
and her lover going whispering by "though Dynasties pass".
John Freeman opened his poem *Happy is England Now* with
a note comparable to the high simplicity of Wordsworth's
sonnets—

> "There is not anything more wonderful
> Than a great people moving towards the deep
> Of an unguessed and unfeared future".

As with Brooke, so with Freeman, all seemed now to shine
more purely. Similarly Binyon prayed to the Spirit of
England in *The Fourth of August*

> "Enkindle this dear earth that bore us,
> In the hour of peril purified".

Binyon rejoiced that

> "We step from days of sour division
> Into the grandeur of our fate".

To Freeman and to Binyon it was the English heritage that
moved the heart in the days of trial. So it was with Masefield. In *August 1914* he looked over the quiet cornfield in
the summer night, and felt that never had he seen "so great
a beauty on these English fields"—"unknown generations of
dead men" had lived there, fashioning the earth and in turn
fashioned by it, and from time to time going to the wars as
now men must go again : an influence right from the very soil
of England and transmitted through the generations, and coming even "from beyond the veils of Death", will uphold the
soldier in the soaking trench or the sailor freezing in the rigging. Alice Meynell, now sixty-seven, expressed in *Summer
in England, 1914* the ironic contrast between the special beauty
of that summer with its fair promise of harvest and the heaped
slaughter, "one wet corruption" : man's race appeared unpar-
donable, but she had no doubt of the nobility of the sacrifice,
or that

> "The soldier dying dies upon a kiss,
> The very kiss of Christ".

Kipling, too, spoke of sacrifice, but of "iron sacrifice", in
For All We Have and Are (1914), concluding :

> "What stands if Freedom fall ?
> Who dies if England live ?"

It was natural that the older poets at home should change less in their attitude to the war than did the younger poets who had actual experience of battle. Inevitably they saw the war with more detachment and with only second-hand knowledge of the main aspects, except in so far as they read the mind and morale of the nation, and shared or understood its emotions. Old Thomas Hardy wrote only a few poems bearing on the war. One, characteristically, imagined a talk between himself writing by night and the moon, in which the moon tells him that, having previously looked for the body of a man who has drowned himself for grief at the death of his son "slain in brutish battle", she is now looking in to see what sort of blinkered mind it can be that "wants to write a book in a world of such a kind". But that Hardy was at one with his countrymen appeared in his verses of March 1917, *A Call to National Service*, in which he called upon men and women of all classes and occupations to come forward, and declared that if only he were younger, he himself would "serve with never a slack". Alice Meynell, too, wrote only a poem or two arising from the war : she thought of those dead by sacrifice, and of the women who must now replace their slain brothers in the crippled world, and she celebrated the martyrdom of Nurse Cavell. But from Binyon came many poems inspired by the war : at his highest he spoke for the soul of England, as when in *The Anvil* he declared

> "more urgent comes our cry
> Not to be spared, but to be used,
> Brain, sinew and spirit, before we die",

and when in *Milton : an Ode* he invoked that great patriot

> "Risen, our spirits to claim,
> To enlarge, to summon, to awaken".

His thoughts were often of the slain, and his poem *For the Fallen* with its famous verse beginning

> "They shall grow not old, as we that are left grow old"

summed up the nation's "proud thanksgiving". He praised the heroic hearts of the women, and the courage of Belgium, and he wrote of the sinking of the *Lusitania*, of Gallipoli, of the long, bitter battle of Verdun, of the ambulance men on the battlefield, and of much else. At the end of the war he wrote prophetically of the difficulties of peace when "the nations ache" and the old greeds still possess men. Alfred Noyes wrote *A Salute for the Fleet* and *Songs of the Trawlers*, but his energies during the war were largely given to putting the case of England in the United States where he had become well known as lecturer and writer.

At home the poet who spoke most nearly as the poet of the people was Kipling, who lost his only son in the war. His heart was for England and the Empire, and for France— "France, beloved of every soul that loves or serves its kind!" he had written in 1913. He had looked upon what seemed to him a weakening of the sinews of the nation, upon slothful thinking and unpreparedness, and now had come the reaping. He hated the slackers and the incompetent, as he hated the enemy whom he did not hesitate to call "the Hun". Like Winston Churchill a quarter of a century later he proclaimed "no easy hope", but "naked days". He invoked the spirit of Bunyan, who so long ago had told how Armegeddon must be faced:

> "The wisdom that he taught us
>   Is proven prophecy—
> One watchword through our Armies,
>   One answer from our Lands:—
> 'No dealings with Diabolus
>   As long as Mansoul stands' ".

His *Epitaphs of the War* with incisive brevity crystallised men's thoughts and feelings : as T. S. Eliot has remarked, good epigrams, such as these, are very rare in English, and they were possible to Kipling because he was very impersonal and could express objectively feelings capable of being shared completely by a wide audience. They spoke of every aspect of the war, of the trenches and the mine-sweepers, of air raids and convoys, of soldiers and civilians, of brave and cowardly, of English clerk in arms and Hindu Sepoy : now the theme is iron sacrifice and willing service, now courage, now grief, and not seldom a bitterness verging on hate for those, whether lying politicians or slack munition-workers, who had been responsible for the slaughter of the young soldiers. Many of these themes he dealt with also in longer poems like *Mine Sweepers* with its vivid picture of "five damned trawlers with their syreens blowing" and *Mesopotamia* (1917) relentless in its angry, contemptuous condemnation of those who left the soldiers "thriftily to die in their own dung". And all the time we feel behind his poetry the conviction, governing his appraisal of every aspect of the war, that

"The game is more than the player of the game".

In the poetry written by those who were soldiers that of Edward Thomas stood apart. He attempted no description of the battlefield ; indeed he rarely acknowledged the war at all in his poetry. Before 1914 he had for some time been a sensitive writer of books and essays on literature and the countryside, and then, thanks to his friendship with the American poet-farmer Robert Frost at that time temporarily settled in England, he realised the innate poet in himself and the possibility of releasing in verse the essential self, which had been so far able to shine only diffusedly through his prose, which was often task-work. The weight of the war could not but lie upon his spirit, and service as a soldier involve at times a hard and irksome sacrifice, but in those last years, as De la Mare has said, "his comradeship, his humour blossomed over. He plunged back from books into life, and wrote only for sheer joy in writing".

The poetry of Edward Thomas arose from his love of the ordinary things and people of the English countryside. When they were not present to the eyes of his body, the memory of them sustained and rejoiced his mind. To quote De la Mare again, "when, indeed, Edward Thomas was killed in Flanders, a mirror of England was shattered of so pure and true a crystal that a clearer and tenderer reflection of it can be found no other where than in these poems". He saw everything with a clear observation, behind which lay a quiet but intense love, so that he saw not only with his eyes but with his understanding, and his poems gave a true picture not only of the scene but of himself. How he loved the sun, and what varieties of quality and music he found to enjoy in rain and wind and water. Trees and flowers were always with him, and it is hardly an exaggeration to say that half our English birds are there by name and nature in his poems. It is a countryman's view of the world where men work for their own and the nation's livelihood, and yet he can like most the corner of a farmyard in which the nettles never lose their dust "except to prove the sweetness of a shower". As for the war, in one poem he talks to a ploughman who tells him "a good few" have gone from that part never to come back, and in another he thinks of that first harvest time of 1914

"when the war began
To turn young men to dung".

Indeed, "now all roads lead to France". For himself, "I hate not Germans", but

"I am one in crying, God save England, lest
We lose what never slaves and cattle blessed".

It was Robert Nichols who gave from the battlefield the most balanced and sustained account of what modern battle was, and of how a noble and sensitive spirit answered the demands made upon it. When in 1917 at the age of twenty-three he published *Ardours and Endurances*, he had seen much service on the Western Front, and had been invalided out of the army because of shell-shock, but he had acquired none of the bitterness or disillusionment which characterised the later poetry of others.

Fine and striking though single poems are, the war poems entitled *Ardours and Endurances* are an integral sequence built up to span a whole experience. The poem begins with The Summons, proceeds to Farewell to Place of Comfort, takes us gradually within hearing of the guns in The Approach, then in Battle gives us in eleven short poems life in and out of the trenches ending with The Assault and the poet's emotional response, after which come two concluding groups, the Dead and The Aftermath. So the whole

of a soldier's life was shown with abundant realism, and the
poet who had himself known such a life presented it with a
heroic, sane acceptance of all that it involved, making no
secret of the loneliness and pain that existed in him side by
side with comradeship and joy. The style varies with the
theme : there is the direct lyric narrative of The Day's March
nearer to the line, the jerky, impressionistic onomatopoeia of
The Assault, the elegiac rhythm of the Plaint of Friendship by
Death Broken, the plain heroic song of Thanksgiving. The
note that rings through is a proud exultation beating down
fear and weariness, finding in the unbroken thunder of the
guns a blast by whose "mighty winnowing being is blown
clean", and able at the end to say

> "I count mere life-breath nothing now I know Life's worth
> Lies all in spending ! that known, love Life and Earth".

It was natural that in the twenties such a reaction to war
was unfashionable. The poetry that expressed it fell under
the same condemnation as descended on Rupert Brooke, and
the poet was not even given credit for the obvious sincerity
which had dictated his attitude. Nor did the other poetry
that made up Books II and III of *Ardours and Endurances*
fare any better. It consisted of *Faun's Holiday*, a long lyrical
narrative somewhat in the spirit of Keats's *Endymion*, and
of *Poems and Phantasies*, among them lyrics of passionate
romantic love and a group of three pictures drawn with a
fine detailed restraint, one of Mary on a hill-top in May singing a lullaby to the infant Jesus, one of Jesus in the upper
room speaking to His disciples, and one of Judas hanging
upon his tree. All these poems were characteristic of the
years when they were written, 1913 to 1916. Nichols found
his poetic masters in such poets as Keats and Rossetti, and
with his own unique imagery expressed beauty of idea and
feeling and scene : he allied himself with the Georgians. The
war matured, but did not change him, and he saw no reason
to abandon the ideals of his Oxford days because of his
experience of battle. In battle he felt that no love counted
save his love of his heroic comrades, but love and beauty

always returned to him in the balancing sanity of his mind, just as in those years Edward Thomas refreshed himself with the love of nature, and as all, whether soldiers or civilians, found comfort in memories and imaginings of the beauty nearest to their hearts. The poetry of Nichols was then truth and beauty, fulfilling men's desires ; if later both this volume and such a volume as *Aurelia* of 1920 failed to appeal to the next generation, the loss was theirs.

The way in which some of Nichols's own generation as well turned against romantic war poetry can be seen in the treatment accorded by Robert Graves to the poetry he had written between 1914 and 1918. Graves, only two years younger than Nichols, had enlisted at the outbreak of war, and he too served in France, being by error officially listed as having died of wounds on his twenty-first birthday. He published two volumes of poetry during the war, but as early as his *Collected Poems, 1914-1926*, he omitted the war poems completely. Analysing himself in the Foreword to the drastically selected *Collected Poems* of 1938 he wrote of "the anodynic tradition of poetry in which I was educated" : his war volumes had for their underlying emotion, he held, "a frank fear of physical death", and that he had included as a contrast to the war poems several on the subject of childhood was "a digression . . . towards wistfulness, in disregard of the pseudo-adult experience of soldiering". For truth and maturity the war poetry of Graves certainly did not compare with that in *Ardours and Endurances*, but it was as natural a product of its time. The titles of his volumes, *Over the Brazier* and *Fairies and Fusiliers*, fairly declare the contents and their nature—topical episodes and compensatory fancy.

Perhaps if it had been the lot of Robert Nichols to stay in France instead of being sent to America on propaganda work, his poetry might have changed nearer to the spirit of what was characteristic in that of Siegfried Sassoon. Sassoon's *The Old Huntsman and Other Poems* of 1917, though some of its war poems went back to 1915, spoke only once or twice in a tone at all near to that of Nichols. Once he could say, "We are the happy legion", and once declare without irony,

"We have made an end of all things base". But in general his mood was to convey the bitter truth, to tear off any mask from the ugly face of reality, and to wreak his anger on the heartless and the hypocrites. Nichols had not failed to convey the horror of the battlefield, but by Sassoon a more varied scene was drawn more vividly, in detail that could leave none unaware not merely of the guns and the slaughter, but of the unwholesome air, the rotten naked corpses, the mud and the rats, the wiring parties in the darkness, the foul dug-outs, the mutilated and nerve-shattered survivors, the agony and ignominy of death. The heroic was gone, and men prayed for a wound that they might be sent home, or were driven to suicide. All this, and more, Sassoon conveyed with a natural, almost conversational directness. The heroism and endurance could be deduced. In one poem, indeed, he told of a soldier, whose face glimpsed by the light of a rocket in a rain-sluiced trench "seemed a mask of mortal pain", and declared the man was Christ, but on the whole he let the stark realities of description speak for themselves. His next volume, *Counter-Attack and Other Poems*, was grimmer still. How much longer would the senseless slaughter go on? "O Jesus, make it stop!" The anger that in an earlier poem had made him wish to see a tank lurch through the stalls where the music-hall audience cackled and grinned in mockery of "the riddled corpses round Bapaume", burnt in poem after poem against civilians insensible to the reality, incompetent staff officers, facile journalists, and bishops who proclaimed

"That 'if our Lord returned He'd fight for us' ".

Above all, throughout his war poetry, Sassoon expressed a most pitiful sense of the terrible lot of the survivors, with their "dreams from the pit" as well as their broken bodies. With such thoughts in his mind he put hardly a poem in his second volume that was not primarily of the war, but in *The Old Huntsman* in addition to the title poem he had included a number of poems in which like Thomas he rejoiced in the beauty of English country scenes and like Nichols imagined dryads and fauns. In the later volume he showed a soldier at break of day reminded by the smell of autumn in the air of a happy day with the hunt, but it was "a happy dream . . . in hell".

The war poems of Wilfred Owen were not published until 1920, when Sassoon introduced them, for it was from Sassoon that Owen had derived a new inspiration. They were together in hospital in Scotland, and, as Edmund Blunden has said, "the impact of Sassoon's character, thought, and independent poetic method gave Owen a new purpose". He had written poetry from the age of seventeen, and his early worship had been for Keats, and then for Shelley, Tennyson, and Arnold. Acquaintance with French poetry made during a visit to France before the war had led him to take a deep interest in the art of poetry, and he had a passionate love of music.

The outbreak of war found him with high poetic ambitions but his memorable poetry did not come yet. At first, like many others, he had "a sense of new crusades and modern knightliness", but the rapid development of his views can be traced through his remarkably honest and vivid letters. Sometimes bitter and despondent, he never lost faith in humanity or the conviction that from this universal suffering the human spirit would emerge triumphant. He wrote of being "kept warm by the ardour of Life within me". By the time he met Sassoon his views had changed greatly. Tennyson now seemed only "a great child". Owen did not seek to turn aside from his path, but by 1917 he had come to a strong pacifist position, holding that "one of Christ's essential commands was : Passivity at any price !" He himself gave the date January 1917 as the time when he first wrote "the *only* lines of mine that carry the stamp of maturity"—the first was,

"But the old happiness is unreturning".

It was a few months later that he met Sassoon. A little over a year later he was killed, a week before the Armistice.

Before he died Owen had conceived of his poetry clearly enough as a volume to draft a short preface for it. With curt clarity he declared : "This book is not about heroes. English poetry is not yet fit to speak of them . . . Above all I am not concerned with Poetry. My subject is War, and the pity of

War. The poetry is in the Pity . . . All a poet can do to-day is warn. That is why the true Poets must be truthful". Ten years later this flat proclamation of poetic integrity summoned Day Lewis and Auden and other young poets of their generation to follow in Owen's footsteps. His poems, as he had prophesied might be so, they then found "consolatory", which Owen had said they were "in no sense" to his own generation. Indeed, these thirty or so poems hardly swerved one iota from their consistent warning and witness of the debt owed by humanity to the victims of this monstrous nightmare.

> "The front line withers,
> But they are troops who fade, not flowers
> For poets' tearful fooling".

Nor were they "troops" to Owen, but comrades even in whose "hoarse oaths that kept our courage straight" he "perceived much beauty". No word of his should fail or misrepresent them. *Greater Love*, the most passionately perfect of all the poems of the war, declared that no love or beauty of beloved woman could be compared with the love and beauty of these English soldiers—

> "Kindness of wooed and wooer
> Seems shame to their love pure".

Owen depicted the battle scene with a terrible, quiet clearness in *Exposure* : we feel the cruel tension in which mind and body ache in the icy, silent darkness, and, as far as words can ever make us do, we see, touch and smell all the patiently given details of this ugly and fearful desolation of mere existence ; it is a seemingly endless moment in hell—"But nothing happens". Always Owen appeals to our senses, but not always quietly. In *Mental Cases* he employed a vivid violence of language to convey the passing of all the physical horror into the mind—

> "Memory fingers in their hair of murders . . .
> Treading blood from lungs that had loved laughter".

But he was more often quiet, and especially in pathos, when indeed "the poetry is in the Pity". So it is in *Futility* and in *Disabled*. Yet Pity is hardly the word, for his pity is intertwined inseparably with irony and anger, an anger as terribly

quiet as the pity. One can hear it even in the opening of
the *Anthem for Doomed Youth* with its incomparable beauty
of mourning :

> " What passing-bells for these who die as cattle ? "

And yet his anger could cry aloud too. The sacrifice of the
young by the old, the insensitiveness of civilians, the whole
business of modern warfare which he called "the unnaturalness of weapons" forced strong, bitter phrasing from him.
In the trenches men ceased feeling and lost imagination that
they might live and endure, but at home there were those who
"made themselves immune to pity". "Cursed are dullards
whom no cannon stuns." But the poem on which he was
still working at the end, *Strange Meeting*, transcends anger.
Sir Osbert Sitwell has declared it "as great a poem as exists
in our tongue", and there, imagining himself being spoken
to by a German he had killed the day before, Owen made his
final plea and gave his last warning : the truth must not be
left untold. In that poem he concentrated his high vision and
his poetic beauty.

It was Owen's technique as well as his attitude that made
him one of the "ancestors" hailed by Day Lewis and his contemporaries. In particular, they adopted his innovation of
alliterative assonance, but they also found his "easy, almost
conversational kind of verse without losing dignity", his
directness, his appeal to the senses, and his ironic understatement features in harmony with their own conception of
poetry. So Day Lewis declared that though "Owen was not
a technical revolutionary . . . he was a true revolutionary
poet, opening up new fields of sensitiveness", and held that
"his unsentimental pity, his savage and sacred indignation
are the best of our inheritance". There was also one of
Owen's poems which could have a particular appeal to those
on the Left : it was the poem *Miners*, showing that Owen
too thought of those heroic fighters, equally as liable to be
overlooked as the soldiers of the battlefield.

Edmund Blunden, a Sussex man who joined the Royal
Sussex regiment and saw service on the Western Front, began

to write in 1914, but he first came into general notice with *The Shepherd and other Poems of Peace and War* in 1922. He began as a poet of the country scene, and he became one of our truest pastoral poets, whose poetic contribution was considerable in the twenties and thirties. His poetry of the war appeared mainly after the war, some as late as 1928 in an appendix to the prose *Undertones of War*, and indeed later than that, drawing from him the following remark in the Preface to his *Collected Poems, 1930-40* : "Some of these writings are concerned with the war of 1914-18 and its after-refrains. It is not a case of morbidly wishing to go back that road, or of want of anxious interest in current events ; but those who saw that tremendous time will know that it does not easily give up its hold".

Blunden's war poetry gives the impression of fulfilling Wordsworth's definition of poetry as being "emotion recollected in tranquillity". Indeed *Third Ypres*, which the poet himself called "one of his most comprehensive and particular attempts to render war experience poetically", is entitled "A Reminiscence". In that poem, after creating an atmosphere of ominous quiet, in which the dreary misery of the troops in the grey, steady rain breaks at times into hysteria, and where the troops in the line find strength only as in a dream "to bear back that strange whim their body" when relieved, Blunden proceeds to tell of the horror of being shelled in a pillbox. It is vivid, descriptively and psychologically, but even in the total effect of such a poem the urgency of feeling which gives such a painful intensity to the poems of Sassoon and Owen seems absent. In general, the poems are meditative and descriptive, as though the pastoral poet could observe and record, as was his nature, but, deeply though he felt, the monstrous business of war was too alien to his spirit to be absorbed and released again in poetry comparable in quality to his poems of the countryside he loved. His awareness of the grim folly and the sickening horror and tedium of war was accompanied by the even deeper and more abiding desire

"To seek and serve the beauty that must die".

Whatever beauty, especially of nature, there was in the scene of war, he loved to describe. So anger and bitterness were foiled in him. The memories of war never left him, but became a living background to all his thinking, whence he could first extract the essence of remembered scenes and later the wisdom of a quiet mind in a chaotic world. In his poetry two complementary themes constantly recur, the mutability of all things, and the strength and beauty that lie in long tradition—in the war he had a shocked sense of mutability magnified to grotesque proportions, and of the upsetting of the decencies of human tradition.

By 1920 the poetic scene was being transformed. The day of the Georgians, now led by J. C. Squire and joined by Blunden, was coming to an end. Already in 1916 Edith Sitwell had begun her rival collection of contemporary poetry, *Wheels*. It was in *Wheels* of 1919 that Owen's *Strange Meeting* and a few of his other poems were first printed. In 1918 Bridges had revealed the astounding treasure of Hopkins's poetry. In 1920 T. S. Eliot's second volume appeared. As for the poetry of the war, it was the satiric, the disillusioned and the unsentimentally realistic that was alone esteemed by those who were to form the critical opinion of the rising generation—the poems not of Brooke and Nichols and Blunden, but of Owen, Sassoon and Herbert Read. Yet for a while the wider public continued to prefer the poems that had acclaimed the heroic aspect of war. The popular Second Series of *Poems of To-day* (1922) included four poems by Nichols, and such other poems as Herbert Asquith's *The Volunteer*, Julian Grenfell's *Into Battle*, Maurice Baring's *In Memoriam A. H.*, and Tennant's *Home Thoughts in Laventie* —of Sassoon's it had only the beautiful, indeed idyllic, *Everyone Sang*, and no poem of Owen's. The new note of 1919, however, was that of Osbert Sitwell, who carried on the message of Owen and shared the spirit of Sassoon. He celebrated the official Peace-day in July 1919 with a poem entitled *Corpse Day*.

CHAPTER V

HOPKINS AND T. S. ELIOT

In *A Hope for Poetry* in 1934 Day Lewis said of the poetry of Auden and himself and those who shared their views that its immediate ancestors were Owen, Hopkins and Eliot.

Gerard Manley Hopkins had died in 1889, leaving his poetry unpublished, and it was the wise choice of his intimate friend Robert Bridges, to whose hands he had entrusted it, that made 1918 the time for its release to the public. Tennyson had for some while been out of fashion, and a Victorian so different from him as Hopkins was readily welcomed. A few years later F. R. Leavis, the Cambridge critic, declared that Hopkins "is likely to prove, for our time and the future, the only influential poet of the Victorian age, and he seems to me the greatest". But, more than that, the poetry of Hopkins had qualities which particularly appealed to the post-war world : it revealed a sense of spiritual tension and frustration ; it combined a powerful intellect with a strong sensuousness ; it possessed a bold originality of technique. In the twenties the poetry of the early seventeenth-century poet John Donne was rediscovered and almost worshipped for similar reasons, but Hopkins could speak even more immediately to those years, for he had been aware of the industrial age when "all is smeared with trade". The greatness of his poetry can be judged from the impact it made upon poets and critics who did not share the religion which inspired and governed all that Hopkins wrote.

The personality of Hopkins was rich and curious. He was at once an artist, with a deeply sensuous appreciation of beauty, and an intensely devout man of religion, ascetic in his self-denial. As a boy he had a passion for drawing, and he wrote poetry under the influence of Keats and the Pre-Raphaelites. It was as an undergraduate at Oxford, where he was an outstanding Greek scholar, that he was converted to the Roman

Catholic Church, and, having been received into the Church by Cardinal Newman, in due course he trained for the priesthood and became a Jesuit priest in 1877. From his youth his life seems to have been one of inner strife, very keenly felt. At first he gave up poetry : "what I had written I burnt before I became a Jesuit and resolved to write no more, as not belonging to my profession, unless it were the wish of my superiors". But after seven years of poetic silence he resumed poetry in 1875 with *The Wreck of the Deutschland*, taking as permission the remark of his rector that he wished someone would write a poem dealing with that disaster in which five nuns, banished from Germany, were drowned at the mouth of the Thames. But even so there were times when he felt that to write poetry was to misuse time for which God's service had other demands, though his letters show how continuously he was preoccupied with an insatiable interest in the very technique of poetry. He feared beauty almost as much as he loved it, and he would punish himself through his love of beauty by sometimes refusing to let himself look upon the beauty of nature when he was walking. Indeed in a poem written in 1866 when he was contemplating the taking up of the religious life, *The Habit of Perfection*, he bade all his senses renounce the world.

The worship of God, and religious experience and service, were the be-all and end-all of Hopkins's life, and yet even here he experienced frustration and felt fear and failure. As his diaries show, his mind could give him no rest ; as some of his poems show, his fears ever welled up for the young, that the blight of sin would mar them ; as his life shows, preaching and teaching do not appear to have given him joy. His last sonnets in the year or so before his early death at the age of forty-four after much ill-health lament the drying up of his poetic impulse. His curious, baffled, striving self-analysis can be glimpsed in such a comment as this in a letter to Bridges in 1870 : "I always knew in my heart Walt Whitman's mind to be more like my own than any other man's living. As he is a very great scoundrel this is not a pleasant confession and this also makes me the more desirous to read him and the more determined that I will not".

The purpose of Hopkins in poetry was to employ his mind and senses with such concentration as to force into words the very essence of the subject he contemplated. So his famous poem *The Windhover* presents the power, beauty, speed and ecstacy of the kestrel's flight, isolated and magnified to more than life-like (as art must magnify): to Hopkins its flight was the distinctive, essential quality of the bird—"the achieve of, the mastery of the thing!" This seizing of the distinctive quality, and as far as possible its concrete, sensuous presentation was said by Hopkins to be "what I above all aim at in poetry", and he called it "inscape". The pursuit of "inscape" resulted in expression in which every word told, and nothing extraneous had a place. *Hurrahing in Harvest* presents first the stooks "barbarous in beauty", then the loveliness of "silk-sack clouds" compared to "meal-drift"; there the poet walks "to glean our Saviour", whose "world-wielding shoulder" is "the azurous hung hills". The whole scene and the poet's rapturous response have been concentrated into ten lines, and in conclusion the poet's heart

> "rears wings bold and bolder
> And hurls for him, O half hurls earth for him off
> under his feet".

The Wreck of the Deutschland, which began his later poetry and is his longest poem, has for its themes the human soul in its relationship to God, and the might and majesty of nature as the servant of God : which is to say that it contains the essentials of all the poetry Hopkins has left us. The tragic event that occasioned the poem had moved him intensely in the very depths of his soul, and he wrote the poem rapidly, fashioning, even as he composed it, his new poetic instrument which proved so startling to its first readers that the Catholic magazine to which he offered it "dared not print it". At that time indeed there was no poem like it in the English language in its technical aspects : more important, but inseparable from the technique, was the unrivalled way in which the passionate self-revelation of a soul is joined to the description of a storm at sea. Part I is the cry of a strong soul that feels the finger of God upon it : for Hopkins the Passion of Christ is the overmastering fact in the life of his soul; Christ is "light-ning and love", and he both adores Him and confesses His terror; he knows that life has value only through the mercy and grace of God, but, when that is understood and felt, discipline is sweet, and the beauty of the world glorious. So the devout priest and the acutely sensitive artist are reconciled, though it is possible to hear within the lines echoes of his inner strife. In Part II, when he describes the storm, he might be in the storm-wrecked ship itself, glorying in the terrible majesty of the might of wind and water, for it is all of God, it is "God's cold", it is indeed God reaping His harvest, the tempest carries His grain, the lost nuns are five even as the wounds of Christ were five. Whatever his poetic talents, the power comes from the personal stress in his own soul.

> "Ah, touched in your bower of bone
> Are you ! turned for an exquisite smart,
> Have you ! make words break from me here all alone,
> Do you !—mother of being in me, heart".

God and his own soul, God and other souls, God and nature, these were his main subjects. For the souls of others he yearns as a priest, reflecting in *Felix Randal* on the spiritual effects of illness and the ministration of the Sacraments. He had a particular tenderness in his love and fear for the inno-cence of youth, a tenderness that can give discomfort to colder natures, so sensitive is his compassion, and so sensuous can be the imagery, as in *The Bugler's First Communion*. The beauty of youth aroused in him an aching fear of what the world's corruption would do both to the handsome face and the handsome heart. In one of his finest poems, *The Leaden Echo and the Golden Echo*, he asks first how it is possible "to keep back beauty . . . from vanishing away" and gives the answer that it must be by giving back all youth's beauty—

> "beauty-in-the-ghost, deliver it, early now, long before death
> Give beauty back, beauty, beauty, beauty, back to God,
> beauty's self and beauty's giver".

So the artist and the priest were ever joined in his poems, and when the theme was God and nature he was nature's noblest worshipper. Religion was the air he breathed, and in *The Blessed Virgin compared to the Air we Breathe* he was rapturously at ease in the happy skill with which he played with his image, adoring the Virgin and rejoicing in all the beauty of air and sky. Not Wordsworth himself was half so rapturous a poet of nature as Hopkins, when his senses responded to "the grandeur of God", and he was impelled to sing, exalted in the knowledge that, despite "man's smudge",

> "nature is never spent;
> There lives the dearest freshness deep down things".

He apprehended all things vividly—their colour, form, movement, touch, taste, and smell. (One critic has even remarked that in *Harry Ploughman*, where his theme is the man's nature physically, his verse can so excite muscular responses that the poem "leaves the reader feeling almost as though he had been exercising himself in a gymnasium".) And as one would expect of a spirit so original as Hopkins's the poet above all loved

> "All things counter, original, spare, strange",

and prayed that "the wildness and wet", "the weeds and the wilderness" might long remain : for where the Holy Ghost "broods with warm breast" over the world all nature is good.

The sincerity of this original poet triumphed over any difference of faith, or lack of Christian faith in his later readers. What impressed them was the unique poetic personality which combined so penetrating an intellect with such sensuous appreciation. That he had felt the pressure of "our sordid turbid time", and had been conscious of the social-political problem of the unemployed (see the "sonnet" *Tom's Garland*), and had suffered an inner strife

> "With this tormented mind tormenting yet"

made him seem their contemporary. To the young poets he had the special appeal of a great original craftsman : as Day Lewis put it, Hopkins "is a true revolutionary poet, for his imagination was always breaking up and melting the inherited forms of language, fusing them into new possibilities, hammering them into new shapes".

Technically, Hopkins was both an innovator and a restorer in both rhythm and language. The total effect was one of revolutionary innovation, but most of the single features were a recovery of older practice. His Sprung Rhythm, as he called it, went away from the syllabic foot back to the stress rhythm of our earliest poetry before the Norman Conquest and of the medieval *Piers Plowman*, and never quite suppressed in English poetry, for such stress is in the nature of our tongue. This brought his rhythms closer to the rhythm of ordinary speech, a feature which in the twenties and later was by most critics regarded as a touchstone of good poetry. With this stress rhythm in Anglo-Saxon poetry had gone alliteration as a basic principle, and Hopkins too made much use of alliteration, employing it with a special power to shock the reader into deeper attention by the binding together of unexpected words by this device. Pursuing his mastery over sound effects, for the sake of driving his meaning home as well as for their own sake, Hopkins used rhyme within the line, and played upon the balance and accumulation of similar sounds, and learned from Welsh metrical forms the possibility of rich consonantal harmonies. In language he went back to the practice of coining compound words which the Elizabethans had used freely and Keats had resumed, and coined them with a bold freshness, as in "dappled-with-damson west", "not-by-morning-matchèd face". He got away from abstract and "poetic" words, and used concrete, sensuous, forceful words, like "sloggering" of the waves, and "rinse and wring the ear" of the song of a thrush. His words are often as unexpected as his alliterations, but they are good words of natural speech, though of a heightened kind when necessary, as he declared poetic language should be. In syntax, he often omitted little words, like relative pronouns, as Shakespeare did.

In all this there was at first a great strangeness not only to his friends Bridges and Canon Dixon, but no doubt to the poet himself, so that, enjoying the originality that burst its way from him, he was also finding himself, and in the process indulging in rather more violence than was necessary. Of *Tom's Garland* he wrote to Bridges: "I laughed outright and often, but very sardonically, to think you and the Canon could not construe my last sonnet : that he had to write to you for a crib." That poem is still very difficult, but the twentieth century acquired by a variety of experiences a greater understanding of this concentrated manner of expression, and even in *Tom's Garland* the reader is greatly helped if he reads the poem aloud, letting the natural stress of speech open the door of the understanding—as Hopkins told Bridges, "declaimed, the strange constructions would be dramatic and effective". His obscurity was in large part the penalty he had to pay for his originality, and for the way in which his mind leapt from image to image leaving the reader to follow by finding the unstated emotional links—which again the reading of much of the later poetry and a change in the mental climate made easier for the readers of the twenties and thirties. But, had Hopkins lived longer, he might have kept his strength and his originality without its defects, for his latest sonnets show him coming to a stern, almost monosyllabic simplicity. That he saw the defects of his qualities is clear from his letters to Bridges : On "inscape" he remarked : "It is the virtue of . . . inscape to be distinctive and it is the vice of distinctiveness to become queer. This vice I cannot have escaped". Reading his *Eurydice* only with his eyes he admitted : "it struck me aghast with a kind of raw nakedness and unmitigated violence" ; but he reassured his friend, "take breath and read it with the ears, as I always wish to be read, and my verse becomes all right".

T. S. Eliot, the last of the "immediate ancestors" named by Day Lewis, had the strongest influence of all in changing the nature of English poetry. To his influence was joined that of the even more provocative earlier poetry of Edith Sitwell, who with Eliot was the leading "modern" poet of the twenties. The new poetry had been inaugurated in 1914 by Eliot's *Love Song of J. Alfred Prufrock*, whose influence upon poetry a later critic declared to have been "almost as disturbing as the murder at Serajevo [the immediate origin of the 1914 war] was to the peace of Europe". It was naturally a little while before its influence was felt, but by 1920 Eliot was a force in poetry, and in 1922 his *Waste Land* appeared and soon became the object of worship as of a poetic masterpiece and the supreme self-expression of its age. *The Hollow Men* followed in 1925, and it was the poetry which culminated in this poem that was mainly responsible for Eliot's influence upon the young poets who came forward around 1930. By 1930, however, Eliot himself had begun to develop considerably away from the thought behind his earlier poetry, for by that year, when *Ash-Wednesday* was published, he was an Anglo-Catholic. His influence continued in the thirties by virtue of his technique, but many came to think of him as a lost leader. He had become accepted and "respectable" : his worshippers could no longer feel that they shared him with the few who understood. Indeed, having taken to the drama, Eliot won himself a much wider audience with a play like *Murder in the Cathedral*. His critical writings too spread to a wider public, and by the outbreak of the 1939 war, and with the death of Yeats and the poetic silence of Edith Sitwell, he was without challenge at the head of English poetry. In the forties the resumption, from *Burnt Norton* of 1934, of his philosophic odes, difficult though they were from the thought as much as the manner, brought him his full fame, acknowledged in the bestowal upon him of the high distinction of the Order of Merit. "Modern poetry" after some quarter of a century had won the day. Masefield, the Laureate, was still respected, but his kind of poetry dated from before 1920.

Before considering the man and the poet it is well to have in mind both the poetry which had helped to form Eliot's conception of poetry and also what he himself said upon the nature of poetry in his time. He owed a great deal to the French Symbolist poets, who in their turn had learnt from Edgar Allan Poe, whose *Ulalume* has been called "the first great poem of the Symbolist school". Following Poe, the symbolist poets regarded poetry as consisting in the musical evocation of moods, vague, subtle and evanescent. To this end they concentrated on the suggestive power of word-music and on suggestion by means of association of ideas. Their whole method was indirect : as Mallarmé said, "My

aim is to evoke an object in deliberate shadow, without ever
actually mentioning it, by allusive words, never by direct
words". It was largely through Arthur Symons that this
influence of the French symbolists reached English poetry.
Symons introduced their work to Yeats, and in 1899 he published *The Symbolist Movement in Literature*, of which Eliot
wrote : "I myself owe Mr Symons a great debt. But for
having read his book, I should not, in the year 1908, have
heard of Laforgue and Rimbaud ; I should probably not have
begun to read Verlaine, and but for reading Verlaine I should
not have heard of Corbière. So the Symons book is one of
those that have affected the course of my life". Indeed, so
much did he appreciate the poems of Corbière and Laforgue
that certain of his early poems show a close correspondence
with some of theirs in tone, metre and even theme, as Edmund
Wilson has pointed out in *Axel's Castle*. In Corbière he
found the combination of romance and mockery, and in both
a tone where irony balanced pathos, and a style mingling
slang with the poetic. Laforgue was his master in conversational rhythm. The work of both no doubt encouraged his
early tendency to be smart and even flippant.

Donne and the other metaphysical poets and the
dramatists of the first half of the seventeenth century also
contributed much to the making of Eliot as a poet. As he
remarked in a critical paper, they "possessed a mechanism
of sensibility which could devour any kind of experience",
and he held that to go back to their example was to recover
poetry from the "dissociation of sensibility" whereby it had
come to pass that poets either felt or thought but no longer
did both at once, thinking through and with their senses.
Donne gave him examples of the complex and subtle mood
poem, at once intellectual, emotional and physical in its
appeal ; of striking imagery, and unexpected turns ; of rapid
transition from image to image and idea to idea by emotional rather than logical sequence ; of "the alliance of levity
and seriousness (to the enhancing of the serious)". The
poetic drama of Webster and Tourneur, too, was an example

to him in the union of thought and passion, and in its dramatic speech rhythm.

But it is difficult to point out all the poetic influences that went to form Eliot's poetic mind. Dante must be given a very high place, for throughout his life Eliot has clearly had a reverence for him, both for the grand simplicity of his style and, with an ever-growing realisation, the profundity of his genius. Baudelaire's influence on his imagery is obvious in his poems ; in prose he paid tribute to him for giving "new possibilities to poetry in a new stock of imagery of contemporary life". The Imagists, too, made their contribution to his style, for he combined their precise little pictures with the vaguer imagery of the Symbolists. In fact, he did his best to fulfil his own definition of a mature poet as "one who not merely restores a tradition which has been in abeyance, but one who in his poetry retwines as many straying strands of tradition as possible". His wide and very sensitive reading made him acquainted with a great variety of such straying strands. It gave him also much material which, if not elements of a tradition, was of a kind to be woven into his poetry for its suggestive value, for he extended the scope of symbolism to include the use of partial quotation and of allusion to create the thought or atmosphere, contrast or illumination, he desired. With the elusive hint often from the depths of learning he rivalled the later masters of the crossword puzzle, which was another product of the new mental climate.

As critic, Eliot, from the period of his early poetry, expressed his views on the nature of poetry, and his own poetry is best understood when we bear these opinions in mind. His view of poetry was very high and exacting. His belief in tradition involved "the conception of poetry as a living whole of all the poetry that has ever been written". "Tradition cannot be inherited . . . It involves the historical sense . . . and the historical sense involves a perception, not only of the pastness of the past, but of its presence ; the historical sense compels a man to write not merely with his own generation in his bones, but with a feeling that the whole literature

of Europe from Homer and within it the whole of the literature of his own country has a simultaneous existence and com-
poses a simultaneous order." He believed that poetry had a
function of its own—"poetry is not a substitute for philosophy
or theology or religion". Its function was "not intellectual,
but emotional". Indeed, "what every poet starts from is his
own emotions", and they are deep-rooted emotions, for the
poet possesses "auditory imagination", which, Eliot says,
"is the feeling for syllable and rhythm, penetrating far below
the conscious levels of thought and feeling, invigorating every
word; sinking to the most primitive and forgotten". Poetry
was therefore not to be apprehended easily by the mind. The
reader must approach poetry in a state of unprejudiced sensitivity. "The more seasoned reader, he who has reached . . .
a state of greater *purity*, does not bother about understanding ;
not, at least, at first"—about understanding, that is, in the
logical way which can express the "meaning" of a poem step
by step as prosaic statement.

This suspension of the merely intellectual understanding
was the more necessary because it was the nature of poetry
to be complex, and in his time, declared Eliot, more than
usually so. His view in 1921 was : "we can only say that
it appears likely that poets in our civilisation, as it exists at
present, must be difficult. Our civilisation comprehends
great variety and complexity, and this variety and complexity, playing upon a refined sensibility, must produce various
and complex results. The poet must become more and more
comprehensive, more allusive, more indirect, in order to force,
to dislocate if necessary, language into his meaning". Finally,
we may note that Eliot abandoned the conception that a poet
should be preoccupied with the beautiful : "the essential
advantage for a poet is not to have a beautiful world with
which to deal : it is to be able to see beneath both beauty and
ugliness ; to see the boredom, and the horror, and the glory".

Eliot was twelve when the century began. His family
traced its history back to an Eliot who emigrated from East
Coker in Somerset to America about 1670. In America the
Eliots were New England Puritans who became comfortably

wealthy. The poet-to-be studied at the University of Harvard, at the Sorbonne, and at Oxford, and from 1914 he was settled in England, becoming naturalised in 1927. His personality, as deduced from his writings, is elusive and contradictory. Above all perhaps one has the impression of a "superior person", austere, detached from common life, sophisticated, a little too self-assured both as poet and critic. He remarks oddly, but no doubt ironically, of the poet Blake that "there was nothing of the superior person about him. This makes him terrifying". Yet of his own appearance as a superior person he makes unaffected fun in the lines "How unpleasant to meet Mr Eliot!" His austerity and refinement are countered by his approval of zest in living and his regret for the passing of the full-blooded music-hall. But when he remarks of the ordinary man that he "falls in love or reads Spinoza", we see how far he was removed from the ordinary man. He tells us that poetry arises from the poet's own emotions, but also that poetry must be impersonal, and his own poetry often seems a baffling combination of both personal and impersonal. At any rate he often gives us apparently personal glimpses of a tantalising nature, for he alone knows their significance :—

> "The moment in the arbour where the rain beat,
> The moment in the draughty church at smokefall".

His assurance seems frequently reversed to self-distrust, and his pride to be equalled by his humility.

With many poets the question of personality does not arise in estimating their work, but in all his writing, and particularly in his poetry, one is conscious in Eliot of a personality so strong, however elusive, as to have been responsible, rather than the poetry itself, for some of the unsympathetic reactions to him. It is a complex personality, sheltering itself behind irony and reticence, and the true clue to its basic nature may perhaps be found in considering his childhood. In New England the Puritan faith still lived on, a religious background likely to be apprehended by a child as giving a simple assurance, austere but not without warmth, of the being of God

and the existence of the soul. The structure of culture and
learning which he built over this led him first to reliance
upon humanism ; the Puritan conscience and temperament
remained but not the faith. But in due course he returned to
a simplicity of faith, though enriched and less austere. Part
of his childhood background physically was the Atlantic sea-
board, and it is remarkable how strongly the sea comes
through the imagery of poem after poem. Like the child of
his *Animula* he took

> "Pleasure in the wind, the sunlight and the sea".

Even when his poems are speaking of rooms, or seem to
come from the poet sitting in his study, the voice of the sea is
nevertheless often there. In childhood, too, there was the
"strong brown god" of the river :

> "His rhythm was present in the nursery bedroom".

When we come to the *Quartets*, imagery of nature and childhood is used to convey the deepest suggestions, as through

> "The voice of the hidden waterfall
> And the children in the apple-tree".

As "the child is father of the man", so Eliot's later poetry
can well be seen as showing a return to his earliest memories
and understanding, leading to wisdom and assurance and
humility regained after much bitter experience.

In his first two volumes of 1917 and 1920 we see Eliot up
to his early thirties. Between the lines his poems present a
picture of an intellectual young man, with inner divisions and
uncertainties, his culture and learning above, his faith steri-
lised below, his heart aching, and his mind keen, observant
and amused. From his very nature he has become the satirist
of his own *milieu* and of himself. There is J. Alfred
Prufrock, slightly bald middle-aged dilettante, feeling himself
growing old, hugging to himself his suppressed yearnings and
romantic memories, but too afraid and too indecisive to
fulfil any of his desires, and laughing ruefully at himself. There
is the woman in *Portrait of a Lady* groping for some hold on
life as it slips into middle-age, trying amid concerts and talk

to find romantic friendship again in the person of the intelligent, attractive young man who speaks as "I" in the poem, and who, though it would be wrong to interpret him as Eliot himself, no doubt portrays some of Eliot's own dissatisfaction with himself. There are "Miss Helen Slingsby . . . my aunt" with her four servants, Cousin Harriet, and Professor and Mrs Cheetah and their guests listening, in a superior way, to the brilliant pagan talk of their charming visiting lecturer. These people amuse Eliot, but they rather frighten him too, with their lives following a convention from which the meaning is evaporating, with their lack of purpose and of faith in themselves. They are a cultured caste that has become exhausted. And the observer fears the more for realising himself as one of them, in danger of becoming a Prufrock. He notes the nervous tension and suppressed hysteria of this world of frustrated, rudderless, cultured, well-to-do people. Looking at the lower strata he distastefully records the footman, when his mistress is dead, sitting on the dining table with the second housemaid on his knees ; he thinks of streets of furnished rooms, where he imagines a woman waking in the morning in her sordid surroundings, and thinks of her soul as constituted of a "thousand sordid images". He reflects of a pilfering street-child he has seen that

> "I could see nothing behind that child's eye".

But with his satire, his irony, his anti-romantic observation, there is a true and tender pity—

> "The notion of some infinitely gentle
> Infinitely suffering thing".

The 1917 volume concentrated most on the signs of a dying class : Day Lewis declared in 1934, "It is very much to Eliot's credit as a poet that he detected this deathwill in Western civilisation before it rose to the surface in the disillusionment of the later war years". But Eliot also pointed out that, outside this society, there were those who felt "the appetites of life", and who had "eyes assured of certain certainties". The 1920 volume, though it opened with *Gerontion* depicting an old man in whom passion and religion had long lost their force, and who had little left but "thoughts of a dry brain", extended the scene more ominously. In *Gerontion* we are made aware of the shady world of cosmopolitan finance ; in other poems we meet broad-bottomed, ape-neck Sweeney, in whom there is crude vitality enough ; Grishkin too has a rank sensuality. If life has drained away from the top, in lower spheres it can be seen, as Yeats declared in *The Second Coming*, that in the worst there is passionate intensity. But the general effect of the 1920 volume is one of decadence and death, and Eliot seeks to emphasise the faded culture of the present by contrasting it with the romantic glamour of the past. Again, however, Eliot could not resist the mood of ironic self-depreciation, implicit with self-pitying humour in the very title *A Cooking Egg*—at thirty he was no longer new-laid.

From the beginning these first two volumes had a twofold appeal. On the one hand they showed a sensitive criticism of the spiritual state of our civilisation ; on the other they were a revelation of a new poetic technique, and, better, still, they were a new poetry. None of his work more clearly shows Eliot as the artist, rejoicing in the sheer perfection of his artistry, in every detail of wit, imagery, sound, rhythm, as well as in the total effect. His aesthetic criticism through his artistry is indeed finer and even more essentially Eliot than his moral criticism, though the moral and aesthetic often seem inseparable as in Pope's poetry, with which Eliot's has much in common. But in *The Waste Land* of 1922 both artist and moralist took on more than they were able to accomplish. Its immediate fame and influence were certainly great, but there is much to be said for Herbert Palmer's view : "Surely Mr Eliot never intended *The Waste Land* to be taken quite so seriously, at least not quite so constructively, especially as it exhibits too many of the features of a hoax. At any rate a hoax and earnest are strangely, hypnotically, and bafflingly blended". It certainly made an enormous demand upon the intelligence, knowledge and patience of its readers.

Shortly after *The Waste Land* was published Eliot wrote, in an essay on James Joyce, of "the immense panorama of futility and anarchy which is contemporary history", and it was this panorama that he had sought to compress into this poem. Partly through his own emotions, partly through those of typical figures, he aimed at creating, not an objective description, but a dramatic self-expression of an age of emotional sterility, devoid of real purpose, and haunted by fear. As the men in the poem melt into one another, so, Eliot tells us, "all the women are one woman", and the whole scene is further represented as being observed by centuries-old Tiresias, in whom "the two sexes meet". As an enveloping symbolism the poem draws on a myth from the legend of the Holy Grail of a Waste Land, stricken by drought, where everything vegetable, animal and human has become sterile, and whose king too is impotent, until all fertility is restored through a knight who seeks at Chapel Perilous the Lance and the Grail. To this is joined the symbolism of the ancient Tarot pack of cards used for telling fortunes, and related ultimately to fertility and water myths : one of its cards was the Hanged Man, whom Eliot associated in his mind with the Hanged God dealt with in Frazer's great mythological study, *The Golden Bough*, from whose sacrifice came the renewal of life. His notes to the poem declared that to read Miss Weston's *From Ritual to Romance* and two volumes of *The Golden Bough* would help towards the comprehension of his poem. Further, to the need of this not inconsiderable preliminary knowledge the poet added the difficulty of his own excessive concentration, his continuous use of often obscure literary allusion and of the past in contrast to the present, his admitted adaptation of the Tarot pack "to suit my own convenience", and the desirability of an appreciation of Buddha's Fire Sermon. Moreover, his presentation involved the passing of fear into hysteria, and, magnificently though he conveys the hysteria, it is yet another element exacting intuitive understanding from the overburdened reader.

Nevertheless, if the reader follows Eliot's own advice upon poetry and does not bother to understand it all, *The Waste Land* has a powerful general effect, and frequently delights by its high artistic achievement. On the one hand, we have powerfully presented the horror of the "Unreal City", the blight of barren mechanical sexuality, the sense of spiritual emptiness breeding fear and hysteria. On the other, the poet finally builds up his own spiritual refuge in a code of living, indicated by Give, Sympathise, Control, and in the humanism of great literature. The poetic beauty comes through with special clarity in the elaborate description of the room where the woman sits at her toilet, and in the universal elegy *Death by Water*, but time and again the lines are rich with a highly suggestive power. Yet, overriding all, perhaps, is the reader's awareness of the poet's own suppressed personality :

> "I have heard the key
> Turn in the door once and turn once only".

A defect of the poem as a true view of the contemporary world is that it concentrates on the cosmopolitan city-dwellers, on suburbia, and the intelligentsia, and ignores both the life abundant which upheld them, and the vitality, destructive but strong, of his Sweeney type. When in 1925 *The Hollow Men* followed, with a similar view of a dying civilisation, drawing to its end "Not with a bang but a whimper", he achieved far greater clarity, with a unique lyric beauty, but, as 1939 was to show not only in the heroic endurance of this country but in the international scene both for good and ill, it had not been a generation merely of

> "stuffed men
> Leaning together
> Headpiece filled with straw".

After 1925 the direction of Eliot's poetry changed. He kept his technique, though often modifying it in favour of greater clarity, but he turned away from satire and criticism to a constructive search for the truth. *Ash-Wednesday* of 1930 records in six movements a spiritual experience, beginning with renunciation and ending with the hope of life renewed. First, he must rest in quiet and humility, forgetting self, with its introspection and self-analysis ; then, even in the Waste Land there shall be joy again ; but still the self dogs him, his senses distract him, and he realises only his unworthiness; and yet the time can be redeemed, and "the new years walk"; but in these days of darkness the voice of God is hard for men to hear, and those who hear it with fear yet cannot surrender themselves; finally, however, he can rest in quiet with a new assurance, which he conveys with a poignant beauty of imagery drawn from nature and of a ship with white sails flying seaward. So the movements alternate between the sombre and the hopeful. Much of the imagery and the concentrated expression makes the intellectual understanding of the poem very difficult, but the colour and life in the imagery and the very sound and rhythm of the lines convey the spiritual movement to the reader.

Four shorter poems between 1927 and 1930 appear as by-products of this spiritual transition. *Journey of the Magi* is related to the sombre movements of *Ash-Wednesday*: with admirable clarity it gives us a picture of the journey of the wise men, but because the birth of Christ means the death of the old gods the conclusion is the painful tension in the death of one world when a new one is begotten. *A Song for Simeon* too is sombre, and looks for joy to death rather than life, the poet again seeming to speak for himself when Simeon says

"Not for me the ultimate vision".

Animula also opens with a bright picture only to close with sombre thoughts of death, often so wilfully sought in this modern world; it resembles Wordsworth's *Immortality Ode* in depicting the closing in of the shades of the prison-house upon the growing boy, but with an even darker sense of the light lost until the soul becomes a "spectre in its own gloom" and without Wordsworth's compensatory philosophic faith. It seems reasonable to link its feeling to Eliot's own and to suspect that the picture of the child is of himself too—the child who took pleasure in the brilliance of the Christmas tree, in the beauty of the pattern of stags on the silver tray, and "in the wind, the sunlight and the sea". Undoubtedly the last of these poems, *Marina*, is related to the hopeful movements of *Ash-Wednesday*, particularly the last with its image of the ship : for in this poem he blends with the concept of Marina, the re-found daughter, the image of a ship making its landfall on an unknown shore to symbolise hope and strength revived and vision refreshed and extended, as well as the joy of new aspiration when that which has been lost is found again transformed. *Marina* and *Ash-Wednesday* showed the emergence of Eliot from the Waste Land with a better hope than humanism.

Eliot, however, did not go straight on to his poetic fulfilment. The two *Coriolan* poems of 1931 and 1932 showed an interest in political problems. The first posed the question of leadership where the people were without vision, and the second satirically underlined the futility of government by committees. It was a digression inadequately worked out, but in the second poem there sang out in lovely contrast to the satire a small voice hinting at the hidden reality behind this weary futility. Here was the theme to occupy him in the *Four Quartets*, the first of which, *Burnt Norton*, appeared in 1934. But he now turned aside to the drama. *The Rock* of 1934 was a pageant play written for performance on behalf of a fund for forty-five churches in the London diocese. In its choruses was much preaching. The Waste Land still oppressed him—

"The desert is squeezed in the tube-train next to you"—

but now he saw everything from the view-point of the right relationship of men to God, and he bade men seek the Light, one of the finest choruses praising both the Light of God and the physical beauty of light, which gives Eliot much of his characteristic imagery. In another chorus can be found the theme of the intersection of the timeless with time, theme too of the Quartets. There followed *Murder in the Cathedral* and *Family Reunion*, in neither of which was poetry the predominant quality. In 1938, it is said, he resigned the editorship of *The Criterion*, founded by himself in 1923, in despair at the international scene after Munich, but the sure resurrection of his faith was declared in the successive appearance of the later Quartets, *East Coker* in 1940, *The Dry Salvages* in 1941, and *Little Gidding* in 1942.

The *Four Quartets* are great philosophic odes so complex in their thought, their development, and their imagery that books are necessary for their full expounding. But the total effect of each separately and of all together is not difficult to grasp. His meditations are now always within the bounds of Christian thought. Whenever he broods upon time and eternity, behind his thinking lies the acceptance of the certain truth of the Incarnation, and because his thinking is Christian thinking there constantly attends upon his thoughts of time the problem of how time can be redeemable—a problem we can feel him aware of, though without any solution, as early as in his portrait of Prufrock.

The complex form of the Quartets is due to the way in which the poet feels his way variously with mind, with imagination and with emotion, his imagination and emotion being largely released by memory. *Burnt Norton* centres on the significance of a sudden moment of illumination, whereby the nature of time can be tested. Thus in the first movement the poet begins by making a statement of the nature of time, present, past and future, and then sinks into the memory of one of his experiences, a moment in a rose-garden with the hidden laughter of children in the leaves, a glimpse of the hidden reality which is timeless. In the second movement, after feeling lyrically the flux of the material world, he tries to express the nature of eternity through the image of the "still point of the turning world", the point which does not move—"neither movement from nor towards"—but yet where there is not fixity, but an eternal movement; he then meditates on the moral implications of this realisation of the still point and of such an experience, and sinks again into memories.

The third movement changes to a mood akin to that of his earlier satires; here he senses the twittering twilight of the contemporary world, and is led to state the doctrine of the way out, by descent into the world of darkness and perpetual solitude, the way of renunciation as in *Ash-Wednesday*. The fourth movement is a lyric, as in all the Quartets, and it is the core of the poem: here he sings as it were in the heart of darkness, feeling the intimate and tender love that speaks in darkness, knowing that the darkness shall be light, that the way of renunciation is the way to the eternal Light, so infinitely greater than even its most beautiful symbol in this world. That lyric ended, in the concluding movement he tries once more to express the sense of eternal life, of the eternal stillness which is eternal movement,

> "The stillness, as a Chinese jar still
> Moves perpetually in its stillness".

He confesses the difficulty of the task, but is not disconcerted by the Waste Land. So he gathers himself for his conclusion, finding in Love a similar quality of being "itself unmoving, Only the cause and end of movement". Another image of continual movement within a pattern occurs to him—a shaft of sunlight within which the motes of dust dance in ceaseless motion. Finally the image of the hidden laughter of the children in the rose-garden recurs to him; compared with such an experience of illumination, how

> "Ridiculous the waste sad time
> Stretching before and after".

So we have had an intricate weaving together of statement, lyric, meditation, and satire; of thought, memory, analysis, and vision. But all turns upon the question what light is thrown by a moment of illumination upon the hidden reality which is beyond time. As with all Eliot's poetry, if the reader lets the poem speak to him as a whole, the intricacies and details will gradually grow clear, for beneath the complexity is a fundamental simplicity.

East Coker was written for Easter 1940, when the war was entering its grimmest phase in the West, a moment when "the poetry does not matter". This comes out in the lyrical fourth movement, the core of the poem, where he uses the image of a sick world—

> "The whole earth is our hospital"—

and proclaims that only through greater sickness can the cure come, and the only answer is Christ's Incarnation and Passion, which took place in time but is an eternal act ever renewed in the Eucharist. But, though this is a particular moment in time, and one where

> "every moment is a new and shocking
> Valuation of all we have been",

his main theme is again the significance of the moment of sudden illumination. The only way now is that of humility and renunciation : the true purpose of life is fulness of living which cannot be achieved in this temporal world. The brief but intense experiences of illumination must be linked together in the pursuit of truth. He concludes, as in *Burnt Norton*, that Love is " most nearly itself" when it reaches beyond time and place, and so, ignoring time, we must move forward into more intense living, into deeper communion with the hidden reality.

So Eliot both kept his eyes upon the days in which he lived, and sought the timeless reality for himself and for all who would follow. In *Burnt Norton* his thoughts had started from a Gloucestershire manor house, and in *East Coker* from the Somerset village from which his ancestor had come. In *The Dry Salvages* he went back to the coast of his childhood memories, where the warning bell was sounded by the ground swell of the primal force of ocean, and again his meditations, based upon "the moment in and out of time", led him to reflect how time could be conquered, and man released, and again the answer was, through "prayer, observance, discipline, thought and action", in "the hint half guessed, the gift half understood . . . Incarnation". In *Little Gidding* he found a spiritual home in the little sanctuary of seventeenth-century communal worship, a very precious place, to visit which was an experience similar to the moment in the rose-garden. The opening landscape is one where in mid-winter the sun flames on ice from a windless sky and all has a supernatural glow as of Pentecostal fire, and the poem draws to its climax with imagery of fire, the fire of Love, until Eliot can conclude the Quartets with the peace that passeth understanding, himself "at the still point of the still turning world", knowing that

> "All manner of thing shall be well
> When the tongues of flame are in-folded
> Into the crowned knot of fire
> And the fire and the rose are one".

The *Four Quartets* thus revealed Eliot solving for himself the problem he had put at the end of *The Waste Land*—how "to set my lands in order". He had gone a long way from Prufrock, but neither the artist in him nor the satirist had ceased to be, though both were transcended. The pictorial artist lived on, as in the remarkable picture of the village in *East Coker*, and the satirist in the mockery of human superstitions in *The Dry Salvages*. The poet's vision, fed though it was by learning from Buddhism, medieval mysticism, and elsewhere, had come to the simplest assurance of peace, at once quiet and intense. Now in all humility he could survey his previous poetry, in the second movement of *Little Gidding*, and, appraising his distant efforts "to purify the dialect of the tribe" and appreciating his "conscious impotence of rage at human folly", tell himself that, until he knew the "refining fire", he must admit

> "things ill done and done to others' harm
> Which once you took for exercise of virtue".

Since completing *Four Quartets* Eliot has turned mainly to the writing of plays (see pp. 306-8 and pp. 368-70). But for Christmas 1954 he published as a new "Ariel Poem" a short poem entitled "The Cultivation of Christmas Trees". Disregarding the wrong attitudes to Christmas, "the social, the torpid, the patently commercial, the rowdy . . . and the childish", he prayed that the child may "continue in the spirit of wonder", and that

> "The accumulated memories of annual emotion
> May be concentrated into a great joy
> Which shall also be a great fear".

CHAPTER VI

POETRY, 1920-1930

It would be hard to dispute that, in this decade, the poets who led the vanguard of poetry were T. S. Eliot and Edith Sitwell. They were the outstanding new poets, breaking fresh ground in a modern way. Yet even from that point of view their rival was the elder poet Yeats and, since their work was only in its first stage, it would be truer to give the poetic crown of this decade to him. Yeats was as sensitive as they to the pressure of the age, his style was as much in harmony with the new vision of things, and his poetic personality the richer in its nature and assurance.

To those who lived in the twenties, however, the poetic stage appeared far more crowded, and merely to enumerate some of the other principal poets shows how various were the kinds of poetry written and admired. Alongside the new poetry appealing at first to the few we see the continuance of the more traditional poetry as written by poets both old and young, the younger poets often introducing new qualities without experiencing so radical a change in outlook as Eliot and Edith Sitwell. Of poets long established there were Hardy and Bridges, now rejoined by the almost forgotten A. E. Housman. Davies and De la Mare were at the height of their popularity. Binyon and Sir William Watson maintained the dignity of poetry. Masefield, in the early twenties, was probably the most widely read poet. Wilfrid Gibson and Gordon Bottomley both made 1925 the year of their Collected Poems, reaching back to the early years of the century. Gibson and Bottomley had both been among the early contributors to *Georgian Poetry*, and in this decade, though *Georgian Poetry* ceased to appear after 1922, others of its poets, such as Drinkwater, Shanks, W. J. Turner and their leader, J. C. Squire, remained prominent. Alfred Noyes added to his songs and ballads and aspired to the heights with his almost epical history of science, *The Torch-Bearers*. Other poets who made a name for themselves without break-ing away from the traditional poetry were Richard Church, Herbert Palmer and Victoria Sackville-West. Of the war poets Sassoon, Blunden, Graves and Herbert Read all followed their notable, but diverging ways. There were the brothers Osbert and Sacheverell Sitwell, and Humbert Wolfe. Roy Campbell from South Africa was perhaps the most forceful poet of the decade, though the strange personality of D. H. Lawrence might well contest the distinction. And then at the end of the decade Auden and his contemporaries appeared. It makes an impressive enumeration, but several notable names could be added, and there were many others who deserved their inclusion in the anthologies of the day. In Ireland there was the friend and contemporary of Yeats, "A. E.".

Though in a survey such as this we must here speak principally of Edith Sitwell, the other poets must not be overlooked either for their intrinsic merits or for the light they shed upon that time. Thomas Hardy was highly honoured as the Grand Old Man of letters and, his last novel being now a quarter of a century old, his reputation as a poet rose to equal his reputation as a novelist. Neither his matter nor his manner had changed in any appreciable way, and indeed among *Late Lyrics and Earlier* (1922) a considerable number were earlier —they had "been lying about for years". But their welcome by young and old was not merely tribute paid to a great writer, but testified, perhaps especially in the young, to an appreciation of the poet's refusal to wear rose-coloured spectacles. As Hardy remarked in his Apology to the volume, it contained "some grave, positive, stark delinea-tions", and he had been unable to stifle his "questionings" in the exploration of reality, believing, as he had expressed himself years before, that

"If way to the Better there be, it exacts a full look
at the Worst".

The Apology, indeed, has a particular interest as showing Hardy's view of "our prematurely afflicted century" to be only a variation of that of Yeats and Eliot. He thought "we seem threatened with a new Dark Age", and as probable causes suggested "the barbarizing of taste in the younger minds by the dark madness of the late war, the unabashed cultivation of selfishness in all classes, the plethoric growth of knowledge simultaneously with the stunting of wisdom, [and] 'a degrading thirst after outrageous stimulation'". If the world were not to perish, he could only put his hope—"it may be a forlorn hope"—in "an alliance between religion . . . and complete rationality" effected by means of poetry.

No doubt, his prefatory remarks received less general attention and assent than his poems, but it was the same critical and tragic cast of mind in them and in his novels which won him a wide general public, not least among the younger readers. When A. E. Housman, after a silence of twenty-six years, followed up *A Shropshire Lad* with *Last Poems* in the same year 1922, different from Hardy's though his poems were, there was similarity enough in their sardonic realism and bitter strength to appeal to the same taste of the age as made Hardy's work acceptable. Housman perhaps as poet was the more popular because his sombre view of life was expressed in a more colourful and melodramatic way. Its element of self-pity too, quite alien to Hardy, met a corresponding feeling in many emerging from the war into the questionable blessings of peace.

But alongside the "pessimism" of Hardy and Housman there were the elder poets Bridges and Binyon to testify to a faith surviving the war undimmed. In 1925 Bridges published *New Verse*, most of the poems having been written in a late burst of creative impulse in 1921, the impulse coming in large part, as always with Bridges, from the artistic excitement of prosodic experiment. For Bridges there was still "the intimate comfort of Beauty . . . the soul's familiar angel", and above all there were "our temple of Christian faith and fair Hellenic art". Putting his trust in these things he could in *Cheddar Pinks* rejoice idly in his rose-garden not caring how the world "toil'd moil'd fuss'd and scurried"—he was approaching eighty—and in *Kate's Mother* could recreate a summer day

of over seventy years ago, when as a small boy he was taken
to pay his "first visit of compliment", so freshly that it
might have been the observation of the moment,

> "England in the peace and delight of her glory".

In *Kate's Mother* he had found the "neo-Miltonic syllabics"
which he employed in *The Testament of Beauty*, written when
he was over eighty. It is a poem like Pope's *Essay on Man*
or Tennyson's *In Memoriam* in that it embodies the philosophy
of an age, though with Bridges it was a philosophy by then
long superseded for most people. Bridges had never attended
to what seemed foreign to his nature, and his pen shows his
contented ignorance of modern psychology and economics.
But with a mind shrewdly wise with long thinking he restated
a noble faith in human nature under the guidance of God, who
is Love and expresses Himself through Beauty. The late
war had been a terrible reminder of evil, but he had an
unshaken confidence that man could so use his reason as to
mould his instincts to a higher way of life, his faith showing
in his finest passages a mystical basis. The reception of the
poem in 1929 showed that many still shared his faith and
found in his prosody some of his own pleasure, but the poem
also had its detractors to whom the conservatism of its thought
was antipathetic, not least in its political aspect.

The readers to whom *The Testament of Beauty* appealed
were those who in the twenties had found pleasure in the
Odes of Binyon. In *The Sirens* of 1924, as exalted and nobly
sustained a poem as this half-century produced, Binyon
faced perhaps more deliberately than Bridges the new world
of mechanised industry, and the doubt and division in the
mind and spirit of the age, but equally with Bridges he
rejoiced in the confidence that man would triumph.

> "Vision that dawns beyond knowledge shall deliver him
> From all that flattered, threatened, foiled, betrayed.
> Lo, having nothing, he is free of all the universe,
> And where light is, he enters unafraid."

Nineteen years older than Eliot, Binyon had not been withered
by the drought of the Waste Land.

Other and younger poets deserve consideration in order
to see the twenties in perspective, but to give its just emphasis
to the new poetic outlook that was, by virtue of its greater
sensitiveness to the changing mind of the world, to make the
more traditional poetry largely outmoded, it is time to appreciate the early achievement of Edith Sitwell.   Between 1916
when she founded *Wheels* in opposition to *Georgian Poetry*
and 1929 when her *Gold Coast Customs* appeared she produced
a large body of very distinctive poetry.   She and her brothers
were highly gifted publicists, who set out to shock.   They
rejoiced in controversy and in the gentle art of making
enemies.   Edith Sitwell gave in 1923 a remarkable and most
effective recital of poems by herself and her associates, her
voice coming, to a musical accompaniment, through a strikingly designed curtain.   It became impossible to ignore "the
Sitwells" and particularly the poetry of Edith Sitwell.

Edith Sitwell was born a great individualist in an aristocratic tradition.   Her father was the fourth baronet of
Renishaw, a great estate in Derbyshire for some six centuries
in the possession of the family—the whole background is
magnificently depicted by Sir Osbert Sitwell in his autobiographical volumes.   It was a setting from which she could
draw the best of a world which was already vanishing in her
youth, a stable tradition of fine living, in which the arts were
a living heritage and beauty of every kind was an open book.
It is no wonder that she could make no compromise with the
vulgarity of the modern world, and often, for choice, went
back in her imagination to the formal grace and the good taste
of the eighteenth century.   But she had equally no admiration
for tradition that had become unintelligent and dull, whether
in life or art, for she was born above all else with the soul of
an artist, bound to strike out as a rebel in pursuit of her
ideals.   Her brother Osbert said of her :

> "Ascetic artist of the painting word,
>   Your whole life bent to this one, selfless, cause
>   Of netting beauty with a phrase or pause".

Poetic artistry became her life's devotion.

Both in outlook and technique she had similarities with
Eliot. She too saw the Waste Land. Her early poems
showed her painfully aware of the artificiality of contemporary life, and oppressed by the dust of mortality. Relying
more on imagination and less on learning than Eliot, she
first conveyed her sense of the human tragedy through the
imagery of a puppet stage, its properties flimsy, its actors
wooden, a world of Clowns' Houses, the title of one of her
poems. In this mood she harmonised all nature to this
artificial "human" world, so that the very sky was paper
and the leaves wooden. With disillusion she saw the world
given over to materialism. Writing of the Russian ballet she
said :

> "This modern world is but a thin matchboard flooring
> spread over a shallow hell. For Dante's hell has faded,
> is dead. Hell is no vastness; there are no devils who
> laugh or who weep—only the maimed dwarfs of this life,
> terrible straining mechanisms crouching in trivial sands,
> and laughing at the giants' crumbling!"

It was a similar view that lay behind her poetry of this period.
The material world lost in its materialism would crumble into
dust, and only dust and the bare bones remain—dust and the
bone were favourite images in her poems, and the ever-tapping
drum.

Like Eliot, Edith Sitwell was close in spirit to the French
poets. She too could best be understood with a knowledge of
Baudelaire and Mallarmé, of Rimbaud and Laforgue. From
these sources in large part derived the use of the often obscure
symbolism, the artificiality, and the nightmare brilliance, and
by them the sardonic wit was encouraged. But her imagination reacted to much else. As the previous quotation
indicates, there was the Russian ballet. There was also
painting—MacNeice has said that when at eighteen he discovered the poetry of the Sitwells he found that their "little
jazz fantasies . . . were in tune with the 'childlike' painting of
Matisse and the sentimental harlequins of Picasso's blue
period". Jazz too made a notable contribution to her

experiments in rhythm. But the most distinctive feature of her style in these years was in her use of sense impressions. She often gave to one sense the attributes of another, as had been done by Milton in the famous phrase "blind mouths" in *Lycidas*. In particular what we see she often described in terms of hearing, as in "crackling green", "braying light", "jangling rain", or, in reverse, "the brass band's snorting stabs the sky". Some critics have over-emphasised this, but it would be hard to over-emphasise her vivid and unusual use of her senses. To quote from her *Essay on her own Poetry*, the supreme interpretation of her poetry up to 1929 : "if some of the images in these poems appear strange, it is because my senses are like those of primitive peoples, at once acute and uncovered—and they are interchangeable". Commenting on the image of "pigeons smelling of ginger-bread" she says : "in the summer, when their feathers are hot from the sun, they *do* smell like ginger-bread, and I am afraid there is nothing to be done about it". Plenty of children still share her "acute and uncovered" senses. Another difficulty experienced by readers not yet accustomed to it lay in her rapid transition from image to image, by an association of ideas whose connection previous writers would have felt it necessary to draw explicitly. But here she was with Eliot, and in harmony with the practice of the seventeenth-century poets now popular again.

In relation to that decade, Edith Sitwell's criticism of the contemporary scene, and the strangeness, eccentricity and experiment in her technique are major aspects of her poetry. Her fantastic dream-world containing marionettes, clowns, wooden horses, nymphs and satyrs can still give delight ; the imaginative brooding on Death and Time will always have its relevance ; there will, no doubt, always be artificiality to be mocked at by greater artificiality ; but her satire was on the whole too oblique to be powerfully effective, though its culmination, *Gold Coast Customs*, is a great symbolic presentation of a diseased society, of "rat-fat" souls, and of greed and corruption. The technical experiments of the volume *Facade* hold their interest, and led her to the technical achievement of *Gold Coast Customs*, but were too much of her own genius to lead others.

But, looking at her poetry from beyond its decade, the major aspects are the beauty and the humanheartedness. Her long poem *The Sleeping Beauty* is a rare continuity of beauty, highly wrought, glowing with colour and dazzling with imagery, a beauty existing equally in the control and harmony of sound, to which she always gave the most exacting and sensitive craftsmanship. For her, beauty existed in many things, as in the stuffs and costumes in her *Elegy on Dead Fashion*, but above all it lay in nature. "I was brought up", she tells us, "in the country, and mine is a country world . . . The world I see is a country world, a universe of growing things, where magic and growth are one". Often it is nature in a great garden, glorious with roses and heavy with bee-song, where peaches and nectarines grow, but wherever it is her senses are alive to the light, colour, texture, taste, and sound of things. Nor should her childhood love of the sea be forgotten. "I was born by the wildest seas that England knows", and she tells us the sound of those seas is to be heard in many of her lines.

As for the humanheartedness of her poetry, it was to become in her later poetry as deep as ever was expressed in English, but it speaks very movingly in these earlier poems. In *Aubade* the country servant girl, whom she shows us coming downstairs in the dawn to light the fire, is observed with sympathy even as she points out how little anything but the obvious can penetrate the girl's mind. She does not sentimentalise the girl any more than she does "Poor Martha", insensible to all "since her love is drowned". She draws them with comic exaggeration, but behind lies pathos. The "Portrait of a Barmaid" concludes with

> "Your soul, pure glucose edged with hints
> Of tentative and half-soiled tints"

but there is none of the distaste which Eliot seems unable to suppress in the portrait of the woman in bed in his *Preludes*. Her figures seem often to have been drawn from childhood memories as in *Colonel Fantock*, which shows how on a lovely summer's day in the garden the poor old man first felt the cold shadow of death from overhearing the careless remark that it was his old age that made him "babble". But her humanheartedness comes out especially in the *Four Elegies*, which she pointed to as instances of the fact that when her poems deal with emotion "they are always the most simple and primitive emotions of simple and primitive people". Here, in tales told with a bare, brief beauty, is love at its simplest and purest, love set off by treachery, love so strong in a mother for the son whom she saw in the moment he murdered her that in death her thought is that "he did no sin", that rather her own love for him had been "not deep enough".

In "The Lament of Edward Blastock", a true story of the eighteenth century, a brother is betrayed to his death for the reward's sake by the sister he loved, and surely the poet was also reminding us of the terrible spiritual evil that may grow out of poverty. These cruel treacheries are worse than death, and add to the anguish of death,

"Melting the last flesh from the bone".

In the cry of "The Little Ghost who Died for Love",

"it is not I
"But this old world, is sick and soon must die !"

we may well hear the undertones of symbolism.

Set against the poetry of Edith Sitwell that of Edmund Blunden may appear purely traditional, but beneath the surface of the quiet pastoral poet there is discernible the tension of spirit characteristic of the post-war years. The war lived on in his memory, an unforgettable experience bringing forth in peace poems of the war, but most of his poetry in this decade was concerned with natural things. For him as for Keats "The poetry of Earth is never dead", and from the pressure of the age and from his memories of France he turned for the balm that gives sanity to little things and to old, rooted things. In *The Recovery* he tells how, that he may escape "the dark mood's control", he finds "medicine for the mind" : it is to lie beneath a "chance-planted, many-centuried tree" so quiet that

> "the mouse stays his nibbling, to explore
> My eye with his bright eye".

The Recovery is a poem after 1930, but there is little that distinguishes his poems of the twenties from those of the thirties. His earliest poetry was more simply descriptive, but it soon became the medium of his shy exploration of reality, showing his hopes and fears, his awareness of things great as well as small, present as well as past. In his Preface to his *Collected Poems, 1914-1930* he said with quiet irony : "Great as is the power of country life over me, and of that stately march of the seasons above, around, below it, yet I have always suspected myself of some inclination to explore other subjects". Yet, as *The Recovery* declares,

> "The meadow-stream will serve
> For my refreshment ; that high glory yields
> Imaginings that slay".

The March bee, a dried mill-pond, a poor man's pig, a mole catcher, a blue butterfly, hawthorn, intimations of mortality, such were the themes of *The Shepherd* of 1922 and *English Poems* of 1925. The thought of change, the ceaseless mutability of things, never leaves him. The changes of nature give him not only comfort and joy, but uneasy fears, and a disturbing sense of mystery and awe. A quiet humour and humbleness often reassure him, but his truest point of rest is in a serene feeling born of the centuries through which men have gone on their quiet country way. However he is pursued by the evidence of change, there lives on in answer a faith and a way of life that is never lost from the countryside. He is a poet of friendship too. From our forefathers, from nature, from friendship comes the strength to face the tragedies Time brings. It is an intuition of a true way of life, not any turning away from life, which makes his poems often echo the warning that "Sufficient unto the day is the evil thereof". He knows its evil, and he acknowledges also the fierceness of nature, but he has a Wordsworthian sense too of the fellowship of nature in joy. Out of this ever-present realisation of opposites comes the tension of his spirit.

Traditional poetry found its most serene exponent in Victoria Sackville-West. In *The Land* of 1926 pastoral poetry came to full flower again in the wake of Virgil, and far exceeding such an English predecessor as Dyer's *Fleece* of 1757. Rarely have love and practical knowledge gone so hand in hand to produce poetry of the land. Here in the Weald of Kent the poet records all the country year of shepherd and yeoman, the toil that knows no intermission.

> "An English cornfield in full harvesting
> Is English as the Bible"

she says, and her poem is as English too. These, she admits, are "clanking times", and thatchers are few, and the crafts decline, but there is little modernism in her scene, and her own manner is timeless with the best kind of impersonality. Her interspersed lyrics especially have the purity and clarity of timeless song. We are nearer Wordsworth's world and thought when we are reminded of what "the bookish townsmen" lose—

> "The power of being alone with earth and skies,
> Of going about a task with quietude".

In these years too came some quiet volumes from Richard Church, building up a secure name for honest, unpretentious poetry, *Mood without Measure* of 1928 condescending so far to modernism as to be "a group of poems in free verse". Ordinary things and ordinary people, and his own everyday scenes and moods were matter enough for his muse, and his poems testified to the satisfaction poetry could still give by the simplest sincerity and lucid artistry. We are with him catching a bus or in a railway carriage, overhearing bell practice in a village church or out in the country in a shower, and the poet is always his unassuming self, with enough to say that sets the mind working and rouses the spirit. The current years make little impression on his poems, for he seems rather a pilgrim soul on life's highway, seeking

> "the joy that never fails;
> The silent speech with vast creation's God".

In love poems he showed not a little of Browning's direct
actuality combined with subtlety of feeling.

Where new and old met perhaps most strikingly in these
years was in the poetry of Osbert Sitwell. We have already
noticed the keen satire of his poetry in the last years of the
war and the first years of the peace. He flayed with shining
whips the money-making philistines who held that their sons
had gone to war to kill, among other things, modernism in the
arts and poetry, and the social "war Horses" laid by during
the war and emerging in the peace to dine and chatter their
platitudes as though the triumph was theirs. In *Green Fly*
he would have cut to the quick, had it been possible to make
the unfeeling feel, "the sentimental wonderless" who could
cry over a hurt dog but who had watched unmoved when
millions went to their death in the agony of battle. His scorn
for the anaemic and featureless, afraid of reality, and insulated
by money and convention, appeared in a poem like *Church-
Parade*. Here was the young poet flashing the sword of his
wit at the old and stupid, at convention and decorum meaningless or masking ill. He began to write with that symbolism which
gives beauty and obscurity to poetry, with brilliant colours and
striking imagery, and still with satiric purpose he achieved
a poem like *English Gothic*. *On the Coast of Coromandel*
showed the dance and dazzle of his lyric, and *Fox-Trot* and
other poems the experimenting in rhythm which he also
shared with Edith Sitwell.

There could be no doubt that he was "one of the Sitwells",
and some of his best poetry passed over contemporary heads.
But he dealt with very serious contemporary themes, and in
his Preface to his *Selected Poems* in 1943 he told how later
some members of the public wrote to tell him of their now
seeing a prophetic quality in his earlier writing. He com-
mented that *Out of the Flame*, written in 1921, "certainly
demonstrates a preoccupation with those problems of poverty
and inequality which the extremely gifted, but more politi-
cally-minded, poets of the following decade were to seize
on as the main theme for their verse". His sequence *Winter
the Huntsman*, written in 1924, told on the surface the story

of the seasons, but below gave reasons for "the plight in which we found ourselves", namely the worship of science and materialism, until "religion, intuition, even superstition had been banished from the modern world". "No one", he said, "seemed then to perceive the substratum". The public, clearly, in spite of the work of Eliot and Edith Sitwell, had not generally succeeded in reading the modern use of symbolic imagery. But Osbert Sitwell showed himself too a lover of the old world and a master of the old clarity of expression. In *England Reclaimed* of 1926 he called back to life from the memories of childhood figures of a world even then vanishing. It is with a good deal of the clear amused observation of childhood that they are drawn, these figures of an old rustic world, farmhand, gardener, housekeeper, carpenter, game-keeper, and others, and the whole is a labour of love. The queer, worthy creatures make a pageant of Old England, and the new style, with all its brilliance of colour and wit, but none of its obscurity, presents them with the happiest effect.

The scope of this chapter allows only the briefest allusion to other poets, and compels many omissions. Sacheverell Sitwell's poetry dates from 1917 when he was seventeen, but it was in the thirties that his work reached its full achievement. From the beginning he rivalled his sister in devotion to the artistry of poetry, sharing her passionate love of beauty and her eagerness to experiment. His early poems were often clear lyrical pictures of ordinary life, of a fisherman, of the crowds on Brighton pier, of a trapeze artist, of barrel organs in a city street—the last looking at a world akin to that in Eliot's *Preludes* but with a richer humanity. *One Hundred and One Harlequins* of 1922 lit up with wit and fantasy a real contemporary world. Often he evoked beauty as rich as Edith Sitwell's as in *Damson and Medlar*, and frequently he evoked the memory world, like both Edith and Osbert Sitwell. Throughout this decade he worked on a long, strange symbolic poem, *Dr Donne and Gargantua*, published as a whole in 1930, its purpose to portray "a contest between good and evil, between the spiritual and the physical".

Siegfried Sassoon's *Satirical Poems* (1926) sardonically exposed the materialism of the age, the rich world of Grand Hotels, the commercial world blessed by broadcasting bishops, the social world of fashion and convention, obsolete but refusing to die, the world in which his "port-flushed friends" discussed the Miners' Strike until he lost his temper, and where a blaring Press expanded its bloated circulation. The years had continued to feed the flame of anger burning in him in the last years of the war. But in *The Heart's Journey* (1928) was heard the song of a pilgrim soul, speaking still to the spirits of the war dead, but thinking, striving, and praying—

> *"Let life be God* . . . What wail of fiend or wraith
> Dare mock my glorious angel where he stands
> To fill my dark with fire, my heart with faith ?"

Herbert Read, in a terse intellectual poetry of austere beauty retaining much of his earliest Imagist style, wrote both satire and metaphysics. He too had come from the war intent to unravel the twisted years and the twisted soul. In his poetry burnt "the white ecstasy of intellect". For Robert Graves the nature of poetry changed radically about 1926 when he became acquainted with Laura Riding and her poetry. Until then his poetry remained, though very individual, not very distant from the Georgians, romantic, and full of fantasy. Most of it he omitted from his *Collected Poems*. After 1926 he submitted himself to an exacting discipline and self-analysis, and a bitterness and contempt for the current world of fools came upon him. This later development will be considered in the next chapter.

Here the poetry of Humbert Wolfe too can receive only brief mention. In *News of the Devil* in 1926 he satirised the Press in exuberant couplets telling of an encounter between the Devil and a multiple newspaper proprietor. In *Requiem* (1927) he sought to see behind the lives he chose of types of men and women who fail and succeed in life, and to reach a reconciling vision in which sinners and saints rest in God's sight. He gave to his theme deep feeling, and much beauty, and no volume of poems in this decade had a deeper religious attitude to life.

The one poet in this decade to break away with full-blooded energy from all current tendencies was Roy Campbell. He was a South African and only twenty-two when his long narrative *The Flying Terrapin* appeared in 1924, to be hailed by one critic with the declaration : "We wanted air ; and here is a southwester straight from the sea". The Terrapin, a sea-monster symbolising the elemental energy of life, is harpooned by Noah from the Ark, and drags the Ark head-long round the world through shrieking hurricanes, until finally the line snaps and the Terrapin bumps into the Devil and hurls him into the Bottomless Pit. In the middle, that he may enjoy the gusto of hatred as well as the wild imagi-nation of narrative, the poet imagines a land where the Devil has begotten industrialism and with it mediocrity and corruption. Here was a romantic with some of the old-time poetic energy of poets like Byron and Dryden. The verse was impetuous, the imagery bold. Here too was one who snatched man out of his social and economic setting, and gave him "proud irreverence" in the face of whatever Fate should befall him. Perhaps both in his attitude to life and in his manner there was something of the posturing of a young man from outside tired Europe, but it was no affected posturing.

His next works were high-spirited satire, *The Wayzgoose* of the commercial and cultural behaviour of the whites in South Africa, *The Georgiad* of the English literary scene. His best volume was *Adamastor* of 1930 in which, the poems being mostly short, he gained from the discipline of concentration. He worshipped strength and even violence, and admired Nature for being fierce and callous. He loved the primitive in South Africa, he rejoiced in bull-fighting in Spain, he saw the horses on the Camargue as "spirits of power and beauty and delight". His poems throb with delight in physical sensation. He also nursed "cold infernal hates". He was scornful of the "dark road of progress . . . cobbled with a line of bowler hats". His anger blazed at all he thought was modern decadence. Indeed he drew near at times in thought and feeling to what came to be labelled Fascist, but his poetry showed none of the impurities of Fascism. When he was at his most objective his pictures had an unexcelled vividness, as in that of the two sisters in the frosty morning before light wading out into the sleeping cove naked on their horses. To find in these years a poet at all akin to him it is necessary to turn to D. H. Lawrence, a deeper and in many ways a different thinker than Campbell, but sharing his reaction from the industrialised world to a worship of blood and the senses. Yeats too had experienced something akin to their feeling in his realisation of "a terrible beauty" born out of violence in Ireland. To note this element, whose occurrence in some was inevitable, may well round off our survey of the twenties.

CHAPTER VII

POETRY, 1930-1940

With the opening of this decade a new group of poets came quickly into notice, Auden, Day Lewis, Stephen Spender, and MacNeice, young men born a few years before the war. Partly heirs of Eliot, and partly reacting from him, their aim was to cure the Waste Land. Very soon followed a still newer poetry, that of Dylan Thomas, accepting the Waste Land as the soil from which poetry must be produced, and near-Surrealists like David Gascoyne. As the decade ended, yet another new poetry was on its way, "Apocalypti-cism", from Henry Treece, J. F. Hendry and G. S. Fraser. The decade was indeed prolific of new poetry, and not all of it new in a way to startle and perplex, as was much of the early work of the poets already mentioned. There was, for instance, the new poetry of Christopher Hassall, which belonged to no movement and was content to be new by the modification of old traditions.

The new poetry deserves here most consideration because it was the poetry of and for the rising generation, but the poetry of their elders was far from negligible. There was Yeats, who, having in the twenties achieved his supreme expression, remained a passionate old poet, younger in heart than ever, admired by the new poets of all schools and respecting them. Kipling in his *Storm-Cone* of 1932 spoke prophetically from the midnight lull between the storms. Sassoon remained the angry satirist of war and materialism. Robert Graves kept on unremittingly in his rather embittered search for the essence of poetry in an evil age. Blunden's quiet volumes proclaimed his poetic maturity, as did those of Richard Church. Sacheverell Sitwell gave the decade its richest poetic beauty in *Canons of Giant Art*. Herbert Read and Edwin Muir maintained the high discipline of a more intellectual poetry. Poets like Ruth Pitter, Herbert Palmer

and Victoria Sackville-West refreshed the more traditional
poetry. Roy Campbell was joined by his fellow South African
William Plomer. Masefield was still Laureate and still kept
his skill in the old manner. Such a list is again, as with the
poetry of the twenties, only a selection of notable names.
There are many names that might be added of elder poets,
and of younger poets too such names as William Empson,
George Barker and Julian Symons.

The group of poets led by Auden was quick in getting off
the mark. Auden and Day Lewis had been joint editors of
Oxford Poetry in 1927, as were Stephen Spender and MacNeice
in 1929. The first outstanding new poem was *Transitional
Poem* by Day Lewis in 1929, and with two others it made his
Collected Poems of 1933. Auden's first notable volume was
Poems of 1930, and Spender and MacNeice followed in 1933
and 1935 respectively. By 1935 indeed all four were well
known. Michael Roberts, himself a poet, had undertaken
very effective work to publicise them by editing two anthologies, *New Signatures* (1932) and *New Country* (1933), and
when he edited the *Faber Book of Modern Verse* in 1936 the
new poets could no longer complain of the lack of a public,
which had in part led Day Lewis to undertake his statement
of their case in *A Hope for Poetry* of 1934. By 1936 it was
Auden, Day Lewis, Spender and MacNeice who stood out,
but there were many others who shared their views and whose
poems appeared in these collections. Above them all Auden
stood out as leader.

This group of poets had a revolutionary and dynamic
poetic creed which the earlier group of Georgians had lacked.
They meant poetry to speak in a new language and rhythm.
Its imagery should draw on modern life and its vocabulary
on contemporary speech, and its rhythm too should be nearer
to that of natural speech. They meant their poetry to make a
greater call on the intellect than on the emotions of their
readers. All modern knowledge should be at their disposal.
In most of these things their master was Eliot, but, as we have
noted, Day Lewis showed in what way Owen and Hopkins
were also their immediate inspiration in their conception of

the nature and technique of poetry. By Edith Sitwell they do not seem to have been inspired, though she could have taught them much about poetic beauty.

It was in poetic technique in the broadest sense, including the use of symbolism, that these poets were mainly indebted to Eliot. By 1930 his attitude to life was not theirs, and in that Owen was nearer to them. They held that, at the time, it was the duty of poets to take sides in politics and to use poetry to that end, and in politics they stood on the Left, and, though themselves mostly university men from professional middle-class families, they espoused the cause of the "proletariat". The contemporary scene could be observed to be dark enough with its grave financial crisis when they began writing, to the unemployment resulting from which the following years added the increasing likelihood of renewed European war, and indeed its prelude in the Spanish Civil War. But if it was a Waste Land in their eyes, they did not despair, but were determined to use poetry to assist in healing it. Many of the group adopted Communism as their faith, and Michael Roberts in his *New Country* selection, which included prose as well as poetry, emphasised their political tendency. Their general attitude was certainly strongly inspired by their reading of Karl Marx, and it gave a positive vital force to their poetry. That in the long run their preoccupation with contemporary life in its political aspects was bound to limit their effectiveness as poets they did not realise until this decade was ended. Then in 1942 it was Stephen Spender who in *Life and the Poet* once more directed attention to the essential nature of poetry and the dangers of such political partisanship. But in the early thirties this new hope in poetry admirably countered the tendency then too widely spread to cynicism and apathy.

The poetry of Auden in this decade followed a clear, strong upward curve. It began with uncertainty and obscurity. Like all young poets he had to work out his technique, and at first he was hampered by a feeling common to his fellows that they were speaking in isolation, with the result that he, and they, sometimes indulged in a private language, whose allusions were shared only by their friends. Few more pain-fully obscure books can ever have been published than Auden's *The Orators* of 1932. As he looked at the bad old world, he indulged in his earliest work in an imagery, more natural to boyhood than youth, of plots, skirmishing, sentries and crossing of frontiers in an embittered civil war. His boister-ousness and liking for practical jokes suggests unease in this crusade. With youthful anger and contempt he threatened and abused the "Enemies", the effete bourgeoisie, the "nice" people. Doom menaced the old world, and it was time to get out or go under. But he advanced rapidly in confidence and in power of expression.

The plays written in collaboration with Isherwood, *The Dog Beneath the Skin* and *The Ascent of F6*, gained him a larger public for his poetry and by 1936 he could lay aside in *Look, Stranger* much of his earlier obscurity and crudity. That was a balanced volume, on the whole clear and confident, looking forward with hope, and replacing hatred and sus-picion by the inculcation of love. It was not surprising that in 1937 he was awarded the recently instituted King's Medal for poetry. Up till the war he maintained this advance. *Another Time* (1940) showed a further development to a more objective poetic approach, the poet expressing himself more concretely through the contemplation of people and places. The questioning seemed deeper, his apprehension of life to embrace a more complex actuality. But the contents of that volume antedated the war, and when the war came this continuous development was checked. Auden had gone to America and he did not return, and from his growing hope and his sense of sharing the aspirations of a progressive community he seemed to fall back into a feeling of isolation, a belief in individualism, or a small group of individuals, though the cure he still preached was love. The fears that appeared, from *Look, Stranger*, to have been banished now returned. The lyric gift which had been so distinctly his throughout this decade became almost silent.

Auden had a wide intellectual curiosity. He picked up ideas, facts and suggestions from an extensive field. On the formal side, it was particularly Eliot, Owen and Hopkins who influenced him. From Eliot came the symbolic method, the use of modern imagery and of abstract expression ; from Owen the use of assonance and internal rhyme ; from Hopkins "Sprung Rhythm" ; and from both Eliot and Hopkins the example of severe condensation, at whatever pains to the reader. But at first he was always ready to imitate what attracted him. So in one poem we find an adaptation of Anglo-Saxon poetry, in another of the sixteenth-century Skelton, and elsewhere we observe the influence of Icelandic saga—his family had originally come from Iceland. To what he took from others he added his own contribution, so that in *Poems* (1930) his style was not one, but several styles. For vocabulary he drew from all layers, including current slang. A personal trick was to use the curtness of a telegram's language and he liked to pun. He certainly opened up fresh possibilities in poetic expression to his contemporaries, and he soon, while continuing to experiment in prosody, found his own individual style. At its best it had a strict functional beauty as of machinery—"strict beauty of locomotive" is a phrase of Auden's.

He showed a similar almost too facile power of assimilation in other fields. His interests included biology and ethnology, which gave an extended sense of time and evolution as a background even to his love poems. His view indeed embraced all current knowledge and the whole contemporary world. When he saw the world as a sick world, it was the whole world, not merely England, and particularly he was aware from personal knowledge of the distress in post-war Germany. To cure this sick world his initial approach was both political and psychological, but later, as in *Spain*, the psychological superseded the political. On the political side he was all for the "proletariat", a favourite expression in the thirties, the "unloved" and "unlucky". They were faced by reactionary "enemies", who must be recognised and dealt with. It was class-conscious poetry, and Karl Marx was behind it. His poetry was dominated by the conception of man in society. But psychologically the state

of affairs was curable. Here he thought in terms of Freud,
and of the psychology of neuroses, and was very strongly
influenced by the teaching of Homer Lane. He believed in
the "pure in heart" and that what was primarily wanted
was a "change of heart". All sickness was due to personal
failure to live properly, diseases being symptoms of psychological illness, of repressions and inhibitions. One must not
pity the sick, but shake them out of their sickness—pity indeed
was a sterile and evil thing, an idea he shared with D. H.
Lawrence. Yet on Marxist lines the origin of the world's
ills lay rather in the realm of economics and politics, and
Auden never solved this dilemma in his poetry. His psychological approach gave his poems the most consistency, and
a background for his satire ; his political approach never
went beyond threats, and a search for "enemies", whom he
saw half politically and half psychologically. Sympathy for
the sick certainly seemed no part of his understanding, and
in a ballad like *Miss Gee* he could try to make rollicking fun
out of a victim of cancer.

As the years passed, it has become easier to value Auden
the artist without being intimidated by Auden the preacher.
At first it was rather sporadically that the artist appeared :
in flashes of scenes remembered, in witty phrases of acute
psychological observation, in glimpses of people drawn with
the skill of a satiric novelist, in fact in many details where
sound, rhythm and choice of word combined to give the
concentrated pleasure and suggestion that only poetry can
give. He was slower in achieving the total effect of a unified
poem : perhaps in his first volume only one poem, "Sir, no
man's enemy", did this really well. But when he did achieve
this in lyric, it was with the magic that it is futile to analyse
and impossible to mistake as another's. In *Look, Stranger*
the title poem is the happiest combination of mood and
picture; "Fish in the unruffled lakes" is one of the most
delightful, in thought and feeling, of love lyrics; "Pro-
logue" has a complex integrity as it pleads for love, evokes
by a series of vivid spotlights the industrial scene of England,
and concludes with a moving vision of the possible birth of

a new age; and "Let the florid music praise" with a brevity
worthy of Shelley sings in less than a hundred words the most
poignant contrast between the royal passion of love and the
lot, and threat, of the unloved millions, in a way that can be
felt in any age without partisan emotions. In sustained poetry
in these years his most ambitious attempt was *Spain*, but
though the total effect is powerful, the details again give
most pleasure ; the use of the father-fixation interpretation
is not too happy, and there is an unevenness of style. But
as his elegy on Yeats showed, his power of sustained lyric
was growing, and his remarkable gift of presenting a vivid
picture, seen at once physically and psychologically, appeared
in such a poem as "The Capital" in *Another Time*, where his
poems as a whole showed him packing more matter, but
clearly, into a small space. But the war came to sever this
happy union of artist and thinker.

Day Lewis, probably even more widely known as Nicholas
Blake the writer of detective fiction, was very different as a
poet from Auden in spite of their association. He shared
almost the same poetical ancestry, and many of the same
features of style, but he was a more human poet, in spite of
Auden's insistence on love and his praise of spontaneous
living. His Eliot-like Notes to *Transitional Poem* and his
mottoes to his poems indicate a very wide reading, but his
poetry does not show the same restless intellect and acquisi-
tiveness of knowledge as Auden's. From allusions in his
poems Auden seems to have loved the countryside of the
North in his boyhood, but with Day Lewis the love of nature
went much deeper, and is one of his strongest features, issuing
in his imagery time and again. It was significant of his love
of nature that he later translated the great pastoral *Georgics*
of Virgil. Auden's writings show a deep love of England,
but in Day Lewis the love of England, as has usually been
so with our nature poets, is transmuted into a quality that is
rootedly English in a way that Auden's poetry is not. Day
Lewis was an open-air poet, above all a poet of the wind and
of bird-song, of everything that shared and inspired his own
nervous vitality.

Transitional Poem, a long cycle of short poems, was a preliminary investigation into the poet himself; he looked back in it upon his "personal experience in the pursuit of singlemindedness", his Notes said. The ideal of life that emerges from the poem is a very Meredithian one, and it may be noted that he was much attracted to Meredith, as his later prose study *The Poetic Image* showed, and was influenced at times by Meredith's rhythms. It is a Meredithian philosophy of blood and brain, an ideal once described by H. G. Wells as that of an "intelligentsia blooded". In the phrasing of Day Lewis it was to "feed austerity on warm blood", but this passionate integrity must be sought not in isolation but in the midst of common life, not abstractly but concretely.

In his next poem, again a linked series, *From Feathers to Iron*, he traced his thoughts and feelings while his wife was bearing their first child. He could not but feel that the child should be born in the country, and the progress of the months inspired his country muse. But into what kind of world would the child be born? and what qualities would he wish for him? It must be a new world with a new kind of beauty, and he had a growing confidence that with blood and brain in a vital integrity this new world could be fashioned. So with often boisterous energy he proceeded in his third poem, *The Magnetic Mountain*, once more a closely linked succession of short poems, to tell how the bad old world must be abolished, and what sort of adventurers were needed to go out and bring in the new world. It was his poem nearest in spirit to the early Auden preoccupied with the sickness of the world. He vigorously satirised the public-school tradition, the Press, the Church, and politicians; he was anxious about mother-fixation; he enumerated the "enemy" and scorned the half-hearted. He was confident—"the integral spirit climbs"—and he ended with the assurance:

"This is your day: so turn, my comrades, turn
Like infants' eyes like sunflowers to the light".

A Time to Dance (1935) showed a rapid poetic advance. Its chief poem was a long narrative of an epical flight to Australia in a crock of a plane, giving evidence, like *Nabara* of a year or so later, of the potentialities of an outstanding narrative poet. To it was joined an elegy on a heroic friend lately dead, from whom his thoughts turned again to the reactionary world of unemployment with its death-will. But, as his narrative and his elegiac tribute declared, Day Lewis loved courage, strength and vitality, and he would "dance in spite of death", he would sing

> "As storm-cocks sing,
> Flinging their natural answer in the wind's teeth".

His spirit was more positive and resilient than Auden's. The scene grew darker as the Spanish Civil War ended and the oppression of Hitler loomed heavier, and *Overtures to Death* (1938) reacted to the course of events. But he faced the threat of death in rich dramatic poetry ; his response was to give the heroic example in *Nabara* of the little Spanish Government vessel fighting with desperate resolution against overwhelming odds ; imagery from nature continued to testify to his rooted love, and his artistry in verse still advanced. It was no wonder that of the new poets of the thirties it was he whose poetry reached a most satisfying fulfilment in the forties.

From the beginning Stephen Spender took the most objective view among these poets of the social and political scene, though he also became the most introspective of them. *Poems* (1933) showed the same political attitude as that of Auden and Day Lewis. The old world "where shapes of death haunt life" must go, and the young comrades must "advance to rebuild . . . advance to rebel" ; giving up "dreams . . . of heaven after our world" they must follow "the palpable and obvious love of man for man", and, as "people ordered like a single mind", they would achieve a world where none should hunger and "Man shall be man". But if the ideal was to be

> "One cog in a golden and singing hive",

Spender insisted that the value of life lay as much in the body as in the fiery soul ; there must be not only "the flowering of the spirit" but

> "The essential delight of the blood drawn from ageless springs".

and his own poetry was characterised by the sensuousness of its imagery. He could invest even pylons with physical appearance, seeing them "like nude, giant girls", for there was much in the machine age that appealed to his sense of beauty, for example, the air-liner descending through the dusk

"More beautiful and soft than any moth".

Spender published less poetry than Auden and Day Lewis. In 1934 his *Vienna* dealt with the clash between the dying civilisation of the bourgeoisie and the new life of the workers, unhappily crushed in this instance by the political rulers of Austria. He notably succeeded in portraying the death-will and he vividly depicted the hunt of the fugitives, but as a whole the poem suffered from its ambitious symbolic method. The choruses in his play, *The Trial of a Judge*, which showed the dilemma of the just judge between the millstones of Right and Left, had not the poetic quality of the choruses in Auden's plays. His only other poetic volume of this decade was *The Still Centre* of 1939, but its contents were various. One group of poems was concerned with the Spanish Civil War, *Two Armies* being a beautifully controlled expression of pity in the very spirit of Wilfred Owen—the pity seems almost an element of Spender's sensuousness, a constant in his poetry. *Port Bou* was a fine example of his power to describe an episode so that the scene and its atmosphere are felt by the senses. Another group was concerned with particular subjects, and poems like *Marginal Field* and *An Elementary School Class Room in a Slum* showed qualities similar to those of *Port Bou*, the ability to bring home an idea through a concrete sensuous presentation. A third group was much more personal, an attempt in lyric to examine himself and to find that still centre which gave the volume its title. Here he tells of his inability to be always self-assured and dogmatic, of his feeling of isolation, of the realisation that he must accept his own weakness : the poems reveal a search for a new attitude to life and poetry, and lead to his prose expression three years later that "the poet is he who realises in his art his own being and the being of other lives and nature outside himself". His poems on the Spanish Civil War had already shown him going deeper than partisanship.

Louis MacNeice always stood somewhat apart from the others. He shared their poetic ancestors and ideals, but even on the purely poetic side there seems a difference : he tells us how as a youth he liked the work of the Sitwells, and his earlier poems have often a colour and brilliance more Sitwellian than anything to be found in the others of this group. For him too Eliot was more than Owen and Hopkins. Like his fellows he grew up conscious of the social sickness and the threat of war, but unlike them he never felt the assurance that he could heal the one and defy the other. He came from Ulster, and Ireland, hated and beloved, remained in him ; he could not deny his heritage, and it included strains of melancholy, romantic sentiment and self-pity, and also a sense of humour. Auden, Day Lewis and Spender had all been, like himself, Oxford men, but MacNeice was a scholar, more academic than they, who became a lecturer in Classics. He himself declared with satirical appreciation in *Autumn Journal* that once anyone has been to Oxford he "can never really again believe anything that anyone says", and in his case at any rate the remark harmonises to some extent with the portrait of him given by his early poems.

MacNeice was too balanced to believe in Utopia, and pointed out that though, like snow, Communism might give the world an appearance of uniformity, that "perfection" could be maintained but "for one day only". He was an idealist who realised that ideals cannot be completely achieved, but who still held to his ideals, which were those of the humanist, longing for a decent possibility of spontaneous living in a world of unassertive individuals. He loved the old world, the world of his classical education, but saw in it isolation, remoteness and weakness, and yet he could not whole-heartedly adopt the new world either. So, frustrated and baffled, with shrewd common sense but some sentimentality, he naturally became satiric.

Notable in his first volume were *An Eclogue for Christmas*, *Ode*, and *Birmingham*. *An Eclogue* is a dialogue between a townsman and a countryman which builds up with many flashes of satiric wit a comprehensive analysis of the illness of the modern world. The townsman notes

> "The excess sugar of a diabetic culture
> Rotting the nerve of life and literature" ;

the countryman declares

> "The country gentry cannot change, they will die
> in their shoes
> From angry circumstance and moral self-abuse".

But in city life the townsman finds a "beauty narcotic and deciduous", and so does MacNeice, for in *Birmingham* there is the glitter and display of shop-windows and the colour of traffic-lights, but it is the houses, rather than their gadget-minded inhabitants, and the traffic, that have the deeper life. *Birmingham* presents the devitalised city, where the workers are slaves to the factory sirens, and the people automata. *Ode*, like Day Lewis's *From Feathers to Iron*, discussed his wishes for his son in this divided and war-threatened world : he could wish little that was positive but "five good senses", and offer little advice but to accept and realise his limitations, renouncing alike the infinite and hypocrisy. Nor had he anything to hand his son except the memory of some incidental pleasures to stand as symbols, but it is these incidental pleasures happily remembered that are often the source of his most satisfying poetry as in *Train to Dublin*—they give brilliant little pictures of "the sea's tumultuous marble", of "fuchsia hedges and whitewashed walls", of the singing lawn-mower

> "Spirting its little fountain of vivid green".

Some of these things he may write off as " a dilettante's lie", but they are likely to last longer than the discontent and satire.

His next volume, *The Earth Compels* (1938), lost some of the sparkle of his first in its greater maturity, but this was more than compensated for by the advance in assurance and artistry. There was the sombre sense of impending storm, when there would no more be any "time for dances". He had been to Iceland with Auden, and in *Eclogue from Iceland* he called up the spirit of the outlaw hero of old saga, Grettir, imagining a talk with him on the contemporary world : Grettir bade him and his friend return to Europe, to stand by "the sanctity of the individual will" and to make their gesture, however small, in asserting human values. The restless dissatisfied humanist still remained, trying sometimes to escape the pressure of the modern world with the fun of his *Bagpipe Music* or the detached satirical observation of clichés and their users. *Autumn Journal* of 1939, giving his thoughts subsequent to the Munich agreement, was mainly autobiographical : looking back upon his Irish origin and his English education, he surveyed himself, seeking light by which to live in that dark scene. But the scene was too dark and too perplexing, and in one whose nature told him not to "hanker for a perfection which can never come" there was no impelling faith to point a way. One of the best passages drew the portrait of a girl with all the fresh charm of individuality.

Auden's poetry had quickly become free of most of its obscurity, and though the poetry of the others was never so inclined to obscurity it had shown the same tendency to become clearer. But with the poets who succeeded them, Dylan Thomas, George Barker and David Gascoyne, poetry again became obscure. It was a purer poetry in that it came from deeper levels of consciousness, was less deliberately intellectual, and had no political purpose. A poet like Dylan Thomas had no such aim as that of healing the Waste Land, but, as Stephen Spender expressed it later, it was the voice not of the doctor but of the patient that was now heard : "the poet no longer stands outside the Waste Land. He is the flower". These were the poets who in this country made the nearest approach to surrealism, which, if practised ideally, meant the release by the poet of whatever welled up from within him without any conscious control or selection. Such pure surrealism was probably very rarely, if ever, achieved, because the conscious mind always insists upon having some share in transmitting material to paper, and the poetry of Dylan Thomas always showed an attention to poetic tech- nique which could not be purely spontaneous. Louis MacNeice compared this near-surrealism to the speech of a drunken man, remarking of a passage in one of Dylan Thomas's poems : "I think . . . it is the almost automatic collocation of a number of emotional (primarily sexual) symbols, thrown up as a drunk man throws up phrases".

Dylan Thomas published his first volume of poems in 1934 at the age of twenty, and though it was a slim volume (his output continued to be small), his poetry made an imme- diate impression. His language was highly symbolic, and so rich and strange that, however unintelligible, it had an almost hypnotic power, which was enhanced by the poet's command over sound and rhythm. It was impossible not to feel that *Twenty-Five Poems* (1936) contained much true poetry, though the reader might well feel at the same time that many of the poems could be understood only by the poet himself. From the Welsh chapel of his boyhood he had absorbed the Bible, and he had also come to know Freud, and Biblical and sexual imagery were wonderfully intertwined in his poetry with imagery from nature. With this knowledge as his equip- ment and a strong and energetic emotional life he seemed to use his poetry as a means of discovering himself. The patient, to use Spender's image, was caught in the fever of adolescence, and he talked passionately to himself in the restless desire to cope with his sense of sin, to conquer his fears, and to reassure himself in his feeling of isolation : particularly he brooded on the dark mystery of sex. Occasionally the expression clarified, and occasionally as in the poem "And death shall have no dominion" there rang out a clarion of triumph, but the general impression was one of dark obscurity both of expression and feeling. But by the end of the decade his poetry too was speaking more intelligibly. The telescoping of images and his Hopkins-like coinage of new compound words were used with more discrimination, and such a poem as *In Memory of Ann Jones* (1938) promised the notable advance his poetry was to make.

George Barker, too, at little over twenty had made such an impression that Yeats included him in his *Oxford Book of Modern Verse*. Like that of Dylan Thomas his early poetry was highly symbolical, and dazzled and bewildered with the richness of its imagery and vocabulary. His lyrics were much clearer than most of Thomas's, but his long *Calamiterror* of 1937, in which, like Thomas, he felt the need to explore himself, was as dark and chaotic as the inner life it recorded. His too was the fever of adolescence, with fear of the body and of the world, to which became added his anguish for "the throes of Spain". *Lament and Triumph* of 1940, which declared his growing victory over his "private rebellion", belongs to the next chapter.

The elder poet nearest to the dark mood of these years was Robert Graves. For him, however, as for his associate Laura Riding, politics could have no place in poetry. She explained her point of view in her contribution to *The Left Heresy in Life and Literature* (1939), saying: "Science breeds despair: politics, hate. In science and politics we forget that life is a process incidental to an end of the fulfilment of which there can never have been any doubt: the identification of truth". So the poetry of Graves, largely inspired by her attitude, had become from the late twenties an intense search for truth. He shook off his early romanticism, and he "had ceased to be a Christian", but, as he tells us in the preface to his *Collected Poems* of 1938, he could not get away from "the old fear theme". Having no political idealism or religious faith, his impersonal and intellectual search for truth led him often into angry satire. He declared: "To manifest poetic faith by a close and energetic study of the disgusting, the contemptible and the evil is not very far in the direction of poetic serenity, but it has been the behaviour most natural to a man of my physical and literary inheritances". He would say that his "health as a poet lies in [his] mistrust of the comfortable point of rest", and he was grateful for "this suspicious habit, this dwelling upon

discomfort and terror". He satirised the artificiality and
lifelessness of people, and the worship of machines. At times
he saw the modern world as a hell, plagued by sexuality.
But his pursuit of truth not infrequently led him to pleasanter
themes, as when in *Flying Crooked* he expressed, as effectively
as Hopkins could have done, the "inscape" of a cabbage-
white butterfly, its "honest idiocy of flight", or when in *The
Cool Web* he found a vividly original way of expressing the
truth that words blunt the edges of apprehension. Moreover
he never desisted from his experiments in technique, partly
perhaps because, as Richard Church suggested, "nothing is
so reassuring to a frightened man as a bag of tools".

Edmund Blunden in this decade added much poetry to
his already considerable achievement. Occasionally he rose
to national themes as in his noble elegy on George V, and in
Exorcized, where he voiced with deep sincerity of feeling
bred of the 1914 war his mistaken hopes after the Munich
agreement, expressing the sentiment of a great body of the
nation. The contemporary world was always present to him,
sometimes so oppressively as to divert the pastoral poet, but
on the whole he remained true to his bent, loving nature and
the common life—"I love . . . unattractive, unnoticeable
people". He turned from "Present Discontents" to the
lasting things of nature and man, but his poems together
gave a sensitive complex impression of a whole world, where
peace was threatened by war, where chance still ruled and
change was constant, and where much was bleak but joy
came unexpectedly. He looked upon it with some irony, and
with a pained, puzzled uncertainty of hope as he thought of
the death of friends. And memories of the last war still echoed
in his mind.

Sacheverell Sitwell in this decade crowned his work with
Canons of Giant Art, twenty poems, inspired some by paint-
ings, for example *The Laocoon of El Greco*, others by
statuary, as *The Hermes of Praxiteles*, others again by music,
and one *Upon an Image from Dante*. His imagination
delighted to call up long past scenes and people, and to load
the picture with beauty. *Agamemnon's Tomb* is a sustained

and subtle meditation on death, culminating in the picture
of the tomb itself in the dark hillside at Mycenae with the
unforgettable beauty of the bees entering the dome through
a hidden crevice

> "With honey of the asphodel, the flower of death,
> Or thyme, rain sodden, and more sweet for that".

Bacchus in India presents the contrast between the Mediterranean world and that of the East as the poet describes the
train of Bacchus on the one side and on the other the Indian
prince who has renounced his father's palace for the solitude
of the lonely forest. *The Hermes of Praxiteles* concludes
with a lament for the beauty of the lost Greek world. Indeed
all is beauty. Edith Sitwell, who declared that their relationship was no reason why she should not state her opinion
that Sacheverell Sitwell was "one of the greatest poets that
our race has produced in the last hundred and fifty years",
praised his "acute sensibility to texture" and "the extraordinary sensuous beauty of the imagery" in his work. But
it is all applied to remote ends. We are in the world of the
complete artist, and, delightful though that is, it is impossible
not in the long run to miss the urgencies of life. Even
after more than three centuries we can feel behind the beauty
of Spenser, "the poets' poet", more urgent criticism of life
than in *Canons of Giant Art*. The modern poet had adopted
the newly rediscovered "sprung rhythm", but the modern
tension was dissolved in beauty, no mean achievement in the
thirties of this century.

The last poet of whom space allows mention is Christopher
Hassall. His *Penthesperon* showed the ranging of a fine and
sensitive mind and spirit. Imagining a group of friends, he
built up within a loose framework a series of poems, mainly
narrative, but including talk between himself and his friends,
personal soliloquy by himself, and lyric. It was that central
kind of poetry which comes from an individual rebirth of
sound traditions, and is informed by a modern spirit breathing
the mental climate of the new age. He gave expression to all
that perplexed and disturbed those years—to the disintegrating
theories that sapped faith and put morals at the mercy of

self-judgment, to the social distress, to the threat of war, and to such a brutish deed as the murder of the Spanish poet Lorca. But his answer was the positive answer of the Christian and the humanist. His interest in men and women was declared in his tales, which were rich in a true psychological insight free from the technicalities of the modern school. His love of the arts, particularly of the theatre and the ballet, fortified his spirit. For him romantic love endured unembittered. Indeed it was the volume of a poet looking forward hopefully, intent to make the best of the years, and able to transmit his vision of life with a fresh luminous sanity. One of his poems was entitled "homage to Crabbe", and not only the narrative gift of that eighteenth-century poet but his keen-eyed, balanced humanity lived again in Hassall.

CHAPTER VIII

POETRY, 1940-1950

Until the years have receded sufficiently for a true perspec-tive to appear, all judgment of recent literature is exceptionally perilous, but, whereas each of the first four decades had produced some outstanding new poet or group of poets, the fifth decade would seem to show no emergence of new poets really comparable in stature or in especial promise to their predecessors. In the first decade there had been not only Masefield but Davies, De la Mare and Brooke, in the second Owen, Thomas and Sassoon. In the third Eliot and Edith Sitwell, and in the fourth Auden and those associated with him. The war was in part responsible for this failure, for it cost the lives of at least two young poets, Alun Lewis and Sidney Keyes, who were of undoubted promise, and yet whose achievement, whatever longer life might have given, was not that of a Wilfred Owen. The war, however, saw the writing and publication of poetry on a remarkable scale : many were the young poets in the Forces and elsewhere who appeared in anthologies and in slim volumes of their own. But the stimulus responsible for this poetry seemed largely to pass away with the ending of the war.

This decade indeed belonged rather to the older poets of twenty and more years before. Its greatest poetry came from Edith Sitwell and T. S. Eliot. Herbert Read, having served in the first world war, fitly passed on his vision in *To a Conscript of 1940*. De la Mare published his *Collected Poems* in 1942, and in 1946, then over seventy, added his remarkable long allegorical poem *The Traveller*. Richard Church wrote with steady inspiration, so that his *Collected Poems* of 1948 contained a notable proportion of poems written in this decade. In fact, particularly after the war ended, the established poets stood out all the more clearly by the publication of their Collected Poems, or of selections from their whole work : Sir Osbert Sitwell's *Selected Poems Old and New* appeared in

1943 with a preface commenting on the prophetic quality of
his earlier poems ; Herbert Read's *Collected Poems* were
issued in 1946 and Siegfried Sassoon's in 1947 ; Sacheverell
Sitwell's *Selected Poems* (1948) made it more possible to
know his work, though nothing new was added. Of the
poets of the thirties Auden, in America, seemed to have lost
both his position as leader and his poetic assurance, but Day
Lewis and MacNeice well maintained their position with further
notable volumes, and MacNeice in 1949 felt the time had come
for at least an interim volume of *Collected Poems*, as too in
1949 did Laurence Whistler. Of the younger poets of the
thirties probably Dylan Thomas, small though his output was,
most advanced his reputation. But again many names could be
added both of poets who had begun to be known in the thirties
and of poets becoming known in this decade, such as Christopher Hassall, Geoffrey Grigson, Rex Warner, Norman
Nicholson, and Anne Ridler. In fact it was by no means a
barren decade, and some of its younger poets may well be
destined to greater eminence, but within its limits no poet,
young or old, really rivalled T. S. Eliot and Edith Sitwell.

Eliot's *Quartets* have already been noticed in Chapter V.
The background of total war in which they were written
hardly appeared in the poems. *East Coker* certainly admitted
it to be a time when "the poetry does not matter" ; the poet,
after his lyric commending the Crucifixion as the only answer
for a sick world, had to regret "twenty years largely wasted".
The Dry Salvages was timeless in its sense of loss at sea, with
no hint of the special hazards of wartime convoys. *Little
Gidding* declared that "History is now and England", but
the intense poetic contemplation inspired by the secluded
chapel was unbroken by any topical reference, and the poet
sought his satisfaction in a vision of history as "a pattern of
timeless moments". As the years pass there will be found
little or nothing in these poems which points to the catastrophic
background, but in their rising above the topical lay one great
virtue of the *Quartets* at the time as well as for the future.
From a village rooted in the past, from rocks immemorial
in the ocean, from a lonely chapel visited three centuries

before by a broken king, Eliot sent his thoughts ranging to seek the truth of things ultimate, and in those dark days his detachment from the contemporary scene could give comfort and strength. To share the poet's intensity and renunciation made the *Quartets* at once a discipline and an inspiration. By encouraging his reader to build upon his own remembered moments "in and out of time" Eliot was "a priest to us all". In the first world war many poets had comforted themselves and their readers by their backward-looking pictures of the English countryside, but Eliot found his own salvation and rendered a not dissimilar service to others by his deeper and more complex meditation—"an occupation for the saint", as he remarked in *Little Gidding*, but not beyond the approach of most of us.

Edith Sitwell, however, showed how it was possible to deal with the contemporary horror of war, and yet in doing so to transcend the theme so far that the spirit entered into a heaven of contemplation as timeless as Eliot's. Indeed her achievement was the more remarkable, for, however high her spirit soared, it never lost emotional contact with earth, as Eliot's did, partly from the strain of the academic in Eliot. Edith Sitwell could be at once in Heaven and in Hell, still suffering the anguish of a world in travail while lifted up to a spiritual vision of love eternal. The best approach to this later poetry of hers is through her *Poet's Notebook* of 1943. There she gave quotations (with occasional comments upon them) from a wide range of authors, culled to express her own conception of poetry, and, for her, poetry had become nothing less than a divine art, divine because it was religious, and a supreme art, because it must not fall short of perfection of craftsmanship.

After quoting Karl Barth's statement that "the theme of the Gospel proclaims Eternity as an event", she asked herself, "Is not this true of the greatest poetry?" We must learn, she quoted Kirkegaard, "to cram today with Eternity and not the next day". Her whole outlook was fundamentally religious, so that she could quote the sentence of Saint Augustine, "O eternal Truth! and true Charity! and dear

Eternity !", and apply it to poetry of the greatest kind. In her Notebook, as in her later poems, the name of Christ rings out, but her spirit seems to have been intent to draw upon all true religious feeling, whether specifically Christian or not, as when she quotes Cocteau to identify the spirit of poetry with "the religious spirit outside all precise religion". It was from the seventeenth-century bishop Jeremy Taylor that she quoted to suggest the experience of the poet during creation : "passing from passion to reason, from thanksgiving to adoring, from sense to spirit, from considering ourselves to an union with God". But the spirit could not communicate without the co-operation of the artist, and she held with William Blake that "mechanical excellence is the only vehicle of genius. Without innate Neatness of Execution, the Sublime cannot exist". In poetry, she agreed with Beethoven, "melody is the sensual life", but "among the principal necessities of Poetry at this time" she would affirm "a return to the savagery of the senses—'a voice that speaks somewhat above a mortal mouth'—and a grandeur of simplicity". Indeed, "in addition to harmony and melody, we need, as Emerson said, 'fire enough to fuse the mountain of ore'". For the art and the poetic spirit must be one, the form and the spirit of the poem inseparable—as Blake said, "the notion that man has a body distinct from his soul is to be expunged".

There is "a terrible beauty" in the later poetry of Edith Sitwell. It is often hard to tell whether the anguish or the comfort is the greater, for they are inseparably interwoven. Her third volume of this decade, *A Song of the Cold* (1945), incorporating *Street Songs* and *Green Song*, declared the dominant theme in its title poem, for it was the bitter cold of the night of the world, in which men starved and froze, dying of

"The ultimate cold within the heart of Man".

Following the onset of the war had come her heart-wringing *Lullaby*, with its "loud discordant cry" of ironic and anguished pity, a most bitter indictment of humanity's fouled nest in the days of the steel birds. Then, inspired by the air-raids of 1940, came *Still Falls the Rain*, equally terrible

in its agony of feeling, but rising above satire and despair in
the assurance that, even as this cruel rain of death falls upon
the world, so does the voice of Christ still sound, to declare,

> "Still do I love, still shed my innocent light, my Blood,
>   for thee".

In three great poems, *Invocation*, *An Old Woman* and
Harvest, she spoke as an old woman, and here again the pain
and the hope were alike unquenchable :

> "I, an old woman whose heart is like the Sun
>   That has seen too much, looked on too many sorrows,
>   Yet is not weary of shining, fulfilment and harvest".

These poems were indeed the "fulfilment and harvest" of
her own earlier work. The *Four Elegies* had held the promise
that her humanity would become as great as her artistry, and
now it embraced all men, no longer according to the rich
merely the ruthless satire of *Gold Coast Customs*. The cruel
desolation of the poor still oppressed her, but in this dark
night of the world,

> "this Cainozoic period
> When we must learn to walk with the gait of the Ape and the
>   Tiger",

Dives and Lazarus were brothers in suffering. Yet "as an
old woman in the light of the sun" she gloried in its life-
giving light and knew that Spring would return, the season
of the young and of love. Now there fell a dark rain "to
cool the delirium of gold", and one could hear "the wolfish
howls the starving made", and there were "man-made chasms
between man and man", and it was a world where hands were
useless because there was nothing for them to hold or make,
but in spite of all that issued from the cold in the heart of
man she watched with the deathless confidence of intuitive
knowledge "for a rebirth of faith and of wonder". Her trust
was still in "the heart of man, that second sun", whence
issued Love and the promise

> "Of the nobler love of Man for his brother Man".

Moreover,

> "Gold-bearded thunders and hierarchies of heaven
>   Roar from the earth : 'Our Christ is arisen, He comes to
>   give a sign from the Dead' ".

Further, as *How Many Heavens* . . . expressed with a glory of colour and with rhythm that matches the imagery, God is in all things, God "our ultimate shore" and "the core of the heart of love".

So assurance was always found in these volumes, though many of the poems were heavy with grief. Yet always too the beauty of the artist co-existed to give that overflow of pleasure that is the prerogative of poetry. Alongside the imagery of the bone and the skeleton and the worm, of cold and darkness and dust, of the ape and the tiger, there is, as earlier, the imagery of her country world, and particularly now of the sun, and of all that gives light, whether stars or emeralds, and of fire and warmth and colour. In some poems indeed all but beauty was laid aside, and she sang outside the cold of "the green ways, the bright April land" of youth and love, or would let a young girl sing in celebration of her beauty to the forgetting of wars and "the new Fall of Man". One such happy poem, however, "Once my heart was a summer rose", ends sadly—"I walk alone now in Lead Town"—and that is as in the high solemnity of her other poems, the sadness cannot but be present, however deep the ultimate assurance. The cure of the world is not easy ; never in Time will the necessary condition be effected, which is that "the fire of the heart and the fire of the mind be one". But in 1947 *The Shadow of Cain*, even with the terrible revelation of the atomic bomb behind it, emerged from its imagery of primal catastrophic violence to renewed assurance that Christ did not die in vain.

Compared with the poetry of Edith Sitwell that of the young war poets must seem minor poetry. Alun Lewis, who died in India while training for action in Burma, had by the age of twenty-six produced a small but notable body of poems and short stories. *Raiders' Dawn* shared with the work of many other young soldiers the constant apprehension of death to come. On sentry or resting in camp or looking at a Tudor mansion the thought of death obtruded. It gave a sombre background to love. In *To Edward Thomas* he recorded his thoughts upon visiting the memorial stone to that poet whose feelings he felt that he shared—"like you I felt sensitive and somehow apart"—and in whose death his own might find a parallel. Nearly all that he wrote was essentially personal, even his poems written in India being more of himself than of that strange continent, whose huge and forbidding problems he did not as poet feel called upon to confront. It was a shy uncertain personality, neither intense nor intellectual, yet possessing a vision alternately radiant and tragic, full of compassion, and sensitively responsive to beauty and to love, and always able to express itself freshly and with a most attractive clarity. As poet he did not concern himself with political or social problems, though he could describe with forceful realism the Rhondda of his native Wales, but he was content to be a poet and, like a knife-grinder, to strike what sparks he could to "warm the night", where beauty was so transient.

Sidney Keyes, who was killed in North Africa in 1943 shortly before he would have been twenty-one, was a more intense and introspective poet than Alun Lewis. He was writing poetry at sixteen, and he rapidly advanced to a remarkable maturity considering his years. His first volume, *The Iron Laurel*, was written while he was reading History at Oxford, before he entered the army. Like Lewis he followed no poetic school, but fashioned his own manner, feeling indeed "rather isolated as a writer". He named Eliot as one of the few living writers he could "accept entirely", and, speaking of symbolism, he declared Yeats and Rilke "the greatest and most influential poets in the last 100 years or so". His "only non-poetic influence" was the psychology of Jung. With such predilections, his poetry was strong, serious, concentrated, inclined to the metaphysical, and technically accomplished, and it showed again the tendency of many younger poets to discard obscurity. From childhood, books and nature had been his loves, and they contributed much to the matter and imagery of his poetry, providing stimulus to his active imagination, but overriding his concrete interests was an obsession with pain, fear and death. The problem of death was common to his generation, as was

the sense of fear, and when in the army he realised more fully
how he shared these things with his fellows his poetry grappled
with them with more assurance. He felt and resisted the death
wish, which Eliot and Auden had earlier expressed, and finally
came to accept death as the destiny of many of his generation. As his friend Michael Meyer put it, he became "the
spokesman of the conscript, the uncourageous anchorite, the
separated lover". He did indeed express the thoughts and
moods of many, but with the subtlety of a personal intelligence
fighting his own fight and finding much in nature, and
particularly in birds, to sustain and energise him in his
spiritual conflicts.

Alan Rook, who took part in the evacuation of Dunkirk,
was a quieter poet. His three volumes of poetry published
during the war expressed the plight of those who loved beauty,
and worshipped the power of love, and yearned to prolong
the moments of faith which could alone lighten the nightmare
of war. His love of beauty was almost mystical, and his
spirit was largely meditative, one of his longer poems, *Green
Mountain*, owing much in manner and mood to the Eliot of
the Quartets. Like Eliot, of whom one can often hear other
echoes in his verse, he felt the virtue of suffering to discipline
and release the spirit, and came to accept it for himself, and,
with a deep human sympathy, for others. His verse was
clear and easy, lacking intensity, but full of body.

Other poets in the Forces, many of them young, were
numerous. Roy Fuller's view of war was grim and disillusioned. *The Middle of a War*, published when he was in
the Fleet Air Arm, gave a sense, through rather fragmentary
expression of moods, scenes and occasions, of something too
vast to be apprehended as a whole. Life appeared to him like
a play of Destiny in which the poet was a mere crowd figure,
without central purpose or directing will, oppressed by
boredom, open to nostalgia, and with the prospect only of
toil and death. The bases of order and conduct seemed to
have melted away. Where men were reduced by routine to
isolated animals, each penned in his body, there was no place
for enthusiasm, or for laughter and joy. A poem like

Defending the Harbour was vividly descriptive of the scene, and a poem like *Harbour Ferry* neatly fused description and mood. The volume *A Lost Season*, the result of his later service in East Africa, gave Fuller in the African scene further opportunity for his descriptive talent, and it was in this more objective poetry that he, like many of the other poets, achieved a truer poetry than in expressing either personal or impersonal reactions to the tragic, distressing and sordid theme of war. Such reactions were too commonly felt, and felt too drearily, rather than intensely, to produce distinctive and vital poetry.

Laurie Lee's *The Sun My Monument*, J. F. Hendry's *The Bombed Happiness*, *Poems* of Terence Tiller—many such volumes were typical of the poetry of the war. Laurie Lee was not one of those poets whose expression the war had made clearer, but he tended to a violence of imagery which begot an obscurity not dissimilar to that of Dylan Thomas and George Barker ; imagery like "the peonies of my anger" matched the sensuous bitterness of his mood. Nor did the war discipline the use of imagery by Hendry and Tiller as much as was needed to produce poetry acceptable to the many. Such poets had their audience, but it was John Pudney who won the most widespread popularity of all the young war poets. Pudney's service was with the R.A.F. and his poetry had much of the clean, swift, air-borne efficiency of that service. His lyric had a spare beauty of music and phrasing, meeting but not condescending to the common man.

Fellow servicemen could readily appreciate his awareness of the deadly chances of war and of the commonplace reliefs from its monotony. He knew how men must cling to the personal against the overruling needs of the impersonal routine; he knew the relation between fear and courage ; he shared the patriotism of Smith and Jones, rooted in home and work, the football field and the pub, the meadows and the street. There, was the background of heroic flying, and Pudney's verse had a message both for the airman and for his family or girl because of its human understanding, unintellectualised,

and conveyed with a moving and attractive simplicity that was
only normal speech heightened into song.

> "I could praise the shy devoted heroes
> Who, from the sky's awareness or the oceans',
> Answer to Smith or Jones:
> And those who wait, dread-heavy, for their homing."

As well as the remarkable number of volumes by individual
poets the war years saw the publication of anthologies too.
In 1941 there was *Poems from the Forces*, selected by Keidrych
Rhys, himself a poet, and as a Welshman one of those who
testified to the resurgence before the war of a national spirit
in Anglo-Welsh poetry, a national poetic resurgence paralleled
in Scotland. In this volume were poems by more than thirty
serving poets, among whom were Alun Lewis, Rook and
Fuller, as well as others known before, who in these years
became still better known, like Hassall, Laurence Whistler,
G. S. Fraser and J. F. Hendry. Here was poetry of personal
experience of war in all its variety and in all its fields. The
intellectual pacificism of the thirties was gone; the unsettlement due to crisis after crisis threatening war had been
replaced by acceptance of war. Much was still left to
question, but this poetry was the poetry of an awakened
democracy expressing itself with resolution, and, therefore,
in the aspect of poetic manner, doing so with far greater
directness than had been characteristic of much poetry of the
thirties. Another notable anthology came some years later
consisting of poems by poets serving in the Italian campaign.

The anthology *Poetry in Wartime* of 1942 edited by
Tambimuttu contained poems not only by poets in the
Forces but by older poets such as Richard Church, Auden,
Day Lewis and MacNeice, and several poems by women poets,
notably Anne Ridler. The editor felt it desirable to deny
his responsibility for "the strain of sadness running throughout", and much seemed flattened by its authors' sense of
futility and frustration, but the finest poem in the volume,
Herbert Read's *To A Conscript of 1940*, spoke with the deeper

vision of a soldier of 1914-18 and rose above the weakness of those oppressed by the present to declare that

"To fight without hope is to fight with grace,
The self reconstructed, the false heart repaired".

To conclude this brief survey of the poetry which came mainly from the young servicemen, Richard Spender calls for special mention because he spoke as hardly anyone else did who got into print in those years. In 1942, when he was in a Parachute Battalion, his volume *Laughing Blood* was nearer in spirit to Rupert Brooke than to any of his own contemporaries. The very title declared the happy warrior, and his dedication thanked his parents for "the happiest first twenty-one years of life that anyone could dream of having". His poetry was not ignorant of tragedy and boredom, of suffering and of slums, but knowing more of beauty and love and the higher human values his dominant mood was proud and exultant :

"Let us repay
Laughing blood with spilt".

He was killed soon afterwards. Christopher Hassall, too, deserves mention for his volume *S.O.S. Ludlow*, in which he was one of the few who made narrative poetry out of the war.

From the poets who had made so considerable an impression in the thirties there came in this decade much outstanding work, but they no longer seemed a group : the poetic personalities of Day Lewis, Stephen Spender and MacNeice drew further apart from one another as they developed their individualities, and Auden was no longer their leader. Auden's *New Year Letter* of 1941 was a rambling exploration, in octosyllabic couplets that rush along tumbling one on top of another, of what the individual, in Auden's opinion, ought to do. His advice culminated in the now familiar inculcation of love : true democracy must be born through small groups of friends sharing in love a common way of life, but the individual, since "aloneness is man's real condition", must learn how to make his choice rightly. The poem sparkled with wit and epigram ; it showed abundantly Auden's power of vividly summarising people, places and periods; it was alive with ideas; it agreeably revealed something of the poet himself with a new humility. It was in fact a very lively piece of topical thinking, hurrying along with a metrical verve and a gay patter of vocabulary that jostled slang with very academic terms. Its substantial Notes culled from extensive reading sought to give depth to the topicality. But Auden was in America, and the poem had no real contact with the events and temper of Europe at that time.

Nevertheless, much continued to be expected of Auden, and *For the Time Being* seemed to promise a new strength. Its first part, *The Sea and the Mirror*, was a commentary on Shakespeare's *The Tempest*, with a re-interpretation of the *dramatis personae*. The lyrics spoken by each of the characters showed Auden's unique lyricism well maintained, his metrical dexterity indeed heightened. One lyric, built up of the ironic comments by Antonio upon each of his fellows, is a masterpiece in its intense expression of the evil of total, rooted Egotism. The long prose address of Caliban to the audience was an ambitious attempt to offer a solution for the contemporary dilemma as it affected both artists and the ordinary man. Art had been evading Reality and it must face Reality. Man too could escape neither into selfish pleasures nor into unselfish but bleak Utopian idealism. The expression was far from clear, but Auden's conclusion seemed to be following Eliot in the direction of a supernatural Christian faith, and this was further developed in the second part of the volume, the Christmas Oratorio, *For the Time Being*.

This, in spite of a questionable use of modern trappings, was a serious and reverent treatment of the Christian story from Advent to The Flight into Egypt, and it was a sermon for the modern world. In the modern darkness, when hatred, fear and death were in the air, and men were sick of soul, feeble, selfish and despairing, it was time to seek redemption, and to learn in suffering the Way, the Truth, and the Life, no more turning our backs upon the Vision. Much to this effect was said clearly and in Auden's best manner, again modified by a humbler spirit than in the thirties. But the hope of major poetry inspired by a fresh positive vision was not fulfilled by *The Age of Anxiety* of 1948. This "Baroque Eclogue" took the form of a dialogue between a woman buyer for a big department store and three men, a clerk in a shipping office, a Medical Intelligence officer in the Canadian Air Force, and a naval officer. The scene was first a bar on Third Avenue, and then an apartment on the West Side of New York. Its total effect, however, was a failure. Here was nothing new. In time the talk was placed back in the war, and unsettlement, frustration and dissatisfaction hung over the whole. The old Auden skill was there, but it had become mechanical, and sparkled with cold lifeless dazzle. It had all been said before, and time had made most of it commonplace and platitudinous.

In contrast the poetry of Day Lewis grew in strength. "For me there is no dismay", he declared ; imagination, his "royal, impulsive swan", had never flown with such exaltation ; the time seeming then in war so short he prayed

> "Love, tear the song from my breast".

This was the attitude to be expected from his earlier poetry. So was the celebration of comradeship and homely courage in the poems that arose from his service in the Home Guard. He had not lost faith in the social and political ideals of his earlier years, but now in the national danger he felt

> "The Cause shales off, the Humankind stands forth
> A mightier presence".

His earlier promise of outstanding narrative poetry was not followed up, for he kept mainly to lyrics and short meditative poems, except for his translation of Virgil's *Georgics*. Nature in its everlasting beauty and its blessed association with man continued to sustain and inform his poems, whatever their theme, and in one of his most notable groups of poems, the sonnets on childhood, *O Dreams, O Destinations*, his love of nature gave him imagery of serene beauty for the expression of his deepest personal feeling. This driving of such a poet upon himself and his essential personal resources was one of the virtuous effects of the war.

Stephen Spender, like Day Lewis, turned away during the war from partisan politics to a more individual poetic expression. In *Life and the Poet*, a long pamphlet of 1942, he said that he was not recanting, but "merely trying to understand why our position was ineffective, why we may even have betrayed our function"—that is, by putting political ideas so nakedly into poetry. Poetry, he held, must not become propaganda : the poet must concern himself with fundamental things, and see everything with a fresh vision which is, inevitably, a critical one. The poet, living fully his own life, must arouse men to a heightened sense of full living; thereby he will give them a faith able to save the individual from the dehumanising pressure of the machine age and its materialism, and he will restore to men the power to rejoice in existence, while facing life fearlessly. In 1946 he wrote an admirable survey, *Poetry since 1939*, in which he expressed his certainty that "everywhere in modern English poetry one comes upon evidence of things truly and sincerely created. Everywhere there is evidence of a restless mental energy, lively invention, sincerity of feeling". These qualities continued to be present in his own poetry. His sequence of poems entitled *Spiritual Explorations* fulfilled his demand that poetry should deal with the fundamental things of human life. His poetry developed the promise of *The Still Centre* and became more introspective; his poems, as in *Ruins and Visions*, gave the impression of a poet facing himself and coming to a fuller knowledge of life through suffering, and winning his way out of chaos.

MacNeice added three considerable volumes of poetry to his credit before collecting his work in one volume in 1949, and during this decade he also made a notable contribution to radio drama. His position as an outstanding poet was consolidated, but his poetic maturity appeared rather in the technical ease which maturity often brings than in a deepening of spiritual comprehension. The earlier MacNeice with all his qualities in all their variety remained, whereas Day Lewis and Stephen Spender had, by sinking into themselves, developed more compact poetic personalities. In this decade

MacNeice in his poetry displayed himself as the modern scholar and wit, the ideal member of a University Senior Common Room, dazzling in his play of ideas and sparkle of words. His poetry overflowed with images and learning; the play on words, the jostling of learned with topical phrases and with proverbs, was exciting. But his rhythms often became prosaic, and his writing entertained rather than illuminated. His idealism seemed still to aspire but still to be frustrated, and the poet to share Pope's view of man as "the glory, jest and riddle of the world" without his having found any basis for hope. Yet his poems still often expressed his zest for life, whether they sprang from the stresses of war or the ironies of the post-war period, and he still took delight in his early memories of the coast and mountains of Ireland, his "inescapable heritage".

The younger poet Dylan Thomas, however, in *Deaths and Entrances* of 1946 showed a remarkable advance both in art and vision. Except for some deliberately symbolic poems, his earlier obscurity disappeared. The result was a rich concentrated poetry, still strongly emotional, but informed by a power of intellect and controlled by an artist of outstanding technical accomplishment. His vision of life was fundamentally religious, and in *A Refusal to Mourn the Death, by Fire, of a Child in London* his faith that, in the words of his earlier poem, "Death shall have no dominion" burnt clearly. Such poetry indeed conquered Death in wartime and opened Entrances to a fuller life. In other poems a passionate love of nature, linked to childhood memories, produced a beauty that touches the heart and stirs the senses, as in the poems *Poem in October* and *Fern Hill*. In his feeling for childhood—"wild boys innocent as strawberries"— we may be reminded of the seventeenth-century poet Traherne or of Wordsworth; in his joy in nature—"a springful of larks in a rolling cloud"—we may be reminded of Hopkins; but Dylan Thomas was unique. His sudden death in 1953 was a tragic and irreparable loss.

David Gascoyne, who in the thirties had by virtue of his surrealism achieved greater unintelligibility than Dylan

Thomas and Barker, in this decade became clearer than either. In his poetry too a religious attitude played an important part.

Of other poets writing in this decade it is impossible to speak here at any length. From Masefield's generation downwards there were a great host of poets whose varied work testified to a remarkable poetic vitality. No picture could be complete without mention of the intellectual poetry of Edwin Muir, William Empson and Herbert Read ; of the continued quiet output of sincere poetry by Blunden and Richard Church ; of the maintenance by Robert Graves of his austere manner of pure poetry and its influence on several younger poets ; of the steady advance in accomplishment of Christopher Hassall's work. Among the younger poets many began to become well or better known in addition to those already spoken of in this chapter : to mention Geoffrey Grigson, Alex Comfort, Rex Warner, Nicholas Moore, W. S. Graham and Norman Nicholson is to name only a few of the more notable. Such a volume as Norman Nicholson's *Rock Face* of 1948, recording with clear beauty the loving observation of Cumberland made by a sensitive and balanced poet, held high promise for the future of English poetry. Anthologies and magazines of poetry also showed that there was much good poetry not always or immediately published in volume form by its authors : one such poet whose occasional poems declared a lyric power all his own was Tom Scott. Moreover it will always remain impossible to estimate the loss to poetry occasioned by the death of young poets in the war : in 1949 appeared an anthology entitled *For Your Tomorrow* drawn from the work of young men from the English Public Schools who had fallen in the war.

This decade saw notable work from women poets. In this narrative the names of Alice Meynell, Victoria Sackville-West and Edith Sitwell have alone stood out, but from the beginning of the century there had always been several women poets of distinction. Among them were Charlotte Mew, Mary Webb, Sylvia Lynd, Rose Macaulay, Frances Cornford, H.D. and Dorothy Wellesley, the last highly praised by Yeats.

Above all, there had been the American Laura Riding, whose influence on Robert Graves had been so considerable. In this decade, with Edith Sitwell showing how a woman could rival if not indeed excel all her contemporaries, many younger women poets claimed attention. Women have, obviously, their own contribution to make to poetry. In war-time they alone know the separation as felt by wife and mother; however "modern" and however intellectual any may be, there is in all a different sensitiveness from that of men in their religious and domestic emotions ; in general their poetic expression seems to incline more to clarity, to achieve a subtler and more refined intensity, and to preserve a personal integrity apart from the dominating poetic schools of the day.

The masculine approach to love, despite its many personal varieties, can seem, at least to a man, a conventional approach in contrast to the sensitive realism of a woman's approach. Anne Ridler spoke of the property of love

"which brings
a new dimension to all physical things"

and in her poetry a fresh personal vision, at once realistic and sensuous, aesthetic and religious, illuminated all that she made her poetic concern. Lilian Bowes Lyon and Kathleen Raine both wrote lyrics notable for their clear beauty. Among other women poets were Eiluned Lewis, E. J. Scovell, Helen Spalding, Susanne Knowles and Sheila Wingfield. The publication in 1945 of a slim volume of lyrics by a girl of seventeen, Diana James, was a notable example of the way in which some publishers were alive to the contribution that could come from the fresh feminine vision of an exciting world undimmed by the conventions of life and literature. The women poets indeed in this decade seemed to have thoroughly learned, if they ever needed to learn it, the truth that poetry is a very personal expression of personally experienced truths, and that the world of politics and external topicalities does not normally concern it.

When Stephen Spender in *Life and the Poet* declared that poetry must return to the fundamental things of life, he would seem to have expressed a realisation which was to become generally accepted. The political poetry of the thirties passed away. The only considerable poetic "movement" of the forties was the Apocalyptic Movement which emerged at the beginning of the war, when J. F. Hendry and Henry Treece edited their Apocalyptic anthology, *The White Horseman*, which was followed by two more. In spite of the expression of the movement's aims by its leaders it was not very easy to discern a distinctive coherent purpose, but in 1946 Henry Treece restated his views in *How I See Apocalypse* and it was certainly possible to recognise and admire a positive aim of the broadest kind. The political position of the movement he declared to be "clearly Anarchic, an antidote to left-wing Audenism as much as to right-wing Squirearchy". The movement acknowledged both worlds, "that of objects and that of dreams". "Apocalyptic writing, then, is the art form of the man who can recognise, without fear, the variety and the multiplicity of life; of the man who acknowledges his dreams and his laughter, and the tiny and almost unmentionable things of life, as being real and desirable for sanity's sake. And the Apocalyptic attitude will teach poetry to be broad, deep, limitless, like true life. It will teach men to live more, and to exist less."

This was very much what Stephen Spender had said a few years before. Henry Treece concluded his book with a "Bird's Eye View of a Romantic Revival". Among the early supporters of the Apocalyptic movement he named, in addition to J. F. Hendry, Nicholas Moore and Tom Scott, and among poetic sympathisers Alex Comfort. He admitted the wide divergences among the Apocalyptists. But from them, and from others not attached to that or to any movement, he looked for a Romantic Revival. Rather enigmatically, he ended that he "would comment on the present-day recognition of God by Anne Ridler and Norman Nicholson . . . who, in a world so apt to think evil, think good; and, in a period of war and suffering, speak tenderly. Theirs, I hope, is the Kingdom to come".

This brief survey, too, may well end by noting the renewed recognition of God by the poets of the forties. It is obvious in the great poetry of T. S. Eliot and Edith Sitwell; in addition to the poets pointed out by Treece there were many to whose work a religious view of life contributed much, for example, John Betjeman, Richard Church, Kathleen Raine, Christopher Hassall, Dylan Thomas and David Gascoyne. An orthodox Christian who as a humanist teacher at Oxford had no small influence was Charles Williams, himself a highly individual poet, novelist and critic. The fifth decade, indeed, ended with the hope of a poetry restored to the fullness of life, renewed in spirit, and disciplined again in expression.

CHAPTER IX

THE NOVEL, 1900-1950

This half-century has been particularly rich in the variety of kinds of novel that it has produced. When the century began, the word "novel" already covered a wide diversity of productions, but most novelists still felt it necessary to make it their primary business to tell an interesting story and to present a number of people whom the reader could see as clear-cut characters such as he could recognise by their clothes, features, mannerisms and talk to resemble, more or less, his own friends and acquaintances. From the very start of novel-writing, however, there had been novelists who could not avoid, or who deliberately aimed at conveying their philosophy of life at the same time as they told a story: both Richardson and Fielding had done so in their different ways, and Hardy was an outstanding recent instance. The novel had also long been used in such a way that its story exposed social evils: Dickens had made many of his novels instruments of social reform, and, though he was probably the most effective writer in that way, he had been only one of many who, since the novel began, had written novels partly at least with such a purpose. Further, there had arisen the kind of novel in which the novelist went beyond particular social problems and made his tale the vehicle of religious, moral and political ideas, as Charles Kingsley did.

To the later Victorians psychological analysis had come to reinforce the earlier manner of characterisation, which had relied on the reader's co-operative understanding of his fellows. Henry James, in particular, had proceeded to make his main concern the inside rather than the outside of his characters, and to replace the primary interest of story by the fascination of the carefully traced reasoning and feeling which motivated a few figures. This was a narrowing of the broader human interest of the novel to a more specialised study of motives and character, and the general tendency, towards the twentieth century, was indeed in the direction of making the interests of the intellect predominate over the love of a story. Even when the balance was well maintained, as it was in Hardy's novels, a new kind of specialisation was apparent in the relative limitation of their background to Wessex.

In the first decade of the twentieth century four outstanding novelists kept fairly closely to the broad traditional kinds of novel as they had developed in the ways just mentioned. They all relied very much upon a story and they all called up before their reader's imaginations a considerable variety of human personages acting in flesh and dress as their creators described them. Arnold Bennett, of these four, kept nearest to the traditional novel : he told his stories for their own sake, keeping himself and his ideas out of them, and drawing his characters mainly from the outside. clearly seen figures in a clearly observed world. By contrast with Trollope's, the world of Bennett's novels was commercial and plebeian, but Bennett's aim as a novelist was similar to Trollope's. While Arnold Bennett was a materialist, H. G. Wells was a Utopian, using the novel to convey his sense of the unplanned chaos of industrial England and to preach his vision of a better way. But Wells too dealt in story and character ; he let his stories ramble on with much of love and abundance of incident, and he made his comic figures as extravagantly vivid as those of Dickens. As a novelist Wells indeed shared the aims both of Dickens and of Meredith : in extending the scope of the novel to include a wholesale criticism of politics, society, commerce and education he followed the precedent of Dickens, but in passing through the body of his criticism a current of dynamic ideas he used the novel more after the conception of Meredith, who had both spoken of fiction as the vehicle of philosophy and himself used it notably for the expression of general ideas.

Galsworthy in his very English way held a middle course, nearer to Bennett than to Wells, and central after a fashion that linked him with Victorians like Trollope and George

Eliot and Meredith yet without his closely resembling any one of them. His saga of the Forsytes was a solidly built tale of living people, but it was the picture of a way of life lived by only one social class and, without his views being forced upon the reader, the implicit criticism was there for all to read. Conrad, telling on the whole more exciting and colourful stories than did the other three, nevertheless paid much more attention than they to the psychological presentation of character and motive and also achieved at the same time a more comprehensive and universal criticism of life. At mid-century Conrad may well appear the most modern of these four by virtue of the painstaking artistry and subtlety of his psychological approach. In this he can be compared with Henry James, whose last novels appeared in the opening years of this century : James was the great master of that art and a powerful influence on the novel of this century.

Though the work of these four stands out thus prominently, there were of course many other distinguished novelists in the first decade of this century. G. K. Chesterton in his *Napoleon of Notting Hill* and *The Man Who was Thursday* displayed a rich combination of poetic fantasy and humour : with zest he turned ideas into romantic dreams and peopled them with strange but human beings. Belloc, too, gave his shining wit and keen intellect to the novel. Somerset Maugham, already prominent by his *Liza of Lambeth* of 1897, slowly built up his reputation. W. W. Jacobs, alongside his short stories, put his comic sailormen and their women folk into short novels like *Dialstone Lane* and *Salthaven*. A. E. W. Mason kept to the highway of fiction, and Maurice Hewlett renewed the life of the historical novel. In 1901 Kipling wrote a great book, if not a great novel, in *Kim*. It was a decade of quite stirring life in the novel, and not least of its productions was the posthumous novel of Samuel Butler, *The Way of All Flesh*, destined by its satiric attitude to the Victorians and by the general tenor of its witty questioning of accepted things to be very acceptable in the twenties, when the disintegration of the old world was in the intellectual air. Above all, from the point of view of the development of the novel, there were the first four novels of E. M. Forster, the last being *Howards End* in 1910.

E. M. Forster set out to modify the traditional novel by giving the intellect a greater share in its creation and direction. As he later admitted in *Aspects of the Novel*, though he kept them, he questioned the real need of story and plot in the novel. Following in the wake of Meredith, he took the conception of the novel as "the vehicle of philosophy" a stage further. With him the theme became more important than the plot and the persons. He started with an idea, that convention was evil and was the enemy of the true natural way of life ; to express this idea he imagined contrasting groups of people who embodied respectively convention and nature and set them in contrasting backgrounds of suburbia and an idealised Italy or Cambridge. Because the idea came first, the story which embodied it was almost bound to have elements of falsity, which were less likely to be present when a novelist either first imagined his characters and then fitted his story to them, or saw the story and then peopled it, or imaginatively created story and people in one process. In Forster's novels the idea reigned supreme, imagination was crippled, psychology became the servant of theme, and the scene was limited by excluding the human bustle which did not specifically contribute to the exposition of the central idea. As handled by Forster such novels were very stimulating, and their appeal grew with the changing mind of the century. He had given a brilliant example of how to talk about life intellectually rather than present life in all its variety as the interaction of definite personalities to produce a story.

The story of the novel in this century cannot be told as satisfactorily as can that of the poetry by considering it more or less decade by decade. In the second decade Bennett, Wells, Galsworthy, and Conrad, remained "the big four". Forster did not publish his next novel until 1924. Most of the rising generation of young novelists such as Hugh Walpole, Compton Mackenzie, Rose Macaulay, and Sheila Kaye Smith, showed individual gifts working within the accepted

manner and mood. Hugh Walpole, in particular, looked
as though he was richly gifted with talents of all kinds :
keeping to story and characterisation in the traditional way
he filled his tales with a spirit of romance and humour and
gave considerable thought to the psychological presentation
of his characters, while he also gave additional substance to
his story by writing it to a theme.

Compton Mackenzie in *Sinister Street* began that devotion of the novel to the portrayal of boyhood and
youth which was to be taken up later by a good
many minor novelists. He made it a substantial story
with a full background, a novel in the traditional
manner, chiefly "modern" in its concentrating on the early
years of its principal figure. But, as in the world of poetry,
so in that of the novel, change was in the air. Even in his
early *Sons and Lovers* D. H. Lawrence, though in no way
revolutionary in the kind and technique of his novel, revealed
an originality and even violence of imagination and emotion
which heralded a dynamic use of the novel as it had hardly
been handled before. Before this second decade was ended,
with prophetic zeal he had made the novel a pulpit for
something like a new religion. Whereas H. G. Wells in *Mr
Britling Sees It Through* reconciled himself to the war and
then in *Joan and Peter* again looked ahead to a better world
more sanely and efficiently planned and educated, D. H.
Lawrence spent these years fighting out a personal battle in
himself, which he transferred to his novels. There the sexual
conflict of man and woman, fierce urgencies of love and
hatred, and a strange worship of blood and blood-brother-
hood gave a foretaste of the welter of ideas and passions
which were to characterise the world of the post-war period.
A single novel in this decade which was significant of the
changing attitude of the times was Norman Douglas's *South
Wind*. A rather fantastic tale, its wit and irony playing around
a Colonial bishop and much else generally accounted respectable, it too pointed to the coming time when the old values
were not only to be questioned but derided. But *South Wind*,

though stamped with an individual personality, was only a variation in the handling of the traditional novel.

It was around 1920 that the attack on the traditional novel began. For some years new influences had been making themselves felt. In the nineties George Moore had been influenced by the French novel, and Somerset Maugham owed much to French example. French influence meant in part an aggressively frank realism after the manner of Zola, but more importantly it meant greater attention to structure and expression. Those who felt the French influence looked with disapproval on the relatively carefree attitude of the traditional English novel, and began to require neater construction accompanied by expression at once more lucid and more subtle. Arnold Bennett, too, came to appreciate and seek these French virtues. In the twenties the sensitive psychological patterning of Proust was to be another potent French influence. But the influence of the Russian novel was in the long run to have a considerably deeper effect than that of the French. In the nineties Constance and Edward Garnett began to publish their translations of Turgenev, which they followed up with translations of Tolstoy, Dostoevsky and Tchehov, the last appearing in the twenties. The effect was cumulative, sinking gradually into writers and readers, until by about 1920 a new world of fiction had been opened to a considerable audience. By the work of the Russian masters it was possible to realise how much more deeply one could penetrate into the human soul than English novelists had so far attempted. Many felt that in comparison with such work the English novel appeared provincial and soulless, half-blind to the psychological wonders of human personality. The influence of the Russian novel came to a head in time to join forces with the psychology of the subconscious mind which was also by 1920 becoming current. The time was ripe for an attempt to revolutionise the English novel.

It was James Joyce who first undertook this task. After he had written his short stories *Dubliners* (1914) and his fictionalised autobiography *A Portrait of the Artist as a Young Man* (1916), both of them showing a distinctive originality more or less within traditional limits, it became known that he was engaged on a remarkable experiment in the novel. This experiment, begun as early as 1914, appeared as *Ulysses* in Paris in 1922, and was hailed with amazement, some scornful, but much almost idolatrous. Tracing a not very attractive, though very human, "hero" through some twenty-four hours of a Dublin day, Joyce portrayed the outer world through the inner workings of his hero's consciousness, introduced into the flow of consciousness a symbolic phantasmagoria, and all the time played with the English language, now with strange effectiveness, now merely with obscure pedantry, and again with puckish humour. Nothing of the traditional novel was left. Humanity remained, at least a section drab and often rank. Listening to the internal monologues of his characters, the reader smelt the flesh and dust of existence, but continuity of story was gone, plot was indiscernible, the theme was deeply buried, and to the ordinary reader many a stretch was unintelligible. In England the book was banned as morally offensive, but many copies came in unobserved from France, and the world of letters and its hangers-on were for many years sure that a great experiment had been successfully achieved. Moreover the sexuality in the thoughts of the characters and in the style of the author had a particularly strong appeal in the twenties. *Ulysses*, indeed, made such an impression that, bearing in mind also the revelation of the Russian novelists, it was no longer possible for many to regard the traditional English novel with the same complete satisfaction as before.

At the same time, in the early twenties, Virginia Woolf dealt the traditional novel another blow, perhaps more effective because she was more restrained. She had early become acquainted with *Ulysses* in its serial publication in *The Little Review*. So, in 1919, she began her attack with an article on Modern Fiction in which she pleaded that "the proper stuff of fiction is a little other than custom would have us believe". Looking at the novels of Bennett, Wells and Galsworthy she found that, in spite of their substantial picture of life and the abundant vitality of their characters, the reality of life escaped them. All three novelists were adjudged "materialists" because of their preoccupation with the outside of life ; and by "materialists" she said she meant "that they write of unimportant things ; that they spend immense skill and immense industry making the trivial and the transitory appear the true and the enduring". For her, the true and the enduring resided in the very essence of life, the ever-changing, ever-fluctuating consciousness, continuously affected from without and ceaselessly working its transformations within. "Life is a luminous halo, a semi-transparent envelope surrounding us from the beginning of consciousness to the end". "Is it not", she asked, "the task of the novelist to convey this varying, this unknown and uncircumscribed spirit, whatever aberration or complexity it may display, with as little mixture of the alien and external as possible ?" Because she found in *Ulysses* an attempt "to reveal the flickerings of that innermost flame which flashes its messages through the brain", she found Joyce, in contrast to her materialists, spiritual.

In another paper, on "The Russian Point of View", she noted that in Russian novels the time comes when "the elements of the soul are seen, not separately in scenes of humour or scenes of passion as our slower English minds conceive them, but streaked, involved, inextricably confused", so that "a new panorama of the human mind is revealed". Here too was spiritual writing in contrast to materialism, and with her attitude to fiction thus changing —she had herself been recently engaged on a traditional novel—she proceeded to try her hand at experiment. *Jacob's Room* was an uncertain start, *Mrs Dalloway* was nearly successful, and in 1927 *To The Lighthouse* showed her in full control of a technique which displayed the inner stream of consciousness, the spirit of life ebbing and flowing; symbolism too played its part in her treatment; a very sensitive artistry added a delight at times akin to poetic pleasure. A new kind of novel had been born in England. Story in the old sense had largely disappeared, but the traditional English gift of vivid characterisation was supremely retained by means of the new technique in the two unforgettable realities of Mrs Ramsay and her husband.

But neither James Joyce nor Virginia Woolf could do more than unsettle opinion about the novel. The new possibilities were obvious ; the limitations of the traditional novel were clearly underlined. But the individuality of Joyce was far too strong to be followed, and the influence of Virginia Woolf worked slowly, reinforcing that of Henry James in the direction of heightened psychological sensitiveness and making readers more accustomed to immersion in the flow of a character's consciousness. Though many critics worshipped Joyce and Virginia Woolf, writers were reluctant to indulge in further revolutionary experiment, and one of the next more interesting experiments did not come till 1936 when Aldous Huxley shuffled three layers of time in the construction of *Eyeless in Gaza*. In the nineteen-twenties Bennett, Wells, Galsworthy and Conrad were too old too change their ways and, though Conrad died while in full production, their work held its wide public and maintained the prestige of the traditional novel with the average serious reader. On the whole the greatest change in the novel in the twenties was not in technique, but in the impact of new ideas upon moral standards in the flux of the post-war mind.

As regards the novel, the nineteen-twenties indeed presented a remarkably rich and varied scene, impossible to summarise with real justice. With Joyce and Virginia Woolf in the vanguard, the novelists who, next to them, attracted most attention were probably E. M. Forster, D. H. Lawrence and Aldous Huxley. Forster's *A Passage to India* crowned his work and ensured the renewed life and influence of his earlier novels, now approaching a generation old. In this last novel the rather complacent preaching of his younger days had given place to a more complex apprehension of life, while the desolating echo in the Marabar caves at the novel's centre held a suggestion of hopelessness even deeper than that expressed by Eliot in *The Waste Land*. D. H. Lawrence, part of the time in Mexico where his dark mystical broodings on the passions of the blood were strengthened, continued to display in his novels the violence of his reaction from contemporary civilisation. Less by their intrinsic merits as novels than by their projection of a passionate personality, half saint, half devil, fighting for sanity in a soulless world, his books fascinated younger readers in particular, and not least the intellectuals in spite of Lawrence's own repudiation of intellect in favour of a more primitive intensity of living.

Aldous Huxley too attracted the rising generation in the twenties : his witty presentation of contemporary ideas had an effect stimulating enough to offset any depression induced by his implicit view of the meaninglessness of contemporary life—and indeed of human life—though the very disillusionment of the world he drew had a strange appeal to those who themselves largely shared it. His *Point Counter Point* melodramatically crowned his scornful analysis of post-war psychology and manners in the intellectual and artistic classes. Aldous Huxley saw human beings rather as human animals, by whose follies he was often amused, though he hated often both their follies and their disgusting habits. His satiric amusement was shared by William Gerhardi, as in *The Polyglots* (1925), and by Wyndham Lewis, and indeed by a large audience happy to be amused even while they themselves were satirised, like the Court audiences at a Restoration comedy. There was a cynicism in this disillusioned laughter, for which the recession of the Christian faith from the minds of a considerable proportion of writers and readers was in part responsible. As the Christian view of the value of personality and of the nature of good and evil came to be held less widely and less surely, the antics of human types were a sport for the intellect. The resultant effect on the novel was a narrowing one : the feverish animation of puppets in a human zoo tended to replace in Huxley's novels the presentation of normal human beings acting more or less purposefully in a world of moral values.

Below these outstanding novelists of the twenties were many good novelists in a variety of kinds of novel. Hugh Walpole continued to develop the traditional novel in his generous romantic way, speaking much of the soul and enjoying the bustle, comedy and colour of the Polchester scene : his deceptively easy style (for it was capable of a good deal of subtlety in psychology and atmosphere) and his appeal to the emotions and moral approval of his readers earned him the disapproval of higher critics, but his novels were very widely read by the average serious novel-reading public. Compton Mackenzie did not rise again to the strength of his earlier *Carnival* and *Sinister Street*, but in less ambitious novels displayed a very human interest together with much humour, a combination that was very acceptable. Several other names of good competent, or better than competent, writers could readily be added, such as Frank Swinnerton, Francis Brett Young, Algernon Blackwood and Louis Golding. It was a decade too in which women novelists made an unusually large contribution, as such names as Rose Macaulay, Sheila Kaye Smith, May Sinclair, Constance Holme, Mary Webb, Storm Jameson, Stella Benson and G. B. Stern readily indicate. With Virginia Woolf and Edith Sitwell especially prominent, these and other women writers made the contribution by women to the literature of the twenties a close rival to the masculine contribution.

Towards the end of the twenties, some ten years having it would seem been necessary to release memory under artistic control and to remove repugnance on the part of the public, the novel of the 1914-1918 war came in a three-year flood. R. H. Mottram's *Spanish Farm* trilogy was perhaps the best, but among other outstanding war novels were C. E. Montague's *Rough Justice*, Henry Williamson's *Patriot's Progress* and Richard Aldington's *Death of a Hero*. The war seen in perspective and with varying degrees of disillusion provided ample scope for narrative, characterisation and description in the traditional manner. The American Ernest Hemingway, however, by his *A Farewell to Arms* (1929), a novel of the Italian campaign, left a deeper mark on the English novel, for the direct realistic recording of the way of natural man, reticent of emotion, but sensuous and primitive, held a greater originality than the English war novels, though its appeal had been prepared for by Lawrence's appraisal of the primitive element in human nature below the veneer of civilisation. *A Farewell to Arms* also reminds us that many other American novels deserve to be included in the story of the English novel in the twenties, for in this decade the work of Sinclair Lewis and Upton Sinclair and Dreiser's *American Tragedy* became well known in this country, an indication not only of their intrinsic worth and interest but of a more international outlook on the part of the reading public and also perhaps of a sense of a relative loss of vitality in the English novel.

Yet this account of the novel in the twenties has not even yet given a full outline of its variety. There were two novelists too individual to classify, the brothers T. F. Powys and John Cowper Powys. Of these T. F. Powys wrote short novels and short stories about a queer rustic world of eccentric clergymen and lewd yokels: his conception was a symbolic one, his method a comic realism blended with fantasy and enriched by wit and irony, and his spirit had a strangely appealing human charity which was paradoxically at once Christian and pagan. John Cowper Powys was equally original and built up at greater length another rustic world, similarly sex-ridden and grotesque, but unlighted by the wit and almost poetic assurance of his brother. The Powyses give the impression of rejecting the ordinary workaday world of reality as a subject because of a peculiar Powysian cast of vision, and Osbert Sitwell's combination of a kind of nightmare realism with ironic wit to describe the old ladies of pre-war Scarborough in *Before the Bombardment* was born of a vision peculiarly Sitwellian. But there were other individual developments in the twenties which, individually and cumulatively, give the impression rather of a deliberate retreat from the pressure of the contemporary world than of inner compulsion. Thus David Garnett's *Lady into Fox* escaped into a hauntingly real world which was however transformed by magic, a world as uncanny in its seeming reality as the world of such a story as De la Mare's *The Return*, in which the soul of a man long buried entered a living man to transform his very features into its long lost countenance. Ernest

Bramah gave a peculiar delight by his Kai Lung books, in
which a very fine understanding of human life was set forth
in a Chinese setting and with a Chinese obliquity of style
that was, and is, irresistible to his devotees. The Kai Lung
books might indeed have come at any time, but they had a
special appeal to this decade, when escape alike from the
traditional forms and ways and from the current reality
awakened a ready response in many. Just as every age has
its best-sellers who carry their readers away on colourful
magic carpets, so this age had them in special abundance.
The historical romances of Rafael Sabatini won wide popularity
in the early twenties and kept it for years ; Jeffrey Farnol's
blend of romance and humour was a gold-mine to its author ;
A. S. M. Hutchinson's emotional stories of modern dilemmas
romantically and morally considered were read by thousands
who had not heard of Virginia Woolf or Aldous Huxley.

In the very wealth of its variety the novel of the twenties
suggested either the ferment heralding a new creative age or
a disintegration preluding decline. Looking back, it would
seem that rather than expanding its scope and treatment the
novel was in fact in process of becoming less broadly concerned
with human life. The regional novel was a healthy development, but it was a narrowing of the novel's scope. Partly
from the stimulus given by Hardy's concentration on Wessex,
several novelists made a particular region their chosen world.
Mary Webb took Shropshire and in *Precious Bane* (1924)
her aim was very largely to preserve a passing age with its
old local customs and superstitions, while her earlier novel
The Golden Arrow had been pervaded by the sense of change
as modern ideas began to intrude into her isolated countryside.
Sheila Kaye Smith too had for some years concerned herself
with Sussex past and present before *The End of the House
of Alard* in 1924 depicted the break-up of an old Sussex
landed family under the force of modern conditions. The
regional novel had begun early in the century as in the West
Country tales of Eden Philpotts, but it was in the twenties
it really took root. Then it continued in the thirties and

forties, Yorkshire being a particularly favoured region, as in Winifred Holtby's *South Riding*, while Leo Walmsley became the novelist of the fisher folk of the North-East coast. The Anglo-Welsh novels of Caradoc Evans and others, though hardly to be labelled "regional", may also well be borne in mind here.

The concentration of many novelists on childhood and youth was also a good development, but again it was a narrowing of the novel's scope. Kipling's *Stalky and Co.* (1899) lay behind, ready to add its influence, when Alec Waugh's *Loom of Youth* (1917), written with a rather crude vigour at the age of seventeen, brought in the school novel, generally with a considerable strand of sex in its texture. The elder novelist E. F. Benson countered with his *David Blaize*, a far pleasanter "loom of youth". Hugh Walpole wrote his stories about the boy Jeremy and his dog. Henry Williamson traced his Willie Maddison through his childhood and schooldays. In the thirties there was still such a novel as Geoffrey Dennis's *Bloody Mary's*. Sometimes the school novel was mainly from the masters' point of view, as in Hugh Walpole's early tragicomedy of *Mr Perrin and Mr Traill*, or Paul Selver's *Schooling* of the late twenties.

The variety of the novel in the twenties further included as a special kind the novel of country life. Here it was not the region which concerned the novelist so much as country life in contrast to town life. It was an aspect of the widespread desire to escape from the pressure of the industrial world, a desire so strong and natural that this kind of story, finding a considerable public in the twenties, held and extended its popularity in the next decades. Adrian Bell was the best and most popular exponent of the appealing theme of how to make one's livelihood and happiness out of the land. His novels had little story, but a healthy almost old-fashioned simplicity of interest in men and things. A. G. Street handled the theme with more complexity, coming closer to the unlimited novel except for his preoccupation with the problem of British agriculture. H. E. Bates too should perhaps rather be included among the less limited novelists, for his early novels were often as much concerned with the life of a small country town as with that of the country side, but he wrote as a countryman, and, especially in his short stories, the poetic realism of country life was the substance of his vision. The early novels of Henry Williamson also owed much to a country vision, for under the spell of Richard Jefferies Williamson made the sun and the open air, the woods and the seashore help in the shaping of his Willie Maddison. His *Tarka the Otter* (1927), and to a less extent the more diffuse *Salar the Salmon* of the thirties, were outstanding examples of the novelist's art applied to the non-human life of the countryside.

The novel of crime and detection too came fully into its own in the twenties. The fame of Edgar Wallace was already established and now commanded a very wide public, and the popularity of the Sherlock Holmes stories had further prepared the way. G. K. Chesterton's poetically intellectual fantasies of detection, the Father Brown stories, had first appeared in *The Innocence of Father Brown* in 1911, and E. C. Bentley's *Trent's Last Case*, by some considered a classic of its kind, came as early as 1913. Now there came to the fore such writers as Agatha Christie, J. J. Connington, Austin Freeman, the Coles, Freeman Wills Croft, and Dorothy Sayers, and in the thirties and forties the fashion maintained its strong hold on readers. Writers like E. R. Punshon, John Rhode, H. C. Bailey, and Margery Allingham, shared notably in the sustained favour of the public, while again in this field too American writers, particularly "Ellery Queen", Van Dine, and M. G. Eberhart, made a large contribution. The variety of kinds within the detective and crime novel gave a wide choice, and in each kind there were several writers, all with a high degree of competence. Some writers concentrated on detection, others on excitement ; some on motive, others on mystery and the unexpected ; some kept closely to a factual treatment, others indulged in imagination. The individual variations of writers in the proportions of the mixture of story, psychology, detection, background, excitement, characterisation, wit and literary ornament were indeed great and were adjusted to various levels in the taste and intelligence of the reading public. That there was money as well as pleasure in catering for this public perhaps diverted to the writing of such stories some novelists who would have concentrated on the novel proper had that continued to hold its old largely unchallenged primacy in esteem. At any rate L. A. G. Strong was one who varied his novel-writing with detective fiction ; Dorothy Sayers was to show that her greater gift lay in the field of religious drama, but she first gave several years to varieties of detective fiction, gradually replacing interest in detection by a more literary approach in which background played a large part ; Cecil Day Lewis the poet, after trying the straight novel, became as "Nicholas Blake" an outstanding detective writer, showing that narrative power to which, considering his talent, he gave too little scope in his poetry. Indeed in the forties the detective novel attracted to the ranks of its writers a Professor of English in "Michael Innes", who gave to it a brilliance of mind, wit and fancy sufficient to dispel any lingering doubts that the detective novel was worthy of being written and read by the highest class of mind and taste. It became natural that a young writer like Edmund Crispin should turn to the detective novel rather than to straight fiction.

The very variety of the novel in the twenties, from the new approaches of Joyce and Virginia Woolf, through the various modifications of the traditional novel, down to the more specialised kinds like the detective novel, encouraged a tendency to disintegrate the reading public. Where one unified serious reading public had supported the work of Wells, Bennett, Galsworthy and Conrad, there now tended to be a series of different publics. The whole of the reasonably serious novel-reading public no longer read the novels of Virginia Woolf as their predecessors had read in succession those of Dickens, Hardy and Wells. The readers of Virginia Woolf, Forster and Huxley were unlikely to be also appreciative readers of Hugh Walpole. The Powys brothers could not be to everyone's taste, nor would the more limited kind of story like *Tarka the Otter* be everyone's book. In fact there came into existence readers of the intellectual novel, readers of the central traditional novel, readers of the romance, readers of the detective novel, and so on. Of course, these were not self-contained groups, but there was overlapping in all directions. Now and again a writer emerged who for a while at least commanded the attention of the majority of all readers, as did Priestley with *The Good Companions* of 1929, followed by *Angel Pavement.*

With the improving facilities in education, the official recognition of contemporary or "modern" literature in the examinations of schools and universities, and the opportunities offered by adult education, the cleavage noticeable in older readers between those who followed the intellectual novel and those whose taste was limited to the more traditional or popular was gradually much lessened as the younger generations succeeded, but that this relative disintegration of the novel-reading public had taken place is to be borne in mind when one views the course of the novel in the thirties and forties. The writers who aimed at the broadest public were henceforth on the whole those whose gifts were of the less seriously intellectual kind, like A. J. Cronin. The younger serious writers of fiction, like the Auden group of young poets of the thirties, wrote more or less consciously for a smaller audience : of such were even Graham Greene and Elizabeth Bowen in the thirties, and Rex Warner in the forties. As with the poets, their public too expanded, encouraged by *Penguin New Writing* and Penguin reprints. In between remained as before the considerable body of competent writers who relied on story rather than ideas, but the prestige of their kind of novel was no longer as high as it had been in the earlier years of the century.

Perspective in regard to modern writing grows slowly as the years pass, and perhaps more slowly in the matter of prose than of poetry. It is certainly hard to see the fiction of the thirties in as well defined a perspective as the poetry. The story seems one of a marked decline from the highest levels of creative, imaginative and interpretative fiction. It was in the early thirties that Virginia Woolf consummated her vision of life and her technique in *The Waves*: she had little more to give. Aldous Huxley replaced his despair by a search for spiritual truth in *Eyeless in Gaza*, but he too as a novelist then largely withdrew. John Cowper Powys produced an outstandingly fine novel in *The Glastonbury Romance*, in which modern psychology was integrated into imaginative portrayal of character. The young novelist Henry Williamson, who in the twenties had inspired hopes of further development, expressed himself mainly outside fiction, having revised his early novels into the linked *Flax of Dream*. Among the older novelists Hugh Walpole stood out, for in his "Herries" novels he fulfilled his earlier promise of recreating the traditional novel in something at least of its fullness and substantiality of vision. Compton Mackenzie, Rose Macaulay, Frank Swinnerton, Francis Brett Young and Louis Golding were among those who kept to their own track on the broad highway. One outstanding newcomer among the best-sellers was A. J. Cronin, in whose work Charles Kingsley's kind of novel dealing with broad ideas and topical problems was presented with eloquence and melodrama. A. P. Herbert too joined the ranks of popular novelists with a purpose with his *Water Gypsies*.

But in the thirties the future of the novel seemed in the hands of a few young writers, chief among them being Graham Greene, Charles Morgan, H. E. Bates, L. A. G. Strong and Elizabeth Bowen. Each of them had distinctive merits above the average, but none was free from the limitations that were narrowing the scope of the modern novelist. Greene had a vision limited by his consciousness of evil in human life: he concentrated on the seamy side of modern life, and his principal characterisation ran to a type, that of the moral defective. Charles Morgan in general wrote his novels to a theme, which he handled with a keen, lucid intellect but in a style peculiarly mannered. H. E. Bates had the limitation of his country vision extending only to the small town. L. A. G. Strong was probably at his best in an Irish setting. Elizabeth Bowen's keen appreciation of the human comedy and its possibilities of tragedy was nevertheless limited by a feminine sensitiveness, though excellent in its kind, and by a class-consciousness. In addition Christopher Isherwood, collaborator with Auden in his plays, seemed to show special promise with his *Mr Norris Changes Trains*, and also there were the varied attractions of the novels of Eric Linklater. Further there was an appearing and disappearing of young novelists without the power to follow up a bright promise. Keith Winter's *Other Man's Saucer* was wittily cynical and sensitive but formless, and he turned aside from the novel. Arthur Calder-Marshall's *Pie in the Sky* of 1937 was typical of another kind of novel. The expression "the proletariat" was then in the air, and *Pie in the Sky* had some claim to be considered a "proletarian novel", for it showed how left-wing and communist theories and contemporary social and economic conditions in the working classes affected the relations between young men and their girls and between the young and their families. Such a novel, both loosely written and topical, was hardly written with a thought to its lasting. The corresponding politically conscious poetry of the thirties had more chance of lasting because of its redeeming virtues of brevity and form.

The forties are still so near that it is even more difficult to see their novelists in perspective. Perhaps the greatest single achievement was John Cowper Powys's *Owen Glendower* (1942), in which he applied his imaginative understanding of modern psychology to a complex, wide-scale portrayal of the early fifteenth century. It is not easy to perceive any new novelist of exceptional achievement or even of more than average promise. Perhaps C. P. Snow will come to stand out in time. Certainly Snow, formerly a research physicist and during the war organiser of scientific man-power, applied himself to the novel with great seriousness and achieved a most impressive sequence of novels in which, through well controlled narrative and effective characterisation, he expressed some of the problems of the day in regard to education, religion and marriage, giving indeed a view of life with breadth and detail of presentation. A young novelist who for a moment looked as if she might rival any woman novelist of the century was Elizabeth Myers : *A Well Full of Leaves* had an emotional intensity and a sensuous vividness which gave almost poetic power to the tragic theme. But when she followed it with *The Basilisk of St James's*, a recreation of the personality and background of Dean Swift, she did not show an equal grasp of her material, and she died young.

Joyce Cary certainly stood out as a new novelist of a limited, very personal kind, as with *The Horse's Mouth* : he gave a passionate vitality to eccentric figures, and there was exciting intensity in his manner. Denton Welch, before his early death, had given a remarkably fresh, bitter-sweet re-creation of childhood and adolescence. But on the whole it was the writers who had established themselves in the thirties whose work was most outstanding in the forties. Charles Morgan well maintained his reputation, and Graham Greene and Elizabeth Bowen added to theirs. H. E. Bates in *Fair Stood the Wind for France* showed that war as an experience and a theme had matured and extended his powers. Evelyn Waugh, mordantly witty in a young man's way in his highly individual satiric comedies in the thirties, added to his achievement in the maturer *Put Out More Flags*, and later savaged the sentimentalism of Americans in *The Loved One*. Aldous Huxley, too, now in the third decade of his fame, in one novel, *Time Must Have A Stop*, blended satire and pseudo-mysticism and in another, *Ape and Essence*, indulged in a grim satiric vision of the future. The latter vein was shared by George Orwell in *Nineteen-Eighty-Four*, while the same writer's *Animal Farm* was a wholehearted satire of the post-war menagerie.

In the forties there was indeed a strong tendency to use the novel for the exposition of general ideas with regard to the trend of civilisation. Three writers, who were also poets, stood out in this kind of novel, Rex Warner, Alex Comfort and Frederick Prokosch. Rex Warner's *The Professor* had appeared in 1938 : inspired by the recent European policy of totalitarian Germany, it had dealt with the peril to democratic ideals of individual freedom. *The Aerodrome,* blending Freudian psychology with melodrama, again sought to expose the threat to the democratic way of life, and at the end of the forties his *Men of Stones* was still concerned with the theme of totalitarianism versus the free life. The appeal of such novels lay wholly in the presentation of ideas through largely allegorical story ; their people hardly existed, for as mere pawns on the political chess-board they were dehumanised in the conflict of ideas. Alex Comfort's *Power House* dealt with France in the days of resistance to German occupation, and as with Rex Warner's novels combined psychology and politics without giving real life to the characters. In 1949 Prokosch's *Storm and Echo* gave an oblique presentation of the problem of civilisation's future by exposing the folly of running away from "the European malaise" to the African jungle : his characters were types, the story was thin and desultory, only the African jungle, grotesquely beautiful and horrible, had a justifying power in the book. But many less gifted writers also turned to the novel with the hope of interesting the reader in fictional presentation of the problems confronting the world, and the general effect was one of tedious seriousness, aping factuality. A reviewer in 1949 was moved to lament : "Once upon a time novels were stories about imaginary people. Now large parts of them often consist of biography, history, philosophical argument or leading articles. They are still read, but it is open to question whether they reach the same audience as they did formerly".

To judge from the lapse of time between the 1914-1918 war and the main treatment of its themes in fiction, the review of the second world war by novelists could hardly be expected before mid-century at the earliest. The protracted course of the war itself inevitably checked the writing of young novel-ists more than that of young poets. Nevertheless there appeared quite a number of war novels during the war. *I'm a Stranger Here Myself* was a convincing novel about life and warfare on an armed merchant cruiser by Anthony Thorne, who had himself served in the navy. Roger Grinstead's *Some Talk of Alexander* applied satirical realism to characters in the Brigade of Guards. Nigel Balchin's *The Small Back Room* made a sensational story out of the stress and strain of a team of research scientists in their work, including their conflicts with bureaucrats, and in their personal lives. Such novels were in tune with much of the war poetry in conveying in the world they depicted a sense of unease, frustration and boredom ; they too were written with the realism of an inside knowledge that bred satire. Some naturally wrote rather of the heroism and pathos of war, and indeed there were few moods, as there were few theatres, of this long drawn out war which were not handled while the topicality made the writing of such stories profitable, and either a pleasure or a purgation to their authors. John Brophy in *Target Island* gave a picture of life in the heroic island of Malta ; Phyllis Bottome in *London Pride* dealt with the children in the ruins and amid the bombs. As already mentioned, H. E. Bates turned his first-hand knowledge to excellent account in *Fair Stood the Wind for France*. But the novel which first sought to extract the very spirit of war-time England as seen in the lives of typical individuals was Elizabeth Bowen's *The Heat of the Day* in 1949, when memory had been given a little time to sift and interpret its vast material.

At mid-century it is the names of Elizabeth Bowen and Graham Greene that may well receive the last emphasis in ending such an attempt to outline the course of the novel. In this brief survey many names have been omitted, some no doubt unjustly. For instance, Charles Williams in the thirties wrote allegorical fantasies which time may retrieve and exalt. Writers, popular in the best sense, like C. S. Forester and R. C. Hutchinson, would deserve serious appraisal in any longer account. In the latter years a best-selling novelist like Richard Llewellyn with *How Green was my Valley* (1939) could not be omitted from a complete story of the novel : it reminds us that, though one novel will come before the film of it, the next novel may have its author's success in the cinema as a fresh influence upon it. Also one of the most widely read novels of the forties came from America, Margaret Mitchell's *Gone with the Wind*. In days when the intellectual novelists seemed afraid to portray the ordinary emotions of ordinary people, and unable to imagine or believe in the reality of human personality, the ordinary reader found his needs better supplied by such large and colourful stories as these best-sellers provided. Their great success was something of a commentary on the absence of great English novels and on the relatively limited appeal of the better English novelists. J. B. Priestley, however, in *Festival at Farbridge* (1951) boldly returned to the manner of his *Good Companions* of over twenty years earlier; there in a very English scene, crowded with figures humorously exaggerated in the drawing, he invited us to recognise that what still matters most is the humanheartedness of ordinary people and that in 1951, no less than before, energy, laughter, and romantic love make the world go round.

Nor would it be right to conclude without special mention of V. S. Pritchett who also in 1951 published in *Mr Beluncle* a novel of the earlier broad kind. Loosely episodic, it is a satiric comedy of suburbia and it is dominated by the title-character, a bumptious genteel humbug conceived on the scale and after the manner of Dickens. Pritchett's earlier novels such as *Clare Drummer* (1929) and *Nothing Like Leather* (1935) had promised some such notable achievement to come. His volume of short stories, *It May Never Happen* (1945), contains some of the best work in the modern English short story, and Pritchett is outstanding as a critic too.

To add Ivy Compton-Burnett at the end is to underline her uniqueness. Her work really dates from *Pastors and Masters* (1925), which was followed by some dozen novels including *Men and Wives* (1931), *Daughters and Sons* (1937), *Parents and Children* (1941), and *The Present and the Past* (1953). She stands apart, a novelist for the few, but by them immensely valued. Keeping to a world before 1910, with a detachment almost cruel she creates families of "nice" people, whose hidden wickedness and weakness she reveals with astringent clarity and wit, and mainly by dialogue.

CHAPTER X

ARNOLD BENNETT

When Arnold Bennett died in 1931 the day of his kind of novel had passed, especially with the critics, and his reputation as a novelist declined. Indeed his best novel, *The Old Wives' Tale* was twenty-three years old. But that novel had been built so firmly and so solidly, with such a grasp of life and character, that it is likely to remain one of the classic English novels. In his own day it stood out among his novels, but the contemporary reputation of Bennett rested on far more than one masterpiece. Bennett was an all-round man of letters, a personality and a power. His output was prolific not only in the novel, including what he called "fantasias", but in the short story, and in little books of "pocket philosophy", as a reviewer, and as a dramatist. As a reviewer he was a born journalist, and it was said that at one time his reviews could make or mar an author. As a dramatist he achieved wide popularity with *Milestones* (1912), written in collaboration with Edward Knoblock.

Arnold Bennett came from the Staffordshire Potteries. There he was born near Hanley in 1867, and the life, character and philosophy of that rather grim area of the industrial Midlands left a deep impression on him. He knew the people of the Potteries and he remained of them in heart, even though, after his early twenties, his life was spent mainly in France or London. When at the age of forty he began writing *The Old Wives' Tale* his memories of the Potteries were still the foundation of his vision of life : he left it on record that he wrote the first part of the novel in six weeks, for "it was fairly easy for me, because, in the seventies, in the first decade of my life, I had lived in the actual draper's shop of the Baines's, and knew it as only a child could know it". Bennett did not come from the working class— his father was a solicitor—but the character of the people of the Potteries was common to its inhabitants in general. They were proud of their industrial progress and efficiency, of their shrewd, tough, sensible, realistic grasp of life. The background was grey, but to them it was not grim, for it was theirs, the product and symbol of their energy and achievement. The pride of the Potteries is declared at the very outset of *The Old Wives' Tale* : "The Five Towns seem to cling together for safety. Yet the idea of clinging together for safety would make them laugh. They are unique and indispensable. From the north of the county right down to the south they alone stand for civilisation, applied science, organised manufacture, and the century—until you come to Wolverhampton". Theirs was the monopoly of supplying the whole kingdom with crockery. No wonder "the inhabitants of the Five Towns in that era were passably pleased with themselves . . . and they were amazed with their own progress".

As Bennett creates and appraises this background, there arises from the pride of the Potteries the nearest approach to a poetic feeling his novels ever have. Certainly he had no more use for the poetry of nature in his novels than the people of the Five Towns had for the countryside around them : "a district capable of such gigantic manufacture . . . is surely well justified in treating the county as its back garden once a week, and in blindly ignoring it the rest of the time". The Potteries preferred comfort to aesthetics, the real satisfaction of practical things well done to the doubtful joys of the speculative intellect and of artistic taste. It was not mere complacency, and it was certainly not inertia : it was rather the healthy attitude of a self-contained area where normal people made the most of their everyday life and with much reason found it good. When Bennett in *Clayhanger* describes the immense satisfaction and wonder with which its owner regards a newly installed hot-water system, the reader feels the author's fellowship with the world of his early years.

Religion, no more than the arts had any considerable place in this world—at least as Bennett portrayed it, for it was an aspect to which he himself seems personally less responsive. The charge of materialism levelled against his work by Virginia Woolf was therefore considerably justified. But the omission is characteristic of the matter-of-factness of both Bennett and the Five Towns. They were believers in the adage that "God helps those who help themselves", and their devotion was to the practical duty of self-improvement. This Victorian ideal of "Self Help" was still widely held in the opening years of this century, and far outside the Potteries, and Bennett showed his belief in it by the several volumes of "Pocket Philosophies", which proved very popular. *How to Make the Best of Life, Married Life, Mental Efficiency*, and their fellow-volumes have been put in their place by the superior, but, though the Five Towns themselves might well, with their self-reliance, have had little need of them, clearly to very many in England they were welcome. Bennett indeed extended his practical helpfulness to the field of literature; in 1903 *How to Become an Author* was published as "a practical guide", and in 1909 appeared *Literary Taste: How to Form It*. Such books were the complement to his own life. By a similar philosophy, some qualities of genius being added, he had made a success of his own life. From a lad from the Potteries he had become a wealthy man of the world, and he was happy to share some of the secret of his success.

The practical man normally has a considerable interest in things, and what distinguished Bennett was the range and the insatiable nature of his interest. It stands self-confessed in the title of his volumes of *Things That Have Interested Me*, but it is to be discerned in all the detailed texture of his novels. Content to leave to others the question how men ought to live, he was fascinated by the material facts of how they did live. It was one aspect of his gift for journalism. The internal economy of houses and hotels down to their plumbing, food as bought, prepared and eaten, clothes and their fashions, means of transport, indeed all the machinery, equipment and paraphernalia of living claimed Bennett's absorbed interest. The fascination of finding out how things were done lasted with him throughout his life, so that his late *Imperial Palace* involved him gladly in finding out all the details of how a big hotel was run, before he sat down to write it.

This attitude to life and literature by no means made him a Philistine in the matter of literary artistry. Instead, his practicality led to and found an ally in a severe apprenticeship to literature. Finding, while he was a solicitor's clerk in London in the nineties, that he had a gift for writing, he became a freelance journalist and editor of a woman's magazine, steadily increasing his output until his journal could record at the end of 1899 that during that year he had written 335,340 words, his work including ''six or eight short stories not yet published, also the greater part of a 55,000 word serial . . . and the whole draft, 80,000 words, of my Staffordshire novel, *Anna Tellwright*''—the last published as *Anna of the Five Towns*. His approach to his craft became a serious as well as a financial one : he read widely, and in 1900 he went to France for some eight years. He was determined that his best work should reach the highest standard of craftsmanship, and that standard was in his opinion set by the work of the French novelists, and living in France and speaking the language he hoped the better to assimilate their virtues. The Victorian novel in serial parts, and therefore liable to diffusion and shapelessness, was outmoded, and Bennett's ideal was the naturalistic novel, presenting people and things as true to life as possible, in a style to match, clear and sensitive yet precise, the whole story shaped and controlled by intellectual intention. It called for hard brain work, wide and curious observation, and a retentive memory, and in the last respect Bennett helped himself by keeping a journal, a device suggested by the journal of the Goncourts.

It was in a Paris restaurant in 1903 that the idea of *The Old Wives' Tale* came to him. When a grotesque old woman entered, her antics, of which she herself was unconscious, soon had the waitresses giggling and the customers guffawing at her. Reflecting that this queer stout figure had been "once young, slim, perhaps beautiful", he saw in a flash the theme of a novel, the pathetic passage, by imperceptible gradations, of a woman from the charm and radiance of youth to the grotesque mockery of old age. Maupassant's novel *Une Vie*, which, according to Bennett, was in the nineties regarded "with mute awe, as being the summit of achievement in fiction", spurred him into rivalry : he would "go one better" than *Une Vie* and write the life-story not of one, but of two women. So, having first thought of Constance, he added Sophia "out of bravado", was for a while intimidated by his own boldness, and then after thinking the idea over for some four years he wrote the novel in two concentrated bursts.

It began with two pretty and lively schoolgirls, daughters of "a respected, bedridden draper in an insignificant town" ; having built up that little world where Constance chose to stay, it showed how "the confident and fierce joy of youth" in Sophia broke the trammels of that world and took her to Paris ; at the end it brought the sisters together again in the evening of their lives, leaving Constance, "too ill to know how ill she was", rambling in her mind with pity for dead Sophia "as a woman whose life had been wasted". Bennett spared no detail to convey his picture of these contrasted lives, but he never lost the firm continuity of his story. Fidelity to fact, without exaggeration, even in describing a public execution by the guillotine, gave the whole massive work an impression of sober truth, all the greater because Bennett kept his own view of life fairly out of the book. The world is seen through the minds of the characters. The theme itself receives direct expression not from Bennett himself but through Sophia as she looks at her dead husband : "what affected her was that he had once been young, and that he had grown old, and was now dead. That was all. Youth and vigour had come to that".

The story of *The Old Wives' Tale* only here and there rises above the common experience of all men and women, in which, in Dr Johnson's words, "much is to be endured and little to be enjoyed", and the background of that life is in general unexcitingly normal and even drab. Where passion might break out or melodrama flash its gaudy lightnings, common sense turns all into sordid reality. As Sophia discovers her husband to be a mean, shiftless, lying cad, her anger is subdued to scorn and her reaction is practical rather than emotional. But this mature and tolerant book is not cold and colourless. It has a subdued warmth and colour from the philosophy of life implicit in the characters and in their creator's manner of telling their story. Treat the world reasonably, take life as a friend, face what may befall with good courage, they seem to say, and life is worth the living, and will give as much as, or more than it takes away; and Bennett shows them, if not dramatising themselves, yet half-conscious of their lives as battlefields and pleasure-grounds, where their steady struggle, with its unheroic heroisms and occasional joys, appears by no means insignificant, either to themselves or to their sympathetic and absorbed creator. This quietly tenacious practical hold on life is conveyed well by Bennett's appraisal of Constance and her husband after years of a life which "had much in it of laborious tedium". She had a sense of vague contentment. "The basis of this contentment was the fact that she and Samuel comprehended and esteemed each other, and made allowances for each other. Their characters had been tested and had stood the test. Affection, love, was not to them the salient phenomenon in their relations. Habit had inevitably dulled its glitter. It was like a savouring, scarce remarked; but had it been absent, how they would have turned from that dish!" So it is with the dish of life presented by Bennett. The "luminous halo" desired by Virginia Woolf was absent, but Bennett gave far more than the surface and the material aspects; he gave men and women in an environment which was at once the making and the atmosphere of their characters and of their lives.

Though *The Old Wives' Tale* quite overtops them, the Clayhanger trilogy, *Clayhanger* (1910), *Hilda Lessways* (1911) and *These Twain* (1916), shows very much the same qualities. Here is the Staffordshire scene in full detail as the setting of the lives of Edwin Clayhanger and Hilda Lessways. Again many years are covered, and Bennett depicts the grimness of the industrial world giving way gradually, but never completely, as progress brings its material benefits in easier working conditions, in better transport and lighting, in cinemas, and the general amenities of life, and in educational and social services. But Bennett is no apostle of progress; his interest remains primarily in the human beings and in the success or failure they meet with in their struggle with life in the Five Towns. A particular aspect of this normal adventure of living is of course love and marriage, and after seeing Hilda romantically through Edwin's eyes in the first book, we see her more objectively in the second, and finally, with some decline of interest, in the partnership of marriage in the last volume. In the end lovers have to live together, and again all comes down to the practical relationship of normal people, fundamentally the same, Bennett held, for all people in all places.

Love, marriage, housekeeping, moneymaking, illness and death—these were the basic realities Bennett kept in mind, and in *Riceyman Steps* (1923) he could leave his Five Towns for the dreary London district of Clerkenwell and concentrate on the relatively abnormal psychology of a miser, and yet remain essentially the same novelist, because the abnormal was so inevitably encompassed by the normal. Seeing Clerkenwell through the eyes of its inhabitants, those who with Bennett's philosophy look upon life as an adventure, we behold "this wonderful Clerkenwell". We see the gripping passion of the miserly bookseller Henry Earlforward through his own eyes and understand its power almost sympathetically. His abnormality is moreover only an intensification of Five Towns materialism : "he was, in fact, a very great practical philosopher, tenacious, it is true, in his ideas, but, nevertheless, profoundly aware of the wisdom of compromising with destiny". So in this novel, more briefly told, limited to fewer figures, Bennett achieved a minor rival to *The Old Wives' Tale*. It is almost sentimental, with its middle-aged miser, who "did not feel middle-aged", and his middle-aged bride, whom he saw as "perhaps a little more than a girl, but not much more", and with its intertwined story of the young charwoman Elsie and her lover, still suffering from shell-shock from the Great War, but it is only the mellowing of a Bennett who had always seen life thus, as an arena of normal people, normally good, with the normal experiences of life. Cancer might ravage to death the middle-aged, but the novel ends with the joy of Joe with his "worshipping faith in Elsie's affection", while Elsie has to carry his heavy bag because he is too weak, and she is full of apprehensions of the future. Such is Bennett's brave, kind, practical, but shadowed view of human happiness.

Among Bennett's other novels *Anna of the Five Towns* (1902) and *The Card* (1911) stand out. Both have their origin in the Five Towns. The latter, sub-titled "A story of Adventure in the Five Towns", mitigates the realism of his greater books and approaches nearer to his Fantasias. Denry Machin, the Card, lives by his financial wits and his flashy personality, and the tale is full of humour and high spirits. What an author writes less for fame than to please himself and gainfully to entertain his public may well reveal his less serious, but still significant, self, and from *The Card* emerges another aspect of the Five Towns and, it would seem, of Bennett, their amused admiration for the Five Towns young man who cuts a dash in the big world without too scrupulous an attention to a code which would restrict his activities. When Bennett classed his works as fantasias, we can cordially agree: such a story is *The Loot of Cities: Being the Adventures of a Millionaire in Search of Joy* (1904). When in *Mr Prohack* (1922) he combined his conception of a product of the Five Towns with knowledge from his own experience of Civil Servants, obtained by useful service at the Ministry of Information in the 1914-1918 war, he pleased his public without increasing his reputation. There were indeed at least three Arnold Bennetts, the serious novelist of genius, the novelist who less seriously wrote out of his own interest and enjoyment, and the novelist who more or less played on the public as a professional writer.

CHAPTER XI

H. G. WELLS

Like Arnold Bennett, H. G. Wells was a born journalist, but they had little else in common. While Bennett accepted the world, Wells was fired by a passion to change it. As a young man, seeing a small girl of the slums, barefoot and tired, he resolved, "I want to change everything in the world that has made that, and I do not care what goes in the process". Later he said to himself, "I want to write novels, and before God I will write novels", but his novels were from the beginning, not objective novels, but part of his campaign for a transformation of all things. Herein lies the great difficulty of judging his contribution to the English novel. On the one hand he had the gifts of a great novelist, a power of creating people and places, an energy of imagination and a command of words that hold the reader despite himself; on the other, he was a supreme publicist of ideas. Again and again his people are left in suspended life, while their creator sets the world right. In the person of the narrator of *Tono-Bungay* he declared:

> "I don't think I'm blind to the fun, the surprises, the jolly little coarsenesses and insufficiency of life, to the 'humour of it', as people say, but that isn't the root of the matter in me. There's no humour in my blood. I'm earnest in warp and woof. I stumble and flounder, but I know that over all these merry immediate things there are other things that are great and serene, very high, beautiful things—the reality."

There was more "humour in his blood" than he admitted, but "the reality" he saw was a vision, and it was a vision born of a certain period in human progress. As time passes, it is the reality of the actual world he saw and re-created that lives on, while the reality of his visionary world of ideas, at any rate in its details, bears the stamp of time, and his novels

suffer from their having been the transmitters, with whatever
brilliance and clarity, of the best progressive thought of his
day. In Wells himself the fire that had blazed with such
incandescence died down, and when he died in 1946 he had for
some years been bitter with disillusionment. At mid-century
it is difficult to recapture, more difficult still to feel for the
first time, the exciting splendour of his vision. The fire of his
idealism may well have an after-life as effectual as Shelley's
did, but Wells willingly gave some hostages to literary immortality by the attitude he confessed to Henry James : "I would
rather be a journalist than an artist".

As Dickens, who was Wells's favourite novelist, did in
David Copperfield, Wells used the background of his early
life to make such novels as *The History of Mr Polly*, *Love
and Mr Lewisham* and *Kipps*. Later he gave a full and
direct account of his beginnings and of his reaction from his
environment in his *Experiment in Autobiography*. As Dickens
felt keenly the neglect and incompetence of his father which
put him as a small boy in a blacking factory, so Wells
grew up to a contemptuous awareness of the muddle and
inefficiency, of the stuffy stupidity and convention, which
characterised the whole of his environment, whether at home
or at school. He was born in 1866 at Bromley, Kent, then
still a country town cut off from the London suburbs by a
narrow green belt. His father was a successful professional
cricketer, an unsuccessful small shopkeeper ; his mother,
formerly housekeeper in a big country house in Sussex, was
well read in the relationships of the royal family but not well
equipped to help a boy more than usually inquisitive about
life.

After a brief schooling at the kind of school Wells was
never tired of satirising, where unintelligent teachers mistaught
a futile syllabus in dreary buildings, at fourteen he became,
like Polly, an assistant in a draper's shop. From this he
escaped to be a pupil-teacher in a country school, like Mr
Lewisham, and like him too made his way to the Science
College at South Kensington. Nothing indeed could keep
Wells down ; from the beginning his energy was tireless, his

ambition soaring, and his ability to assimilate and make use of a wide range of knowledge altogether exceptional. But when, with a mind luminous with thronging ideas and a brave vision of Utopian possibilities, he became a novelist, the world of his boyhood remained vivid in his memory to provide a solid background. His early novels show us a boyish underworld life on the brickfields, where moral problems open, as when the hero of *A New Machiavelli* is set on by a gang of roughs and robbed of a pocket-knife; they present the dawning glamour of sex in meetings begun under the flare of arc-lamps in a shopping street, advanced along by-roads, and ended by irascible parents; they take us into a world of young science-teachers and shop-keepers yearning for a wider scope but frustrated by indigestion and nagging wives, and into stuffy little parlours with an air of fussy propriety, only broken when a wedding party, the final achievement of a predatory young woman, breaks out into giggles or is menaced by squabbles or its hilarity is dowsed by the anticipation of a child's being sick. That world gave his mind its first problems, and in many of his novels it is the medium of his criticism of life.

Wells was nearly forty, however, before he found himself as a social novelist. First came his short stories and his scientific romances. As a science student—he graduated in zoology—he had acquired an imaginative vision of the potentialities of science. He was prepared to suppose almost anything as the start of a story—interplanetary war, war with new weapons, a mermaid brought ashore, stepping into the fourth dimension, the manipulation of time either by enormously speeding up the reactions of the human machine or by transport into the far future. Nothing of this kind had been done in literature before. Swift in *Gulliver's Travels* had imagined strange beings but he did so satirically against the standard of normal humanity, and he touched science only to mock at it. Jules Verne had not transcended a boy's sense of the wonders of mechanical invention. But Wells speculated as one who saw already taking place before his eyes a transformation of the whole world. Scientists had the future of humanity in their hands, and Wells with a fearless fascination imagined some of the results that might ensue, changes not only in material invention but in the powers and nature of the human mind and body. Indeed he confronted the apparent possibility of man at the mercy of scientific magic, and himself possessing a shrewd knowledge of scientific facts and speculations he was able to project his imagination with great plausibility, writing in the spirit of a journalist intent on making the most of a topical enthusiasm which he was particularly gifted to see with more prophetic insight than others.

In some concrete instances, like bombing from the air in *The War in the Air*, he proved a prophet, but it is in a broader sphere that we can now most justly appreciate his vision of things to come. Though his early outlook was optimistic, his scientific romances by no means prophesied a golden future. He saw that science could as easily produce ill as good, and on an equally vast scale. In *The Time Machine* we see the horrors on which Utopia may precariously rest, and in *The Island of Dr Moreau* the brutality to which men can sink. Further it is clear that Wells, despite his fascination by science, was aware of the subordination of man to the machine and to scientific power generally which the advance of science implied. Indeed in an odd way for one whose novels were to declare much human feeling, his tales do not show that he really felt in his heart the problem impending for humanity, the response that would have to be made to the inhumanity of science. His human figures in these stories are little people, like his later Polly and Kipps, dwarfed by the immensities that come upon them, and Wells, rapt in his dreams, sees them scuttle like rabbits from the bombed cities, as though he had neither faith in their human morale nor care for their human plight. Indeed, we who have seen the actual fulfilment of some evil and who live to fear more, are naturally more alive than Wells was to the full implications. In the first flush of vision Wells could be carried away by sheer narrative zest and watch with a-moral detachment. He saw that progress might be evil and disastrous, that certainly it must make the mass of men the slaves of their masters, whether human or mechanical, but he felt no need to make a sermon of the matter. In fact, as his other work shows, he remained optimistic enough to trust in luck and hope that a good dose of luck would bring humanity the blessings and not the evil that lay in the womb of science.

The Time Machine was published in 1895, and several scientific romances and short stories had appeared by 1900, when his first ordinary tale, *Love and Mr Lewisham*, came out. Then his field gradually expanded. He did not give up the scientific romances—*The War in the Air* was published in 1908—but his mind turned largely away from fantasy to the consideration of what kind of better world should be constructed politically, socially and economically, and of the means to achieve it. His views were socialist and republican, and for some time he was a member of the Fabian Society. Before really settling down to the novels in which he was to publicise his ideas while he exposed the deficiencies of the recent and contemporary world, he proceeded to work out his ideas by more direct writing, and only after *Anticipations* (1901) and *A Modern Utopia* (1905) did he make the novel his main platform. *Tono-Bungay* came in 1909 and then for more than twenty years novel succeeded novel.

Behind the story of each lay a consistently developing body of idealism and criticism, but Wells was always journalist and politician enough to keep his eye on the present moment and to put topical problems in the foreground. Thus *Ann Veronica* (1909) and *The Wife of Sir Isaac Harman* (1914) dealt with the feminist movement culminating in the suffragettes; *Mr Britling Sees It Through* and *Joan and Peter* reflected the earlier and later attitude to the 1914-18 war of Wells and of the nation too, for Wells always reflected strong currents of opinion as well as sought to direct them; similarly *Christina Alberta's Father* (1925) took up the topical subject of institutions for mental disorders, *Meanwhile* (1927) centred on the General Strike of the year before, and on *The Autocracy of Mr Parham* (1930) the totalitarian state of Mussolini threw its shadow. All the time Wells kept in touch with the changing scene. After the 1914-18 war he turned again to direct preaching in the *Salvaging of Civilisation* (1921), and on finding no-one else willing to attempt it he produced his incomparable *Outline of History* (1920), which indeed probably no-one else had the mental energy, breadth of vision and concentration of purpose to achieve, for Wells was completely convinced that the World State must come and a knowledge of world history was an essential educational preliminary. He never lost his conviction, but in the thirties his hopes declined. So did his power as a novelist and his hold over his public : a novel like *Brynhild* (1937) no longer raised the enthusiastic interest that had greeted his novels for over a quarter of a century. The final darkening of his outlook is indicated by such ironic and despairing titles, not of novels, as *The Fate Of Homo Sapiens* (1939) and *Mind at the End of its Tether* (1945).

The idea that, from quite early in his life, dominated Wells's thinking was the World State. Man must abolish national divisions and all kinds of local divisions, and rule the world in universal brotherhood. Now that science was advancing with such giant strides, nothing was impossible if man would only use his reason to plan the utilisation of the earth's resources and would shake off the shackles of all hampering traditions. Wells saw the world into which he had been born as a chaos of greed, incompetence and stupidity, but as he grew up it was a time of bustling progress : indeed "tremendous" is no exaggerated epithet for the transformation that came over the Victorian scene as the nineteenth century passed into the twentieth, and, while Bennett and his fellows of the Five Towns equally marvelled at it, Wells became the passionate apostle of its further possibilities, granted an intelligent and co-ordinated effort by those best qualified. His novels showed in detail this almost furiously expanding industrial civilisation in the English towns and lamented the wastefulness, the disorder and the selfish exploitation by which, in the absence of over-all planning, it was accompanied. But how were the new powers to be harnessed efficiently ? It was clear to Wells that a new human type must be evolved, and in *The Research Magnificent* (1915) he drew a picture of his conception of "the new knighthood, the new aristocracy, that must at last rule the earth". The new aristocrat must refuse "to come to terms with the limitations of life" ; instead, in the pursuit of the noble life, he must "refer his life to ends and purposes beyond himself", he must conquer fear and sloth, sex and selfishness. Wells wrote of Benham, his knight of "The Research Magnificent", that "he never faltered in his persuasion that behind the dingy face of this world, the earthy stubbornness, the baseness and dulness of himself and all of us, lurked the living jewels of heaven, the light of glory, things unspeakable". The new aristocracy was to be "an intelligentsia blooded", keen lucid brains and fine fearless bodies. It was "at once the demand for kingship and the repudiation of all existing states and kings", a "conception of an unseen kingship ruling the whole globe", and, though this new kingship, Benham declared, was "latent in all mankind", it must be brought into being by "an open conspiracy" in which "self-appointed aristocrats, who are not ashamed of kingship, must speak to one another".

Later, in *The Undying Fire* (1922), Wells gave this idea of kingship a metaphysical expression. God—Wells had long rejected the Christian faith—was coming to birth in humanity : there was an undying fire in the hearts of men, and that was the only divinity in the universe. So he took refuge from the alternative conception of man at the mercy of a malignant Nature, the thought of which had indeed always impelled Wells to seek a god. This gradual evolution of a divinity in man was an idea to which the task of *The Outline of History* had led him, and on the strength of this faith he was able to contemplate with a triumphant optimism the vision of "Man leaving his ancestral shelters and going out upon the greatest adventure that ever was in space or time". He concluded his *Outline* with the sure hope that "life for ever dying to be born afresh, for ever young and eager, will presently stand upon this earth as upon a footstool, and stretch out its realm among the stars".

Wells took the first World War in his stride. He did not share the pacifism of such progressive thinkers as Norman Angell, nor did his conviction that national states were obsolete prevent his supporting the national cause. The main effect of the war upon him was to give him a still keener sense of how urgent was the need to help bring in the World State. He was conscious of "the generations rushing to waste like rapids", a theme developed in *Joan and Peter*, but his optimism grew rather than lessened as he urged the vital necessity of a new kind of education. In *The Salvaging of Civilisation* he sketched enthusiastically the ideal school, a "syndicated school" using "syndicated lesson notes", "leading the youth of the whole world through a parallel course of schooling". He was in harmony with the general tendency of the nineteen-twenties to throw a great emphasis on youth. History was a race between education and catastrophe, and the young, set free from the stupid restrictions of the pre-war world and provided with proper mental and physical equipment, were to be the heirs of his promise. They should be free too from the outworn personal loyalties of marriage. In fact the preaching of Wells in the twenties in spirit and in many particular aspects was the heir of Shelley's. His influence coincided with that of the still very potent Shelley, and many idealists of the rising generation owed much to both, while many who were not idealists were encouraged by both in those doctrines of personal freedom which coloured that decade with a gay irresponsibility. But Wells himself was in deadly earnest, and the proportion of preaching to story tended to become still higher, as in the three-volume *World Of William Clissold* (1926), which surveyed the past, present and future in the political, social and economic fields.

It is impossible to judge the novels of Wells apart from their ideas. In an early story like *The History of Mr Polly* character and incident have an attractive comic richness that is in itself justification enough for a novel. But even there the ideas and the social and educational criticism are an essential part of the story as a whole, for the aim of Wells in all his novels was to present a total environment, a complex social and educational and, if necessary, political and industrial environment, completed and given atmosphere by ideas. Whereas in some writers it is their personality as transmitted by their style which provides an over-all appeal, in the novels of Wells it is the sense of contact with a mind, a fluid, restless, inquisitive, and, for long, a very hopeful mind. He had supremely the gift of vitalizing talk in print. As G. K. Chesterton remarked, "nobody else could interest and excite us so much without telling a story"; indeed, his arguments and exposition of ideas have an exciting power many a story-teller might envy. We may not share the ideas, but nevertheless the eloquence and zest of their purveyor, his spaciousness of mind, which can give a sense of vastness seen totally and seen luminously, and his gift of sweeping generalisation again and again inspire a feeling of exhilaration. As he sums up a phase of industry, a period of history, a climate of thought, a vision of a new kind of aristocracy, we are dazzled by his grasp. He allowed himself perhaps too much exuberance of style : his pages are gay with bright adjectives and emphatic adverbs—"amazing", "unprecedented", "splendid", an "evening . . . tremendously entertaining, a glory, a thing to remember". But such expression, though it may date and though it occasionally sank to school-girl gush, was no trick but the natural flow of his intellectual gusto. It appears too in his descriptions, which often have a light and a radiant colouring that make one think of Shelley. The supreme instance of his ability to make a novel almost entirely of ideas and argument is his modern Book of Job, *The Undying Fire*, a book without peer of its kind, one flow of living argument. How commonplace a novel of his can become when the ideas are left out, was illustrated by a film made of *The Passionate Friends*.

Wells contributed nothing fresh to fiction in the matter of form. What he did was to follow where Meredith had led in the use of the novel as "the vehicle of philosophy" : indeed, this treatment was as old as the seventeen-nineties when Godwin, Bage and Holcroft had transmitted ideas

through fiction, in some cases not dissimilar ideas of the
perfectibility of man. Wells merely decreased the proportion
of story to ideas. His normal looseness of construction, and
his frequent use of the semi-autobiographical novel had their
examples in such fiction as *Pickwick Papers* and *David
Copperfield.* His criticism of contemporary life as a strand
of his novels was no doubt also encouraged by the example
of Dickens. His admiration for Dickens, however, never
led him to adopt Dickens's other method of elaborate plot
construction. Indeed the novels of Wells generally have
no plot worthy of the name, as a summary of *Marriage*
indicates well enough : a girl, engaged to a man for whom
she does not really care, is carried off by another with whom
she falls in love ; married to the latter, her social ambitions
disturb his scientific research work ; they go away together
to Labrador to think things out and get a fresh grip on life.
Problems and ideas abound, and the function of the story is
merely to generate them. In fact, Wells, preoccupied with
his ideas, goes his own way. His Dickensian debts apart, the
closest parallel between Wells and any earlier English novelist
is that between him and Meredith though there is no need
to suggest the influence of Meredith on Wells. Dr Shrapnel
in Meredith's *Beauchamp's Career* with his optimistic radicalism, eloquently preaching "History—the Bible of Humanity"
and looking forward to "certain nobler races as yet but
dimly imagined", is a curiously close anticipation of Wells
as novelist and of the kind of character he portrayed.

In characterisation, too, Wells was no innovator in method.
His characterisation has little finesse, it is not deliberately
psychological. If there is an innovation, it is in his love
of simple souls like Kipps and Polly and Mr Preemby of
Christina Alberta's Father as his central figures. It is the
beginning of the phase of "the little man" that from the
twenties at least of this century has been current with cartoon-
ists and others, but the suggestion of which might again
be found in Dickens in such simple likeable creatures as
Tom Pinch and Traddles. Wells's comic characterisation is
markedly in the Dickensian manner, with its reliance upon

certain small appealing mannerisms of speech constantly repeated like Polly's murmur of "li'l dog" or Mr Preemby's "h'rrmp". These tricks go well with his simple souls, unversed in social life, seeking with a mild sense of humour to reassure themselves when doubtful of correct behaviour at table, and buoyed up by a half-ashamed sense of the wonderful possibilities of life which they never seem able to realise. Like that of Dickens his sense of humour can in this way easily pass into pathos, but it can also rollick in oddity and action. He has a knack of comic phrasing bordering on caricature, as in saying of Aunt Plessington that "she wore hats to show she despised them", and he has a keen eye for comic situation. But his normal method of characterisation is the old one of hitting off the character on its first appearance and thereafter leaving it to proceed on its own momentum. With the more or less comic figure supported by its endearing trick this method succeeds, or with a minor figure, but his weakness in characterisation comes out in his heroes and heroines.

His heroes, or central figures, whether narrators or protagonists, tend to be so full of ideas that they have no personality at all. They are priggish, superior, and selfish, and very eloquent. Rising above the lower middle-class which Wells could portray so well, they tear up any local roots and deliberately try to transcend mere individual limitations. In fact all their creator's aim and prejudice is against their developing real human vitality, and it is similar with the heroines, who might have taken over where the dashing Dianas and Carinthias of Meredith left off. His Ann Veronica and her kind were born of the same conception as Meredith's of women as the fine and inspiring comrades of men, physically and mentally vigorous, but like his heroes they too are prigs, even in their frankness, and, as against Meredith's heroines, they are further weakened by their descent from social aristocracy to bourgeois intellectuality and by Wells's recurrent despair of women. He cannot help regarding them as in the long run a drag on the hero's "Research Magnificent" : indeed one hero declares that "an aristocrat cannot be a lover". However hopefully a heroine begins in a novel, she is liable to be replaced by an affaire, for the heroines gain their men by an intellectuality and idealism, in part at least unconsciously assumed in support of biological impulse, and once married their feminine materialism drags them back from their earlier heights. Further, as characterisation, they have suffered even initially from their ideas, for when told, for instance, that "the new gale of emancipation sent a fire through her veins" the reader is far from interested in the girl as an individual. So the heroine is "the modern girl", just a contemporary variation of the feminine life force, conditioned at first by her need to play up to the hero's ideals. And so far as the heroine, or hero either, is young, Wells tends rather to present a generalised concept of adolescence : his young people are "full of strong indistinct desires and fears and a gnawing indefinable impatience", and they are little more. But Wells's small children are natural ; exempting them from the pressure of his ideas, when he lets them play an incidental part, he gives the liveliest sketches of childhood in any major novelist, except perhaps George Eliot.

The strength of Wells as a novelist rests, then, on an unusual combination of qualities. Caring little for plot or story, he relies on ideas, and time alone can show whether the bright luminous flame of his hope for humanity will continue to lighten the minds and hearts of readers. Certainly for something like the first quarter of this century at least he carried a torch which many thousands of young people followed with excitement ; in the twenties *The Waste Land* of T. S. Eliot remained unknown by a great host to whom Wells was still the prophet of a splendid world still possible of achievement. Many who did not share his concept of the World State or his socialism nevertheless felt his stimulation. If time diminishes this appeal, there must remain his picture of the English scene from about 1880 onwards, presented with a gusto of critical vision happy alike in breadth and in concreteness of detail. Since he wrote so much, a certain sameness and repetition as well as inequality will cause his many novels to be sifted, but when the rich comedy and characterisation of such a novel as *Mr Polly* have delighted a reader, he may well realise that those qualities will be found abundantly in *Joan and Peter* and elsewhere. The idealistic vision of Wells demanded depersonalised aristocrats directing the human massed millions—indeed as visionary he was out to destroy as much as to build—but, ironically, as novelist he created the very obstacles to his vision, the flesh and blood of little people, whose vitality nothing can subdue.

CHAPTER XII

GALSWORTHY

It was in the first decade of the century that John Galsworthy, like Bennett and Wells, made his name as a novelist, and like them he held his wide public for well over twenty years. Born in 1867, within a few months of them, he too observed the scene of life undergoing its rapid transformation, and like them he made his greatest work the recording of that change. When he died in 1933, though the general reader had continued to the end to be delighted by his novels, his reputation with the critics, in an ironic way he would have appreciated, sank at once. His own virtues were for the time outmoded, and both the virtues and the defects of the older world he had drawn with great understanding stood between him and a younger generation which had absorbed the violence of Lawrence, the bitter disillusion of Aldous Huxley, the "Waste Land" vision of T. S. Eliot, the political and psychological dogmas of Marx and Freud, and the petulant poetic propaganda of Auden. Galsworthy's pre-1914 Forsyte world had been based on the idea of property: by 1930 even those who still retained an insecure hold on property were often half-ashamed of it. It did not matter that the novelist himself had exposed the defects of the property-owning class. Such a gap had opened, with countless fissures, that a restless, insecure, and self-conscious generation was irritated into depreciation of the very spirit and texture of Galsworthy's achievement. Yet his novels may well rise again to share with those of Jane Austen and Trollope the honour of preserving the essential truth of aspects of lost ages, curiously remote in social customs and outlook but undeniably part of the continuous tradition of English character.

While Bennett was content to record, and Wells wanted to change everything, Galsworthy would have welcomed the moral reform of a civilisation in which he saw a great deal of good. If the Victorian upper middle class professional world, from which he sprang and whose summer and fall he portrayed, could have gained a greater sense of the responsibilities of its position and heritage, a more humane generosity of spirit, and a broader and less material vision, then Galsworthy would have felt that true progress had occurred. As a novelist he preached no such faith—he was obviously didactic only in his plays—but that faith is the atmosphere of *The Forsyte Saga*. Educated at Harrow and Oxford, a man of independent means and for a while a lawyer, Galsworthy was no traitor to his class nor was he its antagonist, but he was very sensitive in his conscience to its defects as well as sympathetic to its merits. Moreover he was an ironist, not a satirist. In all ways he had a sensitive balance : if conscience lay ever in his scales, taste and reason were always his equalising weights ; he loved beauty without extravagance, tradition this side idolatry, nature as the setting and solace of man, the arts as the grace and justification of wealth, and he did not forget the poor. The vessel of his spirit kept an even keel, so that the storm of the world war and the troubled waters of the post-war world did not drive him off his course or check his forward movement.

It has commonly been held that in *A Modern Comedy*, in which he showed the younger Forsytes trying to cope with the post-war world, he failed to show an understanding of that world equal to that which he possessed of that of their predecessors, but it is the very balance of his presentation that has probably deceived the critics. Disdaining the mantle of a prophet, whether of the World State or of the next war, rejecting melodramatic emotions and exaggerated sex, and disliking the dreary realism of naturalistic writing, he presented the nineteen-twenties with a cool, ironic, rather sad clarity, which time may well declare to be the nearest to truth of any contemporary writing. As his Preface to *A Modern Comedy* makes explicit, he was no hopeful spectator : "Will things ever settle down—who knows ? Are there to come fresh wars, and fresh inventions hot-foot on those not yet mastered and

digested ?" But his balance was too sure for him to partake
of defeatism. As the idea of a death-will in western civilisation took root in many minds, he could declare that "there
never was a country where real deterioration of human fibre
had less chance than in this island". Yet it was, he held,
"A Comedy", for "an Age which knows not what it wants,
yet is intensely preoccupied with getting it, must evoke a
smile, if rather a sad one".

The Forsyte Saga, completed in 1922, was built up of
several novels. A Modern Comedy, three more novels linked
by two short stories, followed in 1929. The End of the
Chapter, appearing posthumously in 1934, rounded off the
extensive family history. Galsworthy had begun his record
with the England of 1886 and he pursued it almost up to the
year of his death. He did not aim to present the whole of
England : in his own phrase, the world of the Forsytes was
the world "above the Plimsoll line of property". Particularly
as the story passed into the third decade of this century,
he admitted that, even in the limited world of his concern,
"the multiple types and activities . . . would escape the
confines of twenty novels". But the limits suited his genius :
they gave ample scope for a comprehensive study of human
nature within a large and important class stratum of English
life, and Galsworthy was the born biographer of "the man of
property".

The Forsytes had roots in Dorset, where the first of the
family tree farmed in the later eighteenth century. His eldest
son was a master builder, whose eldest son was a tea-
merchant, with brothers who became respectively a solicitor,
an estate and land agent, a "Collector of House Property",
Nicholas interested in "Mines, Railways and House Property",
and a publisher. When we reach the next generation with its
central figure of Soames Forsyte born in 1855, it has behind
it a tradition of steady, prosperous growth. In the Five
Towns, as 1900 approached, material progress, having come
much more rapidly, was a flashier, headier, more plebeian
affair, of which a "Card'" was no uncharacteristic product ;
from Wells's suburbia came ambitious young men and women,

wanting above all to get away from the drab and altogether unhistoric background of their early lives; but the fortunes of the Forsytes had risen with the gradual commercial and industrial progress of over a century, in which they, with their various interests always linked to a sense of property, had played their part. The Forsytes did not forget their roots, they kept their family coherence, they developed a common code of living. By Galsworthy's careful presentation we are soon aware of all that the Victorian Forsytes stood for, and of their sense of a secure, stable society, in which they expected little change, for they could not imagine anything more generally satisfactory.

What Galsworthy invites us to contemplate are the inevitable changes which time and circumstance are, nevertheless, bound to make in men's general and their personal lives, especially having regard to the defects and limitations of the Forsyte kind. Justifying the title word "Saga" as being "used with suitable irony", he remarked that "the folk of the old Sagas were Forsytes, assuredly, in their possessive instincts, and as little proof against the inroads of beauty and passion as Swithin, Soames, or even young Jolyon". Elsewhere he speaks of "the stealthy march of passion". To the dangers to individuals inherent in beauty and passion must be added the disintegrating force of the human spirit that will always resist the exclusiveness of property, so that even among the Forsytes themselves will arise rebels against property. That a world war was monstrously superimposed on the natural forces made the novelist's record of the Forsytes in due course a study of much wider disintegration, but from beginning to end his vision of the Forsytes is primarily that of a philosophic observer of human nature "under its changing pretensions and clothes". He could well have echoed Dryden's famous dictum: "mankind is ever the same, and nothing lost out of nature, though everything is altered". In particular he held that "Human Nature . . . is and ever will be very much of a Forsyte, and might, after all, be a much worse animal".

That remark is from his brief preface to *The Forsyte Saga*, and there, and in the equally brief preface to *A Modern Comedy*, can be found the best light on his work. As he wrote in 1922, many in pitying his Soames Forsyte thought that "in doing so they [were] in revolt against the mood of his creator". His ironic detachment, as so often happens in England with ironists, had been misinterpreted. He had certainly begun with a good deal of direct satire as well as irony, but as the Saga grew and passed into the Comedy his attitude became more and more one of tolerant, if ironic, understanding. In 1922 he could summarise the story of Soames as "the very simple, uncontrollable tragedy of being unlovable, without quite a thick enough skin to be thoroughly unconscious of the fact". But the final picture, when Soames lay dying, as seen through the eyes of loyal old Mr Gradman speaking to Soames's son-in-law Michael, is in a softer, but not sentimental tone :—

> " 'Not an easy man to know, but one felt—'
>
> Something gave way in Gradman and he spoke :
>
> 'Ah ! I knew him from a little boy—took him to his first school—taught him to draw a lease—never knew him to do a shady thing ; very reserved man, Mr Soames, but no better judge of an investment, except his uncle Nicholas. He had his troubles, but he never said anything of them ; good son to his father—good brother to his sisters—good father to his child, as you know, young man.'
>
> 'Yes, indeed ! And very good to me.'
>
> 'Not much of a church-goer, I'm afraid, but straight as a die. Never one to wear his 'eart on his sleeve ; a little uncomfortable sometimes, maybe, but you could depend on him.' "

It is the concluding irony that Soames, giving his life for his daughter, was killed by the fall of a picture from that collection, whose beauty flattered his love of possession as much as it pleased his taste. And as he lay dying in a speechless struggle to convey his love to his daughter, he had the satisfaction of knowing that for once at least in Forsyte story an inroad of stealthy passion had been finally frustrated, and his daughter could face the future with what remained of Forsyte self-possession.

No novelist has laboured more conscientiously to understand the life he portrayed, and in the long run that effort to understand was bound to be coloured with pity. But his pity was, in the novels, always controlled by his sense of proportion, and its expression toned down by that instinctive sense of the value of reserve and reticence, which he shared with the Forsytes. No more than Soames would he "wear his 'eart on his sleeve". Holding the balance between criticism and appreciation, he let his characters face the normal chances of life without their being dominated by any determination of their creator to submit them to any other destiny than the normal working of human nature. "We humans have only ourselves to blame" : our hurts, the more's the pity, come from one another. The ideas that affect his people do not come, like Wells's, from books and other external sources, but are inbred by inheritance and way of life. If there is something lacking in his world, even within its limits, it is real evil. There exist selfishness, folly, passion, but there is no real wickedness, an absence strange in a complex story covering half a century. Yet the absence is only doubtfully to be condemned. On the one hand, Galsworthy's concern was with the normal life, in which positive wickedness is an alien element; on the other, the liberal humanitarian outlook shared by many besides Galsworthy in the pre-1914 world was philosophically averse from the frank recognition of wickedness. Similarly, religion as an element in the Forsyte world, is perhaps understated by Galsworthy, but any positive recognition of religion as a vital force was alien to the Forsytes; religious observance was a social matter, and religious speculation an uncertainty kept for uncertain moments : neither could claim much more place than they were given by Jane Austen in her world. A simple old man like Gradman may say his customary prayers when Soames is dying : Michael Mont, when Soames is dead, reflects in the starry night on what an ironical world it is, and one feels that he rather than Gradman is expressing Galsworthy. We are not sure what God may mean in the author's mind : we are only in the position to say that he believes in goodness, in kindness and in courage, and to feel that he would pray his deity to shed sweetness and light upon Forsyte and Philistine.

Galsworthy's handling of the novel is the flower of the central traditional manner. That is to say, he aimed at a well-proportioned combination of story and characterisation ; he gave his main characters a background both of minor characters and of physical setting and atmosphere and he kept his own part as unobtrusive as possible. Thus the reader becomes the privileged onlooker at a scene so varied and natural as to give the illusion of the fulness of life within the broad limits of Forsyte society. Though the theme of Beauty's inroad, accompanied or not by other themes, lies behind the stories, they do not give the impression of having been written for the theme's sake. Rather the story takes its rise in character. In his Romanes lecture on "The Creation of Character in Literature" in 1931 Galsworthy admitted to suspecting "in common with not a few other people of the older fashion, that the vitality of character creation is the key to such permanence as may attach to . . . the novel".

"Speaking as one who has been trying to write novels of character over a period of more than thirty years" he still could not claim to state with precision how the process of character creation worked in himself, what share the conscious mind had in grouping and welding the odds and ends of experience and observation released from the subconscious mind, but he suggested the following analogy :—

> "That profound instinct for the breeding of blood-stock implanted in every English breast will assist us in understanding how a novelist, in the creation of his characters, selects certain salient human traits, and continually reinforces them ; just as the blood-stock breeder selects certain strains of blood and gets as many crosses of them as he can without falling into the snare of too close in-breeding. But in spite of this breeding to type, everything done, or said, or felt by the character, when once it begins to live, will take it a little farther from the original model."

In such really creative characterisation the character may not indeed run away from its creator, but looking back over each stretch of writing he is surprised at the way in which the character has spoken and behaved, both "by seeming to come out of what went before, and by ministering to some sort of future". His pages are always "adding tissue to character", and so at his best, as in Soames, there is the natural continuity in which the constant slight variations and deflections accord with our experience of human personality. Moralist as he is, it is not surprising to find that Galsworthy ended his lecture by stressing the moral value of creative characterisation.

> "The unending moral assessment which is so deep a part of the life of a human being is more furthered and furnished by the character creations of fiction than most of us realise . . . it is always comforting to a novelist to know that by the creation of character he contributes to the organic growth of human ethics."

It is a remark that underlies the affirmation of the Preface to the Saga that "this long tale is no scientific study of a period". In Soames he has certainly added one more to the rich gallery of individual portraits in the English novel. He stands out as a unique figure among all the Forsytes, typical but distinct beyond possibility of mistake. But there are many others of his people who carry their personality in all their words and acts : it is only when he steps below the Property line that Galsworthy fails to give life. His women, too, especially Soames's first wife, Irene, and his daughter Fleur, are realised in the clear personal separation of their nervous vitality.

The style of Galsworthy matches his material. It has the best qualities of the Forsyte spirit, and something more. It is a civilised style, quiet, reticent, and assured, without tricks or fuss. It has a grace and dignity which never assert themselves too much. Irony and a sensitive reaction to atmosphere continually prevent any dulling of the tranquil surface. When beauty asks it, an almost poetic glow and pulsation inform the still normal prose. When passion and deep feeling need expression, a close restraint of phrasing, a quiet concentration of meaning, produce the required effect. Without apparent striving he can move the emotions deeply. But a true Forsyte appreciates that "nothing is so terrible as a scene", and, while Galsworthy knows this fear of emotion is one of the Forsyte defects, neither will he let a scene get out of hand. When, however, he notes of a character that he is "too much of a Forsyte to praise anything freely", we feel that Galsworthy is absolved of that trait. Yet even as the Forsytes are very English, so is their creator, and both would always prefer understatement to overstatement. Understatement is some safeguard against failure; exaggeration makes the fall greater. In like manner, Galsworthy shunned the symbolic method, of which E. M. Forster was one of the first novelists to set the fashion. If any one, he wrote in 1929, should think there was a symbolic intention in the story of Fleur, he would deprecate it, for "symbolism is boring". Galsworthy's purpose was so sure, and his craftsmanship so dextrous, he had no need in his own day to make any concessions to modernism.

CHAPTER XIII

CONRAD

About 1920 Joseph Conrad stood in general opinion alongside Bennett, Wells and Galsworthy as one of our chief novelists, but his work differed greatly from theirs. Not only had he made the sea and the East Indies the scene of much of his best work, but his approach was essentially different from theirs in spirit as well as in the technique of story-telling. How different his work was Virginia Woolf acknowledged in her essay on *Modern Fiction*, in which she not merely exempted him from her attack on materialism as exemplified in the novels of Bennett, Wells and Galsworthy, but placed him with Hardy as one fit to receive "our unconditional gratitude". Indeed, far from writing in any materialistic spirit, Conrad wrote with the vision and spirit of a poet. He did not concern himself with material progress, except to deplore the passing of the beautiful old sailing ships, or with current ideas, or with property : he wrote of the conflict between man and nature, and of the mysteries of the human soul, and, in his view of man, the word "soul" was an inevitable word to use.

Conrad's becoming an English novelist at all was a remarkable achievement, for he was born, in 1857, in Poland of Polish parents. An orphan by the age of twelve (his father had been a keen worker for Polish freedom) he was educated in Cracow, and it was 1878 before his passionate love of the sea brought him to England and he was about twenty before he learned the English tongue. For a good fifteen years he served in the English merchant service, in which he obtained his Master's certificate ; at first he sailed along the English East coast, but later he was on the Australia route and in the East Indies. Deeply attracted by the English spirit he became naturalised in 1884, and when he was nearly forty

he took an English bride. It was the English novelist Galsworthy who, talking to him as a passenger on a ship on which
he was serving, was largely responsible for encouraging the
writing of his first novel. In 1893 he left the sea, and in
1895 *Almayer's Folly* appeared. The rest of his life was spent
quietly in England, where he died in 1924. His mastery of
English and of the English character is obvious in his novels,
yet to the end he spoke with a foreign accent, and it is said
that, before he decided on English as the medium for his
novels, he had considered the possibility of French instead.
Of Conrad himself, as he saw life and the sea, *The Mirror of
the Sea* (1906) and *Some Reminiscences* give the essence.

His career as a novelist can be seen in fairly clear outline.
At first he kept to the world of his experience since early
manhood. *An Outcast of the Islands* (1896) returned to the
scene of his first tale; Almayer, Captain Lingard, Abdulla
the Arab Trader, Babalatchi the one-eyed cunning Malay
counsellor and others came to fuller life. *The Nigger of the
Narcissus* (1897) and *Lord Jim* (1900) were stories of the
sea and sailors. By 1903 his first "period" was over: it
included the short stories *Youth*, telling of fire at sea and of
a young man's first vision of the East, *Typhoon*, described
by its title and creating the formidable Captain M'Whirr,
and *The Heart of Darkness*, a terrible evocation of the Congo
jungle, visited by Conrad shortly before he left the sea. His
fame might well rest on this early work; its combination of
strength and subtlety, its poetic passion, and its glamour of
setting and style belong to no one but Conrad. The spell it
casts is so strong that only those detached afterthoughts, to
which even the greatest genius is subjected by critics, detect
at times a certain stiffness of manner and a tendency to over-
write his atmosphere.

Having achieved so much from his intimate knowledge, he felt it necessary to make a fresh start
and in *Nostromo* (1904) he turned to the South American
coast, to the evil power of a silver mine and the complications
of revolution. It has great and mature power in its complex
handling of theme, story and characterisation. In *The Secret*

Agent (1907) set in London and *Under Western Eyes* (1911), dealing with political plotters, the psychology of anarchism held his ironic interest. *Chance* of 1914, however, a tale set entirely in England, was a great contemporary success, and in its treatment, if not in its story, shows the real powers of Conrad. His earlier work, though it had won critical approval, had brought him so little money that in 1911 he had been given a Civil List pension to help him. Now that the success of *Chance* had given him security, he went back to his earlier loves, the sea and the East, with *Victory*, *The Shadow Line*, and finally *Rescue* (1920), though *The Arrow of Gold* (1919) was set in nineteenth-century Spain. When he died, he was engaged on a great attempt to create an epic of Napoleonic times. Again the sea was his major inspiration, and Master-Gunner Peyrol is one of his best characterisations of sailors. *The Rover* was published in 1923, the unfinished *Suspense* after his death. He died with his powers undiminished; the fire burned less vividly, but more brightly; the subtlety of his manner was kept, but combined with an epic clarity and assurance—in his sixties he had no need to strain or overwrite.

In the kind of novel which was characteristic of him there was nothing revolutionary, but it was very much a kind of his own making. From boyhood he had read widely and eagerly, yet if he owed any appreciable debt to literary inspiration it was a general one to Russian novelists, and especially to Dostoevsky. The Russians had his interest in the human soul, and a similar view of life as a drama which moved the spectator in his soul to pity and wonder. So, though the influence of the French novel was at its height in England in the nineties (as we have seen from Bennett's tribute), Conrad could gain from that only an appreciation of artistry: its realism was of too materialistic a kind. What writing a novel meant to Conrad was telling a story about people in such a way as to bring out as fully as possible the truth about their characters, the real reasons for their failures. This made psychology at least as important as story to his novels, and realistic treatment of setting was equally necessary, because that was part of the story and because it had no little bearing on character. His emotional attitude to his people, his love and admiration for what was good, his scorn or pity for what was bad or weak in them, his poetic reaction to beauty, his passion for the sea—these things transmuted his realism. The result is the Conrad novel, where more than in any other English novels romance and realism are inseparable.

It is impossible to think of Conrad as novelist apart from his devotion to the sea, for in that intimate love lay the secret of his view of life. The sea was at once the concrete and the symbolical test of character. Faced by that vast, uncertain elemental force, now friendly, now neutral, now hostile, man's soul could rely on nothing but its own spiritual resources—with the very important reservation of "the strong bond of the sea, and also the fellowship of the craft". In the school of the sea the great lessons were the simple basic virtues. In *Some Reminiscences* he declared :—

> "Those who read me know my conviction that the world, the temporal world, rests on a few very simple ideas; so simple that they must be as old as the hills. It rests, notably, amongst others, on the idea of Fidelity."

So the characters in his early tales whom he loved and upheld were simple souls, whose faith lay in courage, strength, honesty, duty : they were men of honour, to whom self-respect was life itself. Captain Beard, in *Youth*, his ship shattered by the explosion from its suppressed fire and soon to sink in flames, was determined to take off every least thing as salvage for the underwriters, for to do so was an article of his fidelity, and he was "immense in the singleness of his idea". His crew ("to an onlooker they would be a lot of profane scallywags without a redeeming point") stood by him loyally, not from any ingrained discipline, and "they had no professional reputation" to uphold, not from a sense of duty, not because they were well paid,—"no ; it was something in them, something inborn and subtle and everlasting", a quality of English seamen, "something solid like a principle, and masterful like an instinct—a disclosure of something secret—of that hidden something, that gift of good or evil that makes racial difference, that shapes the fate of nations". The philosophic narrator, Marlow, through whom Conrad often expresses himself, puts this faith in the simple things vigorously in *Lord Jim* :—

"Hang ideas ! They are tramps, vagabonds, knocking at the backdoor of your mind, each taking a little of your substance, each carrying away some crumb of that belief in a few simple notions you must cling to if you want to live decently and would like to die easy."

It is this view of life, learnt at sea and applied on land too, that makes Conrad's novels stand out with a lasting grandeur amongst such novels, however good, of such novelists as Bennett and Wells and Galsworthy, of which it may well be said in contrast that "the world is too much with them".

The background of Conrad's novels is not the immediate world but the universe, the vast unknown Nature, at once behind all things and objectified in them. At the end of *Youth* Marlow speaks of "the lands of brown nations, where a stealthy Nemesis lies in wait, pursues, overtakes so many of the conquering race, who are proud of their wisdom, of their knowledge, of their strength". This is one of his main themes, the effect of the East on the white men who live there, and Nature in her Eastern guise is a complex power, working through men and things. The natives of the East are one manifestation of Nature, looking down upon the white men as "meddlesome fools", being themselves masters of patient intrigue, against which that white man struggles in vain "whose hand is strong [but] whose heart is foolish and weak". The women of the East are another of Nature's testing forces for white men, for they are possessed of "that great but occult influence which is one of the few rights of half-savage womankind". All around is the Nature of the jungle, "that great dark place odorous with the breath of life, with the mystery of existence", where the white man feels afraid "of his solitude, of the solitude of his body, of the loneliness of his soul in the presence of this unconscious and ardent struggle ; of this lofty indifference ; of this merciless and mysterious purpose, perpetuating strife and death through the march of ages". To win the battle against Nature in the East demands the same heroic simplicity as the battle against Nature at sea exacts. When Conrad is dealing with man's contest with the sea, nothing could be clearer than his theme of how that endless encounter with the lovable treachery of the ocean both breeds and challenges the character of men, but the complexity of such a book as *An Outcast of the Islands* does not obscure the same lesson. Indeed the contest against Nature is Conrad's constant theme as a novelist. Nature is the same mysterious force in the dangerous love of a woman as it is in the East or in the sea, and it matters not where the look of a woman "whips the soul out of the body". "It has the same meaning for the man of the forests and the sea as for the man threading the paths of the more dangerous wilderness of houses and streets."

Conrad, then, may write of Destiny or Nemesis, but what he means is that character is destiny. What a man is in his heart determines his fate. Once he loses courage, once he palters with honesty, once his fidelity slackens, once obsession gets a grip on him, his failure begins and grows and ruins him. Life demands eternal vigilance, the unfailing preservation of the "few simple notions" against all inroads, for, let Captain M'Whirr surmount the typhoon by his unyielding courage and strength, yet at any time the ocean may renew the encounter. Life indeed in Conrad's books is a hostile force ; how malignantly hostile Nature could be is most powerfully shown in *The Heart of Darkness*, in which the evil power of the African jungle converts an idealist into a living pagan deity fit for the savage tribes who worship him. In the battle against Nature many fail, and Conrad's interest, as often with Browning, lies frequently in the failures, in analysing the weakness of a man's character, and, as does Shakespeare, he often pits a man against just those circumstances that are fatal to his weakness. His psychology is the servant of his moral vision.

His technical approach to the novel seems an almost inevitable one in view of his complex purpose. He is a sailor who will tell a yarn. The kind of sailor he is we see in his character Marlow, whom from time to time he uses to tell his story for him—a sailor of many years experience of the sea and life, as simple in his creed as one of his simple heroic sea-captains, but a man who has reflected deeply on life and who matches his simplicity with his complexity of thought. So when Conrad starts to tell a story—and he can hold the reader as surely as any novelist by the excitement of sheer story—he does so broodingly, with a mind that sees all round what he is talking about. He advances his tale not directly, but as it were by a zigzag path, always tacking but never off his course. In something of the same way as Browning in *The Ring and the Book* shows his characters from different angles, through different eyes, so Conrad works.

To take the reader into the recesses of his characters he employs a continual variation of method. Straightforward description alone would not serve to show the cross-currents of emotion, the patchwork of ambition and instinct, the past in the present, the fluctuating struggle in the soul. At times he will analyse his character's feelings, but constantly he gives us his memories, his day-dreams and his dreams, in a way approaching the work to come some years later from Virginia Woolf. The result was that he could either create a clear-cut individual character, robust and masculine, like Captain Lingard, or make us aware of the gradual degradation of a Willems. He could create too the illusion of Malayan character and personality unforgettably in such figures as Babalatchi and Dain, and portray women, whether European or Malayan, Rita of *The Arrow of Gold* or Aïssa of *An Outcast of the Islands*. The subtle, slow, varied method gives us more than illusion of the luminous texture of life which Virginia Woolf asked of the novel, and even his simpler characters are far from static. It is, perhaps, by those economical but very suggestive touches, whereby we are shown his sailors in a domestic setting, that we are most convinced of Conrad's genius for characterisation. In *Youth* Captain Beard's wife is only glimpsed at the beginning, asking for the young mate's socks to darn them and saying to him from the train "If you see John—Captain Beard—without his muffler at night, just remind him from me to keep his throat well wrapped up", but this hint gives to Captain Beard himself that indefinable touch of complete reality.

In his indirect approach, his subtlety of psychological analysis, and his high degree of intellect and artistry, Conrad invites comparison with the older novelist Henry James, whose friendship Conrad enjoyed and from whose example he may well have learned. Henry James must no doubt be acknowleged the greater of the two, the purer, the more assured master of the subtle craft. Yet a comparison between them does help us to see the full stature of Conrad as novelist. Henry James has no poetry in his soul. There Conrad is himself alone. It is not only that the moods of the sea, dawn in the tropical jungle, passionate love and bare heroism make the spirit of lyric poetry pulse in his prose, but his vision apprehends things with such imaginative energy that the spirit of poetry is never long absent. Thinking in terms of the universe, and feeling with a sensitive human-heartedness, he is so free of materialism as to be able naturally to enter the poetic world. His style in his earlier novels sometimes tended towards "poetic prose" not unlike De Quincey's, but such a passage as the following, which concludes *The Rover*, shows his later prose still a poet's.

> "The blue level of the Mediterranean, the charmer and the deceiver of audacious men, kept the secret of its fascination—hugged to its calm breast the victims of all the wars, calamities and tempests of its history, under the marvellous purity of the sunset sky. A few rosy clouds floated high up over the Esterel range. The breath of the evening breeze came to cool the heated rocks of Escampobar ; and the mulberry-tree, the only big tree on the head of the peninsula, standing like a sentinel at the gate of the yard, sighed faintly in a shudder of all its leaves as if regretting the Brother of the Coast, the man of dark deeds, but of large heart, who often at noonday would lie down to sleep under its shade."

CHAPTER XIV

E. M. FORSTER AND D. H. LAWRENCE

In many ways there could be no more strongly contrasted novelists than Forster and Lawrence. Forster, from
the upper middle-class, with the liberal humanism of its
culture irradiated by the "sweetness and light" he found at
Cambridge, has at first sight little in common with Lawrence,
son of a Nottinghamshire coal-miner, and fighting a life-long
battle in his soul to reconcile his arrogant awareness of his
genius with the internal and external circumstances that continuously frustrated him. The luminous intelligence of Forster
seems at the opposite pole to Lawrence's volcanic passion;
the ironic serenity of the one, as of the heir of Matthew
Arnold, to be in a different world from the prophetic fury
of the other, whose creed, as it developed, has been, not
altogether unfairly, compared with the power- and blood-
worship of Hitlerian ideology.

Yet Forster and Lawrence have much in common. With
their work the breakdown of the pre-1914 world becomes
visible. They were precursors, and creators and symbols of
the moral disintegration which from about 1920 proceeded
to transform much in English life and literature. Indeed
the world to which their writings appealed was the world
after 1920. Forster's first four novels, to which only one
more was to be added, had appeared by 1910, and Lawrence's
Sons and Lovers came out in 1913, but neither won any
considerable public for some years. It was after *A Passage
to India* in 1924 that Forster became really well known,
and in the thirties and forties that his effect was fully felt;
his novels were twice reprinted in their standard edition
during the second war itself. The intractable personality of
Lawrence, the German origin of his wife, and the suppression
of *The Rainbow* in 1915 for "obscenity" caused Lawrence
much difficulty during the war, and it was after *Women in*

Love in 1919 that the eager worship of his work began. From about 1920 Bennett, Wells, Galsworthy and Conrad seemed to the young to be acquiring the quality of classics, speaking in an old-fashioned way of an elder world, and by 1950 they had reached the full status of classics, while the novels of Forster and Lawrence retained the provocative challenge of "moderns". Far from his death in 1930 leading to a relaxation of interest in Lawrence's novels, their appeal steadily grew, stimulated at first by the daemon of his personality as it was released by his friends' accounts and by his published *Letters*. The printing in 1950 of a million copies of several of his novels in a *Penguin* edition, which coincided with the appearance of Richard Aldington's biography of Lawrence, *Portrait of a Genius, But . . .* , is proof enough of his continued vitality; and it declared too the continued fascination which lay in his ideas and his attitude to life, apart from the purely literary merits of his novels.

Basically the "modernness" of Forster and Lawrence consists in the discomfort of soul which made them both critics of contemporary civilisation. It is generally the poets who are most sensitive to the changing spirit of the times and who anticipate it. But, as we have seen, this was not so with the English poets of this century before 1914. The novelists too, as a whole, showed no prescience of that manysided change which the 1914-18 war was to accelerate. Wells was certainly critical enough, but not as one who felt that there was any spiritual sickness to be cured ; his optimism was without self-distrust, indeed without any distrust in the possibilities of the achievement of a better world. Conrad might arraign Nature, but his novels expressed no sense of any special weakness in the contemporary way of life. It was in fact Forster and Lawrence who first among creative writers raised this issue, and showed this discomfort of soul in civilisation and in themselves. From their earliest novels their attack upon the materialism of their day is clear, if sometimes implicit rather than explicit. Forster from the start was explicit enough in his denunciation of the life

according to convention and in his preaching of the spontaneous life, and by *Howards End* (1910) undisguised in his
attack on the business mind and the worship of bigness in
industrialised England. Discomfort of soul is obvious in his
characters, and not difficult to feel in their creator's urgent
attempt to "save their souls" in the course of his stories.
As against the cheerful enthusiasm of Wells advocating an
open conspiracy to beget the World State Forster rather
impresses one as preaching a secret conspiracy for culture
and the education of the heart, with a fear, in his last novel,
that the battle may be lost. In Forster's attack on his
Pembrokes and Wilcoxes there is a tension of the spirit quite
absent from Galsworthy's exposition of the weaknesses of
the Forsytes. Lawrence's reaction against the materialism
of the machine age, against the intellectual and scientific
bias of the time, against the unnaturalness of the personal
and social life in modern conditions, soon cried aloud in
novel after novel. In the nineteen-twenties his antagonism
was expressed in a very high-pitched voice.

Not only did Forster and Lawrence share this general
reaction against contemporary civilisation, but they also had
a common positive theme, for the novels of both are really
exercises on the motif of "right personal relationships", a
favourite phrase of Forster's. Their solutions were radically
different : Forster relied on intelligence, culture and an
awakening of the heart, while Lawrence, though he too was
preaching to the heart, relied primarily on the passions of
the blood and was preoccupied with sexuality, a theme almost
alien to Forster. But they had in common a belief in the
necessity for the individual to be free in his inner life ; not
even in love must a man suffer himself to be possessed in
his thoughts and feelings by another, or a woman herself.
Lawrence saw the relationship between the sexes largely in
terms of a fight by the woman to possess the man and of the
man's furious struggle to escape, or vice versa ; Forster
similarly revolted from the idea of marriage as "eternal
union, eternal ownership". Moreover there is in Forster's
first novels a curious Laurentian strain, for, complementary

to the doctrine of sweetness and light, of love and culture, there is an admiration of crude virility in the Italian Gino in *Where Angels Fear to Tread* and of uncouth rustic vitality in Stephen in *The Longest Journey*. Stephen indeed is quite close to the figures in Lawrence's novels who obey little but their passionate instincts and who are quick to hate, and Forster's symbolic presentation of the natural life by a glimpse of young Stephen relaxing naked on a sunwarm roof and of the naked gambols of George and Freddy after bathing in *A Room With a View* is in harmony with Lawrence's use of naked wrestling to suggest the approach to spiritual sincerity between his characters. Forster never approached Lawrence's worship of the gods of darkness, but there is in his thinking in his novels a pull towards a semi-mystical paganism, as exemplified in his writing up of Stephen, and in his last novel his appreciation of mystical non-Christian religious feeling is obvious in his brilliant sympathetic account of the Hindu religious festival of the Birth of the God.

The first four novels of Forster are the work of a young man. He was twenty-four when he began writing *A Room With a View* in 1903, and the last, *Howards End*, appeared when he was thirty-one. Hitherto it had been unusual for a major novelist to begin his work as novelist, certainly his sure and characteristic work, so early as in his early twenties. Dickens and Jane Austen had been the most notable exceptions. Bennett, Wells, Galsworthy and Conrad were all advancing towards forty before they found their true bent. It is not a mere statistical point, but another aspect of Forster's initiating and sharing a more modern tendency, one which had the effect of making the novelist rely rather on ideas than on a comprehensive experience of life, since he could not yet possess it. In part the early writing of novels has, of course, been encouraged by the financial prospects which successful fiction offers of making literature a career while a writer is still young, and this applied to Lawrence, who was writing his first novel, *The White Peacock*, when he was twenty-four.

Whatever the reasons why young men took to writing novels, that the novel did largely pass into the hands of younger writers—Hugh Walpole, Aldous Huxley, Henry Williamson and Graham Greene are typical instances of novelists with a good deal of practice before the age of thirty —meant some change in the kind of novel written. On the credit side can be set such qualities as youth can especially give, freshness, energy, a lively awareness of the passing world: the young novelist will be up-to-date in his ideas, and is likely to be at his wittiest and his most poetic, or least prosaic. On the other hand, lacking adequate experience of life, the young man's fictional scene is likely to be narrower than that of the older novelist, and, though his psychological insight may pierce deep within its field, its field is likely to be a relatively restricted one. Further, almost any young novelist must write largely from inside himself, and will tend to make much use and often his most expert use of the childhood and youth which are his surest personal knowledge—it was on those foundations that Lawrence began both in *The White Peacock* and in *Sons and Lovers*.

The youth of Forster in his first three novels appears in several aspects. All are based on an idea, which they work out in a rather formal pattern ; they sparkle with wit ; they flirt with poetry ; they humorously caricature people like elderly ladies and formal clergymen ; they glow with an attractively self-righteous enthusiasm for their author's view of the good life. In fact, the last element excepted, they are close in quality to Shakespeare's charming youthful fantasia, *Love's Labour's Lost*. Their basic idea is a young man's idea, at least with the exaggeration with which it is conveyed, for, as Forster handles it, convention is seen as an almost evil force, a power capable of inspiring fear, since it can plunge the soul into darkness and destroy it.

In *Where Angels Fear to Tread*, on the one side is Forster's suburbia, Sawston, where Mrs Herriton lives armoured in convention and snobbery ; on the other is Italy, where her widowed daughter-in-law, Lilia, has become engaged to a vulgar Italian, Gino, some years younger than herself. Lilia must be rescued, for the sake of the Herritons' social standing, to appease their outraged gentility, and for the sake of her Herriton daughter born of her first marriage. So Mrs Herriton sends her son Philip to Italy to try and buy off the Italian, only to find they are already married. When Lilia dies in childbirth, another deputation is sent, this time to rescue the baby. Unable to understand the vulgar father's love for his child, Philip's narrow-minded sister Harriet kidnaps it, and as a result of her bungling stupidity the child dies. So at the expense of two deaths Sawston closes this scandalous chapter, but not with total success, for Philip and Caroline Abbott, a spinster friend of the Herritons who has taken it upon herself to show an active interest in the proceedings in Italy, have learned a lesson. They now know that there are human values that Sawston ought to recognise. Caroline reverences the wonderful love of Gino for his baby—indeed, she falls in love with him, with his elemental naturalness. Philip, who had long loved Italy, has been won over to a deep admiration for Gino, and after Gino, in his agony at the death of his baby, tries to murder him Philip is again reconciled to him. Philip and Caroline return to England at least with their souls awakened from the death-in-life of Sawston, but Harriet has lost her soul too many years before and nothing can save her. Told at no great length, with an agreeable irony, the novel makes its point clearly, and its rather inconclusive ending is natural enough. There is, however, something naïve in the way in which Forster depicts his products of Sawston, making Harriet so black and Caroline so open-eyed in her wonder at elemental human nature. The characters indeed are types conceived by a witty young moralist, whose sense of humour is sometimes shut off by his moral preoccupation.

In *The Longest Journey* the same patterned contrast between convention and nature is worked out more elaborately. The first Part, "Cambridge", beginning symbolically with an undergraduate discussion of the nature of reality, introduces Rickie, a somewhat neurotic Shelleyan idealist, who wants to give another young man money to enable him to shorten a long engagement, for he knows that love is a holy emotion and that all emotions must be given full rein, and who loves nature and art for their beauty but with a wholesome sense that he must not avoid the vulgar because "his own vulgarity would be greater if he forbade it ingress".

In Part II, which is "Sawston" once more, this promising soul is in danger of destruction by the deadly forces of convention. He has married Agnes Pembroke, a practical girl who worships success and social orthodoxy. He has become a schoolmaster under the aegis of her brother Herbert, who despite "all his fine talk about a spiritual life" also worships success alone, a man "not stupid in the ordinary sense—he had a business-like brain, and acquired knowledge easily—but stupid in the important sense : his whole life was coloured by a contempt of the intellect". In the resultant struggle for his soul Rickie escapes for a while in Part III, "Wiltshire". In the company of Stephen, once he has got over the shock of learning him to be his half-brother, illegiti- mate son of the dead mother whom he had long idolised, Rickie feels that he has "journeyed . . . till he stood behind right and wrong". Just before the end we are told that he "stood behind things at last, and knew that conventions are not majestic, and that they will not claim us in the end". But ironically Stephen, from whom he had learned so much, gets drunk again, so once more shattering Rickie's faith, for, like Scott's heroes, Forster's young men are much at the mercy of circumstances, not so much acting themselves as being continually acted upon. Then, a page or so later, Rickie is struck to his death by a train in the act of rescuing the drunken Stephen. He had, however, "bequeathed [Stephen] salva- tion", and with a last symbolic touch Forster shows another train with Herbert Pembroke in it passing in the distance— "a lurid spot . . . passed, and the silence returned".

In other words, what the Pembrokes stood for was bound to pass away. It makes a provocative ending to a provocative novel, whose atmosphere is one of ideas, and whose texture is a rich blending of satire and humour, violence and melodrama, idealism and scorn. Gerald, the spiritually crude athlete, Mrs Failing, the clever but malignant aunt who insists "solemnly that the important things in life are little things and that people are not important at all", and Ansell, the good and intelligent friend, who "never forgot that the holiness of the heart's imagination can alone clarify . . . facts", add variety. But again the characters are not vitally created, but are embodied aspects of good and evil as seen by Forster in that fight between the natural and life-giving forces and the conventional and destroying forces which must, in the circumstances of modern bourgeois life, be fought out in the souls of such young people as Rickie.

A Room With a View (1908) is both the most brilliant and the most balanced of Forster's early novels. Again it is in three movements. First he shows us the young girl, Lucy, awakened in her soul by Italy; then, back in England, she refuses to acknowledge her true love and is caught in the toils of convention; finally, on the brink of destruction, of passing into spiritual darkness by lying to herself and to her friends, she is saved by the efforts of the vulgar father of the young man she loves, a rather grotesque high priest of love. It is a modern "Morality" in the form of a novel. A young girl's soul is to be saved—and a young man's too, for George Emerson, in spite of his having an unconventional father, is in darkness until he falls in love, as Italy inevitably helps him to do. In the course of the story, Cecil, a young man to whom in her blindness Lucy becomes engaged, a fairly innocent victim of environment and convention, is given truer light and understanding. Even Lucy's dark angel, Charlotte, spiritual sister to the lost souls of the earlier novels, Harriet and Mrs Failing, ends the book with a prospect of salvation.

The "Morality" atmosphere is broken by two quite ordinary people, Lucy's mother and her young brother, whom Forster allows to have been done no particular harm by convention. But he cannot omit his anti-clerical note, and leaves one of his clergymen, all of them very satirically observed, in the unpleasant grip of an obsessive worship of celibacy. The whole effect of the novel, however, is one of stimulating pleasure, from its delightful opening with the social comedy of the Italian "pension", through the farcical comedy of the Italian picnic, and the lyric beauty of the great slope of violets where George first kisses Lucy, down to the slightly over-written denouement of Mr Emerson senior's enthusiasm for love. Meredith's Comic Spirit—Forster invokes it—broods over the whole, especially where Cecil is concerned, for Cecil's attempts to "re-educate" Lucy, and his very "superior" theories of life remind one of Meredith's figures, Sir Austin Feverel and the Egoist, Sir Willoughby Patterne. Lucy is also akin to Meredith's heroines, for she is the modern girl who requires in love an acknowledgment of her as an equal comrade.

With the publication of this novel Forster had apparently enjoyed to the full his rather one-sided tilting at convention, and in *Howards End* he proceeded to state the case against himself. He gave the novel the motto "Only Connect", and his theme was that, while the practical business mind, typified in the Wilcoxes, was limited, it had qualities essential to successful living, and that what was to be desired was its humanising by the qualities which the Schlegels possessed, a sensitive understanding of moral and aesthetic values. Still with some exaggeration he shows the Wilcoxes to be spiritually empty, too obtuse to know the values of the heart and imagination, but with a parallel exaggeration he makes Helen Schlegel so angry at the Wilcox blindness that she wrecks by her wilful emotion the reconciliation which Forster symbolically presents in the marriage of her sister Margaret to the senior Wilcox. The pattern of the novel is indeed once more based on the attempted saving of a soul, for that is primarily Margaret's aim, to redeem Mr Wilcox from materialism and to achieve in their union the truly balanced life. So too she will gain "Howards End", the house which symbolises the heart of England and which mystically holds the secret of true personal relationships. Between the Wilcoxes and the Schlegels Forster introduces an underbred clerk from depressed suburbia, Leonard Bast, a pathetic aspirant to culture, whose life is wrecked by unemployment due to a chance combination of the well-meant interferences of the Schlegels and the callous indifference of the Wilcoxes.

The whole canvas, indeed, becomes a broad one adequate to portray Forster's view of contemporary England in considerable detail. We see the danger in the selfish worship of money values, the weakness inherent in urban living, the threat of imperialist politics, the uprooting effect of mechanised transport. Above all appear the opposite follies of trying to dominate others by power and force of will on the one hand and to elude practical reality by emotional idealism on the other. It was certainly a fair and telling exposure of peril immanent in the pre-1914 world, and in so far especially as it dealt with the division between the practical and the moral world ominously prophetic of the subsequent human position on the widest scale.

If Forster had stopped there, he had done enough already to encourage the keen questioning of current materialism. *A Passage to India*, however, displaying the mature power of their author, added weight to his first novels. It also modified their conclusions, though their teaching could and did survive its darker thinking. The gist of this last novel, in fact, is that the establishing of true personal relationships is not as hopeful of achievement as had been suggested. The partial failure of the British in India was not due only to the Wilcox nature of their officials, to their administration of justice without emotional understanding. Forster draws in Fielding a character whose sympathies with Indians are true and sensitive, but Fielding in the end finds that intelligence, good-will, and culture, are not enough to connect East and West, not enough indeed we feel, in Forster's view, to solve life's problems anywhere. In the centre of the book Mrs Moore's faith in life is drained away by the desolating echo in the Marabar caves, and some have seen this important symbolic part as the key to the novel's ultimate meaning, so that Forster has been regarded as giving his concurrence with T. S. Eliot's vision of the Waste Land. Certainly Forster frequently gives his characters a sense of the unimportance of men and women, of their littleness in the scheme of things, of the basic weakness of the human soul.

But *A Passage to India* is too great a work of art to render up any simple view of life. On the surface it presents the magnitude, mystery and complexity of India; symbolically it presents the complex mystery of all life and is a study of the problem of evil in the universe. The reader should never, such is Forster's mastery, lose this twofold vision as a simultaneous effect, and, if he is aware of the significance of such a reading of life as coming in 1924, he should equally feel that its vision is timeless. Neither its end nor its total effect depresses. Indeed the last section, through the Hindu Godbole's mystical concentration, hints strongly at an ultimate goodness behind the mystery of the universe. The end is a brusque parting of East and West, but one feels that, if only Western civilisation could learn the uninhibited naturalness of the East, its ability to be happy, its blending of the serious and the humorous, the result might not fulfil the motto "Only Connect", yet it would certainly help the West. Indeed in his own understanding of the East Forster in *A Passage to India* created the one character who exists in the fulness of life in his novels, Dr Aziz, fluid, contradictory and unpredictable. Though we can see it as a novel of the nineteen-twenties, it forbids our labelling it as merely that.

It is questionable whether D. H. Lawrence ever achieved a novel so mature and satisfying as *A Passage to India*. Born in 1885 he had by his death in 1930 published more than a dozen novels or substantial short stories, but most of the time he was grappling with ideas and emotions that shook him too violently for him to gain the control of a master in presenting them. His sheer creative genius was greater than Forster's and forced its way out in poetry too. His productivity, apart from the novel, was also greater than Forster's, for, whereas Forster produced a few symbolic short stories, Lawrence's short stories make up several notable volumes, and the control involved in the shortness of such stories resulted in some of his best work, as did the similar control inherent in verse. Travel books like *Mornings in Mexico* (1927) and three plays extend his output, to which must be added the excellent *Psychology and the Unconscious* (1923), the reading of which is a valuable introduction to his novels, and the pamphlet on *Pornography and Obscenity*. Perhaps his energies were in general too widely dispersed for even his genius to fulfil its maximum potentialities. Certainly the artist and the man in him constantly existed in so acute a state of tension that reconciliation must have been very difficult. The internal storms and frustrations, the search for somewhere in the world where he could find a true background, led him after 1919— he had unsuccessfully tried to leave England during the war —to Sicily, Australia and Mexico. From these wanderings he gained much which his genius absorbed and transmuted into literature, but still when he died of consumption in the south of France he had found no point of rest.

It is not surprising, then, that the one novel in which the artist has complete control of his material is the early *Sons and Lovers*. His later novels, despite their power and often because of it, generally get out of hand before the end, but in *Sons and Lovers* Lawrence never lost his grip on himself. Always so intensely subjective that time and again his themes and characters can be seen clearly in terms of himself, in this novel Lawrence from the vantage point of twenty-eight years surveyed his childhood, the loves of his early manhood and his relationship with his mother. By the time the novel was finished he had broken almost completely with his early life. Having taught for somewhat over three years in a Croydon school he was now in the world of men of letters, with many contacts and friendships. She whom in the novel he called Miriam saw him no more after he had shown her that part of the manuscript in which she appeared and would not alter it. In April 1912 he had met Frieda, whom he was soon to marry. Above all, his mother, the dominating figure of the novel, had died. One chapter of his life had been closed, and the novel has the finality of retrospect, ending with the symbolical picture of Lawrence facing a new world after his mother's death : "Turning sharply, he walked towards the city's gold phosphorescence. His fists were shut, his mouth set fast". Looking back he saw all things in a clear perspective and with the detail that the acute observation of childhood and youth records with special power. Since it is not he or any character conceived in terms of his peculiar vision that dominates the novel, the people and the atmosphere of *Sons and Lovers* are much closer to normality than they are in his later novels. Love and hatred are there with a naked intensity beyond their presentation by any other contemporary novelist, but neither emotion is yet magnified to the inhuman violence to which he later gives expression. Further, the workaday texture of the life shown contributes greatly to give this novel the strength of reality. Here are people earning their living the hard way, and living the confined domestic life of a mining village. Bound by the limitations of actuality, by the characters of the father he hated, the mother he worshipped, and the girl he had known for some ten years, his absorption in the task of setting this all down kept in check for the time being the expression of his growing rebellion against contemporary society.

Once past *Sons and Lovers*, Lawrence let his soul in turmoil fight for truth in his fictional imaginings. His new life with Frieda was both ecstasy and bitterness, alternations of feeling to which he was always liable. When the characters in his novels quarrel with fury and violence, it is no more than Lawrence did with his wife and his friends. *The Rainbow* was in many ways the product of his early married life. In *Women in Love* he projected with apparently little exaggeration the queer intensity of his relations with Middleton Murry, swinging between an attraction which he wanted mystically to consecrate by a rite of blood-sharing and an equally strong repulsion. As novel succeeded novel, he was passionately seeking vital truths about human relationships. What was the naked elemental truth of the right relationship between man and woman, and between man and man in the ultimate sincerity of friendship ? What was the proper relation between blood and brain ? What was the secret of vital living ? What light could old Mexico give him ?—*The Plumed Serpent* (1926) tried to express the last. Often, swept on by the impetuosity of his combined thought-feeling, his novels ended in an indecisive exhaustion. *Aaron's Rod* (1922), for example, begins with as clear a reality as *Sons and Lovers* —the scene of the children and the blue ball is perfect truth —but its end has only the turgid preaching of a prophet trying to believe his own message.

Posterity will in time outlive the power to feel Lawrence's struggle in its full vitality, but at least until mid-century his struggle continued to be shared by very many, particularly the younger generations. Ultimately he was a soul in rebellion against the machine age. He felt a devilish spirit in the machines, and an evil force in the efficient organisation that lay behind them. In *Women in Love*, still thinking of the colliery world of his childhood, he drew the new colliery owner, whose efficiency broke down the old personal relations between owner and miners, and who, in doing so, not only lost his own soul but gave the miners an evil satisfaction which took the very hearts out of them. "There was a new world, a new order, strict, terrible, inhuman, but satisfying in its very destructiveness. The men were satisfied to belong to the great and wonderful machine, even whilst it destroyed them. It was what they wanted. It was the highest that man had produced, the most wonderful and superhuman." Lawrence was writing of the colliery world, but his meaning extended to the whole industrial scene, where machines dominated. "It was the first great step in undoing, the first great phase of chaos, the substitution of the mechanical principle for the organic." He portrays Gerald, "the industrial magnate", as made almost unnecessary by his own efficient reorganisation, a mere will without further desire, an intellect whose "centres of feeling were drying up", and who "felt, with faint, small but final sterile horror, that his mystic reason was breaking".

To what, then, could man in the machine age have recourse in order to save himself? At no time did Lawrence think much in terms of a political solution. In 1921, feeling a longing to take part in some active movement, he did declare: "If I knew how to, I'd really join myself to the revolutionary socialists now", and about the same time in a poem he cried

> "I long to be a bolshevist
> And set the stinking rubbish heap of this foul world
> Afire at myriad points"

but he knew that such an organised idealism was not for him. His views were too anarchic for any group movement, though he did try to lead a party of friends to take up a communal life in Mexico. His was the anarchism which believes in "the sacred and holy individual", lord and victim of his own responsibilities, and yet he also preached fervently the doctrine that men must submit to a leader. In thinking both of leadership and of the individual his thought was rooted in a semi-mystical worship of the blood and of what he called darkness. Horrified by what the intellect was doing to humanity, he turned from the brain to the blood, from the outer light to the inner darkness, for salvation. Even while he was writing *Sons and Lovers* he had reached the position expressed in a letter in these terms :—

> "My great religion is a belief in the blood, the flesh, as being wiser than the intellect. We can go wrong in our minds But what our blood feels and believes and says, is always true. The intellect is only a bit and a bridle. What do I care about knowledge ? All I want is to answer to my blood, direct, without fribbling intervention of mind, or moral, or what-not. I conceive a man's body as a kind of flame, like a candle, forever upright and yet flowing : and the intellect is just the light that is shed on the things around."

The darkness to which he mystically appealed was the inner darkness of the unconscious, the well of instinctive life, in contact with the elemental things. To this he later added something of sun-worship, feeling "a direct dynamic connexion between [his] solar-plexus and the sun". So, largely expressed in the novels but very much in his letters too, he evolved a kind of modern pagan religion to free men from the sterility, from the monotonous boredom and mechanical slavery of the machine age. It was all a rebellion, religious

in spirit, against contemporary materialism. For Christianity
in its organised form he had no use. For such Christian
virtues as humility, pity, and good-will he from time to time
expressed a contempt. To Jesus himself he was drawn, yet
with a kind of jealousy so that he was antagonistic as well
as attracted : one of his last stories, *The Man Who Died*
(1931), depicts Jesus coming alive from the tomb and falling
in love with a young pagan priestess.

This "philosophy" takes up a large part of his novels,
but his other main theme is sex. While at work on *Women
in Love* he declared : "I can only write what I feel pretty
strongly about : and that, at present, is the relation between
men and women. After all, it is *the* problem of to-day, the
establishment of a new relation, or the readjustment of the
old one, between men and women". His preoccupation
with sexuality, reaching its frankest expression in *Lady
Chatterly's Lover*, was so intense that it raised unprofitable
speculations as to whether he was himself sexually impotent
and as to the effect on his sexual views of his early worship
of his mother. Certainly he laid great emphasis on the physical
side of sex, but, as with much of his thinking at any rate
as expressed in the novels, it is never clear what his views
on love were. A character will find himself after physical love
"shattered" as well as "satisfied". Love must be a fusion
of spirit sunk in the "potent darkness". Love must certainly
pay no heed to mere conventions, yet there was a morality
in Lawrence's presentation, even a Puritanism in his insistence
on an innocence in true sexuality, and something of the old
romantic heresy of natural goodness, whereby a man can do
as he likes because the natural man is good. One thing,
however, emerges clearly—that between lovers there must
be "a pure balance of two single beings:—as the stars balance
each other". The class-consciousness of Lawrence comes out
in his fondness for the theme of the man who wins a woman
of a higher class—his own wife was the daughter of a German
baron. His sense of part of the "modern problem" is seen
in his writing of Hermione in *Women in Love* that "she was
a woman of the new school, full of intellectuality, and heavy,

nerveworn with consciousness". And as the modern girl is different, so, of course, is the modern young man. The point is disputed by her antagonist Birkin, but Lawrence saw the part truth in the question he put in Hermione's mouth : "Are not the young people growing up to-day, really dead before they have a chance to live ?"

Lawrence's peculiar strength as a novelist lay in his insight into the emotional life. Plot hardly exists in his novels, nor does characterisation in the normal sense. We do not see or hear his people to know them in the round or even as flat portraits : what we are aware of is naked sensibilities. Indeed Lawrence disowned the old characterisation.

> "That which is psychic—non-human in humanity, is more interesting to me than the old-fashioned human element, which causes one to conceive a character in a certain moral scheme and make him consistent. The certain moral scheme is what I object to . . . I don't so much care about what the woman *feels*—in the ordinary usage of the word. That presumes an *ego* to feel with. I only care about what the woman *is*—what she IS—inhumanly, physiologically, materially . . . You mustn't look in my novel for the old stable *ego* of the character."

Seen in this a-moral way his characters are the human animal—again and again he uses animal similes of them. With his religious bias he would have the animal become spiritualised, but, holding human beings to be first animals, it is their instinctive feelings he records. The feelings of his men and women are like quicksilver, ever on the run. They flash this way and that like lightning. His people love and hate, without knowing in general why they do either. The mother in *Sons and Lovers* is a notable exception in having a moral check on her instinctive emotions. One character is described as "wary in all his senses", and this animal wariness is shared by most others. With this view of human creatures Lawrence naturally shows the awareness and understanding that exist between people below the level of consciousness : without a word spoken there can be "a beam of understanding" or a "diabolic freemasonry". In all this we are no doubt given a true insight into natural man. The weakness lies in the exaggeration of truth, for, whereas men and women have their instinctive moments, and in many the moments are frequent and extended, men and women in Lawrence's novels tend to appear more purely in their elemental and animal nature than is true of them in any human society. No doubt there is truth too in his showing love as only one of the emotions, and one as intermittent as any other, but his novels give such a predominance to hatred as to weaken the truth by over-balance. On the purely literary side, however, his weakness in the matter of the feelings is the monotony and repetition of the enormously exaggerated phrasing peculiar to him. It needs all his excellence elsewhere to make us accept the continual appearance of such a typical expression as :—"Then he went again to look at one of the pictures. Every one of his limbs was turgid with electric force, and his back was tense like a tiger's, with slumbering fire".

His method of concentrating on the interplay of the feelings makes Lawrence at his very best in separate scenes, and it is in separate scenes too that the poet of nature in him makes its full effect. Moreover, as these two aspects of his genius often coincide, some of his unforgettable beauties are those often quite extended passages in which he is conveying a scene of natural beauty and the flow of natural feeling at the same time. Such are the love scenes with Miriam in the country in *Sons and Lovers*, the brief bathing scene in Lincolnshire in the same novel, and the more complex "Water Party" in *Women in Love*. The finest lyric poetry of Lawrence is in his prose when bird-song is his theme. It is the psychologist-poet, freed from the prophet, who will most surely live.

CHAPTER XV

JAMES JOYCE AND VIRGINIA WOOLF

The revolutionary individualism of Joyce's treatment of the novel still awaits a stable assessment. As we have seen, Virginia Woolf acclaimed *Ulysses*, as it began to appear, as being at last a novel conceived by one who rightly appreciated the true function of the novel. After its appearance in Paris in 1922 and its subsequent suppression in England, *Ulysses* enjoyed a great fame with advanced critics and complementary abuse elsewhere. Yet when seventeen years later *Finnegans Wake* was published, it fell flat, at least by comparison. Few claimed the ability to understand it, and it was generally felt that Joyce had carried his new manner to an impossible extreme. When his death in 1941 gave the opportunity for a critical estimate of his achievement as a whole, the emphasis was generally put on his early work and upon *Ulysses*, and *Ulysses* was viewed with less enthusiasm than had been accorded it twenty years before, though its outstanding significance as a product of its time was fully acknowledged. At mid-century critical opinion tended once more to find excellence in *Finnegans Wake* and true success in all his work.

Joyce was born in Dublin in 1882. His education was first in Jesuit-controlled schools and then at the Roman Catholic University College in Dublin, where he graduated in 1902. Then he went to Paris to study medicine, but soon gave up that idea. Apart from a brief return to Ireland in 1904 because of his mother's death he spent the rest of his life on the Continent, never revisiting Dublin after 1912. Thus, though he was rooted in Ireland, he made himself an exile, and added to his Irish heritage a rich cosmopolitan knowledge—though it should not be forgotten that the Dublin of his youth had a quite rich cosmopolitan quality. For some years he was at Trieste; during the war he was at Zurich, where he could preserve an intellectual neutrality towards

the international conflict ; after the war he made his home,
with his wife and two children, at Paris. At no time did he
rely on literature for money, and in his later years he had
enough money to live austerely while devoting himself
rigorously to his writing. So, having no need to consider a
public, he wrote always to realise his ideals as artist and
thinker.

His first book was a volume of poems, *Chamber Music*,
in 1907. His first fictional publication was *Dubliners* in
1914. A firm of Dublin publishers had in 1912 refused to
publish this collection of short stories, but, except perhaps
in Ireland, it is not easy now to see any good grounds for
that refusal. The stories are rich in Dublin life and character
very faithfully observed. The people of whom the stories
are told are in general poor creatures spiritually and in seedy
circumstances, and the mind that deals with them writes not
for edification but with a detached, somewhat cynical amusement, for it fascinates him to see how petty and ridiculous
they are, the human wastage of a city. His presentation
might have an element of the revolutionary by virtue of the
brilliant objective exposure of the common scene, but there
was nothing revolutionary in the literary expression. Nor
was there in *A Portrait of the Artist as a Young Man*,
published in New York in 1916, on which he was at work
at the same time as he was on *Dubliners*. That too kept
to the straightforward, acutely observant realism that the
"naturalism" of the recent French novel had taught Arnold
Bennett also.

In *A Portrait* Joyce, with some disguise, traced his own
development up to his break with Ireland after his mother's
death, and in thus exposing and surveying his growth
in childhood and youth he was doing very much what
Lawrence, at about the same time, was doing in *Sons
and Lovers*. Joyce shows his progressive isolation in his
home as his conflict with his father and his mother grows
with the dissolution of his religious orthodoxy. We see the
growing lad in terms of his education, religion and sexual
awakening. Over all is the theme of the relation of the artist

to his society. Working now on a more complex and on a continuous theme, instead of a short story, Joyce naturally developed his method, and Stephen Dedalus, who is himself, is presented, to a considerable extent, in his thoughts and memories, in which, rather than with a separate existence, the other people in the story have their being. But at this stage of his writing all is still presented with traditional coherence and clarity. *A Portrait* had cost him a good deal of effort, in the course of which he re-cast some and rejected other sections, and after his death part of an earlier version was published as *Stephen Hero*.

Ulysses was begun in 1914. Now Joyce set out to write such a novel as had never been written in English before. Sterne's *Tristram Shandy* of more than a century and a half earlier has a slight similarity in its apparent formlessness and in the highly individual inventions of technique employed by a subtle mind, which, like Joyce's, overflowed with learning. Sterne, however, had behind him the relative solidarity of the eighteenth century, whereas Joyce, a voluntary but embittered exile, was aware with special acuteness of the breakdown of civilisation. Sterne remained in Holy Orders, but Joyce rejected Catholicism and sought a philosophy that would enable the artist to live in the modern world, on whose foundations there remained only rubble. Joyce, indeed, was setting himself an almost impossible task, one which T. S. Eliot, in appreciating *Ulysses*, expressed as "giving a shape and significance to the immense panorama of futility and anarchy which is contemporary history". To do this he went back to the Dublin of his youth, and imagined with unflagging detail the life, for some twenty hours, of an advertising agent of thirty-eight, an Irish Jew, Leopold Bloom. From the early morning in June 1904 when Bloom gets up and makes his wife's breakfast until the early hours of the next day Joyce exposes even more than Bloom himself could know about himself and his environment, and ends with forty pages of the frankest self-communing of Bloom's wife, a singer and a slut. We have the sense of the teeming life of a city seen under a microscope, of being privileged viewers of the habits of human creatures who, as they scurry about, are unable to hide any of their shame and futility, whether mental or physical. As Bloom drifts through his typical worthless day we go everywhere with him : a cemetery, streets, shops, public-houses, lavatories, bedrooms, offices—all are there, the trivial daily round of an ineffective, but bustling sensualist, who, though constantly frustrated and his self-sufficiency insidiously attacked, finds life tolerably liveable, so long as the life force jostles him along. Ultimately he is an isolated unit, aware of his isolation, but he knows everything of at least the seamy side of his city, his contacts are everywhere, and he has sensitiveness enough to respond continuously to the innumerable stimuli of the most everyday kind. As Joyce shows it us, it is a dreary spectacle, in which hardly anything exists to stir the reader to admiration, love, pity, sympathy or even hatred. It joins T. S. Eliot's indictment of the Waste Land, and shares Aldous Huxley's disgust at the human animal. It is the twilight of an age, and its chill has infected its author.

Ulysses may well seem formless at first sight, and that impression is not wholly lost when the reader has mastered the whole book. Joyce indeed planned too carefully : in his own intention, though it is lost on the average reader, incident after incident parallels one in the Homeric *Odyssey*, and in elaborating to this end he confused the trail as effectively as did Spenser in his way in *The Faerie Queene*. The whole is too voluminous and too detailed, and the very everyday drabness of much prevents the imagination of the reader from taking hold of it in the way which gives the form bestowed by perspective. Further, Joyce has now come to the large scale use of symbolism. It is there constantly behind the realistic description, a rich commentary for those capable of perceiving and interpreting it, and causing little or no trouble to those who cannot, but when it overrides the realistic, as in the long and fantastic brothel scene, it adds to the general impression of formlessness. Moreover, the realism itself has an initially confusing effect, for to be at home in the novel geographically is to know Dublin with the intimacy of a native. The reader feels like one in a strange city with a quite inadequate guide book.

The basic technique for the exposure of Leopold Bloom and his wife is at least as old as Chaucer, for it is that of the dramatic monologue. More recently it had served Browning, and at the very time when Joyce was starting Bloom on his interminable self-muttering journey T. S. Eliot was giving the indecisive "love song" of Alfred Prufrock. The reader is inside Bloom's mind, in the flow of his inconsecutive, partially formulated thoughts and transient feelings, and Bloom is at the mercy of his whims and of the chance stimuli of his passage. Bloom's psychological process is one of expansion and contraction: an encounter, a memory, an association of ideas, starts his mind into extra activity, which, having reached a climax, ebbs away. Joyce's method resembles that of the cinema in giving a more or less sustained close-up, to be followed by a fade-out to normal size again, or by a shifting to a different scene or different strand of the story. So there is inevitably an unevenness in the novel's flow, and in the ebb-movement the novelist may be lost in the flat anti-climax and seek relief and continuity in padding. But at his best, which is often, Joyce conveys Bloom's thoughts in a way as nearly true to life as literature allows: he secures an often startling actuality by the combination of psychological truth with sharply observed concrete realism, for, as with Bunyan in *Grace Abounding*, we are never in any doubt of the very place in which feelings are felt or thoughts thought. The most brilliant and sustained piece of internal monologue is the concluding reverie of Molly Bloom, but so sustained a passage could come only this once, for life does not allow in any ordinary twenty-four hours for much extended reverie, and to attempt similarity to life demanded for the bulk of the book a more broken flow, and indeed the intermission of the monologue method for more direct statement. As for the psychology as a whole, it is not only the product of Joyce's obviously deep personal penetration of human nature but the result of an intimate knowledge of the work of Freud, and especially of Jung, whose teaching of psycho-analysis was centred at Zurich at the time that Joyce was writing *Ulysses* there.

The average reader approaching *Ulysses* for the first time had difficulty enough in adjusting himself to the new technique in which story had as good as vanished and, along with it, the old kind of coherent characterisation. But on top of this difficulty was that caused by Joyce's use of language. Again Joyce was too much of an artist. That is, being himself delighted with the artistic joy of playing with words, he indulged his pleasure freely with all the subtlety of an agile mind. He telescoped words together, as in "evoluation" and "heroticism", played with names as in "yung and easily freudened", punned, imitated sounds, coined words, drew on a wide range of foreign words, and made good use of his Irish brogue. In one long passage he imitated the prose style of earlier English writers in such a way that in effect it was a summary of the development of English prose over many centuries.

Many of his linguistic devices had obvious justification. The jostling of meanings when two or more words were telescoped together could give a value to each quite different from their use singly, for the fusion might release irony, mockery, humour or some other feeling. Such telescoping of words frequently takes place in any mind when associated ideas overlap, and its use is therefore particularly apt in the inner monologue. The association of ideas of which Joyce makes great use can indeed be justified on many grounds : it is not only psychologically true, but it is economical, it stimulates the reader, it is clearly a natural characteristic of Joyce himself, and it is a kind of intellectual entertainment which has always been acceptable and never more so than since about 1920 when such different art forms as "modern" poetry, crossword problems, and the "Itma" programmes of Tommy Handley made great play with it. As for the imitation of sounds, Joyce was merely extending the ancient principle of onomatopoeia. But where Joyce erred was in the extent of the continuous demand his language makes, so that he expected of his readers minds both as subtle and nimble as his own and as well equipped with cosmopolitan and often esoteric knowledge. *Ulysses* could provide many years' study to one reasonably well equipped, if he would solve every problem presented by the language alone.

But *Ulysses* is easy reading compared with *Finnegans Wake*. Joyce had now mastered the technique which he had himself been only working out as he wrote *Ulysses*. Now that it was second nature to him to write in this way he still wrote with the intensest self-scrutiny, adding and refining as he revised. Further, being now almost blind, he relied imaginatively to a yet greater degree on the sound of words—he is always more intelligible when read aloud—and his words depend frequently for their full value on what they say to the ear and the eye together, as well as upon any dictionary value of their component parts. So the expression became dense with meaning. Moreover, his whole mental attitude was even far more symbolical than before, and this work was written, not like *Ulysses* primarily to convey a living world, but to express a philosophy of history symbolically—a philosophy expounded in a little known work of a neglected philosopher named Vico of a century before. Above all, *Finnegans Wake* takes the form of a nightmare dreamed by a Mr Earwicker asleep in Dublin. It is not then to be wondered at that on its first appearance it seemed almost completely unintelligible. Now the would-be explorer has at any rate some guidance available which can take him at least into the fringes of its massive and extraordinary jungle. He will succeed the better for a thorough knowledge of psycho-analysis, a good knowledge of world history and literature, and a smattering of several languages.

The work of Virginia Woolf, though she was stimulated by the experimental work of Joyce in *Ulysses* and though she developed a technique in some ways resembling his, is very different in essentials from Joyce's. It too may be for the few rather than for the multitude, but not because of its obscurity. The demands that she makes are upon spiritual understanding and aesthetic sensibility rather than upon the intellect. Her concern is for beauty, and she is worlds apart from the sordid life of Joyce's Dublin. If at times she expresses a feeling of the meaninglessness of life, it is only in a temporary trough in the sea of life : even if she felt herself in the Waste Land she would raise her eyes and her heart to the stars, and because in 1941 her spirit failed and she could not she died.

She was born in 1882, daughter of the eminent Victorian biographer and literary critic, Sir Leslie Stephen. In her home many of the famous regularly met, writers and politicians and painters, among them Meredith and John Morley. Her family was connected with those of Darwin, the scientist, of Maitland, the historian, and of J. A. Symonds, the aesthetic critic. Educated at home she learned Greek, and in her home music was an integral part of life. In fact from the beginning she could inherit the best that Victorian culture had to offer to people with adequate leisure and reasonable wealth. As a young woman sharing a house in Bloomsbury with her elder sister Vanessa, wife of Clive Bell the art critic, she became one of a notable circle to whose fame E. M. Forster, Lytton Strachey and J. M. Keynes the economist particularly contributed in course of time. In 1912 she married Leonard Woolf, who was literary editor of *The Nation* from 1923 to 1930 and who also wrote on industrial and economic themes. On the practical side she took an active part in the Hogarth Press. Thus the social, intellectual and artistic world in which she moved was a wide and a very enlightened one. The term "Bloomsbury group" which was used to depreciate herself and her friends, when it was meant to imply a rarified world too artistic and theoretical to be in touch with common life, had no more truth in it than such labels commonly have.

The kind of woman she was is easily to be discerned from her novels, but in brief it shines luminously in the tribute paid by her friend E. M. Forster after her death, a tribute which cannot be excelled for sympathetic understanding. We see the artist and poet, writing for her own delight alone, as she read likewise for pure pleasure. Literature to her was a joy existing in its own right and needing, as she told a school in a paper entitled "How Should One Read a Book ? ", no further justification, for "are there not some pursuits that we practise because they are good in themselves, and some pleasures that are final ?" This living delight saved her from self-conscious seriousness in her approach to writing, and kept her in touch with the normal life in which she took a many-sided interest. Her novels testify continuously to the vital response of all her senses : the pleasures of the eye are clearly great, but her eye is no more alive than her hearing, her touch, her sense of smell or of taste—she enjoys a meal as well as a landscape, sunshine or the fragrance of flowers, music or a book. It is impossible to read even a few pages without the feeling that nothing in her surroundings escaped her, and that her senses were finely co-ordinated with her intelligence. Her mind was all the time aware of all the reports of her senses, which it was her persistent practice to sift, particularly where human beings were concerned, in order to find out their true implications. It has been said against her as a novelist that she kept within too narrow limits and left the common unsophisticated world out of her books, but that she did so was part of her sincerity. She knew that she could not pass beyond her limits and retain that full under-standing which alone could ensure her success. Hers was a world in which she could maintain a detachment natural to her reserve and to her high sense of the privacy due to the individual. By nature and by birth and breeding she was fitted for her own world, and to have extended her world to include the working classes would have been on her part an affectation, a claim to an understanding she did not possess truly enough to justify the artist in her to use such material. As E. M. Forster remarked, "she detested mateyness" : if she sympathised with the poor or felt with the crowd, she would not wear her heart on her sleeve, or court a public which would not meet her on her own ground. An artist and a lady, she knew the only way that was truly hers. She was a rare spirit : in the words of her friend Victoria Sackville-West,

> "Frugal, austere, fine, proud,
> Rich in her contradictions, rich in love".

When first in her early thirties Virginia Woolf turned to the writing of novels, she did not depart from the traditional form. Her second novel, *Night and Day* (1919), makes a most enlightening study in contrast to her later manner, for it reveals her personality trying to come through, and her personal vision of life, but the traditional form is clearly alien to her vision of things and frustrates her. The result is a novel that in technique stands midway between a Meredithian novel and one of Forster's earlier novels. It is laboured in construction, characterisation and phrasing. The psychology often shows her true understanding, but nevertheless it often creaks. She is indeed trying to impose a pattern on life and to convey the material surface of life, characteristics of the traditional novel which she was herself to denounce.

But, with all its defects, *Night and Day* has an outstanding virtue. It is an honest book. Both the author and the principal characters are above all concerned to be honest, the author about them and they with themselves. The hero is no romantic hero, nor the heroine a romantic heroine, but they are a kind of unsparkling Benedick and Beatrice who doubt and even scorn romantic love. They feel love as something piercing and exalted which is realised only in flashes amid the general flow of a bleak, even blighting, everyday life. For them such flashes are not enough, for they are serious-minded young people, suspicious of such gleams, and the "hero" Ralph definitely tries to cure himself of love as of a mere, but dangerous, hallucination. Thus, with a certain tedium, the story poses the question, Will Ralph and Katherine ever realise that they are really in love with one another? The theme is in fact a "modern" one, with a "modernness" akin to Forster's, that of the peculiar difficulty experienced in the realisation of love by highly sensitive civilised beings given to self-analysis : the world is a Forsterian one in which the conventions and sophistication of society ensnare the natural human being. Comedy, satire and repressed poetry give much incidental pleasure.

After *Night and Day* Virginia Woolf proceeded to try a new method, and only in *The Years* (1937), a comparative failure, did she revert to the traditional form. It was not only what she had seen of *Ulysses* that helped to determine the kind of experiment. Henry James had led the way in entering into the minds of his characters so that their state of mind was the primary interest in one of his later novels. Proust in his long *Recherche du Temps Perdu* had shown how to release the past into the present so that memories lived again in the writer's mind and made that mind, as it evoked the past, a complex recorder in which many levels of experience were co-ordinated. In particular Proust had relied on the impressions of the senses to reveal the fluid personality, without putting upon them that intellectual constraint which gave a fixity of character in the traditional novel. Further, her approach to the novel was influenced by her admiration of the Russian novelists for their "understanding of the soul and heart".

Her first attempt in a new manner was *Jacob's Room* (1922). Starting with a young widow and her two small children, one of them Jacob, on a Cornish beach she takes them to Scarborough, and then, concentrating on Jacob, accompanies him by train to Cambridge, where we see his undergraduate life, thence to London, and finally to Greece. Only at the end is the reader in Jacob's room, looking at the litter of its late occupant, now dead in battle, and hearing Jacob's mother ask his friend, "What shall I do with his old shoes?" It is as though the novelist's idea had begun at that point, and she had then gone back to the time when he was a small child and proceeded to show him in scene after scene through the years. So we see Jacob from childhood, in one place after another, as though a family album of snapshots had been brought to life ; or rather it is as if a recording unit giving both sight and sound showed us Jacob with his friends in his talk and all his various activities.

Each scene is extraordinarily vivid, and Virginia Woolf's exceptional power of conveying sense impressions is already very highly developed, but she is not yet in full control of her medium. The weakness is that the scenes do not all contribute alike to our knowledge of Jacob ; many include

other people who neither have any further part in his life
nor bear any significant relation to it at the time ; in others
he is not the central figure and in others again what we see
around him is not so much the things Jacob himself would
have noticed as those to which the presenting artist cannot
herself fail to respond. Between her unselective method and
her too conscientious adherence to her belief in the ultimate
inscrutability of individual personality we are left with a hazy
picture of Jacob. But in this first attempt she had succeeded
in conveying the intangible spirit of life flowing and ebbing
not only in Jacob but in all around him. An exhilarating
sense of the excitement of living, of the many-coloured
mystery of life, fills its pages, and remains with the reader
when he has come out again from the room whose litter
speaks sadly of a personality now dispersed and fading.

In her next novel, *Mrs Dalloway* (1925), Virginia Woolf
showed that she had learnt how to select only those impressions that were needed to build up the picture. She also
takes us more continuously through the thoughts, feelings
and impressions of the main characters. As Mrs Dalloway
shops, or talks, dresses or eats, we are inside her mind, seeing
her as she sees herself, sharing her memories, and knowing
the people she knows or has known through her own eyes.
Now instead of our following chronologically through the years,
all is presented in the present. We are with Mrs Dalloway for
only some fifteen hours, from nine o'clock on a lovely June
morning when she goes to the florist's to arrange for flowers for
her party that night until the early hours of the next day
when her guests depart. So we are very close to the
experience of real life, for Mrs Dalloway is like ourselves,
reacting, like Bloom in *Ulysses*, to all the stimuli of daily
life, which attract or repel her, and remind her of others or
of her past. But at this stage Virginia Woolf is still unable
to create a true sense of individual personality, for, relying
almost solely, as far as Mrs Dalloway herself is concerned,
on the internal method, she cannot avoid presenting Mrs
Dalloway in a way that is too disembodied. Her essential
being is there, fluid, running this way and that, characterised

indeed by a certain unity in diversity, by certain predominant tendencies, but, as she is largely unaware of how she appears to others and as she is not sufficiently objectified in the thoughts of others or by the author herself, the abundant life she possesses escapes the confines of personality. Even as we do not know how we appear to others, not even how our voices sound to others, so we seem to know Clarissa Dalloway in a similar way, at once too intimate and too remote, rather like a familiar ghost. The objective treatment of character which would have helped to counteract this defect is kept in this novel mainly for minor characters and then tends to be directly satiric.

The novel *Mrs Dalloway* does not, however, consist only of the exposure of Clarissa Dalloway as she was that day. More ambitious than in *Jacob's Room*, Virginia Woolf in this novel worked in a dark strand in contrast to the radiant loveliness of the June day with which the wealthy, relatively carefree life of Mrs Dalloway is in considerable harmony. Septimus Smith, a young survivor from the war, one of whose last battle experiences in Italy had been the death of his closest friend at his side, trudges the same streets with the young Italian girl he had married in the first onset of that panic which now haunts him. The excitement felt by Clarissa Dalloway in her sense of London breathing through all its pores is not shared by Septimus. His will to live has been sapped by the delayed reaction of his war experiences. No longer able to face life he commits suicide, and the news of his death reaches Clarissa in the midst of her party. The link between the two separate worlds on that June day in London is of the very slightest, but the weaving of the dark strands into the light is done with very great skill. Yet one marked weakness is apparent : whereas Clarissa's present holds in solution a rich and varied past, the Smiths exist much more in the present only, their past and their associations with others being inadequate to give them fully expanded vitality. Further, the psychic illness of Septimus solidifies large tracts of his consciousness, and when the free play of consciousness is diminished Virginia Woolf's method of inner psychological presentation is inevitably restricted. She remarks of two characters that they 'would solidify young'', and any characters that so solidify, from whatever cause, need a different treatment. Moreover, though many praise the Smith element for giving greater seriousness to a novel which would otherwise be mainly a social comedy of a rather superficial world, the comparative isolation of this tragic element contrasts with the width, within its limits, of Clarissa's world, and the tragic effect is diminished by the strong vein of satire particularly in Virginia Woolf's treatment of the mental specialist. Satire, comedy, pathos, but above all the mystery and joy of living in a stimulating world, are the main impressions when the book is closed.

After these two attempts Virginia Woolf achieved in *To the Lighthouse* (1927) the complete success of her new method. In *Mrs Dalloway* she had given up the extended space and time of *Jacob's Room* ; now she leaves the bustle of London life for the more self-contained setting of a house in the Hebrides, a small family and three guests. In the long first section we see these people for only a few hours, and nothing really happens. As the scene opens, Mrs Ramsay is knitting stockings for the lighthouse keeper's child ; one of her own children wants to visit the lighthouse the next day, but the weather, in Mr Ramsay's opinion, is unfavourable ; we leave them after dinner, when Mrs Ramsay can finally tuck the younger children in for the night. No event has happened except the engagement of a young couple who have been for a walk. It is the ideal scope for the presentation of people as they really are. The isolation of the Hebrides does not matter, for these people are there only for a respite from civilisation and have their background in their present. It is enough that they exist, reacting naturally to one another, talking, thinking, feeling in silence, sinking into memories, speculating, eating. It is remarkable how much in a small space Virginia Woolf builds up. Especially the figures of Mr and Mrs Ramsay stand out, as living personalities, clearly known inside and out ; there is now no sense of disembodiment. By the end of that evening we feel we know them intimately as their separate selves as seen by themselves and also in all their relations, as husband and wife, as father and mother, and, particularly Mrs Ramsay, what they mean to the others there. Mrs Ramsay is the more dominating figure of the two, an artist in living : she conducts the dinner party like a conductor harmonising the various instruments of an orchestra, and yet all the time we know how she feels inside herself, apart, lonely, facing her enemy, life. Indeed this first section presents the whole life, works and personality of Mrs Ramsay as summed up on that evening.

The novel, indeed, seems in a way complete at that stage, for the short following section is a poetic elegy on the uninhabited house ten years later, Mrs Ramsay being now dead. But when in the concluding section the house is again inhabited by some of the same people, Virginia Woolf has a further purpose, to show the continued force of Mrs Ramsay's personality, as she does symbolically. Lily, an artist, unable to finish a long meditated picture, at last achieves success when she feels the presence of Mrs Ramsay so strongly upon her that she seems actually to see her. From Mrs Ramsay, who was an artist in life, Lily gains the power to consummate her vision on canvas, for life and art are one. The young man, who as a child ten years before had been unable to visit the lighthouse, now visits it with his father and sister, but the symbolism of this, though one feels its pressure, is not so clear. As for the lighthouse, it too has a symbolic and psychological use in the novel : its light could release in Mrs Ramsay a pure ecstasy and delight, and seemed to symbolise for her the final peace in which personality and the fret of life are lost, giving her a feeling of our being in the hands of God, though concurrently she feels that to be an insincere thought, for Mrs Ramsay is a complex figure and her sincerity will allow her no easy resting place. We feel that there is a great deal of Virginia Woolf herself in Mrs Ramsay, but she has projected herself into a clearly conceived figure existing in its own separate individuality.

Excellent though *To the Lighthouse* is, her supreme achievement is *The Waves* (1931). In so far as we are sub-merged almost completely in the waves of consciousness of the characters (a part of the meaning of the title) it is less satisfactory as a novel, at any rate much more difficult of complete apprehension, but as a vision of life it has the complex harmonies, the suggestive mystery and beauty of great poetry. In method it is a further advance in her already developed technique. Where *Mrs Dalloway* had given Clarissa as she was on one June day, and *To the Lighthouse* had pre-sented a small group of people seen twice in ten years, now six lives, beginning with three small boys and three little girls at a preparatory school, expand from childhood to middle age, in a series of scenes spaced over the years. At the boarding school stage the six separate into two groups, the boys at one school, the girls at another. Next they disperse, the young men to the university or into business or profession, the girls to their homes and marriage, but on two occasions they are all brought together again, once at a dinner, and again one evening at Hampton Court. Finally Bernard, in late middle life, rounds off the book with a long soliloquy on all their lives.

Sinking at once into the consciousness of the young children in the sunlit garden of early morning, the reader has to go very slowly, letting himself receive without any resistance the fast flowing impressions conveyed by the children's internal commentary, and all the book must be read as slowly and receptively as poetry, but read thus several times it gives the rich reward of life apprehended in variety from its dawn to its approaching twilight. If the different characters do not stand out as sharply apart as Mr and Mrs Ramsay, it is partly because we are so much inside them, partly because, it would seem, Virginia Woolf's intention was at least to some extent to realise for us the common bases of consciousness on which individuality rests. Moreover, as is the implication of her unique *Orlando*, in which the central character begins as an Elizabethan boy and ends as a young woman of the twentieth century, we must face the fact that at the ultimate levels differences between man and woman are lost in common human consciousness. Bernard in his concluding soliloquy remarks : "This is not one life ; nor do I always know if I am man or woman, Bernard or Neville, Louis, Susan, Jinny or Rhoda—so strange is the contact of one with another". *The Waves* is a prose poem of the human consciousness, conceived and executed by a wise, sensitive and skilled artist.

The image of the sea of life is apt to describe Virginia Woolf's presentation of life. Life is one continuous motion, an endless alternation of flow and ebb ; it has sharply defined edges only at its extremes and even then they are masked in the turmoil of the waves. The voyager in the vast expanses of that ocean, now on the crest, now in the trough of the waves, is unconscious of any form to the scene around him, but terribly aware of his own isolation, broken only temporarily by others passing by, whose departure again gives added sadness to his solitude. On the crest of the wave there is energy and delight ; in the trough disillusionment and a sense of the nothingness of life ; after the happiness of community of feeling comes the desolation of loneliness. It can all happen, this ebb and flow, around a dinner table or in a garden, anywhere that two or three are gathered together with the waters of life isolating and linking them. And the ocean of life bears a constant threat : to both Mrs Ramsay and Lily life is delight and ecstasy, but to both it is also an enemy, ever likely and ready to pounce. Life is ironic : as Bernard reflects, "some beauty must be broken daily to remain beautiful". Life is sad : "it is strange that we, who are capable of so much suffering, should inflict so much suffering".

The fullest coherent presentation of life in her books is probably in Bernard's concluding soliloquy in *The Waves*. As he begins to sum up, he says to himself :—

> "How tired I am of stories, how tired I am of phrases that come down beautifully with all their feet on the ground ! Also, how I distrust neat designs of life that are drawn upon half-sheets of note-paper . . .

> I begin to seek some design more in accordance with
> those moments of humiliation and triumph that come
> now and then undeniably. Lying in a ditch on a stormy
> day, when it has been raining, then enormous clouds
> come marching over the sky, tattered clouds, wisps of
> cloud. What delights me then is the confusion, the
> height, the indifference and the fury. Great clouds
> always changing, and movement; something sulphurous
> and sinister, bowled up, helter-skelter; towering, trail-
> ing, broken off, lost, and I forgotten, minute, in a ditch.
> Of story, of design, I do not see a trace then.''

We can only pretend an orderly life, he reflects. But in his
middle age he has developed no defeatism—that is not the
way of Virginia Woolf's characters. "We have our fundamental goodness surely", Bernard thinks. As his last years
approach, and another day dawns, he can affirm, "this is the
eternal renewal, the incessant rise and fall and fall and rise
again. And in me too the wave rises. It swells; it arches
its back. I am aware once more of a new desire . . . What
enemy do we now perceive advancing against us . . .? It is
death. Death is the enemy. It is death against whom I ride
. . . I strike spurs into my horse. Against you I will fling
myself, unvanquished and unyielding, O Death !" Yet the
eternal renewal, the splendour of love, courage, beauty and
illumination—none of these can deny the sadness inseparable
from change. That is the only sadness which pervades her
books.

Virginia Woolf is the supreme novelist of the mystery of
the personal life, that strange fluid entity that is ourselves.
In those who, in her phrase, "solidify young" she takes
little interest, but otherwise her view is comprehensive. The
individual, as she sees him, is a world peopled by various
selves, and of these there is always one who is a spectator
of the rest : within him is played that continuous ironic
drama in which no man is a hero to himself and yet paradoxically he is the hero of his play. The individual is indeed
a multiple, complex personality whose components merge into
one another : as Bernard expresses it—"it is not one life that
I look back upon ; I am not one person ; I am many people ;

I do not altogether know who I am—Jinny, Susan, Neville, Rhoda, or Louis : or how to distinguish my life from theirs". Again he remarks : "I am more selves than Neville thinks. We are not simple as our friends would have us to meet their needs".

That simplifying to meet his needs was the way of the older novelist. Virginia Woolf inclined to the other extreme, emphasising the complexity. Given sensibility such as Neville's and he can say : "I am clouded and bruised with the print of minds and faces and things so subtle that they have smell, colour, texture, substance, but no name". Bernard expresses the common experience of concentrating on one thing while other factors insensibly make their contribution—"while the fringe of my intelligence floating unattached caught those distant sensations which after a time the mind draws in and works upon; the chime of bells; general murmurs; vanishing figures; one girl on a bicycle . . ." We realise from her method of presenting the inner life how the personal past swirls into the mind, or the historic past, the terrible pounce of memory, and, as the years accumulate, "how the dead leap out on us at street corners, or in dreams". The self is always open to sudden shocks—"there is no panacea against the shock of meeting". The self, indeed, in its ultimate isolation, depends terribly much on others : among others its strength may seem to flow away from itself into others, yet when others are not there to share "how life withers". There are the moods when the self seems drained of everything, the internal drama to be without a single spectator, when no part of one's self seems living to answer the other self. That is the ebb and flow of life : now "to myself I am immeasureable", now "I exist only in the soles of my feet". Nor, though she gives it no prominence, does Virginia Woolf ignore the animal in man, "the brute, too, the savage" : the nice animal is always there in the acuteness of the senses.

Reading thus deeply into the human consciousness, Virginia Woolf keeps two aspects specially before us. Men and women exist in ultimate loneliness, but are incomprehensible except in their full setting : as she says of Mrs Dalloway, "to know her, or any one, one must seek out the people who completed them ; even the places". Secondly, what is visible is but a fragment of the whole, for below the surface are the depths of the subconscious, from which from time to time only small emanations proceed, and these are often unpredictable. Thus she presents her men and women with a humility rare in a novelist, seeming to declare that personality must remain finally inscrutable, beyond complete understanding. We see personality at moments unified, but can never analyse with certainty all the elements that make that unity, or know how many other different unities that same personality can at other times produce. Humble in this way herself, she hated those who would, in her phrase, "force the soul", trying to pierce and rifle its sacred privacy. All her books, including her essays and literary criticism, declare how she herself reacted to a vast range of things big and small, but always one has the impression of the looking forth of a personality which can at any moment retire to its inviolable privacy where its treasure is. She records this ebb and flow too in *The Waves*, where Rhoda cries, "I am sick of privacy", and Neville, "I need privacy", and each might at any moment reverse the feeling. In fact, the supreme achievement of Virginia Woolf was to face the facts of the human consciousness with an utter truthfulness within her limits, and, without preaching, to convey an ideal of sensitive living, open to joy and accepting pain and the mystery of things, and, as her incidental satire makes clear, contemptuous of all sham and of all unintelligent intrusion.

CHAPTER XVI

ALDOUS HUXLEY AND J. C. POWYS

The early novels of Aldous Huxley mirror the irresponsible disillusioned world that emerged after the 1914-18 war. In proportion to the whole nation it was a relatively small world : it was not the world of the hundreds of thousands who put their hopes in the League of Nations or continued their wartime comradeship in the British Legion. In the main it was the world of those who, having been spiritually maimed by the war, sought relief in cynical gaiety, and of the rising generation who had missed active service in the war and grew up to find all the old values questioned and to extend and take advantage of that questioning. It was a world of would-be intellectuals and artists, among whom all ideas were welcome that contradicted the tenets of their fathers. Aldous Huxley selected his fictional world out of this limited aspect of the larger reality.

Huxley himself had missed the experience of military service. Born in 1894 he left Eton at seventeen because of temporary blindness ; in the early years of the war he read for his degree in English at Oxford ; the rest of the war he spent in various useful activities which included work in a government office and teaching in a school. As far as it is possible to judge from his novels, the war made no deep impression on him : at least, references to the war are few there and in general jestingly cynical, though, since the novels are primarily a mirror of a certain kind of people, it is not safe to deduce from them their author's opinion with regard to all his characters say. After the war he turned journalist on the staff of the *Athenaeum*, then edited by Middleton Murry, but after a brief but very intensive spell of miscellaneous writing he soon made himself the most eminent of new contemporary writers by his short stories, novels and essays. Between two volumes of short stories, *Limbo* (1920)

and *Mortal Coils* (1922), came *Crome Yellow*, and the longer
novels *Antic Hay*, *Those Barren Leaves* and *Point Counter
Point* followed between 1923 and 1928. In these years he
expressed his attitude more directly in his essays, as in the
collection *Jesting Pilate* (1926).

His attitude at first was on the whole one of detached
inquisitive amusement at ridiculous, often rather pitiable,
human types, and the current ideas appropriate to each type.
If he was born to live in the Waste Land, Huxley would at
least enjoy it as far as his wit and curiosity could enable him,
without taking up any moral or indeed positive intellectual
position. But as the twenties passed into the thirties Huxley's
attitude changed. He had been greatly impressed by D. H.
Lawrence, whose friend he became and whose *Letters* he edited
after Lawrence's death, and his detachment became modified
by a mystical conception of the universe and by the belief
that what the world needed was a change of heart in individuals. He projected his own changing attitude in the novel
Eyeless in Gaza (1936) and gave his intellectual justifications
in *Ends and Means* (1937). Like Eliot, he had found a
solution in religion, but not in Christianity with its divine
hope. His conception of a change of heart in the individual
was akin to Auden's, but he did not share any of the political
faith or interest of Auden and his associates. In fact in the
thirties, though he changed with the times, he remained
essentially apart, eclectic alike in his mysticism and in his
sociology. In the forties, now in America, he stood apart
too in his novels from the second war, *After Many a Summer*
(1940) and *Time Must Have a Stop* (1945) being quite remote
from it, while his most serious contribution to thought was in
his historical biography *Grey Eminence* (1942). But the
growing threat of scientific invention, as revealed by the war,
intensified the dark views he held of mankind and its prospects, and in 1949 his novel of the future, *Ape and Essence*,
was grim and horrible beyond anything he had previously
written. The essays, *Themes and Variations* (1950), however,
were more constructive.

That Aldous Huxley should have stood out so sharply as one of the leading novelists of the day demonstrates the lapse of the novel from its former standards. From its beginning the English novel had varied greatly with the individual genius who had handled it, but always a healthy interest in human beings and the power to give them imaginative life had been the major justifications of the work of the English novelists. Because of those gifts they could, if such was their bent, dispense with plot. In contrast, Huxley gradually put in more plot and incident to compensate for the absence of vital characterisation. Huxley indeed always saw life at a distance, and used the novel, not because it was his true form, but because it was the popular form and would give him a public, before whom he could profitably indulge his love of writing, and his need for self-expression, and display his abundant ideas and his wealth of knowledge. His novels are primarily talk, at first amusing with its wit and satire, later purposefully seeking a beneficent truth, and then issuing the gloomiest warnings in profound despair.

His first novel, *Crome Yellow*, was little more than a conversation piece. In the manner of T. L. Peacock in *Headlong Hall* he assembled a house party where the odd assortment of guests, a set of self-centred egoists with no principles or aims, spend their time in talk, to which, unlike Peacock, he adds flirtation. All the latest ideas are aired—on art, education, sex, farming, applied science, social problems, church-going : it is a storehouse of current interests and attitudes. The intellectual atmosphere of the book dissolves the old certainties and dogmas. Huxley is amused at his creatures : the "hero", the young ineffective Denis Stone, laboriously trying to make himself a pagan, but "wretched about himself, the future, life in general, the universe", and finding "this adolescence business . . . horribly boring" ; the middle-aged Henry Wimbush wrapt in the past ; the sarcastic Scogan who lives for talking ; the painter Gombauld, whose cult is the eccentric ; the humbug Barbecue Smith, author of books of comfort and spiritual teaching ; Ivor, the young light-hearted amorist with a racing car ; the serious, rather stupid Mary,

who is troubled about her repressions. Silly or malignant
or posturing or out of touch with life, they are not an
attractive house party ; but it is an attractive book, a comedy
sparkling with light and not without beauty. Only an inset
short story, telling how two very cultured and pleasant dwarfs
were driven to suicide by their son, who was not a dwarf but
a big coarse and brutal young man, indicated the darker side
of Huxley's mind.

In *Antic Hay* Huxley expanded his treatment, but did not
change his method. Taking a character similar to the earlier
Denis Stone, he presented the young schoolmaster Theodore
Gumbril, lazy, uncertain of himself, yearning to be a "Rabe-
laisian man" who could enjoy life boldly and richly, and
putting on a false beard to play the part. His search for the
full pagan life, when he has invented pneumatic trousers and
left his school, gives the novel more, but still not much, story.
Again it is a small irresponsible world of the intelligentsia,
with no roots of any kind, and no moral or religious or political principles. But they are puppets rather than personalities,
or, more exactly, they are specimens of the human race,
English, of the nineteen-twenties, seen with unsympathetic
detachment and on the whole with an amused distaste.
When he makes one of his characters declare that "every
man is ludicrous if you look at him from the outside, without
taking into account what is going on in his heart and mind",
Huxley might be almost describing his own effect.

In *Antic Hay* his view of humanity still indeed inclined to
the ridiculous, and the dislike of humanity is rather expressed
by some of the characters than explicitly revealed by the
author. But the scene, though often cheerful and in the figure
of Gumbril senior almost idyllic, is considerably darker than
that of *Crome Yellow*. The recent world war is seldom
mentioned, but the tragic empty desolation of Mrs Viveash
is due to her lover's death in it, and the unsettling effects
of the war are manifest in the whole a-moral atmosphere.
Reaching out with a feverish frivolity for experiences to
alleviate the tedium of life the characters testify to a growing
breakdown in human living, of which another ominous sign

is the loss of human values by the young physiologist Shear-
water, who, wrapt in his research, does not try to understand
either his neglected wife or any other human being. But
Huxley maintains the detachment of an artist, content to
enjoy the ridiculous spectacle. Read now, this novel, like
T. S. Eliot's earlier poetry, reveals disease and sterility in
civilisation, but its first readers rather enjoyed the comedy.
The commercialising of the pneumatic trousers is not prominent, but its fun is pervasive. The charm of Gumbril
senior's passion for architecture and of his joy in the starlings
counteracts the impression of gloom and folly. Bojanus, the
tailor, may talk of class war and revolution, but he cheerfully
admits his attraction towards revolution to be quite frivolous.
In fact, however much the novel was a sermon between the
lines, it could be read with delight by the very kinds of people
it satirised.

Having won his public, Huxley proceeded to treat the
novel more seriously. *Those Barren Leaves*, however, though
much more substantial, differed little in kind. Again he
depended for story on a variety of love affairs. Making
Italy the setting, he gave much more background and indulged
in lengthy descriptions of scenery. He let his people talk
at even greater length. The result was a sprawling novel,
diffuse and discontinuous. He made an experiment in form
by employing the device of insertions from a character's
autobiography, and varied the device of the inset short story
by introducing a lengthy episode. The characters, as before,
are satirically observed types including a bizarre middle-aged
woman, a handsome young amorist, a middle-aged loquacious
satyr, an adventuress, and an ingenuous young girl. Once
more the unpleasant not only outnumber the pleasant, but
take up more of their creator's interest. One cannot help
feeling that there is an element of self-critical confession by
Huxley in Chelifer's entry in his autobiography: "I write
with care, earnestly, with passion even, just as if there were
some point in what I were doing . . . just as if I had a soul
to save by giving expression to [my thoughts]. But I am well
aware, of course, that all these delightful hypotheses are

inadmissible. In reality I write as I do merely to kill time and amuse a mind that is still, in spite of all my efforts, a prey to intellectual self-indulgence".

But now the detached artist is losing some of his humorous relish for the human specimens he puts on his puppet stage, and the disgusted puritan preacher emerges. One feels anger as well as amusement at this world of selfish love-making, with its "classy chats about the cosmos". By the end, it has become a novel with a purpose, that of analysing the disease of modern civilisation and of searching for a cure. From a talk on death between Cardan and Calamy, it broadens out with the contribution of Chelifer to the question of where modern civilisation is going and how such intelligentsia as themselves fit in. Calamy, seeking to end his conflict between asceticism and a love of philandering, decides to become a hermit, to study the interior life and seek personal salvation, but Chelifer holds it cowardly to run away from "the brutish life of humanity". Cardan thinks the dilemma of the sophisticated moderns to be that they are too conscious of themselves to be able to obey blindly, but too inept to behave in a reasonable manner on their own account. Huxley still takes no side, but he has made his characters face reality. To a world oppressed by "the sense that everything's perfectly provisional and temporary" he pointed out the necessity of finding fresh foundations.

In *Point Counter Point* (1928) he made a further advance both in form and in seriousness of purpose. Love of various kinds remained the substance of the story, and talk a principal element, but he built his structure more carefully and crowded his scene. It seemed as though he was determined to give his now big public a big novel, able to rival popular fiction in sensationalism. So he employed the old melodramatic device of a dying child to stop an elopement, brought about a murder and led from that to a grotesque scene in which it is not clear whether the issue is suicide or another killing. He did not greatly change his kind of character or his method of characterisation. The people were still types and specimens, while some were little more than cases from a psychological textbook, such as the permanent adolescent shocked by his mother's remarriage and the woman who never recovered from her uncle's sexual advances when she was a girl. In general, the characterisation was limited by the patterning of the love affairs—among the men, infatuation running parallel with hate, exuberant virility outside marriage, and soulful lechery, and among the women, the cold, the lustful, and the predatory. One of the most human figures was Elinor, a curious mixture of sense and simplicity, who is driven to thoughts of leaving her husband because in her deep love for him she grows soured by his inability to return her feelings. Huxley appeared at once attracted and repelled by the scene of largely irresponsible sexuality which he conjured up, but, although that made a large part of the surface of the novel, his serious concern with the problem of contemporary civilisation predominated over sex-interest in the novel's total effect.

In *Point Counter Point* in fact Huxley followed on from the end of *Those Barren Leaves*. What kind of man was best fitted to cope with the dilemma of civilisation? The answer which the novel seemed to suggest was a combination of the best points of the characters Philip Quarles and Mark Rampion. Philip, Elinor's husband, has a keen, searching, many-eyed intelligence, but is inhuman; Mark, the novelist's projection of his friend D. H. Lawrence, and embodying together with his wife the abounding joy of true marriage, is vital and human, but too flamboyant and headlong. Read between the lines, Huxley seemed to declare: "Humanise and vitalise the intelligence". As Rampion was made to say, there was little time to lose, if the world were to be saved—prophetically he gave only ten more years: and as for the contemporary world, its choice was death, and its destination hell.

Was there any hope in politics? Huxley allowed some serious, but not hopeful discussion between Quarles and Rampion, but he hardly took politics seriously himself in his own account of the British Freemen, with its burlesque humour and melodrama. What of science? Rampion, like

D. H. Lawrence, was bitterly anti-science. The elderly scientist, Lord Edward Tantamount, wrapt in his research, despises human beings, despairs of politics, sees the world squandering its riches, and would favour a revolution if it would reduce the population. He has a young assistant, capable as a scientist, but as a man embittered, class-conscious, jealous and unconstructive. By presenting such people and letting them talk, Huxley posed implicit questions and revealed his own anxiety. His own dislike of the world seemed to be increasing, but he could still be amused, and his satire of the insincerity of social gatherings and his con-temptuous humour at the humbug Burlap and the posturing procession of British Freemen lighten the novel. Indeed, he largely nullifies both the seriousness and the melodrama of the novel by ending with Burlap and his Beatrice splashing together in their bath. He was still disinclined avowedly to take sides, for the novelist, as he made Quarles say, should owe a loyalty only to the cool indifferent flux of intellectual curiosity. But Huxley was learning from Lawrence that the novelist must have more than an insatiable curiosity and an unrivalled power of assimilation : otherwise, he would be as much a misfit as his character, the novelist Philip Quarles.

Eight years then passed before his greatest achievement, *Eyeless in Gaza*, the gap being filled by the publication of essays, short stories, and poems, by the editing of Lawrence's Letters, and by the satiric fantasy, *Brave New World* (1932). The last was very popular, but it added nothing to Huxley's reputation as a novelist. Fully realising the value of science and of the scientific spirit, he was fully as much afraid of the kind of world its abuse and idolatry might produce, but in trying to present his fearful imagination he lacked the per-suasiveness of H. G. Wells. All that he had to say, he had already said cogently in half a dozen pages of talk in *Crome Yellow*. This unconvincing tale with unlikeable puppets did less than justice to his ideas.

Eyeless in Gaza, however, was in the true line of his development. The speculations about the nature of the novel in *Point Counter Point* had led him to a bold experiment in form. The story is told in three layers of time : in the foreground is the diary being kept by Anthony Beavis in 1934; below, are the events of August 1933, which gradually draw up to the time of the diary and finally overtake them ; below those again is the previous life of Anthony and his friends, also told in three layers, one between 1902 and 1904, one between 1912 and 1914, and one between 1926 and 1928. But the novelist does not keep to the chronological order : he shuffles the layers. We are early given an incidental justification of the method, when Anthony, turning over an album of snapshots, finds all kinds of associated ideas pouring into his mind and reflects that "somewhere in the mind a lunatic shuffled a pack of snapshots and dealt them out at random . . . There was no chronology". The novelist, however, controls the shuffling and the result is extraordinarily successful : the method suggests, too, the continuity of life, with the future implicit in the present and the past living in the present so that, looking backwards and forwards, one has a sense of destiny in cause and effect. This shuffling of chronology was Huxley's one striking development. Otherwise his handling of the novel followed his previous practice, but with greater strength. The people are types similar to their predecessors, and so are the varieties of sexual affairs. Satire and comedy again provide some of the most delightful reading, as in the comedy of the young girl who, dared by her sister to steal something from every shop they visit, does so to her own sick excitement and her sister's anguished fear. The physically horrible, pain, suicide and melodramatic possibilities reappear, and the later scenes in Mexico give Huxley, the travel-writer, his usual scope. The great difference is that Huxley had now at last avowedly written a novel with a purpose.

The purpose was to preach a reorientation of the individual life as the only means of saving civilisation. So, at the start, Anthony Beavis is presented as he was in 1933, detached, incapable of true love, refusing to accept any duties, a character determined by years of wasted and irresponsible living. Shocked suddenly out of this, he sets about his own salvation with the help of his diary : technically Huxley had now made his device of the inset extracts from a journal a fully integral feature. In 1934 Anthony is setting down his thoughts on the relation of mind to body, on the problem of true love, on the need of right personal relations. He realises that to obtain self-knowledge must be his first step to self-change. At the moment he has to confess that what besets him is indifference : "I can't be bothered with people", he says—just as the reader must have felt of the Huxley of the earlier novels. Neither the shock given Anthony in 1914 when a friend killed himself because of Anthony's irresponsible trifling with the girl his friend loved nor the 1914-18 war had affected his moral being, but had merely diverted his mind to a study of sociology.

Now in 1934 in his self-exploration he somewhat resembles Calamy in *Those Barren Leaves*, wanting to withdraw from life, but he struggles on to work out a technique of living, in which primary ideas are the need of true love between people, the subordination of personality to a moral order, and the rejection of the worship of the state. The intellectual sociologist has realised that social reform is not enough to cure the world's disease. Under the influence of Mark Staithes, a figure similar in conception to Mark Rampion, he goes to Mexico to join in a revolution, but is frustrated by an accident which leads to the amputation of a leg by a doctor who preaches to him about life-changing and the ill-effects of constipation. Back in England Anthony becomes a pacifist, ready to risk his life for that cause. Huxley's general support of Anthony's developing attitude is clear, and the novel, crowded with ideas and rich in satire, seemed to promise that a combination of heart and intellect might make Huxley a great positive novelist.

This promise was, however, to be disappointed. What his heart had learnt seemed unable to illuminate his intellectual vision. Knowing that he should love humanity, he saw it with his intellect with too devastating a clarity to embrace it. He saw human beings still as specimens of a genus capable of the vilest lusts and cruelties and of the most futile and malignant follies. The human body, which he loathed, came always between him and his spiritual vision. In *Ends and Means*,

which was the direct expression of the changed attitude he
had projected in Anthony Beavis, he had confessed that,
whereas earlier he had thought the universe to have no
meaning, now he acknowledged a spiritual reality behind the
show of things. But, though his view of life had become
mystical, he could not polarise his mysticism, certainly not
to Christianity. Christianity involved the Church, and he
feared institutions. He preferred a mysticism which acknowledged only a diffuse philosophic authority and which did not
exalt the divine possibilities of human personality. This was
the attitude implicit in his essays published in 1950, *Themes
and Variations*. As the outer scene of the world had grown
darker and darker, he had had nothing more positive to offer
than the mystical contemplation of a pacifist, and, like Auden,
the nineteen-forties had seen him withdrawn from England
to America. It was from America that came *The Perennial
Philosophy* (1946), in which he summed up his mystical faith
and denounced the egotism of the individual spirit. From
California came the three novels, *After Many a Summer,
Time Must Have a Stop*, and *Ape and Essence*.

The first two of these novels showed a falling off in scope,
in length, in sparkle, in total effect of meaning and artistry.
Huxley had narrowed his vision again. *After Many a Summer*
mocked at the corrupting effect of great wealth and exceeded
Swift in the horrible vision of bodily life greatly lengthened
until longevity turned its possessor into an ape. In *Time
Must Have a Stop*, a satiric comedy of people who might have
stepped out of *Those Barren Leaves*, he played with his
mysticism in depicting the struggles of the spirit of a middle-
aged devotee of the pleasures of the table and of sex, who
had died of apoplexy, to revisit the scenes of his pleasures and
to resist absorption into unity with the spirit of good behind
the universe. It was an unsuccessful *tour de force*, with some
of the old sparkle in the comedy, but weaker rather than
stronger for its author's conversion from his earlier attitude.

Ape and Essence once more displayed much of his former
power in writing, but the brilliance of his writing seemed
wasted in the extravagance of the contempt for humanity

which characterised the whole book. Imagining that a third
World War had taken place, in which New Zealand alone
had survived the ravages of atomic warfare, he lets some
New Zealanders, two hundred years later, arrive as explorers
at Los Angeles. The novel is a film script of their findings.
In the breakdown of civilisation mankind has become repulsive apes; babies, born deformed and idiot as a result of the
continued effects of atomic release, are sacrificed by eunuch
priests while their mothers are flogged. Nothing is admirable ;
the New Zealanders, if not equally degenerate, are worthless.
The publisher's advertisement described the novel as "a
cautionary tale" ; it was "a warning of what will happen if
we persist in present follies". The mind behind it seems one
in which no pity mitigates the author's contempt for humanity
and which is unhappily apt in the imagination of what is vile.
It was all warning, without hope or hint of escape. The
negative, critical side of Huxley had at this stage triumphed
and reduced the artist to a labourer in hell. Sixteen years
before, in *Brave New World*, he had warningly prophesied
that the growing power of science in a materially-minded
world might result in a world of dehumanised beings, their
happiness and pleasures the degenerate pastimes of slaves in
a soullessly efficient social organisation. In comparison with
the despairing hatred of humanity in *Ape and Essence* it had
been a cheerful vision. After the atomic bomb he seemed to
say that it was not the soulless brain that would triumph, but
humanity's basic devil-possessed brutishness. In drawing his
Yahoos Swift did not so abjure humanity.

From the point of view of the history of the novel,
Huxley's handling of the form was a variation of the traditional. After starting in the manner of Peacock, when he
passed on to a story-character combination increasingly ruled
by the purpose of stating an attitude to life and contemporary
problems as well as of airing ideas, Huxley was using the
novel much as Benjamin Disraeli and Charles Kingsley had
used it some eighty years before. But his personal qualities
were so marked that his kind of novel inclined to be eccentric

from the traditional. It is this quality of individual eccentricity that, together with a preoccupation with the psychology
of sex and a mystical interpretation of life, links him with the
more obvious eccentric, John Cowper Powys, though their
personal differences were enormous.

J. C. Powys never had or could have so wide a public as
Aldous Huxley, but his work was equally a product of the
times, and, like Huxley's, is indeed hardly conceivable out
of relation to the years after 1920. It appealed to a relatively
small, but to a devoted audience, for whom Powys was
something of a prophet speaking to hearts repelled by the
materialism of the age. Powys's output was not prolific,
being rather less than Huxley's in the novel, but the two
novels which stand out, *A Glastonbury Romance* (1933) and
Owen Glendower (1941), are both very substantial creations.
A Glastonbury Romance indeed runs to nearly twelve hundred
pages. Its story is fantastic enough. It centres on a huge
religious pageant culminating in the impersonation of Christ
upon the cross ; it tells of a mayor who is intent on re-creating
the religious glory of Glastonbury so that miracles shall once
more take place in a city of world-wide pilgrimage, which
is also a "commune", for communism is in the air too and
enters the mayor's mystical vision ; it contrasts with the
mayor's efforts the attempt of an industrialist to make
Glastonbury the scene of vast industrial development ;
throughout run love affairs, intense whether in their rare
normality or in their more usual abnormality ; and the novel
ends with a great flood. Yet the strange, often grotesque
improbability of it all, is conveyed with a searching psychological realism. Though many of his characters might, like
Huxley's, be cases in a psychological textbook, in contrast to
Huxley, Powys showed true creative power of a Shakespearian
kind working from within his creatures, so that they live
in their own right. He was indeed the supreme instance in
this period of the creative artist absorbing and bringing to
life the teachings of the psycho-analysts, excelling even Joyce
in his artistic command of his material.

J. C. Powys, indeed, invites several comparisons. Another comparison with Joyce is in the wealth of esoteric knowledge woven closely into the fabric of the novel. Again, the world of Glastonbury has a richly crowded humanity comparable to that of Joyce's Dublin, but without the depressing sordidness of that world. He rivals Virginia Woolf in presenting his people in such a way that we live constantly in their internal world of thoughts, memories and feelings and are immersed in the flow of consciousness. His characters, with all their odd twists and complexities, exhibit themselves as the unity in complexity which we know to be true of ourselves and which Virginia Woolf conveyed with such success, notably in Mr Ramsay. He is one of those moderns in whom the senses are once more fully alive at the end of every nerve, and his pages are full of evocations of sense impressions as near as anything in literature to making the reader apprehend the actuality— again we think of the sense impressions of the children in the first section of Virginia Woolf's *The Waves* in comparison.

That his novels became controlled by a mystical view of life links him not only with the Huxley of the middle period but with D. H. Lawrence, to whom he is in fact closer in "prophetic" quality and in a tendency to over-write both his mysticism and the emotional sensitivity of his characters. Like Lawrence, he makes his characters very keenly aware of the psychic atmosphere, of all that is going on between and below any words spoken. It is a valuable element in his truth to life, but the tendency to overwrite can be seen in such a characteristic passage as the following :—

> "John had his own secret and peculiar method of sounding a stranger's intellectual and emotional nature. It was a kind of etheric, psychic embrace . . . The truth is that for John the soul of every person he met was something that he was doomed to explore. His own soul was like a vaporous serpent, and it rushed forth from the envelope of his body and wound itself round this other, licking this other's eye-sockets with its forked tongue, peering into its heart and into its brain, and pressing a cold snake-head against its feverish nerves."

The mystical philosophy of Powys received separate expression in a series of lectures delivered in America and published as *In Defence of Sensuality*. But the ideas so pervade *A Glastonbury Romance* that sympathetic reading of the book demands at least partial acceptance of the mysticism if the reader is to enter fully into the author's presentation of his characters. He writes in terms of a First Cause with a double nature, benevolent and malicious, in which First Cause everything has its existence. Nothing in the universe is in this view merely material, but all material objects possess an animation which responds to the psychic emanations of the First Cause, "the magnetic energy that moves and disturbs the lethargy of Matter". The sun has "enormous fire-thoughts . . . evoking a turbulent aura of psychic activity" ; there are "the vast, dreamy life-stirrings of the soul of the earth" ; the moon especially has a potent psychic force ; there are "the sub-human breathings of the plants in the conservatory" ; and a room can fall "into the most intense attitude of strained expectancy". Obviously, in this view of the universe human beings are susceptible to an infinite range of influences and those are nearest the secret of living who accept the First Cause, whether it sends pain or pleasure, sinking themselves in the primal forces : distress, and disaster lie in the struggles of non-acceptance. For the First Cause is not impersonal, but "a Personality, a living Person ; and there is *that* in Personality which is indetermined, unaccountable, changing at every second", and it is therefore a fundamental need of all men to respond to it. His mystical philosophy also in part accounts for the predominating place held by the sex life in his creatures ; in fact, the philosophy demands it, for "what mortals call Sex is only a manifestation in human life, and in animal and vegetable life, of a certain spasm, a certain delicious shudder, a certain orgasm of a purely psychic nature, which belongs to the Personality of the First Cause".

All this commentary on the First Cause is an integral part of the novel. It may be overdone at times, but it could not be separated from the whole. That it tends to be overdone was perhaps rather a tribute to the need felt by the novelist of countering the current materialistic philosophies. But the abundance of the commentary is also due to the generous scale on which the author's talent works : his mind is creative, massive and subtle and requires space to spread itself. Lacking the passionate impetuosity of his fellow anti-materialist and worshipper of a "natural" sexual life, D. H. Lawrence, he shows a more sure control of the novel as a whole than Lawrence, and his subtle-minded humour counterbalances his tendency to excess in the philosophic or sexual direction.

Though *A Glastonbury Romance* was a great achievement, *Owen Glendower* was superior, and it is perhaps the greatest example of the historical novel in this century. Owen Glendower is the Welsh prince of Shakespeare's *Henry IV*, and in the hands of Powys the man, the prince and the age, the early fifteenth century, are shown with all the vital complexity characteristic of the treatment in *A Glastonbury Romance*. Indeed all the qualities already referred to appear there, except that the author's attitude to life is more intimately absorbed into the novel. It is on the grand scale : one has the national scene, English and Welsh, the political, religious and economic aspects, soldiers, courtiers and peasants, fighting, loving, worshipping, singing, plotting. Medieval religion and Welsh mysticism clearly had a great appeal to Powys and he is deeply learned in them. His technique is as before, presenting both the inner and the outer life, and many of his historical figures have dark twists of soul and a tortured eroticism like his moderns. The novel is indeed a wonderful application to the past of the psychological and historical knowledge of a penetrating modern mind, humorist and mystic, which is drawn to the darker aspects of human nature but reacts with a fascinated sensitiveness to all life. His great virtue as a novelist lies in his deep and sympathetic knowledge of human nature and his conviction that life, even in pain, is a glorious experience. He did not try to run away from modern civilisation like Lawrence, or hate humanity like Huxley, or help to paralyse the nerves of living like Joyce.

CHAPTER XVII

GRAHAM GREENE AND ELIZABETH BOWEN

By 1940 Graham Greene had come to stand out as the most individual of the younger novelists. Each novel he wrote, strong and clear-cut in its apprehension of good and evil, and efficiently direct in its streamlined expression, had added to his stature. The first was *The Man Within* in 1929, when he was in his middle twenties. *It's A Battlefield* appeared in 1934, *England Made Me* in 1935, *Brighton Rock* in 1938. *The Power and the Glory* of 1940 was generally recognised as marking the fulfilment of his great promise. The war broke the continuity, for he was employed first at the Ministry of Information and later worked in West Africa. In 1943, however, he published a thriller, *The Ministry of Fear*, which he called an "entertainment", under which name he also classed *Stamboul Train* (1932) and *A Gun for Sale* (1936). His next novel was *The Heart of the Matter* (1948), which fully confirmed, but hardly raised his earlier reputation. His other principal literary work was *Journey Without Maps* (1936), a record of a journey through the jungles of West Africa and containing valuable autobiographical material, and *The Lawless Roads* (1939), also a travel book. In 1950 he published the script of his notable film, *The Third Man*. *The Lost Childhood* (1951) is a volume of literary criticism.

His first novel, *The Man Within*, had a historical setting of eighteenth-century smuggling, whereas all the others are of contemporary life, but it started the theme on which the later novels were to play their variations, the theme of betrayal, betrayal of the better self as well as of others. There is internal and external conflict : on the one hand, a young smuggler is divided within himself ; on the other, is the conflict of the excisemen and the law against the smugglers. In *It's A Battlefield* we are in the world of twentieth-century police involved in suppressing communist-inspired rioting; there is again the betrayal by a man of his better self, and, in the figure of the Police Commissioner, an exemplification of the idea of impersonal duty, anticipating the study of the Mexican lieutenant of police in *The Power and the Glory*.

The full possibilities of Greene showed first in *England Made Me*. Centring on a story of high international finance, this largely consists of a study of the moral decline in certain English types as met in Sweden, which is the scene of the novel. Krogh, who from the humblest beginnings has built up a great concern whose finances run into millions, symbolises the ruthless impersonality of international finance. Krogh is happy only with figures: "there was nothing he couldn't do with them, there was nothing human about them". He is the slave of his own success, hardly able any more to enjoy human pleasures, but driven on by the momentum of his vast industrial concern to make it vaster still. In that pursuit he has no scruples: legality and honesty go overboard automatically, and lies and frame-ups are a natural technique, devoid of any personal feeling for or against his victims. The novel ends with the elimination of a potentially dangerous man by the passionate loyalty of an old friend of Krogh's, now subordinate to him, who commits the murder as a matter of simple necessary expediency. This is the background to the group of English figures: Kate, secretary and mistress to Krogh; her twin brother Anthony, taken on for a few days as Krogh's bodyguard; Minty, a shabby journalist; Loo, a girl on holiday from Coventry with her parents. There is also a glimpse of the English legation at Stockholm.

It is not a wide range, but there is variety enough to suggest several aspects of the moral decline from the standards of the previous generation of the England that made them and which continues to exert on most a nostalgic appeal. Kate and Anthony have their living to make. Kate makes hers efficiently, as a business woman without scruples: it was a changed world, "a new frontierless world, with Krogh's on every exchange; one believed in having no scruples while one got what one wanted most: security". For her, no more of the "old honesties and the old dusty poverties", and to her it seemed that "love's no good to anyone". But her weakness lay in her devotion to her brother Anthony, who had "resigned" from one job after another all round the world, and whose "charm" and fluent salesmanship of himself inspired distrust at first sight. Anthony too was unscrupulous in his way, but with him there was always a point where his conventional conscience intervened: as Kate saw it, "he wasn't unscrupulous enough to be successful. He was in a different class to Krogh". He held that "one couldn't go lower by any club standard than to ask for work from your sister's lover", and, though he did so, it rankled and when his latest lover told him his work was also not "respectable" he decided to return to England and follow up his affair with the girl from Coventry. The hunger for irresponsible, easy, sensuous, but "respectable" living led to his betraying the secrets of Krogh and so to his death, a failure to his sister as well as to himself. His failure had begun at school and so had Minty's. Minty is haunted by his sense of inferiority born of bullying and contempt at Harrow. A shabby, compulsory ascetic, a woman-hater, and a superstitious Anglo-Catholic, he trembles on the edge of seedy nonentity: "he had been slowly broken in by parents, by schoolmasters, by strangers in the street. Crooked and yellow and pigeon-chested, he had his deep refuge, the inexhaustible ingenuity of his mind". As for Loo from Coventry, in spite of her worship of respectability, she has no use for the stuffiness of her parents, and lives for the physical satisfaction of casual affairs.

These characters emerge, partly by direct description and dialogue, partly through rather bare inner monologue, with a somewhat thin but lively credibility, but it is not so much they and their story as the general idea of the novel that remains in the mind. This is the decline of a class. Kate could not help reflecting that "there had been a straightness about the poor national past which the international present did without. It hadn't been very grand, but in their class at any rate there had been gentleness and kindness once". She and Anthony are adrift in this new world. "We're done, we're broke, we belong to the past, we haven't the character or the energy to do more than hang on to something for what we can make out of it." "Her dusty righteous antecedents pulled at her heart, but with all her intellect she claimed alliance with the present, this crooked day, this inhumanity." That is the final impression, "this crooked day, this inhumanity". It matches the impression left by some of Eliot's earlier poetry : we are reminded of that world of dying culture, international finance, fruitless sexuality. The failure is within the soul and the will, and in Greene's handling of it there is something of Eliot's pity, pity for the very human fumbling in a twilight between two worlds. It is as Anthony reflected :—

> "They [such as he and Minty] hadn't the resources to hold their place, but the world had so conditioned them that they hadn't the vigour to resist. They were not fresh enough, optimistic enough, to believe in peace, co-operation, the dignity of labour, or if they believed in them, they were not young enough to work for them. They were neither one thing nor the other; they were really only happy when they were together: in the clubs of foreign capitals, in pensions, at old boys' dinners, momentarily convinced by the wine they couldn't afford that they believed in something : in the old country, in the king, in 'shoot the bloody Bolsheviks', in the comradeship of the trenches."

They are pitiable in their dying loyalties. It is the new world's loyalty, as in Krogh's associate, which is strong even to violence ; the loyalty of Minty to the Harrow where he was bullied is a mere refuge, like his devotion to St Zephyrinus. Greene does not force our pity. He does not overdo the self-pity of Anthony ; he leaves Kate on the last page "simply moving on", seeing with a sad clarity, "We're all thieves. Stealing a livelihood here and there and everywhere, giving nothing back". Greene, indeed, handled *England Made Me* with an artistic detachment which could allow the intrusion of the farcical comedy of Hammarsten, the decayed teacher of languages and part-time journalist, with his dream of putting on the Swedish stage his translation of Shakespeare's *Pericles*.

In his next three novels Graham Greene maintained his detachment as a narrator, avoiding emotional colouring and direct sympathy, but, himself a Roman Catholic, he presented life in terms of the faith of the Roman Catholic Church, in the main objectively through the minds of his characters, yet with some restrained personal commentary. The general effect is of a Roman Catholic telling a story with a severe care for fact, making no parade of his faith, which, however, he cannot conceal, and preaching no obvious moral, since the grimly pathetic stories should arouse in any thoughtful reader an anxious questioning of his own faith and a testing of his own values in the light of the events and people he has met. Each of these three novels is, indeed, a commentary in novel form on the world, the flesh and the devil. In each there are people who know that God exists and who, even if they sin against him, do so in full knowledge of their sinning; and over against them are set the materialists, who do not believe in God and cannot therefore think in terms of sin. It is this clear, constant religious approach that differentiated these novels of Greene's from those of most of his contemporaries. Other novelists dealt with the underworld, as Greene did in *Brighton Rock*; others too treated of the destructive force of materialistic tyranny, as Greene did in *The Power and the Glory*. Only Greene wrote in terms of heaven and hell.

Brighton Rock was a further development in the narrowing of the novel, as already seen in the regional novel. Here one small class, the parasites of the gambling world, are studied almost exclusively as seen in a thin two-mile stretch of Brighton bordering its promenade. The main impression given is of a sordid underworld where some aspire to power by violence and to the wealth which will open to them the luxury suites of the Cosmopolitan. It is the author's purpose to make us aware of this cancerous growth in modern civilisation, and in concentrating to that end he has no scope to introduce the ordinary everyday human life of Brighton. One is aware of the crowds on the promenade, but they serve only

to give a grim contrast of empty, noisy sunlit life against the
dark world where razors slash, and fear and violence contract
the heart. For it is this dark world that engages not only
Greene's artistic energies but his avowed sympathy. In the
dark world there is knowledge of God : the open daylight
world is a godless world, an irresponsible world responsible
in its ignorance of God for the mortal sins of the dark world.
So he presents a vivid picture of the slum-girl Rose, badgered
by the breezy, "normal" Ida : "The Nelson Place eyes stared
back at her without understanding ; driven to her hole the
small animal peered out at the bright and breezy world :
in the hole were murder, copulation, extreme poverty,
fidelity, and the love and fear of God : but the small animal
had not the knowledge to deny that only in the glare and open
world outside was something which people called experience".

On the story level *Brighton Rock* has two main themes
which are entwined : the hunting down of the young gangster
Pinkie by Ida, a story whose elements of crime and detection
are as well handled as in a good thriller, involves the story
of Pinkie's efforts first to fulfil his ambitions and hatreds and
then, as Ida presses on, to escape the pursuit by further
murder and by marriage. But neither story nor psychology
was Greene's primary concern : they were the vehicle for his
exposition of the problem of good and evil in a world predominantly godless. The huntress Ida personifies for Greene
a type of middle-class materialist common in the modern
world : full of vitality, quite sure that life is worth living,
hail-fellow-well-met, confident that she knows the difference
between right and wrong but sexually free because "it's
natural", she finds in the hunting of Pinkie fun, another of
the excitements of living. Instead of in religion, she believes
in law and order : she upholds the law of "an eye for an eye"
with "terrible lightheartedness". Greene speaks of her "ruthless vitality" and declares "there was something dangerous
and remorseless in her optimism". That her pursuit has led
to another murder and ended in the suicide of Pinkie and the
misery of Rose is nothing to her. Not once does she reflect
on what has made Pinkie and Rose what they are. Nor

indeed does Greene himself present that aspect as fully as he has analysed Ida.

Simply stated, it is the terrible slum of his childhood that filled Pinkie with anger and hatred against the world and with a furious loathing of the "game" of sex. At seventeen, Roman Catholic as he is, he will commit mortal sin and accept damnation with a proud, soured egotism. We have to accept that life has so conditioned him that nothing else is possible. Revisiting the slum to bargain with Rose's parents, "he looked with horror round the room : nobody could say he hadn't done right to get away from this, to commit any crime". But if he oversimplifies the presentation of Pinkie, Greene does not sentimentalise it. The weakness in characterisation is rather that he depersonalises Pinkie ; we never quite lose the sense of the impersonal given by the anonymous epithet "the Boy" at the beginning. Pinkie is a soul driven to choose damnation, and slum-bred Rose, the good which he feels to be an inevitable complement to his evil, must follow him. What Greene leaves us in no doubt of is the unbridgeable abyss between the religious and the unreligious. As Rose says of Ida, "I'd rather burn with you [Pinkie] than be like Her . . . she's ignorant", so, when Rose whispers to Ida "Confession . . . repentance", Ida's reply is one of total failure to understand : "That's just religion . . . Believe me. It's the world we got to deal with". Successful as the novel is as a thriller, it is the religious mind behind which leaves the final impression, when the priest assures Rose : "You can't conceive, my child, nor can I or any one—the . . . appalling . . . strangeness of the mercy of God". That Greene sends Rose to a last pitifully cruel disillusionment at the very end is an indirect token of his pity for the victims of the social wrong which breeds such evil.

In *The Power and the Glory* Greene made an advance in nearly every way. His new theme, that of the struggle between Church and State, transcended the earlier themes. Those had been indeed wide themes : the lowered moral standards of English people of a tired generation in the new world of international finance were a symptom of a disease stretching far outside the circle Greene drew; the gangster-dom of Brighton was another symptom of disease in modern civilisation equally worldwide. But these were diseases of classes and special ways of life. All might certainly be said to share in responsibility for the social evil exposed in *Brighton Rock*, but comparatively few were directly affected by it. In contrast, by the authoritarian suppression of religion the way of life of a whole nation must be affected, men, women, and children. Moreover, though the theme of the contest between religious faith and secular tyranny was a painfully topical one, it had not the more limited topicality of the earlier themes: what he had dealt with before had been diseases particularly arising in current civilisation, whereas the contest of Church and State is a universal and timeless contest. Greene's method was the same as before: to take a particular place, this time Mexico, and to let the universal meaning spread out in the reader's consciousness.

Writing with his customary artistic detachment, Greene would not heighten his effect by any stimulus to be drawn from topical instances whose grim threatenings were nearer at hand. He seems deliberately, though he himself had visited Mexico, to have chosen a setting remote from the doorsteps of his audience. The alien landscape and setting, as usual overdrawn neither in colour nor in sordidness, with the alien types of people predominating over the few English types, check facile reactions on the reader's part, but in compensation there is on Greene's part a more freely flowing sympathy of interpretation. The whisky priest in particular is drawn with an understanding approaching love and pity, which exceeds that accorded to Pinkie and Rose—and the portrait of Ida had been partially touched with a quality of caricature by her creator's apparent antagonism. Finally, the story was freed from the limits which crime and detection are bound to some extent to impose. Here, as the whisky priest is hunted to his death, the hunt still holds some of our interest, but now the psychology of the man is of far more interest than what happens to him.

It is the priest's belief in God and the Church that controls his life. He is weak in the flesh , a "whisky priest" with a daughter; he is deeply afraid of pain; he is "aware of his own desperate inadequacy"; but, the only surviving priest not to compromise with the secular power, he knows he can still give God to the people and absolve their sins. Very different from the martyr of edifying religious stories, he is nevertheless one who unhesitatingly goes into the trap which must lead to his death, because he cannot refuse a dying man confession and absolution. As with Pinkie, there is something of anonymity about him, and Greene's concern is as much with his faith as with the man himself, yet he has personality and a life-history as Greene draws him. Greene's insistence, indeed, is on the undying power and glory that shine through lives however flawed by weakness : they cannot be quenched, and if apparently the last priest is caught another will come. Against this the secular power is bound to fail. The lieutenant of police who burns with zeal to extirpate the Church is disinterested in his ambition; the priest acclaims him "a good man"; he has human feelings; he hates poverty. But he has a superior who is corrupt; the secular tyranny has created distrust between all men. Talking to the lieutenant, the priest makes the telling comment, as Greene sees it, on the difference between the two sides : "It's no good your working for your end unless you're a good man yourself. And there won't always be good men in your party. Then you'll have all the old starvation, beating, get-rich-anyhow". Against and amid the everlasting temptations of the world, the flesh and the devil, the Church's work can go on with weak servants, but the only end of secular power is corruption.

How far that corruption can go, Greene shows by abundant restrained detail. But Greene declared a faith that humanity will always triumph, and so this novel differed totally from a book such as Huxley's *Eyeless in Gaza*. When Huxley had come to see that godlessness was the cause of human disaster, his mysticism had neither the strength of Greene's certainty nor the humility of his sense of the mystery of God's mercy.

In *The Heart of the Matter* Greene, except for making the scene of the novel West Africa in the recent war, gave up topicality. His theme is embodied in Scobie, who commits the mortal sin of suicide that he may solve, as he hopes, the problem of securing the happiness of the two women he loves : what if a man accepts damnation for himself (Scobie is a Roman Catholic) out of love and pity for others ?   The answer is hinted in the priest's words to the widow :

> " 'For goodness sake, Mrs Scobie, don't imagine you —or I—know a thing about God's mercy'.
>
> 'The Church says . . .'.
>
> 'I know the Church says. The Church knows all the rules. But it doesn't know what goes on in a single human heart'."

It is the human heart that is Greene's primary concern here. Major Scobie, a police officer whose devotion to duty wins the respect of all, is corrupted by love and pity both into sin and into breach of duty. He is not a hunted man, as in the earlier books, though he is spied on, but he is hunted by his conscience and his love of God. It is the human soul fighting its battle alone for the ultimate truth underlying the surface presented by the circumstances of the world, and in showing this Graham Greene brought the novel close again to the example set by Conrad, the spectacle of man at odds with destiny, though without the colour and poetry of Conrad. Greene's Roman Catholicism disciplines his approach, as his austerely effective style does his treatment, but neither constricts his handling of the human heart. He cannot, like Virginia Woolf, let the waves rise and fall outside the will of God, but there is no defined limit to the pity with which he looks on the dilemma of sinful humanity. After all, as Scobie reflects, the riddle of the world's unhappiness may extend far beyond this world.

> "Point me out the happy man and I will point you out either egotism, selfishness, evil—or else an absolute ignorance.
>
> Outside the rest-house he stopped again. The lights inside would have given an extraordinary impression of peace if one hadn't known, just as the stars on this

clear night gave also an impression of remoteness,
security, freedom. If one knew, he wondered, the facts,
would one have to feel pity even for the planets ? if one
reached what they called the heart of the matter?''

Elizabeth Bowen, except that she too from about 1930
came to stand out as a novelist of exceptional individuality,
had little in common with Graham Greene. Certainly for both
the human heart was what most interested them, and
both felt the pressure of the times upon human character ;
both, but Elizabeth Bowen especially, watched keenly the
disintegration of the survivors of the Edwardian middle class
as the conditions which had bred them passed away. But,
while Elizabeth Bowen, like Greene, had an artistic detachment, she had as well a satiric aloofness of judgment in strong
contrast with his Roman Catholicism. In place of his hard,
often laconic style, she wrote a delicate, subtle style, with a
feminine sensitiveness that sought precision not by brevity
but by a patient use of little strokes. To put the contrast
broadly, Greene, his Catholicism apart, drew near to the
"tough" writing of Ernest Hemingway, while Elizabeth
Bowen was close to Virginia Woolf. Chronologically, however, they ran a parallel course. Elizabeth Bowen got off the
mark the better of the two with *The Last September* in 1929,
and then in the thirties in their very different ways their novels
came out similarly spaced, Elizabeth Bowen's including *The
House in Paris* and *The Death of the Heart* (1938). After the
latter, like Greene after *The Power and the Glory*, Elizabeth
Bowen let several years pass until *The Heat of the Day*
appeared in 1949.

What Elizabeth Bowen had in common with Virginia
Woolf was a similarity of background and outlook. Elizabeth
Bowen, as *The Last September* shows, had Ireland too as part
of her heritage, but the younger woman shared Virginia
Woolf's acquaintance with the cultured, stable English civilisation of comfort and leisure which survived, with increasing
disintegration, the impact of the first World War. It was
her pleasure to depict this slowly changing scene with an
ironically sympathetic understanding, and part of the pleasure

given by her work is in her comedy of manners, as when, notably in *The Death of the Heart* but frequently in all her work, she presents the clash of new and old in the social scene : on the obsolescent graces of the older generation and the brash crudities of the younger she turns an eye sparkling with amusement and wit and she is particularly diverted by the clash of class differences. But her approach to life is far more comprehensive than that of the social satirist. With less intensity, less warmth, less richness in her humanity than in Virginia Woolf's, she still has those qualities, and with them an interpretation of life, again less penetrating than Virginia Woolf's, but nevertheless getting well beneath the surface. Life, in her clear mirror, flows rippling on. The mirror cannot but impose something of a pattern, but the impression her tales always leave is, as with Virginia Woolf's novels, that of continuity : nothing breaks off sharply, the edges of life are undefined, its continuations are indefinably hinted. Tragedy and comedy intertwine inextricably : life is never, for any sustained space of time, either the one or the other. Though she employs only in a considerably modified way Virginia Woolf's technique of the flow of the inner consciousness, she does similarly take us into the minds and feelings of her people and thus we again realise that there is no simple black and white about life, but the texture is complex, the constituents everlastingly shifting : there is a continuous ebb and flow, the inrush of the past, the pressure of the "unapprehendable inner wills of the dead", the diffused influences of a present environment at the mercy of chance. So we have a view of life closely similar in essentials to that behind *The Waves* : life carries on the young to middle age, the middle-aged to death, and it is enough to watch the course of things reflectively without speculating beyond the present world's limits. Above all we are aware of the isolation in which the individual stands : however men jostle, come into contact, influence and are influenced, they remain islands, between which any bridges are temporary.

Elizabeth Bowen has other qualities in common with Virginia Woolf. She too has her mind and her senses in an intimate union, so that, while we know what her characters think and feel, we are at the same time alive to the reactions of their senses and to the whole atmosphere of their being, in sky and landscape, house and garden, clothes and meals. She could hardly rival the extraordinary fulness of the life of the senses as Virginia Woolf reveals it, but the lesser vitality of her characters does not ask for such fulness ; a character like Stella in *The Heat of the Day* does not vibrate to London life as vividly as Mrs Dalloway—as excitedly as Mrs Dalloway would have reacted to that later London world Elizabeth Bowen portrays. But our senses are always being appealed to by an observer who is more obviously feminine than Virginia Woolf : physical details of the body, careful appraisal of dress, match the insight into feminine moods.

Like Virginia Woolf, she brings out clearly the differences between men and women, and like her too sees more surely into her women than into her men—indeed, on the whole, she falls below Virginia Woolf in her presentation of men, and she seems too feminine to attain Virginia Woolf's sense of the ultimate duality of masculine and feminine, at least she does not express it. Where she rivals Virginia Woolf, however, is in the portrayal of childhood and youth, though again it is with girls that she excels : one of her favourite themes is the isolation of children in their child's world within but apart from the adult world. A similarity between the two novelists in psychological approach lies in the acknowledgment of the real existence in human intercourse of the words that have not been said ; it is part of the fundamental sincerity with which they seek to reproduce as far as possible the actuality of life. In the like sincerity, she also kept her social scene within the fairly narrow class limits of her own knowledge, and in doing so avoided, like Virginia Woolf, any tendency to use the novel for propaganda.

The Heat of the Day showed Elizabeth Bowen's way of handling the novel to be unchanged after her eleven years' silence. Her picture of war-time London has the quality given by emotion recollected in tranquility, as has the Irish picture in *The Last September* : we breathe the essential atmosphere, but only now and then does she give that peculiar vividness which endows a scene with the urgent freshness of the actual moment, as when we read how Stella "scooped up the cat and stood with it held against her : its fur seemed to shrink and dampen as a stick of bombs fell diagonally across the middle distance".

The outer things of London are not stressed, the crowds, the noise, the bustle and business of life, but we are aware of the war-time camaraderie, the sense of a beleagured community, living in the moment, convention and morals loosened, where all are too busy to bother about their neighbours' private affairs, though ready to share and alleviate their pains and sorrows. Indeed, the autumnal quiet of the opening in Regent's Park sets the tone of the whole novel, even as autumn is the setting of many of her tales, as though that season were particularly satisfy-ing to the novelist's quiet eye that lingers with a steady brooding reflectiveness on her subjects. What would in others be an excuse for sensationalism, she tones down so that the thoughts and feelings of her characters can be apprehended the more sensitively. Perhaps because of this natural aversion from overstatement she does not achieve the full possibilities of her theme, the cancer of treachery which can destroy a man otherwise lovable. Through Stella's thoughts she speaks of the period between the wars as twenty years of "a clear-sightedly helpless progress towards disaster", and of "the fate-ful course of her fatalistic century", but neither this theme nor the reasons which lead Robert to work against his country are fully developed. Instead we are let into the secrets of Stella's heart, from the time she is warned of her lover's treachery until he confesses it to her. That is the core of the book, a psychological study at once detailed and reticent. suggestive rather than analytical. Stella, as lover and mother, lives with a quiet reality, which, however, is hardly given to Robert and still less to her would-be lover, Harrison. As a supplementary story we have the working girl, Louie, and her friend Connie in Civil Defence, a strand woven in some-what after the manner of the story of the Smiths in Virginia

Woolf's *Mrs Dalloway* but without so obvious an intention as there, though Louie's relapse into feckless affaires is due to her finding that Stella's life too was outside moral convention.

The comedy of the novel resides mainly in the picture of Robert's mother and sister, in sketching whom Elizabeth Bowen enjoys, as she had often done before, the diversion, to the verge of caricature, of laughing at the absurdities of middle-class women. And again characteristic of her is the charm with which she invests her sketch of the Irish estate bequeathed to Stella's son, which settles in the memory with an appeal almost out of proportion to its place in the novel. Yet the settled neutral peace of that Ireland stands as positive against the negative disturbed values of the war-time world. There lies continuity by the modifying of established traditions, but still we cannot fail, in the context of this novel, to remember that, in that world too, the same law holds, namely that "the relation of people to one another is subject to the relation of each to time, to what is happening". So the novel, in a way typical of all her work, shows us people acting under the pressure of the current time, "creatures of history" and creatures of the day. This contemplative vision of human life, focussing on the individual but making us aware of the wide fringes of his life, expressed with exceptional artistry, lifted Elizabeth Bowen above most of her contemporaries. In her technique one of her outstanding gifts is her skill in developing character and story simultaneously by dialogue : while her people talk, they take on life, they change, and the mechanics of the story move. To sum up, where Virginia Woolf found it necessary to revolutionise the writing of the novel, Elizabeth Bowen showed how it was possible to employ similar talents in the revivifying of a traditional novel.

CHAPTER XVIII

THE SHORT STORY

The short story was a late development in England. Until about 1890 it had only a casual existence as the occasional by-product of a novelist. In the eighteenth century Fielding, following the example of Cervantes, had used the short tale as an insertion in a long novel, and a century later Dickens did so too. One of the best short stories inserted in a novel was Wandering Willie's Tale in Scott's *Redgauntlet*. It was the middle of the nineteenth century before even the short story which is a novel in brief was written to stand by itself or to be grouped in a volume like George Eliot's *Scenes of Clerical Life*. Anthony Trollope and Mrs Gaskell were among the first to write a few self-contained short stories. By 1860, however, in America, France and Russia the short story had become a notable literary form. In America there had been the tales of Edgar Allan Poe, in France those of Balzac, in Russia those of Gogol and Turgenev, and in all those countries much more was done in this form by the end of the century, above all by Bret Harte and Ambrose Bierce in America, Maupassant in France, and Tchekhov in Russia. In the twentieth century Maupassant and Tchekhov were to have a particularly strong influence on the English short story, but when about 1890 the English short story first showed signs of becoming an important and popular literary form it was from the originality of Kipling and Wells that its power came, with some indebtedness on the part of Wells to Poe, just as the Sherlock Holmes stories by Conan Doyle owed something to Poe.

Individualism indeed marks the first considerable development of the short story in England. The early years of the twentieth century saw the humorous stories by W. W. Jacobs about his sailor trio Sam Small, Peter Russet and Ginger Dick and his rascally poacher Bob Pretty, the fantastic tales of G. K. Chesterton, whose *Club of Queer Trades* (1905) was, however, partly in the wake of R. L. Stevenson's *New Arabian Nights*, the deliciously ironic, whimsical and wise *Wallet of Kai Lung* (1900) by Ernest Bramah, Conrad's *Youth* and *Typhoon* volumes, preceded by *Tales of Unrest* (1898), and Kenneth Grahame's sketches of childhood in *The Golden Age*. Kipling, too, now well past his first journalistic anecdotes, *Plain Tales from the Hills* (1887), had produced a wide variety of short stories, opening up Indian life more fully and deeply, both human and animal, writing of machines and sea-serpents and many moving and adventurous matters on land and sea, and in *Puck of Pook's Hill* (1908) he achieved the high and difficult work of recreating the past of England in a way to delight the imagination at once of children and their elders.

"Saki" (H. H. Monro) applied a highly stylised individual wit to the English upper class social and domestic scene, and of his very different social scene Arnold Bennett contributed the two volumes of short stories, *Tales of the Five Towns* (1905) and *The Grim Smile of the Five Towns* (1907). The first short stories of Katherine Mansfield, *In A German Pension*, came as early as 1911, when she was only twenty-three, but her new kind of short story was not to make its full impact on the reading public until the twenties. On the whole, the second decade of the century saw the continuation of the earlier tendency to apply an individual power of narrative in an English way, neither influenced by nor akin to the French or Russian examples in any marked degree. Thus Chesterton passed on to his Father Brown stories, P. G. Wodehouse conveyed his comic vision with his peculiar twist of phrasing, and Galsworthy showed how he could contain his sense of character and occasion in lucid and civilised brevity. E. M. Forster's collection of six short stories, *The Celestial Omnibus* (1911), was another individual experiment, for the most part sketches in fantasy of the kind of people and themes of his novels. The most dynamic contributions of the second decade were D. H. Lawrence's *The Prussian*

Officer of 1914 and Joyce's *Dubliners* of the same year, but the full impact of both was delayed until after the war.

It was in the nineteen-twenties that the short story came fully into its own. Then a writer could make himself known entirely as a short story writer, as did A. E. Coppard and Katherine Mansfield, or could owe a considerable part of his reputation to his achievement in the short story, as did Somerset Maugham. The public had come to recognise the pleasurable existence of the form, and, while popular magazines like *The Strand* had for some time offered scope to writers of the more direct story, now a literary periodical like *The London Mercury* gave an outlet to writers of the more "modern" short story. Of the dominant older novelists of the third decade, Wells and Galsworthy contributed largely to the widespread vogue of the short story, the omnibus volume of Galsworthy's *Caravan* (1923), leading the way in the publication of omnibus volumes. Just as Galsworthy's stories had accumulated slowly until this publication in bulk, so, once the short story had become a popular taste, what had attracted little attention before now came to the front. Thus in one direction the short stories of Lawrence now made headway, and in another those of Edgar Wallace swept all before them.

Among writers who now expressed themselves in the short story alongside their other work were De la Mare and Osbert Sitwell and Aldous Huxley. Somerset Maugham, already securely established as novelist by *Of Human Bondage* (1915) and as a dramatist, published his first volume of short stories, *The Trembling of a Leaf*, in 1921. More short stories came from D. H. Lawrence. C. E. Montague made a distinguished contribution by his short stories of the war, *Fiery Particles*. But perhaps above all kinds of short story, the trinity of detection, mystery and horror made the most spectacular advance in public favour, as Dorothy Sayers's first large collection published in 1928 testified. That volume contained a small, but noticeable proportion of work by earlier writers such as Mrs Henry Wood, Mrs Oliphant, Dickens, Poe and Quiller-Couch; but her second and third series of

1931 and 1934 respectively, in drawing almost entirely on more recent work, showed the swift growth of achievement in this field. The *Collected Ghost Stories* of M. R. James in 1931, which were steadily reprinted, further testified to the avidity of the public for this genre of the short story. The great appeal of detection, mystery and horror may well have been that such tales provided some escape from the monotonous drabness of industrialised civilisation, offering a wider release than the books and essays of country life whose popularity had a similar origin, but their appeal was no doubt in part increased by the turn which the short story was taking in the hands of those who wrote for the more consciously literary public. The "modern" short story, often very far from being a story in the normal sense, was not for all, and it appealed naturally rather to the younger readers than to their elders and to the literary rather than to the average reader.

In the thirties a new generation both of writers and readers had arrived, a generation whose boyhood or youth had been in the years of the first world war. With their appearance the new short story, after the example of Katherine Mansfield and A. E. Coppard, took pride of place in the field of the short story. Among new names around 1930 were those of H. E. Bates, Rhys Davies and L. A. G. Strong. Soon afterwards came Dylan Thomas. E. J. O'Brien by his collections of short stories, *Modern English Short Stories* (1930) and *English Short Stories of To-day* (1934), and by his annual selections of "Best Stories" did a great deal to make the right public conscious of this new phenomenon : it was valuable work similar to that of Michael Roberts in bringing forward the young poets of the early nineteen-thirties. The publishing of short stories was facilitated by the appearance of more periodicals and magazines, *Penguin New Writing* standing high in the list, as did later *Horizon*. Indeed in the nineteen-thirties the writers of the short story rivalled the new poets in exciting and fecund activity. In addition to those in magazines and periodicals and to collected short stories of single writers there were many volumes in each of which examples of some twenty different authors' work were to be found, including volumes of *Welsh Short Stories*, *Irish Short Stories* and *Scotch Short Stories*, which showed that regional inspiration had passed from the novel to the short story. From among so many talented writers it is hardly fair to choose but Mary Arden, Norah Hoult, H. A. Manhood, Liam O'Flaherty, Caradoc Evans, Glyn Jones and Richard Hughes are certainly among those who deserve first mention. But probably the most distinguished of all the short story writers of the thirties was one of an older generation, T. F. Powys. Of the new novelists, Elizabeth Bowen in particular excelled.

In the forties the output of short stories naturally diminished as war interrupted the writing of the younger authors or turned their literary energies into different fields. Nevertheless war service itself inspired some new writing in this line as in poetry, the short stories of Alun Lewis being an outstanding instance. H. E. Bates was commissioned specially to write short stories of the R.A.F., which appeared under the pseudonym of "Flying Officer X": his first collection of these, *The Greatest People in the World*, was reported very soon afterwards to have sold three hundred thousand copies. The aftermath of the war, with its paper shortage, also severely limited the chances for a writer, especially a new one, to get his short stories published.

The record of the short story in this fifth decade was therefore rather one of the consolidation of established reputations like those of Rhys Davies, T. F. Powys, James Hanley, Glyn Jones and Kate Roberts. Of new talent the most striking example was the work of Denton Welch, who died in 1948 at the age of thirty-one. He left only one volume of short stories, *Brave and Cruel* (1949), but his early short novels, *Maiden Voyage* and *In Youth is Pleasure*, had the quality of linked short stories of autobiographical fantasia. The nervous tension inside the individual, so characteristic of much modern writing and reflecting so truly much modern experience, is intensely present, together with a sharp sensuous impressionism of unusual acuteness and rare precision of expression. Like

Dylan Thomas in his autobiographical short stories, Denton Welch wrote from inside a self fed by the absorbed memories of childhood and thinking in images, but he wrote with a clarity alien to the symbol-loving soul of Thomas and in that difference his work was characteristic of the turn which writing had taken, in some ten years, from obscurity to clarity both in poetry and in personal imaginative prose. That the short story seemed on the whole to need a fresh impetus might be ascribed in part to the great weight of example which by 1950 must lie upon any who chose this form. The last new impetus had reached England in the late twenties from the work of the American, Ernest Hemingway, an influence more in the brute force of style than in conception of treatment. America had indeed, apart from Hemingway, found its own remarkable innovators in Thurber, Damon Runyon and Saroyan, but their work was both too individual and too American to allow its easy influence on the short story in the hands of English writers.

Yet in spite of the prolific and distinguished output of short stories from 1920 onwards it may well be held that the two volumes of 1914, Joyce's *Dubliners* and Lawrence's *The Prussian Officer*, excelled all the later work in originality and force. One of the best of the later practitioners, H. E. Bates, owed much to Tchekhov and Maupassant : in his own words, "for me Tchekhov has had many lessons ; but it is significant to note that I learned none of them until I had learned others from Maupassant". There were also before Bates the examples of Katherine Mansfield and A. E. Coppard. But, though Joyce may have owed some inspiration to the short stories of Gogol, his work came more directly from his own vision of life, and there had been nothing like it before in English. *Dubliners* contains only fifteen stories, of which the longest is *The Dead*.

The Dead, one of the greatest short stories the half-century was to produce, is typical of the form the new short story was to take. A picture of a jolly Christmas party given by three women teachers of music, it is crowded with personalities who exist not for their own sakes but to give the atmosphere. For story there is simply the arrival of guests, the fussing of hosts, the flattery of the elder hosts by their guests, culminating in a little speech by one Gabriel, and finally the dispersing of the guests and the emotions of Gabriel and his wife in their hotel bedroom. Indeed in the normal sense there is no story, but the close is a moment of revelation to Gabriel. Exalted by his speech, by the company, by the wine and song, into a flash of renewed romantic love for his wife, he is first frustrated in this emotion by his wife's aloofness and then shaken to his soul by her sad memories, released by a song at the party, of a youth who years before had died of love for her. As she sleeps, "generous tears filled Gabriel's eyes". "He thought of how she who lay beside him had locked in her heart for so many years that image of her lover's eyes when he had told her that he did not wish to live . . . His soul had approached that region where dwell the vast hosts of the dead . . . His own identity was fading out into a grey impalpable world." Meanwhile outside the snow is falling over all Ireland and that young man's grave. "His soul swooned slowly as he heard the snow falling faintly through the universe and faintly falling, like the descent of their last end, upon all the living and the dead." So the short story ends with a music and phrasing of poetry to conclude a spiritual experience, and the realistic details of the scene which led up to it not only blend in full harmony with but take on a deeper interpretation from the final poetry. The technique resembles Virginia Woolf's expansion of a moment to grow like a drop, which at last fully expanded and shining vanishes in time but remains in the perfection of art.

So the short story had grown nearer to the lyric and close to a psychological mood-poem like Coleridge's *Frost at Midnight*, enriched by an element of narrative No other story in *Dubliners* was either so sustained or so poetic in conception and finality. The short *Araby* gives us a glimpse of a boy's idyllic love frustrated in the manifestation he would give of it because, prevented from getting to the bazaar in time, he cannot bring back a present for the girl he shyly adores, but realism here darkens the treatment, though the boy's emotions shine clearly through. The realism of a shabby Dublin of drunkards, commercial travellers, truant schoolboys, electioneering canvassers, and questionable priests, is indeed a striking quality of the whole book. Joyce had looked closely at the world he knew intimately and he selected scenes, not stories, which would reveal the essential human quality. One often feels as though looking through a peephole at people in a room for just long enough to see how out of the temporary relationship some sharp stirring of the emotional consciousness arises in one or more. Sometimes a brief introduction preludes the moment as in *A Painful Case*: first we see how James Duffy came to know Mrs Sinico till a passionate demonstration on her part made him withdraw completely from her, and then at our peephole we watch his reactions four years later to the newspaper account of her fall to death beneath a train. That is the essence of the story, a glimpse of the human soul in a moment of shock.

Lawrence in *The Prussian Officer* volume similarly united poetry and realism, but the fusion is one of greater passion. In *Odour of Chrysanthemums* he too selects the moment of revelation, but in a way characteristic of him makes it arise out of violence. The miner's wife waits with her children for her man's return, suspecting him to be drinking their money away, but afraid also that he may have met with an accident in the pit. When her fears are realised, the sight of her husband's body—"he was a man of handsome body, and his face showed no traces of drink. He was blond, full-fleshed, with fine limbs"—she was shocked into an entirely new estimation of him :—

> "'Who am I? What have I been doing? I have been fighting a husband who did not exist. *He* existed all the time. What wrong have I done? What was that I have been living with? There lies the reality, this man'. And her soul died in her for fear : she knew she had never seen him, he had never seen her, they had met in the dark and had fought in the dark, not knowing whom they met nor whom they fought."

Through the violence of this death there is more of story than in Joyce's pieces. But Lawrence too could choose a

moment which had the minimum of story in its shaping.
Second Best opens with a talk between two sisters, of whom
the elder has lost the young man whom she loved; the
younger in a flash of anger at being bitten by it kills a mole;
walking home they encounter a young man, and the elder
sister, who had expressed a personal repugnance to killing
moles unnecessarily, is brought, in a brief exchange of words,
to ask, "Why, would you *like* me to kill moles then?" "And
the next day, after a secret, persistent hunt, she found another
mole playing in the heat. She killed it, and in the evening,
when Tom came to the gate to smoke his pipe after supper,
she took him the dead creature." After that Lawrence needs
only a few lines to bring the two together in a passionate
embrace, fulfilling the careful but unemphasised implications
in the earlier part of the eight-page story. Again there has
been violence, if only to a mole, and further, in so far as
action has resulted, the Lawrence short story certainly tends
to have more narrative force than Joyce's. Yet Lawrence
could also present the scene in which emotions are stirred
without resultant action, leaving the reader, as the modern
short story commonly does, to speculate for himself what
followed when the emotions were again dissipated and the
flow of life resumed. For instance, in *The Christening* we
look into a collier's home and watch the conflicting, violent
emotions aroused by the christening of the illegitimate baby
of one of the daughters; nothing happens except the uprush
of feelings.

The Prussian Officer volume indeed contains a wide variety
of short stories. It includes the rather old-fashioned novel
in brief, the long *Daughters of the Vicar*, and the episode short
story *A Sick Collier*, in which we see an outbreak of madness
in which the man tries to kill his wife. The title story is a
psychological study of the hatred of the Prussian officer for
his young orderly, which breeds an answering hatred in the
lad, resulting in his murdering the officer with his bare hands
in the woods; in this the interest again lies not in what
happens, but in the tension between the two and in the reactions in the tortured soul of the young soldier. The volume

is in fact a true expression of Lawrence's variety in all the characteristic themes and manners of his novels : the antago- nism between the sexes, the wife who is socially above her husband, the animal passions of humanity, the crude reality of life in mining villages, the sheer beauty of the countryside, all emerge, but, as in his later stories too, largely unspoilt by his preaching side. The short story constrained Lawrence to concentrate upon the essentials, and the force of his genius, fusing the poetic and the realistic, made his selection of the significant moment, when he chose that as the core of his story, achieve an intensity of effect which the later short story writers could seldom rival.

But after 1920 the short story entered the atmosphere and influence of the Continent, that is to say principally those of Maupassant and Tchekhov. These two influences were largely contrasted, but, as is shown by Bates's just quoted remark, they could be complementary: Bates held both writers "in equal affection and esteem". The short story of Maupassant was in tone materialistic and realistic ; it did not seek to draw its readers' affections sympathetically to its characters ; its treatment was clear and logical ; it was a story cleverly climaxed. The short story of Tchekhov was spiritual, it offered a sympathetic insight into the soul ; rely- ing on atmosphere and suggestion, though its details were realistic, it was elusive ; it tended to have no sharp ending, because it had no "plot", but, like Joyce and Lawrence at their best, to leave the view open, to dissolve and re-form in the reader's mind. Both were great masters of their form, using no more words than were absolutely necessary to secure their effect, and neither coming between the story and the reader.

The writer who outstandingly accepted the inspiration of Maupassant was Somerset Maugham, but on the whole, however much a writer like Bates owed to Maupassant, the English short story evolved much more closely after the kind of Tchekhov. It chose the significant moments in the lives of people, invested them with the appropriate atmo- sphere, and dealt with them with a notable sensitiveness, which was economically controlled. It was natural that women writers should excel in this form with its semi-poetic sensibility. It was natural too that this new form should come into its own in the days of the cinema, with whose technique of the selective psychological spotlight it had much in common. It may be noticed too that it came in the time of a happy rebirth of the essay, with whose technique also it had its similarities, for as the true essay is a patterning of reflection, carefully but unobtrusively controlled, so the short story broods reflectively, like a prose lyric turning on a single theme.

It does not matter whether or no Katherine Mansfield was directly influenced by Tchekhov. Middleton Murry, her husband and editor of her excellent Journal and letters, has denied it. She certainly greatly admired the work of Tchekhov and her handling of the form was akin to his. Her reputation rests on a few volumes slight in bulk. Her early *In a German Pension* she herself declined to reprint; *Bliss and Other Stories* appeared in 1920, *The Garden Party* in 1922, and *The Doves' Nest* (1923) and *Something Childish* (1924) were both posthumous collections in which many of the stories were unfinished. They were not, even allowing for the growing strain of her tuberculosis, easily written, but were very carefully, even anxiously, brooded over in her mind and subjected to severe self-criticism in the writing. As the months passed in her last years, her Journal recorded the increasing intensity of her desire to write nothing but the best as she saw it, to present her story as a crystal unflawed by the least falsity of feeling. Above all, "all must be *deeply felt*"; she must get "the deepest truth out of the idea".

Katherine Mansfield had come from New Zealand, and it was in the nature of her genius that she should produce her best in stories which drew on the stored memories of her childhood and early youth in that country. Among those the long story *At The Bay* stands out as a triumph in the sustained use of her method, for, while its separate little sections are all part of the same day, each a picture complete in itself, they are inseparable parts of a total living idea. Here is the essence of a New Zealand day in a typical family from early morning until night. In the very early morning, the sun only just rising, an old shepherd heads the sheep to their next pasturage : everything is sensitively presented, the white sea-mist, the dew on bushes and flowers, the "Ah-Aah !" of the sleepy sea, the lean, upright old man with his frieze coat and his pipe, its "bowl as small as an acorn", the old sheep-dog waggling past the disdainful cat, the softly stirring breeze, a goldfinch ruffling its small breast feathers as it turns to the sun, and the bleating of the sheep. It is a delicate water-colour, a gently modulated prose lyric. Then from his bungalow races Stanley Burnell to the sea for his early morning swim, to be irritated by finding a neighbour already before him in his own stretch of sea. Back in the bungalow he fusses over his breakfast, his three little girls at their porridge, until in the nick of time he catches the coach to business with the aid of his sister-in-law, and the little household relaxes in relief. Then the family go down to the beach, where the three little girls are shown "an old, wet, squashed-looking boot" by "two little boys, their knickers rolled up, [who] twinkled like spiders". So picture succeeds picture, and we feel the pulse of a typical day's life. The people are ordinary people, the bustling husband, the dreamy wife, the inhibited young sister-in-law, the daring neighbour with her question-able husband, the restless maid with her elderly crony. They have their reality as individuals, but it is the total idea of how such a community's life goes from sunrise to night that is Katherine Mansfield's purpose, so well achieved that it appears to the reader's inner eye like a perfect example of artistic television. Katherine Mansfield has a satiric eye, but her satire ripples without apparent effort and without drawing our notice : we rather feel that we, only as we read, impose any satiric interpretation.

Of the stories set in New Zealand at least two others stand out, *The Doll's House* and *The Garden Party*. Each illustrates another way of working out the short story. The essence of *The Doll's House* is in its end, which crystallises the wonder-ing joy with which a small child cherishes in its heart the

vision of a special beauty gained, after yearning, at the
expense of fear and shame.

> "Presently our Else nudged up close to her sister.
> But now she had forgotten the cross lady. She put out
> a finger and stroked her sister's quill ; she smiled her
> rare smile.
> 'I seen the little lamp', she said, softly.
> Then both were silent once more."

The perfect simplicity of "I seen the little lamp" makes an
ending which on first reading seems unexpected but which
immediately is felt to be the true and the to-be-expected
ending. So this short story resembles a Shakespearian sonnet,
in which, similarly, a slow exposition culminates in a flash
which throws back its illumination on the whole. Here the
picture of the doll's house, of the excitement of the children,
of the snobbish exclusion of the washerwoman's children by
the others, of Aunt Beryl relieving her feelings by bullying her
nieces and the little Kelveys, is given an altered value by the
sudden concentration at the end on a quite different feeling ;
the satire upon pride as it appears variously in the children
and their elders, which at first seems a leading theme, gives
way to the deeper reality of childish emotion, and the final
effect blends our sense of a child's thrill in life with our sense
of pity. To this treatment that of *The Garden Party* offers
a contrast, for, instead of leading up to a climax, it dies away
on the inexpressible. When Laura, leaving the cottage of
death, meets her brother, she is crying :—

> " 'Was it awful ? '
> 'No', sobbed Laura. 'It was simply marvellous.
> But, Laurie—'. She stopped, she looked at her brother.
> 'Isn't life', she stammered, 'isn't life—'. But what life
> was she couldn't explain. No matter. He quite under-
> stood.
> '*Isn't* it, darling ? ' said Laurie."

Here Katherine Mansfield has deliberately left the edges of
her picture blurred, and though her short story attains fuller
meaning towards the end, as the young girl looks on the
beautiful peace of the dead young man, its meaning has been
diffused almost throughout, from the moment the news of

the fatal accident reaches Laura in the midst of the excited preparations for the party. This is more akin to Virginia Woolf's method, once more the drop growing till its time is full. When the drop is full, it contains much—the excitement of youth, the different values of youth and age, and of a young girl and an older girl, the innocent affectation of youth, and youth's sensitiveness and charm, the contrast of rich and poor, and through all the pulse and mystery of life, and a soft brilliance of light and colour.

Katherine Mansfield's human scene is not a wide one. Hers are mostly well-to-do people and the poor are generally present for the sake of contrast, though *Life of Ma Parker*, which depicts an old charwoman reeling under fate's last blow in her hard life, the death of her little grandchild, shows how deep was her sympathy with the poor. Of her well-to-do people she writes in something of Virginia Woolf's spirit, liking them, but aware of their vanities and prides. Her stories often expose selfishness and affectation. Her psychological insight is clear and subtle, and can be ruthless. In one story, *The Fly*, she concentrates on a glimpse of human nature in its least pleasing working : a business man, whose memory has stirred in grief for his son lost in battle six years before, finds a fly in his inkwell, takes it out on to blotting-paper, and then drenches it in ink from his pen, watching its successive attempts to clean itself until finally it dies, and when the sadistic spasm has passed, seized by "such a grinding feeling of wretchedness . . . that he felt positively frightened", he finds himself unable to recall of what he had been thinking. But on the whole, though her view of life inclines to sadness, she does not probe the darker spots, and even when her scene is grey there is always the tremor of life. Especially the frequent appearance of children and the young gives her work tenderness. Had she lived longer, she might well have gone deeper, if not wider, but as they stand her short stories fulfil Matthew Arnold's requirement of a "criticism of life".

The short stories of A. E. Coppard, coinciding in their first appearance with the recognition of Katherine Mansfield, ensured the wide approval of the short story. He became known quickly after the volume *Adam and Eve and Pinch Me* of 1921, and in the twenty years between the wars he had published twelve volumes, among which *The Black Dog* (1923), *The Field of Mustard* (1926) and *Dunky Fitlow* (1933) were particularly notable. Born in 1878, he was ten years older than Katherine Mansfield, and his manner was already formed when in his early forties he settled down to his new career of short story writing. He had not the delicate artistry of Katherine Mansfield, her luminous precision and subtle power of suggestion, but in his greater earthiness lies a solid strength. If in comparison with her he sometimes seems clumsy, his patient progress with a story has a convincing cumulative effect, and, if none of his stories has the perfection of *At The Bay*, any group of them makes an impression of substantial richness.

His is a country world, extending to small county market towns; at times his scene may be Whitechapel or an Austrian circus or "the backyards of Australia Street", but mostly it is the countryside of woods and moors, of fields where "the grass [is] sweet as an apple", of a village with its vicarage "hung over with pastoral elms", of "a little harbour at the mouth of an Anglian river", where we hear the talk in the quiet tap-room of the Ferry Inn. In this setting he gives us ordinary people moved by the ordinary concerns and passions of life, particularly the passion of love and all its consequences of joy and sorrow, frustration, jealousy and hatred. It is a tragicomic view of life of the Shakespearian kind, in which the normal humorous realities, sometimes crude, sometimes pathetic, sometimes ironic, are inseparable from the passion and beauty. He tends indeed, as stories of country life have done from Shakespeare onwards through Hardy, to make the comic loom large by his liking for the odd and even grotesque in rustic character and circumstance. But, especially through the countryside, the poetic always lies submerged in his treatment and breathes from the rich earth of all the seasons.

His short stories vary considerably in length and kind. Some, like *The Black Dog* and *The Higgler*, take the form of full accounts of an episode in a man's life : *The Black Dog* of the love of a gentleman for an innkeeper's daughter, who is drawn tragically to suicide by his very goodness and its lack of passion, *The Higgler* of a man's largely, but by no means wholly, comic distraction between his love for two girls, the poor girl he marries, and the daughter whom a comfortable widow offers him as a wife, a girl too shy to declare her own love, so that the higgler feels there must be some snag in the mother's proposal. In such stories the story element plays a large part and the conception of character is important too. Indeed in the stories in which he gives himself the scope Coppard leans towards the manner of the novel, even approaching plot in his concern with the interaction of character and circumstances, but the unifying semi-poetic atmosphere and the concentration on essentials make them short stories and not novels in brief. In *Doe* he gives one short story within another ; inset is the tale of a man's tragic love, its pain arising from the temperamental incompatibility between a man and a woman (one of his favourite themes), but the surrounding sketch of the two old men, years before friends at college, and now brought together when the one is an almost saintly country vicar and the other has come into haven with him, bearing this tragic memory from the past, could almost stand by itself, as a modern short story, a picture of peace and friendship which needs neither end nor beginning, existing as a sustained moment appealing to our sympathies, our humour and our senses.

In other stories he can discard story almost entirely, and concentrate on the moment where past and present strive in revealing tension: *Christine's Letter* shows a waitress, who has deserted her husband, brooding, as she serves her customers, on a letter she has just received from him; the essence of the incompatibility of the pair having been vividly conveyed, both by the letter and the girl's reactions, the curtains are drawn across this glimpse of the strong feelings surging under the girl's controlled exterior—asked to repay the surcharge made on the letter, she replies, "O, dear . . . It wasn't of the slightest consequence. I wish you hadn't. It was from . . .

from someone I didn't know''. *The Cherry Tree* too is a glimpse of a woman's emotions, its ending tantalising in the uncertainty of its psychological implications. Again he can tell the kind of short story which is a brief anecdote with an ironic unexpected ending, after Maupassant. *Adam and Eve and Pinch Me* has an unexpected ending, but here it makes the perfect conclusion to an unusual dream experience, where the dream dovetails into a revelation of fact at the moment of waking. With all this varied and highly successful achievement it was not surprising that the work of Coppard soon became very influential on the growing host of practitioners of the short story.

A few years after Coppard began H. E. Bates appeared as a close rival. By 1934 he had published two volumes, *Day's End* and *The Black Boxer*, and in that year a selection of his tales was introduced by Edward Garnett. Bates had put himself to school to the best masters; Garnett remarked that "there is hardly a single story in which there is not a subtle reference to one of his favourite authors: to Tchekhov, Turgenev, Tolstoy, Conrad, or Stephen Crane. If you have a good ear, you will catch a number of such allusions, for Bates has read a great deal, and never hesitates to adopt and adapt another man's methods for his own purposes". He showed less originality and strength than Coppard, and was less of a story-teller, more of a writer of prose lyrics expressing simple harmonised moods and scenes with a delightfully fresh sensibility. Like Coppard, he treats of passion, but it does not seem so natural to his genius as to Coppard's; he seems to rely more on the material supplied by childhood memory and later observation than on imagination; humour in many tones often lightens his stories but it stops short of the truly comic; though his world too is mainly the country world, in his poetry of earth there is more of fragrance, less of earthiness.

If there were nothing else, his pictures of the woods and fields, farms and roads, would still show his mastery of setting: it is lively and loving in its details. "In the midday heat of a June day a farm-boy was riding down a deserted meadow-lane, straddling a fat white pony. The blossoms of hawthorn had shrivelled to brown on the tall hedges flanking the lane and wild pink and white roses were beginning to open like stars among the thick green leaves. The air was heavy with the scent of early summer . . ." So one story opens typically. But his gift as a short story writer lay in his being able to expose before us a mood or quality of the human soul as the circumstances of at most a few hours create it. Generally it is quite an ordinary mood, but it is handled with exceptional skill; at the close of *The Mower* there is indeed a complex of emotions—"as she listened her dark face was filled with the conflicting expression of many emotions, exasperation, perplexity, jealousy, longing, hope, anger"—but there is nothing extraordinary about it, and Bates has shown the simple cause with the utmost naturalness. *Fishing* may stand as a satisfying example of his work at both its slightest and its best: two elderly widowers, friends since youth, recall one summer evening the joys of fishing when they were young; surely those joys could be relived again, and so they lay their lines, reminding one another to be out early next morning, not later than four, with a basket; but "birds wake, cattle pass across the meadows, in the village a bell rings for an early service. But along the river-path nobody comes".

As has been said, many writers deserve to be named alongside Bates, but it must suffice to add the name of Henry Williamson to those already mentioned, for his achievement in the field of the short story whose persons are birds and animals—in one notable instance an indomitable weed. His volumes like *The Peregrine's Saga* (1923) had been preceded by the admirable tales of the Canadian, C. G. D. Roberts, but Williamson took this kind of theme nearer to the modern short story.

The exceptional individuality of T. F. Powys, however, demands special mention. He created a country world of his own, where queer loveable clergymen sought to save the souls of parishioners of the greatest bucolic oddity or simplicity, or, despairing of that, preached to the birds and animals. All is seen in a rare distorting mirror : we are invited to think in terms of a strangely inverted Christianity, which keeps love as its core and regards death as the supreme boon, while assuming a pagan a-morality towards the sins of the flesh. Powys is indeed a preacher who employs fantastic parable as his medium, and he hates above all cruelty, malice, selfishness, and all the meanness of materialism. Humour and wit, ironic and poetic, fill his work with a white light, and every short story is a masterpiece of suggestive brevity. No writer in this half-century made words trip so easily in the invisible fetters of artistic control ; no short story writer constantly saw the idea of his story with more intellectual and imaginative clarity. From an early collection like *The House With an Echo* (1928) to *Bottle's Path* (1946) he maintained his characteristic manner. His novels, such as *Mr Weston's Good Wine*, have the same qualities on an extended, but still brief scale.

CHAPTER XIX

THE DRAMA, 1900 TO 1950

The first decade of the twentieth century was a period of great promise and of considerable achievement in drama. With the plays of Bernard Shaw, Barrie, Granville Barker and Galsworthy in England and those of Synge in Ireland. drama, after the lapse of over a century, became once again something more than mere theatrical entertainment. Intellect re-entered the theatre and plays resumed their place in literature.

The way for this almost spectacular advance had been prepared slowly for some time. As far back as 1865 when Robertson's *Society* was produced, to be followed in 1867 by *Caste*, there had dawned the possibility of a new drama realistically concerned with the problems of contemporary life. Henry Arthur Jones had followed in the wake of Robertson with such a play as *Saints and Sinners* in 1884. Pinero, forsaking farce, and the sentimentality of *Sweet Lavender* (1888), in the nineties followed Jones in the half-way house of realistic melodrama, where love and religion encountered the conventions. But by then the influence of Ibsen had arrived in England after a time-lag of some years. His *Peer Gynt* had appeared in 1869, *Pillars of Society* and *A Doll's House* were respectively produced in 1877 and 1879, and *Ghosts*, *An Enemy of the People*, *The Wild Duck*, *Rosmersholm* and *Hedda Gabler* followed between 1881 and 1890. But the first performance of Ibsen in England was that of *A Doll's House* in London in 1889. Then Grein put on *Ghosts* at his Independent Theatre in 1891, and in the same year Shaw published his *Quintessence of Ibsenism*, and they were joined in their propaganda work for Ibsen by the dramatic critic William Archer who also translated Ibsen. Slowly but effectively the force of Ibsen's genius triumphed over the angry denunciation which the first knowledge of his work evoked both from audiences and from the average critic in this country as Grein continued to stage Ibsen. By 1900 the fight for a new drama had been fought and won. From the turn of the century the drama of ideas could go ahead with confidence, challenging moral and social conventions, and dispensing with the theatrical paraphernalia of stagey plots and outworn devices like the soliloquy.

In the theatre itself in the last decade of the nineteenth century the outstanding achievement was the success of Oscar Wilde's plays. This owed little or nothing to Ibsen, but Wilde too was of the greatest value in raising the standards of the drama. Not since Sheridan's *The School for Scandal* in 1773 had there been any comedy of comparable artistry, and indeed Congreve's plays just two hundred years before Wilde's were perhaps his nearest forerunners in witty comedy. *Lady Windermere's Fan* came first in 1892 and, with its implicit criticism of social convention, it had some contact with the work of Henry Arthur Jones; but from the beginning Wilde's genius lay in the brilliance of his dialogue and any seriousness and sentiment were increasingly overlaid by pure comedy as he went through *A Woman of No Importance* (1893) and *An Ideal Husband* (1895) to end with the gay artificial absurdity of *The Importance of Being Earnest* (1895). With such outstanding encouragement comedy revived and both Jones and Pinero produced noteworthy comedies, such as Jones's *The Liars* in 1896 and Pinero's *Trelawney of the Wells* in 1898. But these two dramatists, without capturing the spirit of Ibsen, learnt a good deal from him too and they proceeded also to question the conventions with Jones's *The Triumph of the Philistines* (1895) and Pinero's *The Second Mrs Tanqueray* and *The Notorious Mrs Ebbsmith* of 1893 and 1895 respectively. Audiences were responding favourably to treatment of sex and religious problems on the stage provided that the treatment was not "too daring".

But in the long run the most important development in the nineties was the steady progress of Bernard Shaw. When, after having written some unsuccessful novels, he wrote his first play, *Widowers' Houses*, in 1892, he was already thirty-six and success came to him slowly. On the stage his only financial success was in America, mainly with *The Devil's Disciple* in 1897. In this country his plays for the most part secured only a few performances. *Arms and the Man* had a run of eleven weeks in 1894 and it made him fairly widely known, but it was produced at a loss of about £4,000, which was borne by Miss Horniman, who was then financing a season of modern drama at the Avenue Theatre. *You Never Can Tell*, written in 1896, got off the mark with six matinees in 1900, and *Mrs Warren's Profession*, written in 1893, had to wait for a performance until 1902 when the Stage Society produced it privately. Shaw, however, was steadily consolidating his position, and by 1900 he had made his plays available to the reading public. In 1898 he published *Plays Pleasant and Unpleasant*, supplying full stage directions and adding prefaces explaining the meaning of the plays and his attitude to the theatre and to a wide range of contemporary problems. The Pleasant Plays were *Arms and the Man*, *Candida*, *The Man of Destiny* and *You Never Can Tell* and the Unpleasant consisted of *Widowers' Houses*, *The Philanderer* and *Mrs Warren's Profession*. In 1900 *Plays for Puritans* followed, which added *The Devil's Disciple*, *Caesar and Cleopatra* and *Captain Brassbound's Conversion*. Moreover, after earlier work as musical and literary critic, he had been given the opportunity for three years, from 1895 until he resigned in 1898, of constructively criticising the drama as dramatic critic of *The Saturday Review*.

Thus in 1900 Bernard Shaw, by now forty-four, was a force to be reckoned with, and all he needed was a theatre to put his work before London audiences. This need was supplied by the Court Theatre, which in 1904 came into the hands of J. E. Vedrenne, who was its financial manager, and of Granville Barker, actor and playwright, who was its producer. With this opportunity Shaw rapidly won outstanding success, and his plays provided the main part of the Court Theatre's season, which ran under this management till 1907. *Man and Superman*, which he had been writing between 1901 and 1903, had a long run in 1904 ; in the same year *John Bull's Other Island* was a popular success, and *Major Barbara* and

The Doctor's Dilemma followed in 1905 and 1906 respectively. In America his earlier success was now exceeded, four of his plays, *Candida*, *You Never Can Tell*, *Arms and the Man* and *The Man of Destiny*, running at the same time in New York in 1903-4.

Shaw's reputation was indeed international, *The Doctor's Dilemma* being produced in Berlin in 1908, and in 1912 Shaw had *Pygmalion* given its first production in Berlin in preference to London. In London his outstanding theatrical success before the First War was *Fanny's First Play* which ran for two and a half years, totalling six hundred performances. His other plays before 1914 were *Getting Married* (1908), *The Showing Up of Blanco Posnet* (1909), *The Dark Lady of the Sonnets* and *Misalliance*, both in 1910, and *Androcles and the Lion* produced in 1913. In fact by the time the war came he had become not only the leading playwright of the day and the most distinguished figure in English drama for well over a century, but also a great propagandist for modern ideas of social progress and reform, using the drama to that end just as H. G. Wells was in the same years using the novel. His greatest plays were still to come, but he had already produced some of his most perfect work, such as *Candida*. Above all, he had accustomed a large and growing proportion of the English play-going public to expect, when they went to the theatre, to be provoked into thinking by a lively and penetrating exposure of the questionable bases of established views of wealth, property, the relationship of the sexes, family life, the medical profession, religion—indeed of nearly every aspect of life.

But though Shaw in this way came into his own in these first fourteen years of the century and though, in the perspective of time, most other dramatists of that period have become dwarfed in the comparison, the serious theatre had much else to offer in the years leading up to the war. Above all there were the plays of Sir James Barrie (he was created a baronet in 1913) to hold the balance with Shaw. In the changed mental climate of the thirties when he died, the charming sentimentality of Barrie's work was anathema to perhaps a majority of the public, but when his early plays first appeared they delighted a wide audience. The year 1903 saw the production of *Quality Street* and *The Admirable Crichton*, and in 1904 began the run of the probably immortal *Peter Pan*. *Alice-Sit-by-the-Fire* (1905), *What Every Woman Knows* (1908), *A Slice of Life* (1910) and *The Twelve Pound Look* (1910) were among the best of his plays that followed before 1914.

While Shaw whetted the intellectual appetite of his audience, Barrie played on the sentiments of his and gave little more than a hint of social criticism. In *The Admirable Crichton* he might put the butler, as the one efficient person, in charge of his social superiors on a desert island, but it was for the sentimental fun of it : when the episode was over, the butler would contentedly resume his proper status. In *The Twelve Pound Look* he presented a woman who had escaped from an uncongenial husband by making herself independent of his money by the earnings from her typewriter, but the contemptuous picture of the stupid, overbearing man is, for Barrie, exceptionally satiric, and in spite of its concentrated scorn the little play is only a slight contribution to the plea for economic freedom for women in comparison with the weightier treatment by Shaw and Wells and the ardour of the contemporary suffragettes. Indeed, Barrie in general sought neither to criticise nor to penetrate below the surface of life. He would rather soar on the wings of fantasy, and enchant his audience to follow him by the dexterity of his theatrical craftsmanship, in which in his own way he rivalled Shaw, and by the tender poetic whimsicality of his imagination.

It is impossible not to suspect in Barrie a more searching criticism of life than his plays as a whole contain, but the daemon that inspired him as a dramatist was akin to his own Peter Pan, an elusive spirit which preferred not to grow up in this modern world. As soon as his imagination began to create illusions for the stage, Barrie usually turned his back on the disagreeable in life and set about pleasing an audience which, like himself, wanted its heart moved, but without pain, and its fancy lit up with rosy lights. So in *Quality Street* he evoked a charmingly idyllic picture of love in the days of the Napoleonic wars. In two of his best plays, *Dear Brutus* (1917) and *Mary Rose* (1920), he typically checked his development of the themes from giving rise to any deep uneasiness, in *Dear Brutus* speculating on the responsibility of each of us for his failure in life and in *Mary Rose* letting the supernatural sport with mortals, but in both plays leaving his audience only pleasantly bewitched by his artistic playing upon their feelings. His last play, *The Boy David* (1936), produced the year before his death, was a failure in the theatre, partly because of its uncertain and unequal handling of its Old Testament story, but even more because the spirit of Barrie was by then quite out of tune with the darkening day. His reputation as a dramatist may well rise again, for he was a true creator, who made a world of his own ; but it can hardly rise as high as it was in the days of his prime, when he could delight his audiences as irresistibly by his peculiar charm as Shaw did his by his provocation, and when he ranked without dispute as one of the outstanding creative artists of his time. His influence on other dramatists, however, was negligible; perhaps only the early plays of A. A. Milne owe anything to his inspiration.

Barrie, indeed, was an individualist, while the strongest tendency in English drama in the years before the First War was a group tendency to deal with problems of social morality in a realistic but generally humorous manner. Granville Barker as playwright harmonised with Shaw, as might have been expected from the producer of Shaw's plays. In *The Voysey Inheritance* (1905) he presented a highly respectable solicitor, who, after juggling with his clients' investments for many years to his own great profit and the comfort and education of his family, died leaving the burden of righting his wrongs to his son : we see the realist corrupted by his love of wealth and by his own skill in finance, and in contrast his idealistic son, whom the burden turns from a prig into a man who has come by experience to realise the curious complexity into which right and wrong can be woven in the world of modern finance. *Waste* (1907) dealt with abortion and fell under the censor's ban. *The Madras House* (1910) explored again the way in which men and their families become involved in moral problems by the dependence of their wealth on business, this time a large millinery establishment where a mannequin parade before the directors lightens the serious satiric comedy. Again Barker showed an idealistic younger man waking up to the need for practical steps to improve the current way of the world : the young man declares that "Whitechapel High Street's our civilisation", and he will henceforth go in "for sordid, municipal politics, dull hard work over drains and dentistry in the schools and such like". The implication of the play was that it was time to realise that the comfort of the wealthy industrialists and professional men and their families must no longer exist at the cost of the workers.

The working class, indeed, became the material for several dramatists. Miss Horniman, who in the nineties had financed the production of Shaw, and who in the early years of this century also helped to finance the Irish Literary Theatre, was behind the repertory company established at the Gaiety Theatre, Manchester, in 1907, and here Stanley Houghton, St John Hankin and St John Ervine were among the dramatists to whom her venture gave scope. Among their plays were Houghton's *The Younger Generation* (1910) and *Hindle Wakes* (1912), St John Hankin's *The Cassalis Engagement* (1907) and *The Last of the De Mullins* (1908), and St John Ervine's *Mixed Marriage* (1911) and *Jane Clegg* (1913).

Choosing generally a background of the industrial or business world, these playwrights dramatised stories which showed rebellious youth striving against repressive parents, the clash of man and master, the stupidity of convention, the needless unhappiness caused by difference of social class, and the emergence of bold independent womanhood. *Hindle Wakes* put the question whether a girl should marry her seducer just for convention's sake. *Jane Clegg* showed a wife, deceived and deserted by a weak, lying, gambling husband, who has

embezzled a cheque belonging to his employer, rising courage-
ously above the sordid circumstances of her lower middle
class life to prefer life alone with her children. She is the
"new woman", despising the convention that a wife exists
only for her husband and therefore seeming to her husband
and his mother "unnacherel" ; for she has a mind of her own
and declares that "it doesn't seem right somehow to have a
mind and not use it". *Jane Clegg* was, indeed, a play which
in a very competent manner encouraged its audience to think
seriously not only of the problems of the immediate story
but of the industrial civilisation of which that story was a
symptom. Its conclusion raised a wider issue still, that of
the relationship between partners in marriage, for, in excusing
himself, the husband asserts that "it doesn't do a chap much
good to be living with a woman who's his superior . . . I ought
to have married a woman like myself, or a bit worse". So far
had the influence of Ibsen and Shaw, reinforced by that of
Wells and E. M. Forster and others, made it possible for
dramatists to criticise contemporary society and raise broad
issues of civilised living.

In the same years Galsworthy came to use the drama for
very much the same purpose as these Manchester playwrights.
Already dealing with the propertied classes in his Forsyte
tales, as a dramatist he concentrated more sharply on certain
aspects involved by their wealth and its making. *The Silver
Box* (1906) showed how different the attitude of the law was
likely to be as between two men, both led by drink into taking
the property of others, but of whom one was the son of a
wealthy Liberal M.P., and the other was an unemployed
groom whose opinions were Socialist; the delinquency of the
son is hushed up, but Jones, the unemployed man, who stole
"out of spite", is given "a month with hard labour"—as Jones
cries out in the magistrate's court, "I've done no more harm
than wot he 'as. I'm a poor man. I've got no money an'
no friends—he's a toff—he can do wot I can't". *Joy* (1907),
subtitled "A Play on the Letter *I*", is lighter in its presentation of a group of well-to-do individualists, but fundamentally
it is not a very agreeable world in which a young girl hates

her mother's lover, who is trying to get rid of shares in a dubious gold-mine. *Strife* (1909) dealt with the conflict in industry between masters and men, Galsworthy again putting an emotional weight in his balance against the propertied class by making a strike-leader's wife die of starvation due to the strike. In *Justice* (1910) one theme was the prison system and the treatment of prisoners. *The Mob* (1914) dealt with crowd psychology.

Thus Galsworthy explored various ways in which society, through its laws and institutions, its conventions, its distinctions of wealth and power over against poverty and dependence, in fact by its very nature of being a society, which, even if divided into classes, was always a power to support some and oppose others, shaped and determined the destinies of individuals. Galsworthy looked at this scene as impartially as he could, but his pity was always on the side of the underdog, of the victims of self and circumstance. His treatment was serious and affecting, but his lack of passion deprived his plays of the power to rouse anger against the wrongs he exposed. Indeed, he showed too clearly that there were always faults on both sides and that all his audience too must be to some extent sharers of the blame for the way things were. What he gave was good theatre, and it was educative ; each play was a very presentable plea for a more Christian approach of class to class and of man to man. But his balanced moral preoccupation and the limitation of the dramatic form as he handled it worked against the creation of vital individual characterisation. As compared with his novels, his plays were cramped and formal and approached the reasonable sermon. To the end they ran, like his novels, on the same lines. Thus in the twenties with *The Skin Game* (1920), *Loyalties* (1922) and *Escape* (1926) he was still the dramatist of *The Silver Box* and *Justice*.

Alongside this realistic drama of the middle classes there was, however, in the first decade of the century a poetic drama, quite apart from the fantasy of Barrie. But its home was Ireland, not England, and it had no considerable effect on English drama. In England there were indeed the plays of Stephen Phillips, notably his *Paolo and Francesca* (1900), and similar productions such as *Ulysses* (1902) and *Nero* (1906). They were very popular, but they can be dismissed as colourful spectacles in blank verse. Ireland, however, experienced a revival of drama, in which the poets played a great part. The Irish Literary Theatre had its opening season in 1899 and in 1903 began its tenure of the Abbey Theatre, Dublin. Among those active either in the management or in writing plays or in both were Yeats, Lady Gregory, "A.E", Lennox Robinson and Padraic Colum, but the outstanding dramatist whom the movement produced was John Synge.

Yeats indeed as early as 1892 had written in dramatic form *The Countess Cathleen*, and in 1904 his play *The Land of Heart's Desire* had been acted. Then, with the more determined setting on foot of the movement, he largely turned for a few years from lyric to dramatic poetry, as with *The Shadowy Waters* (1900, acted 1904), *Cathleen Ni Houlihan* (1902) and *Deirdre* (1907). But despite his creative genius Yeats was not a great dramatist and the value of his plays lay chiefly in their poetry, in the way they set free the imagination to roam in Ireland's mythological or historical past, and in the stimulus given by such an attitude towards the theatre from so gifted a man who devoted his practical energy to the success of the Irish National Theatre. Lady Gregory had a talent for comedy, as in *Spreading the News* (1904), but her contribution was rather in her warm support of the movement than in her own achievement. Padraic Colum's work included *The Land* (1905) and *The Fiddlers' Home* (1907): he took Irish problems realistically and seriously but could see the humour too of Irish characteristics even when deploring the way in which the towns, by their attractions, were emptying the Irish countryside of young people.

If Synge had lived longer, his work might well have achieved even greater heights than it did, for his career as a dramatist lasted only some six years, at the end of which he died in 1909, still only thirty-eight. Yeats had discovered him as a struggling journalist in Paris, and on the advice and with the help of Yeats, Synge went away to the Aran Islands off Western Ireland to soak himself in the pure Irish life of that remote region whose peasant population was still unaffected by the modern world. There he lived as one of the peasants, his soul was refreshed and he saw life anew and objectively in its beauty, its comedy and its tragedy. Soon his imagination flowered, and its expression was clothed in the speech and speech-rhythms of the islanders, a speech long in contact with earth and the simplicities of primitive living.

His first play, the brief *The Shadow of the Glen* (1903), was neither comedy nor tragedy, but the tragicomedy of life as it might reach a strange climax in "the last cottage at the head of a long glen in County Wicklow". A woman, disturbed by a knock on the door on a wild evening of rain, puts in her pocket a stocking of money before letting in a passing tramp. For that money she had married the old farmer whose body rests on the bed in the room. When, after a little talk, the woman goes out supposedly to tell the neighbours, the "dead man" throws off his sheet, takes the tramp into his secret and gets a stick to be ready to deal with the young man whom he knows his "bad wife" will bring back. Then the old farmer bids his wife leave his cottage for ever—and she goes with the tramp; and the scene closes with him and the young man drinking together by the fire, for the old man's anger dies down and the other is really an "innocent young man". All is too real and moving for laughter, too desolately strange for tears, and the wild beauty of the lonely countryside is part of the atmosphere. The four characters live for us in a vivid present but impress us as people ripened and ripening by time and experience, unselfconscious creatures going as their several natures bid them.

Then in his next play, *Riders to the Sea* (1904), he expressed the purely tragic vision of the way in which the sea claims the lives of all an old woman's sons. As before, the action is concentrated into one fairly short scene in a cottage : one son has but recently been drowned and his clothes are identified as the play begins, but still the last son will make a journey and, before long, he having been knocked over into the sea by his pony and washed out into a great surf, his body is brought back. The old mother, telling herself that "they're all gone now, and there isn't anything more the sea can do to me . . . I'll have no call now to be up crying and praying when the wind breaks from the south, and you can hear the surf is in the east, and the surf is in the west, making a great stir with the two noises", is left with the further comfort that this son at least "will have a fine coffin out of the white boards, and a deep grave surely". Like all Synge's plays it is in prose, but the diction and the rhythm exalt and attune it to the theme, and the poetic concentration is so intense that we do not notice how the time of the action has been condensed into mere minutes on the stage. It is age-old experience given new expression through characters whose individuality is felt beneath the austere suppression of personal differences which suffering and grief impose on all and especially on simple natures.

In *The Well of the Saints* (1905) Synge took the wider scope of three acts, and let his irony play on the theme of a man and wife, both blind beggars, who, their sight being restored by a saint, found that instead of each being beautiful, as they had thought, both were hideously ugly. At the resultant scene of their fighting each other, at their satisfaction in losing their sight again, and their final departure from the people they had seen too clearly, Synge looked with appreciation of the essential humanity of it all, without mockery or moral judgment.

It was the same in his masterpiece, *The Playboy of the Western World* (1907). In that play the kind of life he saw clearly he presented only too clearly for some of his countrymen, who attacked the play with bitter anger, but its excellence was quickly acknowledged outside Ireland. The Playboy comes to a poor country publichouse on the wild coast of Mayo, and there all the action takes place. There the young man confesses he has wandered miles after murdering his brutal father in a spasm of anger. Previously a poor-spirited lad, shy to the point of stupidity, he expands in the flattery of the village girls and the wonder of the men, and wins promise of marriage from the bold beauty Pegeen, the publican's daughter, who is captivated by his poetic speech and supposedly wild courage. In his new character the Playboy carries off the honours at the village sports, but in the hour of his triumph is exposed by his father's appearance intent on revenge for the blow with which his son thought he had killed him. Then the villagers will have him hanged, but the Playboy fights back and, his new spirit reviving, he marches off to his home again with his father.

But now he is his father's master, and, as he leaves, he says, "Ten thousand blessings upon all that's here, for you've turned me a likely gaffer in the end of all, the way I'll go romancing through a romping lifetime from this hour to the dawning of the judgment day". But Pegeen, who had turned against him when she found he was no murderer of his father, is left wildly lamenting, "I've lost the only Playboy of the Western World". No doubt neither Pegeen nor the other girls, nor indeed any of the characters, throws glory on a countryside where such characters are even likely, but, whatever Ireland thought, the outer world could rejoice in the vitality and humour of the conception. Here was human nature, simple and crude, cunning and brutal, greedy, spiteful and changeable, but warm in the blood and capable of poetry. For any comparable human beings we need to go back to Shakespeare, who in a Sly or an Audrey or a Barnadine or in Falstaff and his uncourtly associates could bring to life common earthy humanity and let it flout its mingled grace and gracelessness of unredeemed flesh and blood and mother wit before the virtuous and judging world, while its creator, like Synge, did not stand aside to judge. And even more than in Shakespeare we are aware of the external scene, of the bogs, the potato field, the hedges and ditches, the straying sheep, the rabbits in the furze, of the smells and the noises of country life, and the lonely landscape beneath a lovers' moon.

Synge was hurt and checked by the attitude of many in Ireland to *The Playboy*, and also his ill-health grew worse. His last play, the tragic love-story of *Deirdre of the Sorrows*, a tale of olden times involving the supernatural, was therefore unfinished when he died, though it showed no decline of his powers. But his other play, *The Tinker's Wedding*, written earlier and revised in 1909, is the least inspired of his work.

The one English play which seems to owe its existence largely to Synge was Masefield's *Tragedy of Nan* produced by Granville Barker in 1908. Masefield was a friend of Synge's and shared his view that "before verse can be human again it must learn to be brutal". So in his play he took English peasant life, comparably crude to Synge's, and, using prose like Synge with a poet's vision, attempted a country tragedy. He had not the sure touch of Synge, partly no doubt because the English scene, invaded by the modern world as Western Ireland was not, lacked the integrity of the Irish. But that more writers turned to poetic plays may well have been due to the encouragement of Synge's and the general Irish example. Among them were Gordon Bottomley, Wilfrid Gibson and Lascelles Abercrombie, all of whom wrote verse plays, but rather experimentally and for the pleasure of the few than with an eye to the ordinary public stage.

Abercrombie and Bottomley indeed did not seek to bring the common life back into poetic drama but to examine morality through stories remote from the modern scene. They aimed to present good and evil and to give their presentation a greater cogency than that of ordinary prose drama by the peculiar potency of poetic imagery and a more universal value because the remoteness of their stories emphasised the symbolic quality of their themes. Flecker, however, stands out among these experimental poetic dramatists. His *Hassan*, which was not produced until 1923, eight years after his death, was a success in the commercial theatre. Subtitled "The story of Hassan of Baghdad and how he came to make the Golden Journey to Samarkand" it had plot, passion and song, and it was spectacular in presentation. It had behind it Flecker's own knowledge of the East. Before *Hassan* he had written in 1911 *Don Juan*, of which he said "My Don Juan is the modern idealist". Opening with a shipwreck off the Welsh coast the play ends in Trafalgar Square and its characters include a fisher girl, a Prime Minister and his beautiful daughter, and a radical-socialist leader, while Don Juan is a young nobleman. Written mainly in prose which is often vividly colloquial it contains also some rich poetry and its total effect is one of poetic tragedy. Flecker, however, was unable to find a producer for it. Meanwhile Masefield went on writing occasional plays, but not on the lines of *Nan* ; his prose *Pompey the Great* of 1910 was followed in 1914 by *Philip the King* in verse and by *Good Friday* (1917) also in verse.

In 1914 the war inevitably checked the development of the drama. The theatre was by no means suppressed, but soldiers on leave from the Front required relief from reality and relaxation by humour, colour and music, and theatrical managers catered for what they thought to be their needs. Nor, with the increasing strain of the war, were the needs of civilians very different from those of the fighting men. Outstanding popular successes were the two revues at the Alhambra, *The Bing Boys are Here* (1916) and *The Bing Boys on Broadway* (1918), and the spectacular and tuneful *Chu Chin Chow*, all of which had long runs. Indeed it was no time for the social themes of Galsworthy and the Manchester dramatists. Moreover St John Hankin and Stanley Houghton had both died before 1914. St John Ervine joined the army. The war called the services of many other dramatists away from the theatre. One of the most successful dramatists in the commercial theatre before the war had been Somerset Maugham, with ten plays to his credit after his first success, *A Man of Honour*, in 1903, but he produced no new play during the war. Barrie's *Dear Brutus* in 1917 was an exceptional success by one of the older dramatists. At the end of the war Drinkwater's *Abraham Lincoln* (1918) stood out as a serious play which could match the hour by its dramatic picture of a character who, by his courage, integrity and moral vision, provided an inspiration to a people

exhausted by war. From the Irish dramatists some good
work came, including Lennox Robinson's comedy *The White-
headed Boy* and Lord Dunsany's one-act play, *A Night at an
Inn*, both in 1916, while St John Ervine's earlier written *John
Ferguson* was produced at the Abbey Theatre in 1915. But
the general position of the English intellectual drama is suggested by the silence of Bernard Shaw. His serious dramatic
consideration of the way civilisation was going, *Heartbreak
House*, was written in the middle of the war, but he was
unable to secure its production until 1921.

When the war was over, the serious drama in part began
again where it had left off. Galsworthy was soon back with
The Skin Game (1920) and Barrie with *Mary Rose* in the
same year. Alan Monkhouse with *First Blood* (1924) followed
in the kind of Galworthy's *Strife*. Bernard Shaw, unchanged
in essence but now abandoning his attacks on contemporary
social ills, crowned his work in the eyes of the wider public
with *Saint Joan* in 1924, while in his great cycle of plays
Back to Methuselah, published in 1921 and produced in 1923,
he had made what he called "my contribution to the
scriptures of Creative Evolution". Drinkwater followed up
the success of *Abraham Lincoln* with *Mary Stuart* (1921) and
Robert E. Lee (1923), on the whole maintaining the power of
solid, healthy dramatic workmanship he had shown before
but not rising above it. An older dramatist who revealed
greater powers than before was Somerset Maugham, who
passed on from his earlier competent melodramas and farces
to plays that cut deeper into life and exposed it with biting
satire. Among his plays were *The Circle* (1921), *Our Betters*
(1923), and *The Constant Wife* (1927). His work was the
comedy of manners at its best, reproducing as naturally as
possible current social behaviour. In *The Circle* his irony
borders on the cruel. A young wife is contemplating elopement from her stiff, priggish husband, a young politician with
a passion for, but no real knowledge of antique furniture.
The husband's father seizes upon the opportunity presented
by a visit of his divorced wife, now a garrulous woman
fighting a losing battle with middle age, who is accompanied

by the man with whom she had eloped years ago and who is
now a querulous old fellow running to seed, to try and save
his son's marriage by disillusioning the daughter-in-law as to
her own prospects if she too insists on eloping. But the father-
in-law loses, though, as the curtain falls, he is laughing in the
confidence of victory, while the others laugh with him in the
knowledge of his defeat. *The Breadwinner*, one of his last
plays, is largely a satire on the families of comfortable middle-
class professional men ; the brash young, with their unrealistic
theories of life and petulant patronage of their elders, and their
materialistic elders treading the ruts of suburbia's society
are all rather grimly amusing. Maugham's breadwinner, a
stock-broker, deliberately lets himself be "hammered" on the
Stock Exchange so that he may break away from the wife
he has lost any mental contact with and his adolescent children
who bore him.

On the other hand, St John Ervine as playwright became
less serious than before with *The Lady of Belmont* (1924) and
The First Mrs Fraser (1928). Eden Philpotts, who had been
a dramatist since the eighteen-nineties followed up the great
success of his rustic comedy *The Farmer's Wife*, first produced in 1916, with two similar broad comedies rich in
characterisation and West country dialogue, *Devonshire
Cream* (1925) and *Yellow Sands* (1926). An outstandingly
delightful, but slight comedy was J. B. Fagan's *And So To
Bed*, which brought the flirtatious diarist Samuel Pepys to
life again in 1926. The poetic drama continued to live mainly
on paper or in small productions outside London. Thus
Lascelles Abercrombie published his *Phoenix* in 1923, and
finished *The Sale of St Thomas* in 1930. Among the best plays
of Wilfrid Gibson were *Krindlesdyke* (1922) and *Kestrel
Edge* (1924), neither of which was written to be acted.
Gordon Bottomley, whose *King Lear's Wife* was exceptional
in being produced in London at His Majesty's, was deeply
interested in the possibilities of poetic drama acted by local
talent, and for many years he was associated with The British
Drama League. Perhaps the most successful poetic play
intended for acting was Hardy's *The Famous Tragedy of the*

Queen of Cornwall (1924), retelling the old story of Tristram and Iseult; it was not, however, intended for the ordinary stage, but was "arranged as a play for mummers, in one act, requiring no theatre or scenery".

But alongside the older dramatists there came forward a new generation of playwrights, outstanding among whom were Noel Coward and Sean O'Casey. Noel Coward, born in 1899, had the theatre in his blood. His unerring sense of theatrical effect, his wit and dance of dialogue, his sparkling presentation of the hurly-burly of the bright young moderns and their disillusioned and fantastic elders delighted playgoers in play after play. *The Young Idea* (1922) was followed by *The Vortex* (1923); then came *Fallen Angels* and *Hay Fever*, both in 1925, and he closed the decade with *Bitter Sweet* (1929) and *Private Lives* (1930). By these (*Bitter Sweet* excepted) and other pieces he had, by his own brilliant talents and helped by the absence of any dramatist of equal talents to give a truer picture, created the legend of the "hectic and nervy" twenties, when morals had been thrown to the winds and human marionettes danced fantastically away from reality, the middle-aged straining every nerve to keep young and the young posturing at the mercy of their cultivated temperaments. At least, if he did not inspire such a legend, he exaggerated facts by the selective process of his art.

The world Noel Coward portrayed was one in which a young man took to drugs because his mother took young men as lovers, in which a house-party was a whirl of perverse flirtation and desperate chatter, a world where "there's no peace anywhere—nothing but the ceaseless din of trying to be amused", but which could provide much amusement to the audience, who were required to exercise little moral judgment but were dazzled into almost thoughtless enjoyment of the spectacle of fashionable people acting with disillusioned abandonment and talking in deft dialogue. *Hay Fever* is a good example of Noel Coward at his lightest, happiest and most dextrous : as he himself said of it, "it has no plot at all, and remarkably little action. Its general effectiveness therefore depends upon expert technique from each and every member of the cast''. All we have is a country house, where the father is writing a novel entitled *The Sinful Woman* and the wife, an actress in retirement, is hoping to entertain to herself for the week-end an athletic young man, but the son has invited a young woman, the daughter a young man, and the husband a young woman, so that all is a jangle of cross-purposes between mainly temperamental people so irritated by their juxtaposition in the domestic circle that at the end the visitors are glad to sneak away, while the family forgets them in hysterical reminiscence of a play the mother had acted in. It is comedy passing into farce as these superficial and affected people change their flirtations in a moment, and are caught on the wrong foot, while neither the young nor the middle-aged seem to have any moral stability. The daughter is disgusted at her mother's flirtations, but her mother spiritedly retorts : "If you mean that because you happen to be a vigorous young *ingénue* of nineteen you have the complete monopoly of any amorous adventure there may be about, I feel it my firm duty to disillusion you".

The characters created by Noel Coward, pitiful seekers after a good time, drinking and flirting to ward off boredom, were in their own persons a sufficient criticism of the post-war futility which certainly existed, and in leaving them to condemn themselves and in letting them excuse themselves on the ground that their parents were responsible for the existing state of things, Coward gave the appearance of to some extent sympathising with the dilemma of the young. Nicky in *The Vortex* indeed suffers so genuinely that he wins a good deal of our sympathy, and he is given a plausible case to state when he says to his mother, "You've wanted love always—passionate love, because you're made like that—it's not your fault—it's the fault of circumstances and civilisation —civilisation makes rottenness so much easier—we're utterly rotten—both of us . . . We swirl about in a vortex of beastliness".

Noel Coward did not make it his business to go any further in analysing the cause, symptoms or cure of the post-war malaise, or to indicate where he thought the "new morality" passed the limits of approval. But he did in *Post-Mortem* ruthlessly attack the hypocrisy and cant that had battened on the soldiers in the war itself and which had seduced many of the survivors of battle to its own complacent creed of money-making in journalism and business and to support the suppression of the truth about the war if it was published. Noel Coward later confessed "the hysteria of its mood", but the play showed the force of its author's fundamental ideals of a decent world, and in his own words "let off a great deal of steam which might have remained sizzling inside me". Its emotionalism harmonises with the tendency to sentiment to be found in *Bitter Sweet* and elsewhere.

In the thirties Noel Coward continued to present the a-moral world of the twenties after its day was really over, as in *Design for Living* (1933). But his ever experimental talent also produced the patriotic pageant play *Cavalcade* (1931), which matched the changing spirit of the times, and which in due course had its successor in kind in *This Happy Breed* of 1944. Among his later plays the perfect farce, *Blithe Spirit* (1941), makes one of his happiest achievements.

Sean O'Casey, the other outstanding new dramatist of the twenties, was very different from Noel Coward. Another Irishman of genius, he was a worthy successor to Synge. His background, however, was not the Aran Islands but the slums of Dublin, crowded noisy tenements where women quarrelled and loafers drank, and the tragic violence of civil war was ever at hand. With altogether remarkable success he handled with penetrating power events still fresh in the memory of all. *The Shadow of A Gunman*, produced at the Abbey Theatre, Dublin, in 1923, showed a girl and a young poet caught tragically in a typical military raid in 1920 on a tenement whose inhabitants were suspected of Republican activities : the girl is shot as a result of her love for the young poet, and he is left with the agonised knowledge that, partly by his own cowardice, he has been the instrument of her fate. *Juno and the Paycock*, produced at the Abbey Theatre in 1924, had its setting in 1922, and again the final scene brings violent death out of civil hatred, the "execution" of a young man by his Republican comrades for treachery, a doom which has haunted him in anticipation from the opening of the play. In *The Plough and the Stars* (1926) the scene was laid further back, in Easter 1916, when the new violence first broke loose in Dublin, but its theme was the same, the cruel and brutal folly of civil war.

Like Synge, O'Casey did not directly preach in these plays, though their consistent presentation of one theme made their very objectivity a sermon in dramatic form. Indeed, like Synge, he gave his characters their own lives, which seem predestined from within and not by their creator. They are individuals at the mercy of themselves, and of chance and circumstance. In general they are crude, pitiable, weak, comic creatures speaking a rich lingo of the Dublin slums, in whose very richness there is poetry. They strut about, boasting, singing, quarrelling, drinking, with an unflagging vitality ; their fear itself is a thing of life ; and whenever true love speaks, the poetic beauty of the Irish countryside comes into the squalor of the tenement rooms. Few writers have so intimately fused realism and pathos, tragedy and comedy, for his world is a basically comic one whose atmosphere is a sky laden with fate ever ready to strike almost at random, and therefore it is a most pitiable world. We feel the Shakespearian sense that in civil strife it is the poor people of the country who suffer and who, if their lives and reason are spared, are made into beasts by the violence, killing and looting with an inhuman remorselessness.

On the whole in these plays O'Casey took no side, but let the various points of view come appropriately from the characters. In *The Plough and the Stars*, however, the total effect was one of less detachment on the playwright's part. There one is made to feel that the people involved in this tragic clash of politics are not only to be pitied for their sufferings but are also to be blamed for having recklessly allowed such a state of affairs to develop. Moreover, in the scornful protests of the young Marxist, though they are a natural contribution and in part a comic one, there can be sensed, at least in retrospect, the intervention of O'Casey himself. Certainly his plays after this underwent some change. He began to mix symbolism with his realism, to rely less on story and to employ a literary speech as well as the rich dialect of his Dublin slums. As a result his later plays had less effect than his earlier ones, but *The Silver Tassie* (1929), *Within the Gates* (1934) and *Red Roses for Me* (1946) were notable plays, and *Cock-a-Doodle Dandy* (1949) showed he had not lost his grasp on Irish character, for in that play the comic disreputable figures of Marthaun and Sailor Mahan are worthy to stand alongside Fluther of *The Plough and the Stars* and the Paycock and his treacherous crony "Joxer". O'Casey's own background and his attitude to life, politics and the drama are to be found in the autobiographical *I Knock at the Door* (1939) and succeeding volumes.

Among other new dramatists in the nineteen-twenties who deserve mention were A. A. Milne and Clemence Dane. Milne, later to gain perhaps his widest public by the Winnie the Pooh books for children, began as a dramatist with *Mr Pim Passes By* in 1921, and for over ten years he produced well-liked plays. They were good theatre, neat, romantic, whimsical and untroublesome : they included *The Romantic Age* (1920), *The Dover Road* (1922), *The Great Broxopp* (1923) and *Michael and Mary* (1930). Clemence Dane raised the question whether divorce was not justifiable on grounds of insanity in *A Bill of Divorcement* in 1921, and in the same year her *Will Shakespeare* appeared. Among other notable plays were Sutton Vane's *Outward Bound* (1923) on the theme of survival after death, and Van Druten's *Young Woodley* (1928). As the novelists waited some ten years before dealing with the war, so it was not till 1928 that R. C. Sheriff produced the outstanding war play in *Journey's End*. Here, without heroics, the agonised strain of trench warfare made a moving and exalting drama, which the revival of the play in 1950 proved to have a lasting value. The end of the decade saw the appearance of plays re-creating figures of the past in an agreeably lifelike way, as in Rudolf Besier's *The Barretts of Wimpole Street* and Joan Temple's *Charles and Mary Lamb*, both in 1930. Indeed, 1930 was reached with little more revolutionary in English drama having been achieved than the genius of O'Casey had to offer.

Outside the more commercial theatre, however, there had been considerable activity and progress. The Festival Theatre at Cambridge had offered fresh scope both for new plays and for original production of old plays. The Birmingham Repertory Company had contributed much of value, including the presentation of Shakespeare in modern dress, notably *Hamlet*. In 1929 the Malvern Festival began, also making both old and new plays part of its programme. The British Drama League had been founded in 1919 and it was followed by the Scottish National Theatre Society and the Scottish Community Drama Association. Further, repertory companies and amateur societies by their number and enthusiasm throughout the country testified to a widespread and ever growing interest in drama.

The nineteen-thirties saw the appearance of two new dramatists of distinction, J. B. Priestley and "James Bridie" (O. H. Mavor). While still writing novels, Priestley followed up a dramatisation of his *Good Companions* with a series of original plays. Sometimes he kept to the normal presentation of character and circumstance as in *Laburnum Grove* (1933) or indulged in pure farcical comedy as in *When We Are Married* (1938). From the beginning, however, he was ambitious to develop his own kind of play. He wanted to present ideas about life, to wake up his audiences to the possibilities of their altering their lives for the better, and to suggest that human life can be a fuller and finer thing than it normally is. His first play, *Dangerous Corner* (1932), developed the simple truth that at any point in ordinary human affairs there may always be alternative developments possible : first he lets a conversation among his characters take a turn which leads to disaster, but then he shows how, instead, the dangerous corner was safely turned in a different direction. So he expressed the mysterious risks in life, the lurking "might-have-been" which is the shadow of actuality. In *Time and the Conways* (1937) he illuminated the old truth that what we shall be is implicit and discernible years earlier in what we are, but to this he added another point of view : as one of the characters puts it :—

> "now, at this moment, or any moment, we're only a cross-section of our real selves. What we REALLY are is the whole stretch of ourselves, all our time, and when we come to the end of this life, all our selves, all our time, will be US—the real you, the real me".

So this play posed questions about the reality of life and time ; it showed the Conways first young, then in middle age, and finally young again so that the audience, knowing what they became, may re-read them in the light of that knowledge.

It was a dramatic experiment, well executed, though the action is small and Barrie's *Dear Brutus* had in some ways anticipated the theme. *I Have Been Here Before* (1937), as its title suggests, used the theory of human life as a cycle of reincarnation : can people, then, by knowledge of disaster experienced in a previous existence reshape their current lives to a better issue ? That is the idea round which the play is built. Again in *Johnson Over Jordan* (1939) Priestley made his audience think beyond the limits of life in time as we know it : in Tibetan religion there is a state after death, called Bardo, and in that strange world Priestley places most of his play, showing the real world only in introductory scenes in the house from which on the day the play opens Johnson's funeral has taken place. What can a man carry over from this life to Bardo ? What, that is to say, have been his real spiritual values which alone can fit him to share and understand, indeed to help keep alive, the values and personalities which those already dead have taken with them to Bardo ?

The play was a bold experiment, which Priestley's own values, his broad human sympathy and his dramatic skill enabled him to present effectively ; but it was not wholly original for it was partly anticipated by Vane's *Outward Bound*, nor was it fully effective as drama because of its hovering between the real world and the shifting scenes of ghost-crowded Bardo. *Music at Night* (1938) put the characters in a trance, induced by music, in which they contact both past and future and become part of the eternal flow of life. In *The Linden Tree* (1947), however, Priestley went back to the normal world and a straightforward treatment, and succeeded in presenting a firm, finely characterised drama, richly suggestive in its appreciation of the problem of life as the characters and circumstances of a family evoke it for its members and for us all.

James Bridie, born in 1888, was a more truly original dramatist than Priestley. His death in 1951 no doubt deprived the drama of further notable achievement and of much encouragement to all keenly interested in the drama, for his own enthusiastic interest in plays and acting meant much to all those whom his far-reaching influence touched. After first writing for the Birmingham Repertory Company, he quickly made a mark with *The Anatomist* and *Tobias and the Angel*, both in 1931, and in the succeeding years he kept steadily to the fore with play after play, his last published collection of plays being *John Knox and Other Plays* in 1949. Among his other most notable plays were *A Sleeping Clergyman* (1933), *Susannah and the Elders* (1938), *Mr Bolfry* (1943) and *Jonah and the Whale*, first produced in 1932 and later adapted for broadcasting and for television. From Biblical history through the Arthurian legend and sixteenth-century Scotland to a Free Kirk Manse in the West Highlands in the Second World War no story or setting came amiss to him. Indeed, his great characteristics were his versatility, his wide, lively intellectual interest and his power of holding an audience by his stagecraft even when they were baffled by his ideas. Certainly the intention of his plays was often by no means obvious, but each was nevertheless stimulating to the mind. Whether he gave a story or, as frequently, dispensed with one, the talk among his characters had the excitement of a good Brains Trust. He was an intellectual without being a bore, and plain people could enjoy, even if some remained rather puzzled, the clash of ideas and personalities out of which he fashioned drama : the title of one of his volumes of collected plays, *Plays for*

Plain People (1944), was no misnomer. True characterisation, wit, comedy, lively talk, a whimsical but shrewd and agile mind, allied to a natural and imaginative talent for the theatre, will ensure the continued life of his work.

Apart from the plays of Priestley and Bridie, the most interesting development in the drama of the nineteen-thirties was in poetic drama. The Canterbury Festival had been established in 1928, when Masefield's *The Coming of Christ* was performed in the Cathedral; there, too, T. S. Eliot's *Murder in the Cathedral* was performed in 1935, Charles Williams's *Thomas Cranmer of Canterbury* in 1936, Dorothy Sayers's *The Zeal of Thy House* in 1937 and Christopher Hassall's *Christ's Comet* in 1938. Except for the fragmentary *Sweeny Agonistes* in 1930 T. S. Eliot had first turned his attention to the dramatic form with *The Rock* (1934), a pageant play written for performance at Sadler's Wells Theatre on behalf of the forty-five churches fund of the diocese of London. As a pageant, it was intended to be spectacular rather than dramatic, and a frank didacticism somewhat weakened even its fine choruses and lyrics. It was with *Murder in the Cathedral* that he turned to drama proper, and achieved an austere masterpiece, promising the development of dramatic power, but rather stiff in movement and rhetorical in expression, with its choruses again claiming much of the praise due to the total effect. Like *The Rock* it was written partly in verse and partly in prose. Then in *Family Reunion* (1939) he chose a modern domestic scene, but his treatment became more obscure and the dramatic development was hindered by the ideas and the Aeschylean parallelism: carefully studied it assists in the understanding of much in the later poems, *Four Quartets*, but at that stage it seemed as if its author would never gain a wide audience as a dramatist.

In 1949, however, *The Cocktail Party* was produced at the Edinburgh Festival and a few months later was enthusiastically received first in New York and then in London. Part of Eliot's difficulty in expressing himself in dramatic form had lain in the need of finding a verse medium. He himself said: "Anyone who tries to write poetic drama even to-day should know that half of his energy must be exhausted in the effort to escape from the constricting toils of Shakespeare". Now Eliot had successfully created his medium—verse without any specifically poetic language or rhythm, fit for prosaic contexts, but also able to enhance dramatic tension by its precise and suggestive poetic condensation. It helped rather than hindered the audience. With this instrument Eliot set out to teach his audience a lesson in living basically similar to the teaching of *Four Quartets*, but presented very much more simply and directly.

Thus Act I of *The Cocktail Party* introduces an ordinary cocktail party, at which the husband, Edward, a barrister, suddenly deserted by his wife, Lavinia, after five years of marriage, tries to persuade his guests that she has merely gone to visit an aunt. But there is also present an Unidentified Guest who, when he gets Edward alone, tells him his situation can lead "to finding out what you really are. What you really feel. What you really are among other people". But when Lavinia returns next day, she and Edward can only indulge in quietly exasperated analysis of one another's failings. Celia, a girl with whom Edward had thought himself in love until Lavinia's brief absence disillusioned him, is a further complication. In fact, these three are dwellers in the Waste Land, self-deceivers interested only in themselves.

So, in Act II, they are introduced to a specialist (none other than the Unidentified Guest) who probes their spiritual illnesses. Edward has to face the fact that his relations both with his wife and with Celia have clearly shown him to be incapable of fully loving; Lavinia has to confess that her breakdown is due not so much to her unspoken knowledge of her husband's affaire with Celia as to her realisation that she had been incapable of inspiring love in a young man, Peter Quilpe, who in Act I thought himself in love with Celia; Celia, after the exposure of Edward's emptiness, is desolate with a sense of her own emptiness, failure and sin. The advice given by the specialist is simple: Edward and Lavinia are ordinary people, let them realise of life that "the best of

a bad job is all any of us make of it—except, of
course, the saints", and then let them make the best of it,
learning "how to bear the burdens of [their] conscience" and
striving to "work out [their] salvation with diligence". But
Celia, with her peculiar awareness of solitude and her sense
of sin, has the makings of a saint : for her the way of redemption must match her greater spiritual potentiality—the lines
in which she talks of her vision of love and the specialist
replies are almost the only lines in the play which are obviously
verse. But then, with the prayers for their salvation which
conclude Act II, the real drama is over.

Act III, however, shows how far redemption has been
attained: as another cocktail party is about to begin two years
later, Edward and Lavinia are at their ease, making a very
good job of marriage, and Peter, back in England for a week
before returning to his successful script-writing in California,
is moved to consider his own life afresh at the news of
Celia's death in the East, crucified on an ant-heap in an
insurrection which had attacked the austere nursing order
to which she had devoted herself. So Eliot, without any
deliberate show of religion, had preached his familiar
doctrine, "redeem the time", and had made of his sermon
a play really dramatic by virtue of its human insight and its
masterly technique, a play which, lightened by comedy and
movement and stage business, kept close to the everyday
world, yet rose above the commonplace and indeed penetrated unobtrusively to deeper levels. In 1951 it remained an
incomparable achievement.

Alongside T. S. Eliot in time and supported by the Group
Theatre, formed in 1933 to try out new theatrical forms,
which also produced Eliot's *Sweeny Agonistes*, came the
younger poets. Auden's *Dance of Death* was produced in
1933 ; gloomy in its theme of the death-will in modern
civilisation, for which Marxism was the cure, its treatment
was bright, fantastic and mocking, influenced largely by ballet
and musical comedy. *The Dog Beneath the Skin* (1935) was
a high-spirited comic extravaganza, capable of delighting
even some of those to whom its left-wing propaganda was

anathema ; the musical comedy theme of the young villager seeking the lost young squire, to be rewarded if successful with the hand of the squire's sister, rattles along through a breath-taking series of scenes and in a variety of forms and stage business. Then in 1936 with *The Ascent of F6*, written like its predecessors with the collaboration of Isherwood, Auden achieved a play of considerable distinction. Here, as in his poetry, Auden blended politics and psychology, attacking big business and imperialism, and interpreting his hero in terms of mother-fixation. In the last Act his symbolism, psychology and unusual technique make a somewhat baffling combination, but the earlier part of the play is clear and striking, the tension of feeling among the climbers of the mountain being particularly dramatic, and in total effect the play was original and stimulating. *On the Frontier* (1938), however, was less successful.

Stephen Spender and Louis MacNeice also had plays produced by the Group Theatre. Spender's *The Trial of a Judge* (1938) depicts the clash of Right and Left, between whose violent extremes impartial liberal justice was crushed. It had enough dramatic power to justify presentation on the stage, but the human individuality of the characters struggles unsuccessfully against the political ideologies they hold, and in contrast to O'Casey's men and women of the Irish Civil War they are little more than puppets. Probably the most satisfying achievement lay in the choruses and in some of the long speeches. MacNeice's *Out of the Picture* was produced at the Group Theatre in 1937, but his talent for drama was shown to better effect in his radio plays of the forties, notably *The Dark Tower*. The Group Theatre had to stop its work with the outbreak of war in 1939 and did not resume until 1950, when it turned to the producing of plays by Jean Paul Sartre and Calderon.

Somerset Maugham, when he abandoned playwriting in the early nineteen-thirties, with *The Breadwinner* (1930) and *For Services Rendered* (1932) as two of his last plays, condemned the tendency to base plays on ideas. His Preface to his fourth volume of Plays in 1932 regretted the poverty

of contemporary English drama, which he held to be largely
"due to the fact that the playwrights have been influenced
by false theories to adventure in a field which the nature of
the drama forbids". In his opinion "prose drama is one of
the lesser arts, like woodcarving or dancing, but so far as
it is an art at all its purpose is to afford delight. I do not
think that it can concern itself with the welfare of humanity
or the saving of civilisation". At any rate, when Maugham
withdrew, it was to leave a considerable gap in the commercial
theatre except on the level of ephemeral entertainment. Among
the best popular plays of the thirties were the rather sentimental productions of "Dodie Smith" (C. L. Anthony), such
as *Autumn Crocus* (1930), *Call It A Day* (1935) and *Dear
Octopus* (1938): the comedy of family life, the amusing
pathos of middle age, and the lovable awkwardness of
children made acceptable fare. A. P. Herbert's comic zest
and witty lyrics as in *Tantivy Towers* (1931) was peculiarly
his own. Terence Rattigan's *French Without Tears* (1937)
was admirable farcical comedy. Among notable plays
there were also Eric Linklater's *News of the Devil* (1934)
and Charles Morgan's *The Flashing Stream* (1938).

The war inevitably checked the possible emergence of new
dramatists and new developments in drama. That the theatres
kept on at all in the years of the blackout and the bombing
was a great tribute to the indomitability of actors and
audiences. Priestley and Bridie continued to write; Terence
Rattigan depicted the tragicomedy of war in *Flare Path*
(1943), and maintained his popularity with *The Winslow
Boy* (1946) and *Who Is Sylvia?* (1950); Emlyn Williams,
notable in the thirties for his *Night Must Fall* and *The Corn
is Green*, produced further plays in the forties including *The
Wind of Heaven*; Esther McKracken enlivened the war years
with the cheerful comedy of *Quiet Wedding* and *Quiet Week-
end*. On the more intellectual and experimental side there
was Peter Ustinov, with *The House of Regrets* (1940) and
The Man Behind the Statue (1945) among his plays. The
drama began to receive some help from the state after the war
through the Council for the Encouragement of Music and the

Arts, which in 1946 became the Arts Council of Great Britain, but new dramatists of exceptional talent were not immediately apparent. Some of the younger poets, turning away from the political propaganda of poetic drama in the previous decade, showed a quiet determination to pursue the possibilities of dramatic poetry. Ronald Duncan, Norman Nicholson, Anne Ridler and others were associated with the Mercury Theatre, but on the whole their work was of a kind for amateur production and to be read. Ronald Duncan first made his mark with *This Way to the Tomb* (1946); in 1950 he published the play *Stratton*. Norman Nicholson, the Cumberland poet, followed up *The Old Man of the Mountains* (1945) with *Prophesy to the Wind* (1950), a play in four scenes which shows a rural civilisation in which industrialism has almost vanished, but where the rediscovery of a dynamo dramatically threatens to bring back the age of scientific power. Anne Ridler's *Henry Bly And Other Plays* (1950) contained shorter, less ambitious pieces. None of these authors really secured adequate theatrical effect; they remained primarily poets.

There emerged, however, after the war one dramatist, who made poetic drama an exciting theatrical entertainment. Christopher Fry, born in 1907, after a varied career as a member of a repertory company, a teacher, a cabaret entertainer, and director of the Tunbridge Wells Repertory Theatre, took gradually to dramatic writing. His earliest work was written, like T. S. Eliot's *The Rock*, with a particular local purpose, for *The Boy With a Cart* was a pageant to commemorate the founding of a village church. *The Tower* was a pageant to celebrate the history of Tewkesbury Abbey. At the beginning of the war Fry was director of the Playhouse at Oxford, and during the war he served in the Pioneer Corps, working on bomb damage clearance : by faith he is a Quaker. After the war came *A Phoenix Too Frequent* (1946), slight and still only promising outstanding achievement. Then *The Lady's Not For Burning*, his first full-length play, was produced in 1948 at the Arts Theatre, London, and its brilliant and unusual qualities secured a wider success at the Globe Theatre,

London, in 1949. The production of *Venus Observed* followed in January 1950. The achievement of Fry is both technical and comprehensive. As with Noel Coward, the theatre seems in his blood, and he can conceive plot, situation and dialogue in the way that excites and holds an audience ; his verse is born for speech, rising and falling, alive with wit and vivid with imagery. Plot and speech alike renounce the naturalism which had reigned so long since Ibsen put his stamp on modern drama. Instead we have a conception of comedy that harmonises with that of Shakespeare in a play like *Much Ado*, where through romantic improbability we are given the fundamental reality of the human heart. Indeed *Venus Observed* brings its characters face to face with themselves in a way close to Shakespeare's handling of Benedick and Beatrice and of Jaques and of the Duke in *Twelfth Night*: sham and selfishness are stripped bare with ironic sympathy. Above all, one feels behind and through these last two plays of Fry's a positive, healthy view of life. To Fry life is a joyous miracle ; faith in God supports the old values of love, beauty and goodness, and, where man errs, there can be forgiveness and redemption. There is a spiritual assurance behind the laughter, a solidity beneath the dazzling surface of the plays.

Fry calls them comedies, and on comedy he has remarked: "Comedy is an escape, not from truth, but from despair : a narrow escape into faith. It believes in a universal cause for delight, even though knowledge of the cause is always twitched away from us". In other words, Fry is no escapist from the contemporary dilemma, but, sharing the peculiar spiritual and intellectual tension of our age, he will by preference go forward unafraid. Indeed *A Sleep of Prisoners*, produced in a London church in 1951, is a bold step forwards. It tells with great dramatic power the dreams of four soldiers who are prisoners in a bombed church in enemy territory, and its theme is the crime of the shedding of blood.

In attempting to survey the drama of half a century in this one short chapter much has, reluctantly, been omitted. Frederick Lonsdale, with his delightful and highly competent craftsmanship, is one obvious omission. Laurence Housman's *Little Plays of Saint Francis*, his *Palace Plays* and *Victoria Regina* deserved not only notice but appreciation. Ashley Dukes's *The Man With a Load of Mischief* is only one of several notable single plays which merited mention. The One-Act Play would be worthy of a chapter to itself. The drama of these years needs indeed not a chapter, but a book to itself.

CHAPTER XX

BERNARD SHAW

When a great writer dies high in honour and in fame, criticism is for a while at a loss; as the applause dies down, praise and blame both sound unnaturally loud and hollow. So it had to be with Bernard Shaw. For fifty years he had had so great and pervasive an influence upon thought in its widest ranging from the eternal to the topical that, when his presence was removed, it seemed more than usually difficult to detach his work from his personality and the texture of his times and to assess its permanent values. Even now, however, he begins to assume a position in English drama second only to Shakespeare. Posterity will judge how close he stands to his great predecessor. Here it is possible only to suggest one or two points of comparison.

In the history of our drama Shaw may well claim the greater achievement, for, where Shakespeare had in Marlowe, Kyd and Lyly notable English forerunners, Shaw built up his own new drama ; true, Shaw followed the inspiration of Ibsen, but he would seem to have been himself ready to be the English Ibsen. But in so far as Shaw's drama relies predominantly on ideas it is less universal in its appeal and less outside the stream of time than Shakespeare's. Again the modern dramatist has so stamped his personality upon his plays that it must for ever be impossible to disregard it, and, whereas the fluid and elusive personality of Shakespeare flows into his creations, the shade of Shaw stands by us as an extra *dramatis persona* in nearly every play. Thus by virtue both of his ideas and his personality Shaw is always likely to divide his audiences while Shakespeare unites his. Perhaps the difference is only that between kinds of genius and not one of greater and lesser genius, and yet one thought suggests that Shakespeare outtopped Shaw in sheer creative genius : does not Shaw seem almost a magnificent serio-comic creation from Shakespeare's own mind, a kind of Puritan Falstaff ? Of course, Shaw was no Falstaff but in most things from morals to meat and drink his very opposite, yet Falstaff and Shaw rival one another in power of intellect and argument, in wit and realism, in fascination of personality, and in love of performing before an audience. Shakespeare could have created the essence of a Shaw out of the wonders of his genius, whereas in that magnitude of creation Shaw created nothing as great as himself.

Bernard Shaw was born in Dublin in 1856. His father's family had been small landowners in Ireland since the late seventeenth century and they had intermarried with the Irish. But previously they had lived in Hampshire, and they claimed an ancient Scottish origin. His father, after employment at the law courts, became in middle life a grain merchant. His mother was the daughter of an Irish country gentleman. She was twenty years younger than her husband and she lived largely for her art, that of an opera singer. Shaw's schooling was ordinary enough, but as a boy he loved to frequent the Irish National Gallery to study the pictures there and by the time he was fifteen he had a sound knowledge of some of the great composers too. To great writers such as Goethe and Molière he introduced himself by following up the sources of and libretti of operas. He was indeed left to a great extent to find his own way, and he spoke of his early years as "rich only in dreams". Religiously the family background was Protestant, but Shaw early rejected the Christian faith.

At fifteen, his mother having gone to London with her two daughters, who were both older than their only brother, Shaw was left with his father and he worked as clerk in a Dublin estate agent's office, where his efficiency soon promoted him from rent-collecting to the position of cashier. Four years of this employment were enough for him. Determined to be a writer he resigned and in 1876 he joined his mother in London. He tried journalism, but in the ten years up to the age of twenty-nine it is said that he earned only £6 by that means. His inner confidence, however, sustained him through those hard years till his writing began to bring him in a small income about 1885. Between 1879 and 1882 he wrote four novels. The first, *Immaturity*, dealt with the problem of marriage. It remained unpublished until his collected works appeared. The second, *The Irrational Knot*, written in 1880, first appeared serially in 1885-87; it was published as a book in 1905. The third, *Love Among the Artists*, was also serialised in 1887-88. It was the fourth novel in the order of their writing, *Cashel Byron's Profession*, that was his first published book, for that appeared soon after its serialisation in 1885-86, and it is decidedly the best of his novels. None suggests that Shaw would have won the success as a novelist that he achieved as a dramatist, but these novels anticipate many of the themes and ideas he was to express in his plays. They contain too some strands of disguised autobiography.

The important events for Shaw in these years of struggle were his meetings with people and his discovery of ideas. In 1882 he went to a meeting addressed by Henry George, of whose speech he later declared that it "changed the whole current of my life". He then began to study Socialism and economics, and he read Marx's *Capital* in the British Museum. He became acquainted with leading Socialists. Henry Salt, an apostle of Shelley's ideas, and Edward Carpenter, another progressive idealist, were among them. It was the newly founded Socialist journal *To-day* which accepted *Cashel Byron's Profession*, and it was through that acceptance that Shaw met William Morris. He already knew Sidney Webb, to whose very clearly conceived Socialist and economic ideas he owed much, and of whom he has said: "Sidney Webb was of more use to me than any other man I have ever met". His membership of the Fabian Society, to whose Executive he was elected in 1885, further extended his contacts and activities. He read papers to the Fabian Society, his outstanding aptitude for debate showed itself, and he became a public speaker on platforms and at street corners, where his tall figure, red beard, clear and self-assured mind and abounding detailed knowledge mastered his audiences.

By 1890 indeed his knowledge of contemporary economic matters was considerable, and it was controlled by a comprehensive philosophic outlook. Like his friends he envisaged a better world to be brought into being by the co-operative efforts of realistic thinkers activated by a selfless love of humanity. This lofty moral idealism had at first no religious basis on Shaw's part, but it was not long before he found a belief which lent it for him a strong support. In the writings of Samuel Butler he saw an escape from the Darwinian theory of evolution which made chance, not purpose, the determining factor, and when in 1891 he came to know the thought of Nietzsche he realised that he had already been thinking in terms of a purposive Life Force behind the workings of the universe. This Life Force he moreover perceived to explain the place of woman in the world, for it accounted for woman's ruthless pursuit of man. Men like himself must therefore, by intelligent co-operation with the Life Force, use all their endeavours to hasten the evolution of mankind to higher moral, intellectual, economic and social standards. To this stage in his thinking he had practically come when he turned to the drama as his medium of expression.

That Shaw chose the drama as the means whereby to criticise and educate society was due to a most happy combination of experience, coincidence and chance. His own experience had taught him that he had no promising future in the novel. It may well seem now a destined coincidence that, just when Shaw was approaching the time when he must find a channel for his enormous vitality, the plays of Ibsen became known to him. It was more or less a result of chance that, when he had finished his *Quintessence of Ibsenism* (1891), he had by him the first draft of a play, which had been laid aside since 1885. William Archer, the dramatic critic, had then asked him to write the dialogue for an adaptation of a French play, but had rejected Shaw's unfinished attempt. Perhaps the predominating influence in determining him to turn to the drama was the example of Ibsen; perhaps his love of debating, in which he had shown how irresistible it was for him to counter his arguments himself if no one else would, influenced him towards choosing the kind of play in which the characters undertake this dual task of proposer and opposer. At any rate, taking up this early effort in 1892, he made it into *Widowers' Houses*, and thereafter for nearly sixty years with unflagging energy he made the drama peculiarly his own province.

The way in which, though his plays were for years little acted, he slowly became known, at first largely by published volumes and criticism, until with the Court Theatre productions of 1904 to 1907, especially *John Bull's Other Island*, he became a popular playwright, has already been outlined in the previous chapter. It was not till after *Saint Joan* (1924) that he became the revered elder playwright, a highly respectable figure whom, however, the dramatic critics did not cease to condemn as sharply as before. By then, the old world having been transformed by the war, a new generation had grown up to accept him. Supreme though he had been in his own publicising of ideas, the parallel preaching of H. G. Wells and others had further helped to make his Socialism and his general attitude to ideas and society part of the mind of the age. But Socialists, as well as others, could still be amazed as the old man, with the energy and the unpredictable originality of his genius, produced such plays as *The Apple Cart* (1929), *Too True to be Good* (1934), *Geneva* (1938), and *In Good King Charles's Golden Days* (1939).

In this long period of dramatic writing, more than twice the length of Shakespeare's, Shaw displayed the manysided-ness of his genius in a great variety of plays. It is hard, however, to discern any clear "periods" or trends in his development. At most there is on the whole a change of theme from the particular to the general, from the contemporary scene to the future (with intervals of looking at the past), and of attitude from the satiric and destructive to the philosophic and constructive, from the materialistic to the mystic. Yet these changes seem not to arise so much from any change in Shaw himself as from his mood of the time in relation to concurrent circumstances. Coming relatively old to the drama, his mind mature and liable to little subsequent change, Shaw was indeed always Shaw, and one gets the impression that he could have written many of his plays in a different order had he felt like it at the time. For example, though *Caesar and Cleopatra* and *Saint Joan* are separated from one another in composition by about a quarter of a century, they are by no means so distant from one another in the nature of their conception and treatment. It was natural that at first Shaw should be particularly "revolutionary"; it was only natural, too, that success should sometimes slacken his craftsmanship and encourage him to overdo his brilliant talk as in *Misalliance*; in his old age the streak of irresponsibility which had always run through his high seriousness quite naturally ran more easily away with him as in *Buoyant Billions*. Indeed, if there is any real division to be made in Shaw's dramatic development it is the First War that marks it. Unable to produce any new work in those four years, when he resumed with *Heartbreak House*, he was on the whole as a dramatist more philosophic than before, and more concerned with the future. But even the gigantic *Back to Methuselah* (1921) had behind it the same Shaw as first dealt with the Life Force in *Man and Superman* at the beginning of the century. As Shaw himself said, he had decorated the earlier play "too brilliantly and lavishly" with the result that "nobody noticed the new religion in the centre of the intellectual whirlpool". The work, therefore needed re-doing, but the dramatist who tried again was unchanged in his essential attitude and qualities by the intervening years.

In his own account, indeed, Shaw refers to *Man and Superman* as marking the emergence of what he himself aimed to be as a dramatist, one of "the artist-prophets" in the succession of men like Goethe and Ibsen. Till then the plays he had written had only "established [him] professionally". In his summary (in the Preface to *Back to Methuselah*) of his first years as a playwright he remarks that in the early nineties he found the existing state of the English theatre "intolerable". "The fashionable theatre prescribed one serious subject: clandestine adultery: the dullest of all subjects for a serious author . . . I tried slum-landlordism, doctrinaire Free Love (pseudo-Ibsenism), prostitution, militarism, marriage, history, current politics, natural Christianity, national and individual character, paradoxes of conventional society, husband-hunting, questions of conscience, professional delusions and impostures, all worked into a series of comedies of manners in the classic fashion, which was then very much out of fashion, the mechanical tricks of Parisian 'construction' being held obligatory in the theatre.''

This summary covers his work as far as 1914. *Widowers' Houses* was his attack on slum-landlordism. The pseudo-Ibsenism was contained in *The Philanderer*. Prostitution lay behind *Mrs Warren's Profession*, for Mrs Warren's quite considerable wealth was derived from brothels. *Arms and the Man* gaily demolished the romantic glory of soldiering. *Candida* was an Ibsen-like consideration of marriage. *The Man of Destiny* and *Caesar and Cleopatra* were adventures in history. Husband-hunting was the comic aspect of *Man and Superman*. *John Bull's Other Island* dealt with current politics and national character. Christianity was examined in relation to moral, economic and social problems through the presentation of an officer of the Salvation Army in *Major Barbara* and in a broader way in the later *Androcles and the Lion*. "Professional delusions and impostures," and questions of conscience make up *The Doctor's Dilemma*. *Misalliance* has as its theme education, which is more extensively discussed in its Preface "Of Parents and Children". In two plays at least, however, Shaw largely let the wicked foolish world go by, namely in *You Never Can Tell* and *Pygmalion*, to which might be added *The Dark Lady of the Sonnets*, *The Man of Destiny* and *Caesar and Cleopatra*, for they too all escape the direct pressure of the modern world.

The exuberant high spirits which characterised his plays before 1914, often bringing into his comedy a lively element of farce, did not appear so much afterwards. Instead something of grandeur and poetry found expression in famous passages of *Saint Joan* and *Back to Methuselah*, though his comic vision still played freely and variously, fully exemplifying the Shavian wit and humour. Before *Heartbreak House*, which, though not produced till 1921, was finished during the war, he had certainly never written a play with such deep underlying seriousness. He called it "a fantasia on English themes in the Russian manner", by which he alluded to his being partly inspired by Tchekhov, and symbolically through its characters it presents a world which has lost its direction, a world of futilities and insincerities struggling to find reality, a world which to one of the characters appears "this cruel, damnable world". No play could be more serious in its general intention than *Back to Methuselah*. In writing it, Shaw said, he "threw over all economic considerations, and faced the apparent impossibility of a performance during [his] lifetime". Its five parts, indeed, demand days to perform, as the cycle proceeds from In the Beginning in the Garden of Eden, through the Gospel of the Brothers Barnabas, A.D. 1920, and two intermediate stages of the future in A.D. 2170 and A.D 3000, until the last play presents As Far As Thought Can Reach, A.D. 31,920. Yet it was soon acted, first in New York in 1922, and then by the Birmingham Repertory Theatre in 1923. In this cycle Shaw felt himself to be co-operating with the Life Force, for through his drama he was declaring that, if only mankind had the will to control its evolution, it could in time achieve perfection, and his "metabiological pentateuch" therefore became part of this purposive process.

When he had thus fulfilled his great wish to express his fundamental religious faith as a Creative Evolutionist, Shaw returned in *Saint Joan* to a drama of his normal scope and manner. Its heroine, played by Sybil Thorndike, was a great success. Portrayed "as a sane and shrewd country girl of extraordinary strength of mind and hardihood of body . . . a thorough daughter of the soil in her peasantlike matter-of-factness and doggedness", she was however, in her creator's mind an instrument like himself

of the Life Force. But, having preached his doctrine directly
in the cycle, he now let his re-creation of history speak for
itself through the spiritual vision of the Saint.   In *The
Apple Cart* (1929) he turned again to the future, and to the
dismay of those who had regarded him as an advanced
advocate of democracy showed that the highest ability could
be found as well in a king as in a peasant. His brilliance
was undiminished, and to the end his extraordinary vitality
of mind animated all he wrote.

Shaw's ideas can never cease to form an important part
of his dramatic legacy, any more than we can appreciate
Shakespeare without reference to the view of life which lies
behind his work. Nevertheless it is as dramatist upon the
stage that Shaw demands primary consideration. In his own
day Shaw's command over audiences which by no means
consisted only of those who shared his ideas was an obvious
fact. That this was so suggests that it was the dramatist and
not the preacher who exerted the real power, though it must
be admitted that no small part of the pleasure felt by contemporaries lay in the stimulus given both to disciples and
opponents by the sparkling irreverence of the wit playing on
topics of particular current interest. But this wit was always
subservient to the total working of the genius of the comic
playwright. His dramatic instinct, indeed, was altogether
transcendant and so wilfully fashioned its own play that the
audience almost forgot in its delight the seriousness of the
lesson it had been offered. Shaw himself wrote to Ellen
Terry : " On my honour *Arms and the Man* was a serious
play—a play to cry over if you could only have helped
laughing ". Those who saw *Man and Superman* at a performance in which the Third Act of Juan in Hell was omitted
were quite justified in not realising how much lay behind the
farcical comedy of John Tanner trying to flee from the
pursuing Ann. Hence, the Prefaces, which not only took
advantage of the success of a play to make a more comprehensive and detailed attack but which had often to make the
public fully conscious of matters which the inspired Comic

Muse had transmuted into laughter. Shaw once spoke of the "lightness of heart, without which nothing can succeed in the theatre", and in his own paradoxical union of the prophet and the jester lies the assurance of his dramatic survival.

Shaw's plays, as a whole, give the impression of his creative powers working in a spontaneous unity. We can well believe that, when he told Ellen Terry that "*Candida* came easily enough", he was expressing a general truth about his work. The component elements of plot, stagecraft, characterisation and dialogue grew into one natural unforced creation. Shaw himself, in the Postscript to *Back to Methuselah*, declared: "When I am writing a play I never invent a plot: I let the play write itself and shape itself, which it always does even when up to the last moment I do not foresee the way out. Sometimes I do not see what the play was driving at until quite a long time after I have finished it." Certainly his method of developing a play often involves a turn which takes the audience half by surprise, as it may, from his own account, have taken the dramatist himself. Thus his success lies partly in the command of stagecraft which instinctively knows how to turn stage situation to profit.

His characterisation sometimes lacks the power of fully convincing us, because it does not always arise from such immediate creative insight as does the general idea of the play, but is to some extent dependent on that idea for the nature and variety of its figures. But once started on their career, his people share the vitality of the whole even when that is a vitality not of action but of talk. They may, indeed, be carried away by the zest of the argument and talk too much like Shaw and not enough as individuals, but this only enhances the unity of the play and its dramatic effectiveness. Of outstanding individual characters Shaw has fewer than Shakespeare, but many surely have that individuality which lives in its own right—a Bluntschli, or a Father Keegan, or a Shotover or Saint Joan. Women, above all, he read and presented with a cunning unromantic realism which suggests that, like the novelist Richardson, he understood women even

better than men: to Saint Joan may be added among his
many acutely and vividly realised women Raina, Cleopatra,
Candida, Ann Whitefield, Major Barbara, Jennifer Dubedat,
and Eliza Doolittle, to name only a few.

In two directions his characterisation possessed special
power—in evoking our sympathetic interest in unattractive
people like Mrs Warren and Louis Dubedat, and in creating
beings of broad comedy of a Dickensian vitality like Candida's
father, Straker and Alfred Doolittle. Other gifts affecting
characterisation included his ability to allow for the existence
in a character of the intuitive, that "sort of sixth sense" which,
when it is possessed, gives an extra dimension to personality,
and his understanding of good simple souls, as pre-eminently
in the Saint. Indeed, his creative power and psychological insight in the matter of character are very great, and when, as
from time to time, he relied on stock figures of angry parents
or the rebellious young or amusing servants he gave them a
fresh existence, as Sheridan had done with stock figures in
his plays. In fact his characterisation, like his playwriting
as a whole, arose, as that of great writers always does, from
a unified working of the unconscious and the conscious
whereby each element takes a larger or smaller share as the
intensity of creation grows or slackens.

As for Shaw's style, it never failed from the earliest plays
to the last, or in his pamphlets, prefaces or letters. No
doubt the previous writing of novels and criticism had already
made it second nature by the time it was put to the service
of his dramatic muse. Shaw himself refused to admit the
existence of style apart from matter. Style arose, he held,
from the having something to say. "Effectiveness of
assertion is the Alpha and Omega of style. He who has
nothing to assert has no style and can have none; he who
has something to assert will go as far in power of style as its
momentousness and his conviction will carry him. Disprove
his assertion after it is made, yet his style remains." But in
his opinion this was not all : he who has something to say
should give the edge of provocation to his assertion. "In
this world, if you do not say a thing in an irritating way, you

may as well not say it at all, since nobody will trouble themselves about anything that does not trouble them. The attention given to a criticism is in direct proportion to its indigestibility.''

With this union of assertion and provocation his style is never dull. In the plays it rarely has a chance to be dull, for there is the further animation given by the dramatic clash of dialogue: the dialogue indeed shares the general effect of spontaneity. In the Prefaces, too, he is always arguing a case, and by separating the many heads of the argument into fairly short sections he keeps the pace brisk: they are a born debater's prefaces. Nearly always one seems to hear the talking voice behind the prose even when the writing is not for the stage. If he is ever dull, it is not in the plays, however long the speeches become, but only when in a preface he overstrains the virtues of his manner by too prolonged a brilliance and too persistent an irritation of his opponents. A notable exception, however, is the treatise *The Intelligent Woman's Guide to Socialism and Capitalism* (1928), in which the length and the unusual aim of persuading rather than provoking his readers does result in some degree of dullness. But what he could do without any aim of irritating is shown many a time in the serious parts of his plays, as in Caesar's meditation by the Sphinx, and the speech of Joan immediately before her execution and Lilith's long soliloquy concluding *Back to Methuselah*. In such passages the poet replaces the debater, and a style which in general combines the virtues of his two great Irish predecessors, Swift and Congreve, takes on a power beyond theirs.

In the briefest summary of Shaw's work it is not enough to mention only the plays and the prefaces. After a journalistic beginning as a critic of painting and a book reviewer he was given in 1888 a weekly column to write on music in the recently founded evening newspaper *The Star*, and in 1890 he gave this up to write a weekly musical article for *The World*. These criticisms were later published in two volumes, *London Music in 1888-1889* and *Music in London*,

1890-1894, which are full of lively and stimulating appreciations. There had been no such musical criticism in England before. In *The Perfect Wagnerite* (1895) he was more concerned with revolutionary ideas in the spheres of politics, economics and sociology than with music. As dramatic critic, too, he displayed a penetrating personal judgment, and his collected notices of Shakespearian performances in particular abound in stimulating remarks. Further, there is the wide range of his pamphlets and newspaper articles, in many of which he never hesitated to express an unpopular attitude, when, as always, he thought he was right. *Commonsense and the War* (1914), published as a supplement to *The New Statesman*, is a typical example of his mingling of what was at the time palatable with a fearless statement of points of view in which he was either peculiarly Shavian or in advance of his contemporaries. Among his writings on religion there stands out *The Adventures of the Black Girl in her Search for God* (1932), in which he presented ironically how the conventional teaching of orthodox Christianity in all its varieties was likely to appear to an unsophisticated mind. In its pellucid brevity it displays attractively both what Shaw felt was wrong with the attitude of the churches and his own yearning for the enlightenment of humanity.

Where Shaw has himself so fully and directly expressed his ideas on religion, politics, science, economics, education, eugenics, doctors, vegetarianism, journalism—in fact, on everything—the reader can very quickly acquaint himself with his ideas. To sum up his attitude, he loved humanity, though perhaps with too detached and impartial a love. He thought mankind very weak and foolish and in need of a leadership which might even be ruthless to individuals and classes. Yet far from despairing of humanity he believed it could be brought to higher and better things. Men must, however, follow reason, and control their emotions. At times he propounded different panaceas for humanity's ills, now socialism, now eugenics, now dictatorship. Like anybody else he was inconsistent. But as he was primarily an artist, it is not his particular ideas but the free play of his spirit that matters, and that is manifested in the joyous vitality that is the over-all impression of his life's work. In the close of *Back to Methuselah* there is solemnity in the joyous assurance that " of Life only is there no end " ; at the other extreme is the light-hearted gaiety of *You Never Can Tell*. The latter play Shaw classes along with *Pygmalion* among his "shameless potboilers". He also wrote once of "that atrocious *Man of Destiny*, a mere stage brutality ". No doubt he half-meant what he said, but posterity may well come to prefer the genius of the theatre to the once influential but outmoded prophet.

CHAPTER XXI

VARIOUS PROSE WRITERS

As with the drama, so prose-writing outside the novel would require a small book to itself if the varied excellence in all the different fields of the essay, biography, history, literary criticism, travel, philosophy and science were to receive adequate notice. Thus the writer of a short chapter is faced with the alternative either of limiting himself to a fairly comprehensive catalogue or of giving to certain writers a prominence over others which is bound to issue from more or less personal preferences. This chapter takes the second course.

An outstandingly admirable writer whose work defies any classification other than that of wide human interest is William Henry Hudson (1841-1922). He was born in the Pampas of La Plata, and lived there until he was a young man, and the record of his early years makes one of our best autobiographies in *Far Away and Long Ago* (1918). This early background also produced among other work *The Naturalist in La Plata* (1892) and *Idle Days in Patagonia* (1893), while the forests of South America inspired the story *Green Mansions* (1904), which was to be one of his best-known books, its character of Rima being chosen by Epstein for the memorial erected to Hudson in Hyde Park. But Hudson left South America for reasons of health in 1869, and he spent the rest of his long life in England, quietly studying men and nature. He wrote steadily, but he was an old man before he received any wide recognition. This may have been partly because his work was thought of as appealing mainly to naturalists, for among his early books were *British Birds* (1895) and *Birds in London* (1898), but the real nature of his work is more truly implied in the title of *Birds and Man* (1901). Then he proceeded to write of several parts of England, as in *Hampshire Days* (1903), *The Land's End* (1908) and *A Shepherd's Life* (1910). *Afoot in England*

(1909) and *A Traveller After Little Things* (1921) are both, particularly the latter, collections of delightful sketches of various places and people. His last work was *A Hind in Richmond Park* (1922).

Hudson was a scientific observer of wild life, especially of birds, but he saw all wild life as part of the human scene, and, as his writing advanced, birds, animals, and insects, were only one strand of his very detailed picture of English life. All the time in reading him one is aware of his personality : his clear, rational, agnostic mind, his temperamental prejudices like his anger at anyone's killing a wasp, his wide-ranging curiosity about ways of living, his cool humour, his love of beauty, his sense of the human characteristics of creatures and of the animal characteristics of human beings, his knowledge of little read authors, especially in the eighteenth century—these qualities give one a sense of contact with a rich and charming "character", which his letters confirm. "The friendship I observed between the two birds at Wells reminded me of the case of a pheasant who had human friends"—so he talks out of a well-stored sympathetic observation of all his fellow creatures, not like one to whom creatures and men are specimens of their respective genera, but like a friendly and understanding commentator. If sometimes he seems primarily interested in the reasons why his fellow creatures, for physical or economic causes, act as they do, in the long run it is the active appreciation of their interesting habits and qualities that inspires his writing. Now a chat with an old shepherd will raise questions of master and servant, of conditions of living and working; now little girls dancing on the wet sand will give him a thrill of pleasure. And all the time he writes the purest English prose style of the century, scientifically precise without jargon, sensitive without aestheticism, concrete and detailed without loss of clarity and ease.

Like Hudson, Gilbert Keith Chesterton (1874-1936) wrote a delightful autobiography and in all that he wrote conveyed his personality: but his *Autobiography* (1936) covered his whole life, and his very different personality from Hudson's perhaps tended to appear in most of his writing a little larger than life. From St Paul's School he went to the Slade School for Art, and his later illustrations to some of his friend Hilaire Belloc's books showed his amusing talent for drawing, but he soon turned professionally to writing. His interest in art appeared in books like those on G. F. Watts and William Blake. Throughout his life he wrote with warm appreciation upon literature, as in his studies of *Browning* (1903), *The Victorian Age in Literature* (1913) and *Chaucer* (1932). But it was as a literary journalist, particularly in the columns of the *Daily News*, that he first came to the fore. At school and later he was a brilliant debater and he was a remarkable extemporary talker on a platform. Indeed he loved argument, and with him a topic of the moment became at once a matter of fundamental faith and reason. So as a journalist he triumphed over the ephemeral, and his essays, in their various collected volumes from the early *All Things Considered* (1908) to later garnerings like *Fancies Versus Fads* (1923), will on the whole wear well despite the little figures and the topical disputes which gave rise to many of them. The essay, with its tradition of personal talk, was for him the ideal form, and when he wrote longer books like *The Everlasting Man* (1925) each section much resembled a substantial essay. As for his themes, he said of one collection of essays that "these notes . . . concern all sorts of things from lady barristers to cave-men, and from psycho-analysis to free verse". He was a laughing cavalier who disdained no antagonist and pursued his opponent at once with unflagging zest and with the greatest good nature. To those out of contact with the fundamental beliefs which inspired his joyous argumentativeness, he might appear a buffoon intoxicated by his own flow of wit and paradox, and he did develop so marked a style of paradox as to invite parody, but his dazzling fancy and play of words was the sword-play of a sincere and single-hearted fighter for his faith.

From the beginning Chesterton was a religious man, and in his later years he was received into the Roman Catholic Church. His faith was centred on the Incarnation, and in humble wonder he rejoiced in the way of life which that great fact illuminated. He declared that the chief idea of his life, the doctrine he would always have liked to teach, was "the idea of taking things with gratitude, and not taking things for granted". He believed indeed in "having a great deal of gratitude even for a very little good", and at the end of his life he could say, "I have grown old without growing bored. Existence is still a strange thing to me; and as a stranger I give it welcome". When he began to write, the progressive thinkers like Wells and Bernard Shaw were on the crest of their materialistic optimism, and he lived to see that faith shattered by world war and in its place arise the barrenness and despair of the Waste Land, but his own faith only deepened. It was a faith in man as well as in God; not in the human perfectibility of man, but in the democratic self-reliant independence of men, with a right, under God, not to have their lives shackled, planned and dehumanised by industrial or governmental masters. His position was that of the older humane Liberalism which upheld the poor against the power of wealth and bureaucracy, the common man against the State, innocent pleasure against repression and common sense against faddists. As the great material forces put their trust more and more in quantity, his was one of the last and loudest voices to cry out for quality in even the meanest and poorest of human lives. In his later years, in *G.K's Weekly*, he lay open to the charge of a too facile ignoring of the complex problem of modern economics in his advocacy of a self-supporting community of smallholders. Good-tempered and sensible as he was he could not really compromise with the modern industrial monopolists.

Chesterton's friend and literary associate Hilaire Belloc, born in 1870, half French by birth (he served his term in the French army as a young man), loving France deeply, and equally a sturdy Englishman in love with Sussex, and a Roman Catholic from the beginning, had much in common with Chesterton. Belloc, too, was a born essayist, but rather less personally and idiosyncratically than Chesterton. As an essayist he ranged widely, full of ideas, a traveller, a historian, a hearty lover of the good things of this life and of the sound traditions of Western civilisation. He progressed through his essays rather more seriously than Chesterton, not without occasional high spirits and with abundant pugnacity, somewhat after the manner and spirit of the early nineteenth-century liberal political journalist, William Cobbett. He too was for the rights of men to live their lives fully and freely, under God, as their minds and bodies reasonably urged them. His *Servile State* (1912), warning men prophetically of the encroachments of the modern bureaucratic State, was in harmony with Chesterton's point of view. He too, in the light of the Catholic Faith, opposed the modern progressive materialistic philosophy, and he attacked H. G. Wells particularly over Wells's *Outline of History*. But he was most himself in two books of personal travel, *The Path to Rome* (1902) and *The Cruise of the "Nona"* (1925). The former must be a classic of its kind; his account of his walk from France over the Alps to Italy is not only full of good things said and described but it is the younger Belloc himself; the latter book is an older Belloc, not fundamentally changed, but more inclined to cantankerous digressions and fulminations against modern follies. Both, however, are noble expressions of an ideal of spirit, brain and body, enjoying and contending with the world. As a historian, as in *James II* (1934) and *How the Reformation Happened* (1928), his work was vivid and substantial, but somewhat too much controlled by his Catholic faith. Perhaps his best history is *The French Revolution* (1911).

Chesterton and Belloc stand out among the essayists by the range, depth and energy of their genius. But their all-round power as men of letters should not make us forget the many others who as essayists made this half-century a golden age of the essay. Among the older essayists Augustine Birrell and Austin Dobson had both made their names as bookmen of taste before 1900. Maurice Hewlett, the historical novelist, was a wise and happy talker in the traditional way. E. V. Lucas garnered many a harvest from his periodical writing, collections of light, entertaining chatter of this and that, often wise, but never really leaving the world of literary and artistic culture to contact the hurly-burly of modern life. A. G. Gardiner ("Alpha of the Plough") was nearer to contemporary affairs: he was editor of the *Daily News* from 1902 to 1919; but he was more interested in writing of the personalities of public figures than in handling general ideas, and a typical collection of his essays such as *Pebbles on the Shore* (1916) is again the light easy talk of an ordinarily thoughtful man. But two writers before 1920 really had high distinctive qualities of their own. Sir Max Beerbohm, born in 1872, wrote little, but all that he wrote had a wit and a style to which only his own name could be attached; he lived to make occasional broadcasts which showed his remarkable skill as an essayist, mellowed by the years, to be able to delight an audience wider than his earlier rather select reading public. *Mainly on the Air* was published in 1946. Edward Thomas, before he found his truest expression to be in poetry, wrote several essays rich in his loving understanding of country life.

Of the later writers of the essay J. B. Priestley, A. A. Milne, E. V. Knox and Robert Lynd perhaps stand out most clearly as real essayists, though there were many others, such as Edmund Blunden and C. E. Montague, who made excellent but less constant use of the form, and others again who wrote essays which, like some of Aldous Huxley's valuable sociological essays, hardly fall within the category of the essay proper. (And one should not forget among the true essays the admirable anonymous Third Leaders in *The Times*.) Priestley had a good deal of the essayist in his make-up as a novelist, and in the essay itself the broad humanity, the shrewd sense of true values of living, the knowledge of men, the power of narrative and the humour that were his strength as a novelist appeared in attractive condensation. Like all the best essayists he is a lover of literature, as his studies of T. L. Peacock and Meredith showed, and in *The English Comic Characters* he produced a very happy variation of the essay in evoking some of the

great comic figures like Toby Belch and his associates and
Jane Austen's Mr Collins and discussing them as though they
were living people. Indeed nearly all his essays are enriched
by allusions drawn from his wide reading in a manner
resembling Hazlitt's. In comparison with Priestley's the
essays of A. A. Milne are considerably slighter, but their
whimsical humour and agreeable sentiment are conveyed by
a durable grace of style that may well make them outwear the
years. E. V. Knox, editor of *Punch* for several years from
1932 and with Sir John Squire a perfect verse parodist, had
his own manner of wise and witty causerie, while Sir Alan
Herbert's contributions to *Punch*, including his brilliant Topsy
papers and his humours of the law, provided some of the
best literary humour of these years.

Robert Lynd (1879-1949), however, was the greatest in
stature of these later essayists. Like Chesterton he had
Fleet Street for his background: for many years he was literary
editor first of the *Daily News* and then of the *News-Chronicle*,
as "Y.Y." he also long wrote a weekly essay in the *New
Statesman and Nation*, and he had his column as "John
o'London" in *John O'London's Weekly* from 1942 till his
death. Those who knew him have testified to the natural
sincerity and sterling worth of the man, and his essays are
the man. *The Pleasures of Ignorance* (1921), *The Money-
Box* (1925), and *The Green Man* (1928) are typical collections of his periodical writings. What he wrote on any topic
was the expression of a quietly formed pervasive philosophy
of life. He knew himself, or rather the several selves which
cohere in all of us, but in him there was none of that warring
among the selves which has been so common a feature of the
modern personality. Instead, knowing himself, he liked himself and the world, and went about his business with an
integrated assurance. Writing of two of the selves we all
have, the spender and the saver, he remarked that "life
would be intolerable if our two selves were for ever dragging
each other into court and laying complaints against each
other before that grave magistrate, conscience", and personally he rejoiced that in him the spender had won an early

and assured victory. So, at ease with the world and himself, he wrote with a detachment that gives a timeless wisdom to his commentary on life. Unlike so many of his contemporaries, he did not want to change the world, but only to encourage it to live sanely, decently and happily. He would have men more humane and tolerant, like himself, but he had an ironic whip for cant, humbug, malice and intolerance. As he wrote, he would dip easily into the reservoir of his memories, frequently those of his childhood, displaying himself with a happy unselfconscious absence of egotism. The ordinary round of daily life supplied him with abundance of interest and adequate sensations. In an essay "On Going Abroad" he admits that if he had a fortune he would go to Italy and he "might even be tempted as far as Athens. But no further"; and he adds, "If I were offered a free trip round the world, I might accept the offer through weakness, but I do not wish to go round the world. Have I not been round the sun once a year ever since I was born?" He could adventure far enough in books, and much of his writing, still retaining the quality of an essay, lay in the interpretation of writers. *Dr Johnson and Company* (1928) is one of his best books of that kind, but he could penetrate the mind and imagination of such a modern as Yeats. That a wide selection from his work was in 1950 added to the "Everyman Library" was a just tribute to his broad and enduring appeal.

To pass from these essayists to Walter Ralph Inge (*b.* 1860), who was Dean of St Paul's from 1911 to 1934, is to encounter the sustained lecture as against the discursive personal causerie. In his weekly article in the London *Evening Standard* Dean Inge for some years outshone many professional journalists. These articles were a journalistic adaptation of the Baconian essay, being serious thoughts on serious subjects seen in the light of current events; to illustrate his points he drew, like Bacon, freely on his stored and sifted knowledge of history and literature, and if he had not quite the condensed aphoristic style of Bacon he was not far from it. His journalistic style is that of his *Lay Thoughts of a Dean* (1926). But his finest work is in the sustained essays in the two volumes of *Outspoken Essays*, 1919 and 1922, some of which were originally lectures, " The Victorian Age," for example, while others had first appeared in the *Quarterly* and the *Edinburgh Review*. Outspoken these essays certainly were, for the Dean wrote without fear or favour, and with a strong mind and a clear eye regarded the world through no rose-coloured spectacles, though he was far from being the " gloomy Dean" as he was nicknamed by the populai press. In some matters, like his advocacy of eugenics to improve the racial stock and of emigration to decrease over-population, he wrote rather from his reason than from his heart, and on religious topics he could display the scorn of a controversialist, but on occasion he could reveal a tender and humble spirit.

His *Confessio Fidei*, in the 1922 volume, takes us very close to the secret places of his heart, and has much, despite its history, theology and philosophy, of the personal charm of the essay. " I begin this essay", he tells us, " on the terrace in front of an hotel at Mürren. A lonely holiday, almost without books, among the grandest scenes of nature, is a favourable opportunity for setting one's ideas in order. Solitude and freedom from interruptions give a chance of continuous thinking. The absence of books compels thought to take the form of self-examination ". So, having begun with the assertion that " we cannot make a religion for others, and we ought not to let others make a religion for us " he concludes that " the true religion for each of us is the most spiritual view of reality that we are able to realise and live by ". He frankly says of mystical experience, " I am very far from claiming that I have had these rich experiences myself ", but he admits that " the mystical experience is the bedrock of religious faith". Sentence after sentence is crisply provocative of thought: " There is a considerable element of agnosticism in true Christianity "; " anthropolatry is the enemy; it has vitiated much modern philosophy "; " no scientific discovery is without its religious and moral implica-tions "; " the worst enemies of Christianity are Christians ". Finally, his view of the future was far from a " gloomy " one: "Nothing could destroy the Christian Churches except the complete decay and submergence of the white race, a most improbable contingency". As for the mystical side of religion, if not himself a mystic, he gave a great impetus to the study of mysticism by his scholarly Bampton Lectures on Christian Mysticism in 1899 and by his study of Plotinus. One of his *Evening Standard* articles in 1930 was a shrewdly penetrating approval of the mystics as experts of the spiritual life. He wrote almost to the end and died in 1954.

Another field in which some particularly notable work was done in this century is biography, and the finest of all the biographers is Sir Osbert Sitwell. It was Lytton Strachey (1880-1932), however, who first broke away from the heavy laudatory biographical monuments which had become the rule from Victorian days. His *Eminent Victorians* (1918) was something entirely new in biography. His subjects, Cardinal Newman, Arnold of Rugby, General Gordon and Florence Nightingale, had all been idolised, but Strachey took them off their pedestals. He saw them instead as very human figures, with amusing weaknesses, with comedy in their grandeur. He shone a strong searchlight on them, which caught them off their guard and revealed details that the sober conventional biographers had thought unworthy of notice or better omitted. The result might be as much a distortion as the conventionalised picture was in its different way, but the lay figure had come to life, and Strachey's portraits were hailed as exciting masterpieces of ironic art— and by many of the older generation were denounced with anger. He followed up his success with *Queen Victoria* (1921), a movingly human revelation of the queen and the woman, leaving her, for all his ironic manner, a figure to be liked and admired, and presenting his portrait in far fewer pages than had formerly been considered necessary for serious biographical work. It was to be his best work, for in the dazzling but over-written *Elizabeth and Essex* (1928) he seemed rather out of his depth historically, and his *Portraits in Miniature* (1931) is a collection of relatively slight sketches, including brief studies of some of the older English historians.

After Lytton Strachey's new biographical attack—his own expression was that "if the historian is wise, he will attack his subject in unexpected places; he will fall upon the flank, or the rear"—even the conventional manner could hardly remain as heavily sombre as before. Strachey's great achievement had been to reinstate biography as a literary art, to present truth in a vision that had a personal perspective, and in a style full of colour and contrast. In his own writing, notably in *Elizabeth and Essex*, it was clear that the danger in the new method lay in the natural conflict between Art and Truth, in which Truth might be the loser, and the weaker of those who were inspired to imitate Strachey aped his irreverence of approach and his dazzle of style without sharing his power of penetrating and illuminating the subject. The nearest to Strachey was Philip Guedalla (1889-1944), whose early work outwent Strachey in glitter and irreverence. *Supers and Supermen* (1920), *Masters and Men* (1922) and *A Gallery* (1923) consisted mainly of short sketches of Victorians and contemporaries, of politicians like Disraeli and Asquith, and writers like Hardy and Wells. They were startlingly readable, but the continual glitter of wit and epithet was overdone: his subjects deserved something better than the manner of a brilliant undergraduate, irresponsibly scoring point after point in a tone of superior amusement. But in his full studies of *Palmerston* (1926) and *The Duke* (Wellington) in 1931, Guedalla had sobered down and his treatment, preserving only the merits of the new approach, admirably matched his subjects.

Among biographies which, without being directly influenced by Lytton Strachey, nevertheless, coming as they do after his example, probably owed something to the stimulus it had given, were Lord David Cecil's *The Stricken Deer* (1924), dealing with the poet Cowper, and *The Young Melbourne* (1939), Sir Duff Cooper's *Talleyrand* (1932), John Buchan, Lord Tweedsmuir's *Montrose* (1928), *Oliver Cromwell* (1934) and *Augustus* (1937), Arthur Bryant's *Charles II* (1931) and his *Samuel Pepys*. A very popular development was the combination of biography with literary

criticism as in Michael Sadleir's *Trollope, A Commentary*
(1927) and P. P. Howe's *Hazlitt* (1922). No doubt with
many it was the changed mind of the age rather than the
stimulus given by Lytton Strachey that was responsible for
the greater vitality of biography after 1920.

Sir Osbert Sitwell's *Left Hand, Right Hand* stands apart
from all other biographical work. Its very scale is impressive, for it occupies five volumes, beginning with the title
volume of 1945 and ending with *Noble Essences* in 1950. Its
author styled it an autobiography, but it is more than that,
for it builds up a full portrait of his father, its last volume
concentrates on the portraits of ten friends, and it is moreover in intention the picture of an age. Sir Osbert is indeed
writing an elegy upon "that halcyon age in which [he] grew
up", in contrast with which the present seems to him "this
cruel and meaningless epoch". Those late Victorian and
Edwardian days of his childhood, especially his earliest years
when in England at least the violence of history seemed to
have subsided into a golden peace, were a time in which men
developed rich and often grotesque characters, and the author
in declaring, "I should like to emphasise that I *want* my
memories to be old-fashioned and extravagant—as they are",
knew that he had abundant material to use. At these ex-
travagances he may laugh, or rather he may smile, but he
loves and respects them, for in his vision there is none of
the irreverence of Lytton Strachey's. Instead, he has an
abiding reverence, a quality without which in his opinion
"no true artist can live", and he is above all an artist, even
a greater poetic artist here than in his poetry. So the picture
grows under his hand, a crowded and detailed canvas,
elegiacally toned, but grained with the enjoyment of good,
gracious, friendly living, in which all the arts and foreign
travel play an inevitable part. Inclusive, and to some extent
digressive as it is, this great work never escapes from the
artist's controlling plan, and the style, with all its variations
from the simple to the elaborate, matches the complex
handling of the material. It should be mentioned that, in
portraying his own father, Sir Osbert had been anticipated

by Sir Edmund Gosse who also drew his own father in *Father and Son* (1907), but Gosse's, though a classic of its kind, is a minor classic in comparison with *Left Hand, Right Hand*. There were other good autobiographies too in this period, for example Robert Graves's *Goodbye to All That* (1929) and John Buchan's *Memory Hold-the-Door* (1940), but they are not in the same class of great artistic creation. Work which perhaps ranks nearest to Sir Osbert's is that of the poet Siegfried Sassoon, who in several volumes, including *The Weald of Youth, Memoirs of a Fox-Hunting Man, Memoirs of an Infantry Officer* and *Sherston's Progress* built up a fine autobiographical panorama.

Historical writing in this half-century reached a very high standard. With some writers it is hard to draw a line between the biographical and the historical. Lytton Strachey's historical biographies, for example, enter the province of history. Philip Guedalla was not only a biographer, but in *The Second Empire* (1922) a historian. Arthur Bryant portrayed in *Charles II* not only the king but the age, and in *English Saga* he surveyed the century from 1840 to 1940, while in *The Years of Endurance* and *Years of Victory* he dealt with the conflict between England and France from 1793 to 1812, and in *The Age of Elegance* (1950) which recreates the decade 1812 to 1822, he completed a trilogy which was popular history at its best, vivid narrative and exposition which thought of the present while expounding the past. Much historical work came from professional academic historians, and in this field of specialism it is rash to intrude a judgment. When such admirable work has been done, it is for time to declare what will live to the general reader by those enduring qualities which make a Macaulay, for all his bias, readable a century later. One of the outstanding academic historians was G. M. Trevelyan: his *History of England* (1926) and *English Social History* (1944) were deservedly popular, and his history of Queen Anne's reign, taking up where his great relative Macaulay had left off, was a substantial contribution to history, but it may be doubted whether, as a writer, he gives so much delight in those works as in his essays in *Clio* and in his little book on *The Poetry and Philosophy of George Meredith*. A great specialist in the medieval period was G. G. Coulton (1858-1947), who with vast learning robustly countered the idealising Catholic interpretation of the Middle Ages as presented by Chesterton: Coulton's *Chaucer and his England* (1909) and the massive *Five Centuries of Religion*, of which the concluding volume was published posthumously, were only a part of his notable work.

Perhaps the academic historian who in recent years has most impressed the wider reading public is A. L. Rowse (*b*. 1903), author of a good autobiography, *A Cornish Childhood* (1942) and also a careful individual poet. *The Spirit of English History* (1943) was a small but inspiring distillation of the English Spirit, which gave strength in the dark days of the war. On the whole he has concentrated on the sixteenth century, as in *The England of Elizabeth* (1951), in which, apart from his defective understanding of the religious spirit in individuals, he shows that masterly power of handling history which brings historical writing within the sphere of literature. But since 1930 there have been many outstanding historical writings. In comprehensive treatment there are H. A. L. Fisher's *History of Europe* (1935) and H. Butterfield's *Christianity and History* (1949) and *The Origins of Modern Science* (1949). Denis Brogan's *The Development of Modern France, 1870-1939* (1940) and *The American Problem* (1944) are examples of his lively individual manner. Among economic historians R. H. Tawney and J. L. and Barbara Hammond stand out, while Sir John Clapham covered a wide field in his *Concise Economic History of Britain* (1944). Important studies in constitutional history include Sir Maurice Powicke's *King Henry III and the Lord Edward* (1947) and J. E. Neale's *The Elizabethan House of Commons* (1949).

But there were many other distinguished volumes, and a notable collaborative achievement has been "The Oxford History of England" in its successive volumes. Perhaps the chief distinguishing characteristic of the newer historical attitude lay in an awareness, on the part of all writers, of the

social and economic backgrounds. Individual figures and
political and military policies were seen in the context of the
social system as a whole. But English historical writing pre-
served its traditional characteristic of individuality. There
had always been a Tory or a Whig bias in earlier history, but
it has been truly remarked that "in England there are no
schools of history: there are only individual historians",
and in this half-century, even in a work like the Oxford
History, it was the individual view that shaped the work of
English historians. There was a considerable attempt at
impartial history, but, to the advantage of literature, the
personal view still coloured the best history.

Certainly the most remarkable, and perhaps the greatest
historical writing of our century came from boldly original
minds, that is from H. G. Wells and Winston Churchill, both
far from being professional or academic historians, and from
Sir James Frazer and A. J. Toynbee, both similarly men of
outstanding originality, though they devoted their lives to
an intense searching into and brooding upon the history of
mankind. Wells's *The Outline of History* (1920) was an
extraordinary task for one man to achieve, surveying as it
does the whole world from the earliest days of pre-history
down to the end of the first World War. G. K. Chesterton,
remarking that he had often disputed Wells's view of history,
felt he must "congratulate him on the courage and constructive imagination which carried through this vast and varied
and intensely interesting work". Chesterton could not
approve the anti-Christian attitude of Wells, which coloured
the whole vision of a history designed to further the Wellsian
conception of a World State, but he found the book "splendid
as a storehouse or treasury of history . . . a fascinating dis-
quisition on history", and he praised Wells for "having
asserted the reasonable right of the amateur" to use in his
own way the facts provided by specialists. Some academic
historians pointed to many errors of fact, though Wells had
his own small board of critics to argue with him in footnotes,
but whatever its defects either in its philosophical notions or
in its details the appearance of this book meant a new

historical outlook: it made a view of the whole of human history possible and henceforth necessary.

With that of Wells the work of Sir Winston Churchill has, of course, no affinity, but it is the product of a powerful mind long experienced in men and affairs and always in touch with the past traditions of the British race. The comprehensive vision, the penetrating analysis of cause and effect, the majestic sweep of narrative, the colourful description, the vivid detail, which made the five volumes of *The World Crisis* the premier history of the First War, characterise also his volumes, beginning with *The Gathering Storm* (1948), which deal with the Second War. In the later work, because of the supreme control he himself came to wield, the international story contains inevitably a strand of autobiography, even as the author had earlier shown his skill in autobiography in *My Early Life* (1930). The power of portraying men shown in his great war volumes is also exemplified in *Great Contemporaries* (1937), while as biographer he had begun with the life of his father in *Lord Randolph Churchill* (1906), and he went on to the portrait of his great ancestor in *Marlborough: His Life and Times* (1933-38), which is second only to his *World Crisis* in the grand scale of its execution. In the ability to present a clear picture of military or naval strategy and deployment, and at the same time to depict the courage, the horror and the pathos of the whole battle scene as it affects the greatest and the least of its participants, and to relate the battle to the continuous theme of the policies and progress of nations, Winston Churchill has hardly a rival in English.

Whereas Wells wrote history with the shaping zeal of a prophet and Churchill with talents a great novelist might envy, Frazer was scientific and Toynbee philosophic. Sir James Frazer (1854-1931) began to publish *The Golden Bough* in 1890, but he had undertaken a work which expanded with his investigations and the thirteenth and concluding volume did not appear until 1915. The result was a massive accumulation of well sifted knowledge of ancient civilisations and primitive societies, their religions, myths and legends,

from which theologians, philosophers, psychologists, anthro-
pologists, students of the classics, and creative writers could
all draw valuable material.   In particular it had a great
influence upon the study of comparative religion.   Scientific
in method and treatment and factual in its general nature, it
is, of course, shaped and pervaded by Frazer's own conclusions and commentary.   Toynbee too went back to the
great ancient civilisations in the six volumes of *A Study of
History* (1934-39), seeking from a study of the rise and fall
of previous civilisations to deduce a comprehensive philosophy
of history.   Both Frazer and Toynbee brought their work
to bear on a wider public by producing abridged versions of
their original presentation.

A great book which may well be mentioned next in passing
on to the literature of travel is T. E. Lawrence's *Seven Pillars
of Wisdom* (1926), abridged as *Revolt in the Desert* (1927).
It is indeed autobiography, contemporary history and travel,
presenting   the   strange   personality   and   extraordinary
achievements of "Lawrence of Arabia" when he played a
determining part in the revolt of the Arabs against their
Turkish overlords in the years of the first World War.   Only
in Doughty's *Travels in Arabia Deserta* (1888) had there
previously been in English any comparable revelation of the
Arabs and their country.   In *Seven Pillars of Wisdom* the man
and the matter are inseparable: it is a book no one else could
have written.   In the more limited field of travel literature
proper there was much good writing but none with the
daemonic power of Lawrence.   W. H. Hudson's descriptions
of South America, Belloc's *Path to Rome* and *The Cruise of
the "Nona"*, and the travel records of Conrad, D. H.
Lawrence and Graham Greene have already been mentioned.
Among other writers there stand out R. B. Cunninghame
Graham (1852-1936), Norman Douglas with his *Old Calabria*
(1915) and other books about the Mediterranean area, Freya
Stark who wrote of Arabia, Rosita Forbes who dealt with
Egypt and the East, the popular H. V. Morton as with his
In the Steps of the Master (1934) and *In the Steps of St Paul*
(1936), and Evelyn Waugh the novelist.   But two writers

deserve more particular mention, H. M. Tomlinson and
Sacheverell Sitwell.

H. M. Tomlinson was born in 1873 in London, near the
Port of London, and from childhood he grew to love ships
and to know sailors. Professionally, however, he became a
journalist on the staff of the *Morning Leader* and then of the
Daily News. In 1914 he served as a war correspondent on the
Western Front, and for two following years he was an official
correspondent at the General Headquarters of the British
Army in France. From 1917 to 1923 he was literary editor
of the *Nation*. He has two very good novels to his credit,
Galleons Reach (1927) and *All Our Yesterdays* (1930), the
latter a product of his personal knowledge of the war in
France, about which his novel is one of the best. But he
had first made his name as a writer with *The Sea and the
Jungle* (1912), which recounted a voyage right up the
Amazon on which he was sent by his editor to see how far
it was possible for an ocean-going steamer to penetrate into
the South American continent. *London River* (1921) was an
intimate appreciation of a port whose ships went to the Seven
Seas. *Tidemarks* (1924) had as its subtitle "some records
of a journey to the beaches of the Moluccas and the forest
of Malaya". *The Face of the Earth* (1950) tells of a trip
from England to Spain in a small vessel with a few friends.
Malay Waters (1951) celebrates the courage and endurance
of ships and sailors in the years of the Second War. In these
and all his books Tomlinson writes as a born traveller, who
might have been bred in the traditions of the sea, as one who
knows all the technicalities of seamanship and who is moreover a most observant man of all he encounters. He never
overwrites, but his style is the man, original, philosophical,
humorous: he loves to describe, but in a way that is that of
the good talk of a natural storyteller.

Tomlinson's books, indeed, are very different from those
of Sacheverell Sitwell, who does not give the same impression
of loving travel for its own sake, for its adventures and
achievements. On the contrary Sacheverell Sitwell's prose
works are on the whole an extension of his best poetry in

Canons of Giant Art. He is interested in the people and the scenery of foreign countries, but he is even more interested in their architecture, their art, their music, their theatres and their festivals. He likes to slip from the present into the remote past, and loves especially those places and those peoples where the past can still be felt below the surface, and even on the surface, of the present. Then his spirit broods in enchanted contemplation, his prose takes on music, while the scene rises before our eyes in all its sensuous detail in a shimmering tapestry of words.

> "The antique magic is in the air again. Forget the present and the future. Nor, in particular, is this the past. Like music, it must live in its own melody and make its shape. The ram's horn trumpet blows. It is the Bacchanale . .
>
> "Where, then, is wisdom ? In the arts, and not in war. In the cold and in the heat. In this music and its lilies. In shocks of corn and in the golden locks of children. In the arts and in the senses. In the bright wing and in the golden leaf."

Such lines as these from *Sacred and Profane Love* are typical of his prevailing mood. His books include *Southern Baroque Art* (1924), *The Gothic North* (1929-30), *Touching the Orient* (1934) and *Primitive Scenes and Festivals*. When he is writing of art he conjures up other lands, and when he is writing of foreign places he thinks in terms of the arts. He is a travel-writer of his own kind. His own book of selections from his prose, *The Homing of the Winds* (1942), makes an excellent introduction to his work.

Of writers about country life in this island the novelists H. E. Bates, Adrian Bell and Henry Williamson have already been mentioned, as have also W. H. Hudson, Edward Thomas and Siegfried Sassoon. To these several names might be added: they would include H. J. Massingham, Sir William Beach Thomas, A. G. Street, George Sturt, Alison Uttley, Robert Gibbings, Eric Parker and Eiluned Lewis. One notable little book which speaks devoutly of the country life alongside other topics is Viscount Grey of Fallodon's *Fallodon Papers* (1926). Here it seems best to say a little

more of Henry Williamson as the writer who has probably
dealt with the theme of country life and nature most compre-
hensively.

Born in Bedfordshire in 1897 Williamson's boyhood was
spent on the edge of the Kent countryside, with long
holidays in the West country, as his more or less autobiographical *The Flax of Dream* recounts. After serving in
France in the First War, he tried Fleet Street for a while, but
soon withdrew to a cottage in North Devon where he remained
until the call of farming took him to Norfolk in 1936 as the
books *Goodbye West Country* (1937) and *The Story of a
Norfolk Farm* (1941) tell. He began publishing with a
volume of slight sketches *The Lone Swallows* (1922), and for
some years, apart from his four novels which make up *The
Flax of Dream* and which contain much careful description
of nature, he kept mainly to nature writing, that is to dealing
with animals and birds, in volumes of short stories, *The
Peregrine's Saga* and *The Old Stag*, and in the full-length
Tarka the Otter. Then with the two volumes of *The Village
Book* (1930, '32) his work tended to become more diffuse.
Now he produced books which were partly still about wild
life, but into which fellow villagers and their children and
the author and his family freely entered, together with the
author's commentary on life. In *Salar the Salmon* (1935) he
recaptured something of his success with *Tarka*, but his
general tendency to let his vision and his thoughts extend
beyond wild life continued and it weakens artistically his
study of a pheasant in *The Phasian Bird* (1948). At his best,
in *Tarka the Otter*, an unrivalled book of its kind, Williamson
was a fine artist—how exacting his confession of constant
rewriting of that book testifies. Always he has written only
after careful and loving observation of wild life, and with
serious thought about human beings and their problems too,
but what he has thought and felt about modern life has not
always helped to produce artistic and harmonious books.
This defect, however, has the virtue of arising from a sincere
determination to be more than a writer on nature, and it
reflects the age: Williamson as a boy absorbed the spirit of

the Richard Jefferies of *The Story of My Heart* and *Bevis*, as a young man he learnt by personal experience the horror and futility of war, and as a man, and a countryman, he felt the disease of modern civilisation and was especially conscious of the urban materialism which was antagonistic to the farmer and therefore to the heart of England. Not all his deep devotion to nature could still his questionings or calm his nerves. His friendship with T. E. Lawrence is of the essence of Williamson.

Among writers upon science there stand out in this half-century several who may well come to rank with such Victorian giants as Huxley, Darwin and Tyndall. Leading scientists naturally responded to the need to keep the educated public in touch with the rapid developments in the sciences, particularly in physics, in mathematical theory, in astronomy and in biology. Above all, Einstein's theory of relativity and the new concept of the physical basis of matter, which had taken the older materialism out of the scientific view of the universe, involved a new approach to life as a whole, but they were by no means the only aspects of a revolutionary change in scientific thought. The impact of the new science fell particularly on religion and ethics, but its effects extended to every sphere, especially in the rapidly developing study of sociology, and the practical bearing of the new science upon society demanded consideration. There appeared, therefore, many books explanatory and popular, which aimed either at explaining new scientific knowledge or theory as clearly as possible to the layman or at presenting the philosophical or practical implications. It became the general tendency for scientists to expound the broad implications of their specialised studies.

The mathematician A. N. Whitehead (1861-1947) was a leading exponent of the philosophical approach: his books include *The Concept of Nature* (1920), *The Principle of Relativity* (1922), *Science and the Modern World* (1926) and *Process and Reality* (1929). Sir James Jeans (1877-1946) won a wide audience with *The Universe Around Us* (1929) and *The Mysterious Universe* (1930). Sir Arthur S.

Eddington (1882-1944), mathematician, physicist and astronomer, was author of *The Nature of the Physical World* (1928), *Science and the Unseen World* (1929) and *The Expanding Universe* (1933). Julian Huxley (born 1887) wrote among other work *Essays of a Biologist* (1923), *Essays in Popular Science* (1926), *Scientific Research and Social Needs* (1934) and *Man in the Modern World* (1947); he also collaborated with H. G. Wells and his son G. P. Wells in *The Science of Life* (1929) and his *Soviet Genetics and World Science* (1949) illuminated the differences which ideology could produce even in the sphere of science. J. B. S. Haldane (born 1892) contributed *Possible Worlds* (1927), *Science and Ethics* (1928), *The Causes of Evolution* (1933) and *Science and Everyday Life* (1939). Lancelot Hogben (born 1895), like Huxley and Haldane a biologist, achieved the very difficult task of making mathematics readable, though hardly literature, in *Mathematics for the Million* (1936), and he followed this up with *Science for the Citizen* (1938), again reaching a remarkably wide public. Indeed the great audience for scientific literature which had grown up received further testimony from the success of *Penguin Science News*, and the work of popularising scientific knowledge was also notably advanced by the B.B.C. as by the series of talks by F. Hoyle, published in 1950 as *The Nature of the Universe*. Such names as have been mentioned are those of only some of the outstanding writers, to whom might be added Sir Oliver Lodge, Sir Richard Gregory and Sir Arthur Keith of the elder generation and J. D. Bernal among the more recent.

There is, however, one writer on philosophical and scientific subjects who stands pre-eminent in this field as a man of letters. Bertrand Russell, third Earl Russell, was born in 1872. His grandfather was Lord John Russell, the Whig statesman who fought for the Great Reform Bill in 1832, and being thus related to the ducal family of Bedford he inherited a long aristocratic tradition. His roots seem to lie in the eighteenth century, the age of reason: his attitude is sceptical, he distrusts religion and emotion, his faith lies in logic, he appeals to common sense, he demands liberty of thought, and all the time with an acute mind he writes prose easy, precise, clear, vigorous and witty. Yet for all his reliance on reason he is a true Russell in his liability to unreasonable prejudice, and his writings convey not only his thoughts but also the sense of a very independent and unmistakable personality. Like an eighteenth-century nobleman he has been able to devote his life to the things of the intellect, though as a twentieth-century advanced political thinker he does not use his inherited title. His thinking has always been directed to contemporary affairs and probably no other philosophical writer of this century has possessed anything like his influence on progressive thought, and yet there is a cold detachment in his attitude to mankind, for he sees it not in terms of individuals but abstractly, almost mathematically. Much of his earlier work indeed was upon mathematics; it includes *The Principles of Mathematics* (1903), and he collaborated with A. N. Whitehead in *Principia Mathematica* (1910-13), while in 1919 he published his *Introduction to Mathematical Philosophy*. A book by him on the philosophy of Leibnitz appeared in 1900 and another on that of Bergson in 1914, and he himself by his original work ranks high among British philosophers in the tradition of the eighteenth-century empirical philosophy of Hume. His philosophical writings include *Philosophical Essays* (1910), *The Analysis of Mind* (1921) and *Human Knowledge: its scope and limits* (1948), two expository works, *An Outline of Philosophy* (1927) and *History of Western Philosophy* (1946), and *The Scientific Outlook* (1931).

From the beginning, however, the practical problems of contemporary civilisation had concerned Bertrand Russell. His first publication in 1896 was on German social democracy; in the First War he expressed his pacifist faith and was deprived of his Cambridge lectureship because of his pacifist activities; later came *The Practice and Theory of Bolshevism* (1920), followed by other writings on the Russian system; and his books *On Education : especially in early childhood* (1926) and *Education and the Social Order* (1932) arose from his desire to help the world to proceed on more sensible lines by dealing from the start with essentials as he saw them. *Why I am not a Christian* (1927), *Marriage and Morals* (1929) and *The Conquest of Happiness* (1930) were part of his general propaganda for a more enlightened world in which the individual should be able to achieve the good life. Particularly he kept considering what was the right relationship between the individual and the state, as in *Freedom and Organization, 1814-1914* (1934) and in his Reith Lectures of 1949 *Authority and the Individual.* In fact it was no wonder that his wide-ranging and continual output, made so persuasive by the lucid charm of his style, won many converts to his view of life. His way of looking at things with a mind always open to fresh evidence had the power which free intellectual examination always has of dissolving insecure conventions of thought. Those less accessible to his larger and more serious books could nevertheless be influenced by his brilliant essays. Somewhat like H. G. Wells and Aldous Huxley he too in his later years found his hopeful vision of possible human progress clouded, but in his *Unpopular Essays* (1950) his intellect still flashes as luminously and provocatively as ever.

Finally, though it has been necessary to forego mention of much good prose writing, the literary critics must be considered. To treat them at once justly and with brevity is perhaps the hardest task among the many difficulties of this little book, for the critics are so many that it is hardly possible to do much more than name some of them and so good that any mere grouping and enumeration becomes particularly unsatisfactory. If none has the stature of a Dryden or a Johnson, a Lamb or a Hazlitt, several have done invaluable work for their contemporaries by advancing the understanding and appreciation of literature.

In the early years of the century Arthur Symons, the poet, whose *Symbolist Movement in Literature* (1899) largely helped to introduce the French symbolist poets to an English audience, published studies of Blake and Dante Gabriel Rossetti, as well as *The Romantic Movement in English Poetry* (1910). Later studies from him include his books on

Baudelaire (1920), Hardy (1927) and Walter Pater (1932)
A. C. Bradley's *Shakespearean Tragedy* (1904) made an outstanding contribution to Shakespearian studies, and his
Oxford Lectures on Poetry revealed a similar deeply sympathetic interpretation of later writers. In fact these were the
years when literary critics were mainly concerned with bringing out the literary and human values of the greatest writers.
The time had not yet come when, as a result of the increasing
study of literature in the schools and universities, not only
the major writers but many secondary authors too were so
well known to a wide public that it began to prefer critical
theory, psychological biography and studies of the social and
economic background of literature to a direct appreciation of
literary values. So a typical work of this time was Masefield's
fresh and enthusiastic little book on Shakespeare, while
Walter Raleigh, though rather more academic, had a similar
broad aim of introducing a great writer as an attractive whole
in his books on Milton, Johnson and Wordsworth, all of which
appeared by 1910 and remain among the best critical writing
on their subjects. G. K. Chesterton's *Browning* and *The
Victorian Age in Literature* belong here too, and J. W.
Mackail, C. H. Herford and W. P. Ker were among others
who helped to make the study of literature a pleasure, Ker's
small *Medieval English Literature* being a pioneer work in
popularising our earliest literature. One work which had a
great vogue as a comprehensive book of introduction and
reference was Saintsbury's *Short History of English Literature*
(1898).

George Saintsbury (1845-1933) indeed deserves a special
tribute. He was a giant in his labours for literature. Some
of his work is truly monumental in scope and thoroughness,
for example his *History of English Prosody* (1906-10), his
History of English Criticism (1911) and his *History of
English Prose Rhythm*. But his immense learning (perhaps
no man has ever read more widely or with a more tenacious
memory than he) was married to a deep, catholic yet dis-
criminating love of literature—and to him a love of wine was
inseparable from a love of literature. He was a great human

being who stamped his personality on his learning. Tory of the old school and High Churchman as he was, his principles were never obscured or compromised, but his love of literature was so wholehearted that he could not withhold praise where praise was due, and he preferred to write of what he loved and of that in which there was something to praise. Among his best works are *The Peace of the Augustans* (1916), his introductions to the novels of Thackeray and his volumes of *Collected Essays*, while his *History of the French Novel* is full of pleasure. His *Scrapbooks* are highly personal talk on many topics, rich in learning and anecdote pungently applied to what he held to be the follies of the modern age. *Notes on a Cellar Book* too is typical of him. His style is sometimes crabbed and involved, but it is the man himself, a matured scholar richly grained.

Sir Arthur Quiller Couch (1863-1944), poet and author of many good novels including *The Astonishing History of Troy Town* (1888) and others based on Cornwall, was appointed Professor of English Literature at Cambridge in 1912 and as a result published several volumes of stimulating literary appreciation and criticism, which were originally lectures. His pages talk to the reader just as their author spoke to his audiences, arousing interest in and liking for his subject by the genial humanity of his treatment and the free use of illustrative quotation. His approach was not so much intellectual or even aesthetic as humanistic, insisting on the intimate connection between literature and life and between books and their authors. His three series of *Studies in Literature* (1918, 1922, 1929) cover a wide field, which is extended by some other volumes. *Shakespeare's Workmanship* (1918) examines several plays in some detail. *On the Art of Writing* (1916) and *On the Art of Reading* (1920) will long deserve to be read for their wise and often humorous common sense. His editing of *The Oxford Book of English Verse* set a high, if now somewhat old-fashioned, standard for the popular anthology of the best English poetry. He was also for some years associated with J. Dover Wilson in editing the *New Cambridge Shakespeare*.

As in literature as a whole, so in criticism the years following the First War saw a change in general attitude, but the
older manner naturally did not disappear. Sir Edmund
Gosse (1849-1928), who with such books as *From Shakespeare
to Pope* (1885) and *A History of Eighteenth Century Litera-
ture* (1889) had been one of the Victorian pioneers in
popularising the study of English literature, continued to
cover a wide field as an authoritative elder critic in *The
Sunday Times*, a typical volume of his being *Books on the
Table* (1921). W. P. Ker kept to the broader approach in
The Art of Poetry (1923) and his posthumous *Collected
Essays* (1925). So did the poet Lascelles Abercrombie in
The Idea of Great Poetry (1925) and *Romanticism* (1926).
George Gordon, who succeeded Walter Raleigh as Merton
Professor at Oxford, was only too sparing in publication, but
his *Shakespeare's Comedies* and his reviews in *The Times
Literary Supplement* maintained the tradition of the happy,
almost conversational expression of a humane love of letters,
while his *Anglo-American Literary Relations* was a charac-
teristic introductory talk on a wide literary subject. To these
more conservative critics appealing in general to a wide
audience may be added John Bailey and some of the
Professors, for example, Oliver Elton with his *English Muse*
(1933) and his massive but very readable *Survey of English
Literature* from 1730 to 1880 in six volumes, and Sir Herbert
Grierson whose *Cross-Currents in the Literature of the
Seventeenth Century, Milton and Wordsworth* and introduction to the metaphysical poets easily win other than academic
readers. One of the wisest books of the century in the field of
literary studies also came from a Professor, namely R. W.
Chambers, whose *Man's Unconquerable Mind* (1942), passing
from the Venerable Bede through *Piers Plowman* and
Shakespeare to A. E. Housman, enshrines the continuity of
the English tradition. Such a book is the fruit of years of
loving scholarship, for R. W. Chambers was a very learned
scholar to whom students of *Beowulf* and all admirers of Sir
Thomas More are greatly indebted for his inspired industry
of research. Here too may be mentioned Sir Edmund

Chambers, whose work also was for the wide public as in *Shakespeare: a survey* (1925) as well as for the scholar as in his authoritative and exhaustive *The Medieval Stage* (1903) and *The Elizabethan Stage* (1923).

From about 1920 the volume of critical writing published by Professors and lecturers at the universities became very noticeable, and not unnaturally it tended to be less popular in quality. The intellectuality, austerity, subtlety, and striving for originality which characterised much modern poetry pervaded the higher criticism too. It was appropriate that the seventeenth-century metaphysical poets now received much attention. The considerable advance in the teaching of literature had made it possible for lecturers and writers to assume a fairly wide basis of knowledge and a preliminary acquaintance with critical theories on the part of their audiences and on that assumption they proceeded to a more detailed and to a more theoretical examination of literature. Specialist knowledge of bibliography, history and psychology became tools of literary criticism. Books were often studied not so much for their intrinsic qualities as in relation to their age and by standards derived from a comparative study of literature which might extend far beyond English. Research was in danger of becoming an academic industry. Indeed in their anxiety to be so "critically aware" that nothing but the purest principles of literary judgment were applied some of the academic critics parted company with the older generations of English critics and were much more intent upon the profit than upon the pleasure of their readers, and they were rather of the company of the new biographers who could not resist the desire to expose the flaws in greatness and to reverse established opinions.

Nevertheless, perhaps indeed because of these changed attitudes and conditions, much excellent critical writing appeared. Professor Dover Wilson in *The Essential Shakespeare* (1932) gave the best popular picture of Shakespeare as modern scholarship was seeing him, his *What Happens in Hamlet* (1935) is among the best of several psychological interpretations of that perplexing Prince, and *The Fortunes of Falstaff* (1943) was a characteristic product of the original mind which helped to make the *New Cambridge Shakespeare* a really new editing of the plays: to that editing knowledge of bibliography and early printing made a valuable contribution. Tillyard's studies in Milton testified to the power of research to bring fresh understanding even where so much had been known before, and his *Elizabethan World Scene* and his studies of Shakespeare's histories and last plays are among his other distinguished writings in which learning is made attractive to the ordinary reader. Sir Maurice Bowra too appealed to a wide literary public by *The Heritage of Symbolism* (1943), *From Virgil to Milton* (1945) and *The Creative Experiment* (1949). Basil Willey in *The Seventeenth Century Background* (1934), *The Eighteenth Century Background* (1940) and *Nineteenth Century Studies* (1949) traced the relationship between the currents of thought in the age and the creative writings of that age, and was luminous to scholars. C. S. Lewis, even better known probably for his *Screwtape Letters* (1942) and other popular religious writings, produced an invaluable aid to the understanding of medieval literature in *The Allegory of Love* and a very careful and balanced study of Milton's *Paradise Lost*. Lord David Cecil, already noted among the biographers, gives perhaps the most quietly satisfying pleasure of all the academic writers.

In all these writers the more academic approach and the more specialised knowledge are to some extent present, but otherwise they kept the traditional critical attitude. Almost entirely of a new kind, however, was the critical attitude of I. A. Richards of Cambridge, who was born in 1893. In collaboration with C. K. Ogden he published *The Meaning of Meaning* (1923), which he followed up with *The Principles of Literary Criticism* (1924), *Science and Poetry* (1926), *Practical Criticism* (1929) and *Coleridge on Imagination* (1934). Richards was much concerned at the decline which, it seemed to him, had taken place in the ability of averagely well educated and intelligent people to understand poetry. He held this decline to be due partly to very defective understanding of the meaning of words by readers, partly to the disintegration of the earlier cultural coherence which had given all the members of a community a common understanding of its speech and ideas, and very largely to "bad training". It was certainly a state of affairs which needed to be remedied, since the good understanding of literature, and especially of poetry, was essential to the mental health both of individuals and of society. So Richards set out to find a new training, which would "make men's spiritual heritage more available and more operative". His approach to the problem was primarily psychological, being based on a study of the various factors which hindered the full understanding of a poem. The new discipline which he advocated consisted of the dissection of a poem with the utmost scientific objectivity, a process which involved an "intellectual analysis of the Total Meaning into its contributories"; thereby all the various elements of a poem, aesthetic, moral, mental, sensory and technical, were appreciated, while the reader learnt to be on his guard against false reactions due to such factors as preconceptions, stock responses, inhibitions, and irrelevant associations of ideas. He admitted that, viewed in this light, "the critical reading of poetry is an arduous discipline", but it would have the virtue of making us "less easily imposed upon by our fellows and by ourselves". Certainly one may question whether any but the most gifted can apply his method without losing the pleasurable effect of a poem as a whole.

The teaching and example of I. A. Richards, however, had a great, if limited, influence both in the universities and outside. His closest follower was the poet William Empson in his *Seven Types of Ambiguity* (1930), which was a subtle analysis of the various layers and shades of meaning which can exist in a statement and the appreciation of which is essential to the proper apprehension of the total statement, especially in poetry. This was analytical criticism, which was to complement appreciative criticism, and of the analyst Empson said that "he assumes that something has been conveyed to the reader by the work under consideration, and sets out to explain, in terms of the rest of the reader's experience, why the reader has had the effect on him that is assumed". By thus supplying a "machinery of analysis" Empson hoped to restore to readers an assurance of critical judgment, which he held the average contemporary reader to lack. "What is needed for literary satisfaction", he declared, "is not, 'this is beautiful because of such and such a theory', but 'this is all right; I am feeling correctly about this; I know the kind of way in which it is meant to be affecting me' ". Empson had been Richards's pupil at Cambridge, and the influence of Richards was particularly strong at Cambridge, where he was followed by F. R. Leavis and other contributors to the journal *Scrutiny*. From Leavis especially (see For Further Reading) there came much valuable, penetrating analysis.

But whether of the more conservative or of the more revolutionary of what we may call the more or less professional academic critics it is impossible to say more here, for there still remain to be considered two other notable classes, the journalists and the creative writers. Among journalists there have not been lacking at any time in this period true critics. Robert Lynd has already been mentioned. To Sir Edmund Gosse there succeeded in due course in *The Sunday Times* Sir Desmond MacCarthy, born 1878, who continued, with a rather conservative taste, to enjoy literature and to relate it to life: among his collected papers are *Portraits* (1931), *Criticism* (1932) and *Experience* (1935). Sir John Squire, editor of *The London Mercury* for many years, was long a leading reviewer. C. E. Montague, of *The Manchester Guardian*, left behind a tantalisingly small volume of literary criticism, *A Writer's Notes on His Trade* (1930), which despite its slightness is rich in suggestion. John Middleton Murry (b. 1889), husband of Katherine Mansfield and friend of D. H. Lawrence, of both of whom he wrote, may also be included here, for he was editor of *The Athenaeum* (1919-21) and of *The Adelphi* (1923-30): his *Keats and Shakespeare* (1925) and *Studies in Keats* (1930) were outstanding contributions to the appreciation of Keats, and his two series, *Countries of the Mind* (1922, 1931), contain some of his best work. Murry, too, was one of those who produced a personal survey of Shakespeare, as was the vogue in the thirties. Imaginative and sensitive, his love of beauty is inseparable from his constant search for religious truth His approach is indeed a fourfold one, aesthetic, biographical, moral and religious. John Palmer was author of two admirable groups of studies, *Political Characters of Shakespeare* (1945) and *Comic Characters of Shakespeare* (1946), in which the former dramatic critic of the *Saturday Review* and the public servant who had seen much of men and affairs as a member of the Secretariat of the League of Nations joined late in life to produce commentaries free from any contemporary fashion.

It is from the creative writers that we get, as we might expect, some of the very best criticism. Writing of literature in the light of their own experience of the joys and difficulties of creation and with an intimate knowledge of their predecessors in their particular craft, they speak with special insight and authority. The numerous little volumes of *Collected Essays* by Robert Bridges contain many penetrating glances at a wide variety of writers: like Dr Johnson, Bridges could be very dogmatic in his prejudices, but the purity of his taste and the strength of his judgment make his appreciation particularly stimulating. E. M. Forster's *Aspects of the Novel* (1927) is an outstanding consideration of its subject. Granville Barker, the dramatist, wrote valuable critical work on the drama, and in his series of *Prefaces to Shakespeare* examined several plays as no one else had done with the authority of a great producer who saw them in terms of the stage.

T. S. Eliot was heard as a critic almost as soon as he became known as a poet, *The Sacred Wood* appearing in 1920. His *Selected Essays* (1932) contains a good deal of his best work, but it is only a small proportion of his writings in which literature is a principal theme, for example *The Use of Poetry and the Use of Criticism* (1933) and *After Strange Gods* (1934). But as Eliot increasingly felt the need to consider how to maintain or redeem the highest values of civilised society his more purely literary criticism was largely replaced by such studies as *The Idea of a Christian Society* (1939) and

Notes on the Definition of a Culture (1948). As a critic, however, he had from his earliest writings wielded a great influence. In general his conception of literature was a classical one, placing a high value on tradition, on content and on form; in particular he was eminent for his appreciation of the Elizabethan dramatists, the metaphysical poets and Dryden and for his condemnation of Milton for bringing about by his great example that "dissociation of sensibility" which in Eliot's opinion weakened nearly all English poetry for long afterwards. Edith Sitwell wrote particularly of technical aspects of poetry such as the use of sound and imagery. Her introductory notes on her own poetry and on that of her brother Sacheverell are invaluable, and in all that she wrote she spoke out of her own experience in poetic craftsmanship. In *A Poet's Notebook* and *A Notebook on Shakespeare* (1948) she provides a wealth of suggestion for the understanding of poetry. Sir Herbert Read, the poet, made a notable contribution to the psychological approach to literature in his study of Wordsworth, and in *Collected Essays in Literary Criticism* (1951) and *The True Voice of Feeling* (1953) he often weds the psychological to the aesthetic in criticism. Day Lewis's *The Poetic Image* (1947), too, goes far beyond technicality, for, in being perhaps the best consideration of poetic imagery yet written, it is really a consideration of the essence of poetry. Edmund Blunden kept largely to the biographical in *Charles Lamb and his Contemporaries*, *The Life of Leigh Hunt* and *Shelley: A Life Story* (1946), while the essays in his *Votive Tablets* (1931) talk of English men and books with a quiet contemplative insight like that of his poetry and a similar respect for tradition and for all that is worthy in those of less fame than the great.

The critical writings of Virginia Woolf rank as high as her novels. Her view of the novel has been referred to in its appropriate place. In her two volumes, *The Common Reader* (1925, 1932), she ranges from the fifteenth century to the twentieth, and her almost poetic imagination recreates the most diverse figures, bringing to life their personalities and settings. She had indeed a very keen perception of both individual and general values, and she wrote her critical papers as she wrote her novels out of the sheer love of literature, just as in *Orlando* she wove literary appreciation through her tale in the happiest possible manner. The posthumous collections of her essays and talks, especially *The Death of the Moth* (1944), though they are often brief, show how joyously and naturally she linked life and literature, and on topics like how to read and the meaning of words they speak her characteristic sensitive wisdom. The critical essays of Charles Morgan many may find of even higher worth than his novels. His two series of *Reflections in a Mirror* (1944, '46) are classical examples of the essay in which a full and thoughtful mind ranges over life and literature. Not all are on purely literary topics, and indeed perhaps in not one is he able to keep within the limits of literary considerations, for with Charles Morgan as with Matthew Arnold literature must be "a criticism of life". So his first volume opens with an essay "In Search of Values" and the second with one on "Ideas at War". *Liberties of the Mind* (1951) was a natural sequel: described as "a re-statement of the philosophy of freedom and a justification of man as a spiritual being", it considers among other themes the place of the artist in the community and romanticism in art and in society. The novelist George Orwell, had he not died early, might also have appeared more considerably as a critic, for his *Critical Essays* showed promise of more to come. Frank Swinnerton, successor to Robert Lynd as "John o'London", wrote a very lively comprehensive survey of much of this half-century in *The Georgian Literary Scene* (1935), recording often his personal impressions of authors he knew. Earlier he had published critical studies of George Gissing (1912) and R. L. Stevenson (1914).

This brief enumeration may well appear inadequate treatment of the criticism by the creative writers, but, if in space they have not been given their due prominence, their very names should secure their proper regard.

POSTSCRIPT

THE NINETEEN-FIFTIES

By Frank Whitehead, m.a.

What you see of any spectacle depends on where you are standing. Naturally, I cannot pretend to any detached or objective vantage-point from which to survey the literature of the past decade, and what follows is essentially a personal, and by no means impartial, assessment of certain writers who seem to me (from where I am standing at the moment) worth reading and discussing. Both the inclusions and the omissions will be found surprising by some readers, but it seems to me that in dealing with the immediately contemporary all one can usefully do is to offer one's own judgment, imperfect and mistaken though it may be, and hope that time will not deal too unkindly with it.

Whatever the ultimate verdict on the literature of the decade, it already seems fairly certain that the nineteen-fifties will be seen as a period in which new moods were stirring into consciousness and in which a younger generation of writers were formulating aspirations consciously different from those of their predecessors. Yet, writing in the closing year of the decade, I find it easier to sense the atmosphere of innovation, of shifting landmarks and dissolving perspectives, than to pinpoint the nature of the changes or to estimate their likely value. We may suspect, indeed, that the neat ten-year period which chronology imposes on our thinking is too arbitrary to contain the real pattern of recent social and literary history. Should not 1945 be our datum-line? Does not the Second World War make a more natural watershed for the historian, marking off the atomic from the pre-atomic era, and irrevocably separating the generations one from another by its epoch-making new awareness of power and guilt? Certainly in some obvious senses we live to-day in a post-war period whose identity has defined itself as a reaction against the characteristic assumptions of the now unfashionable thirties. The nineteen-thirties were determinedly political: the nineteen-fifties have been no less determinedly anti-political —unashamedly apathetic or cynical in regard to all larger affiliations, vehemently sceptical of all 'isms. On the other hand, this recognisably post-war cast of mind seems, in retrospect, to have taken a surprisingly long time to emerge, so that the early post-war years can perhaps more properly be seen as an extension, a transitional period during which earlier attitudes and preoccupations worked themselves out, and in so doing gradually lost their apparent relevance.

In the thirties the consciousness of all thinking people was dominated (one way or another) by the bitter social realities of economic depression, widespread unemployment, the spread of fascist dictatorships, and the gathering threat of war. There were two main ways in which the writers of the time responded to this all-pervasive background of insecurity. On the one hand, there was what we may loosely call the progressivist response—a grouping optimistic in outlook and humanist in its concerns, broad enough to embrace both Marxising intellectuals and liberal-minded Christian reformers, all of whom were united, despite other disagreements, by a common desire to improve the material conditions of human existence, to tackle social evils directly and find the appropriate social remedy. On the other hand, there were those (fewer in number, but influential nevertheless) whose instinct was to reassert the superior reality of the individual spiritual life, and to "take refuge" (as their opponents put it) in religious belief or mystical contemplation. The utterances of these writers were often tainted with an unattractive sympathy for authoritarianism, yet when we recall T. S. Eliot's *Four Quartets* it cannot be denied that from this stable came the supreme literary achievement of those years.

Both these intellectual currents persisted during the war, but it was the "progressivist" viewpoint which became the

more closely identified with the wartime national consciousness. From 1941 onwards the war came to be seen increasingly as a continuation of the anti-fascist movement of the
thirties; the alliance of Britain, the U.S., and the U.S.S.R.
against the Axis powers looked to many like a belated large-
scale realisation of earlier dreams of a Popular Front, and
soldiers and civilians alike were sustained by the expectation
of a post-war world in which war and poverty would be out-
lawed, democracy and social justice would be secured, and
the "common man" would at last come into his own. This
was the mood which lay behind the return of the Labour
Government in 1945, and which survived to a considerable
extent even the first years of austerity and peacetime readjustment.   Gradually, however, disillusionment set in: international disagreements proved to be as intense as ever,
austerity seemed destined to go on and on, the benefits of
the Welfare State could be represented as either unexpectedly
meagre or dangerously suspect. In this period, too, began
the reversal of feeling in regard to our wartime Russian ally,
which ultimately was to undermine the whole basis of "progressivist" thinking. In this respect, the coup-de-grâce was
not administered until 1956, when Krushchev's revelation of
the tyranny and injustice of the Stalin regime became public
knowledge; but long before this an image of Russia had begun
to form which was very different from the idealised wartime
version, and this was persistently reinforced by the widespread
impression of intransigence in Russia's international attitudes.
As a new realignment of international groupings took shape,
it once more became almost respectable to make the tacit
assumption that between 1939 and 1945 we had been fighting
"the wrong war"; and a good deal of quiet re-writing of recent
history took place along these lines.

In this developing climate of opinion it is hardly surprising that formerly "progressive" writers either faltered or
turned an intellectual somersault; no attempt at a witch-hunt
on McCarthyite lines could get very far in this country, but
the suspicion of "fellow-travelling" proclivities certainly

became something that had to be lived down. By most, however, this dilemma was quietly shelved, and the issues
involved in it allowed to go by default. Even now, remarkably few of the writers whose adult consciousness was formed
in the pre-atomic era have made any serious attempt to
re-examine and re-define their position in the light of post-
atomic realities and sentiments. Of those who have tried,
Angus Wilson and John Whiting are perhaps the only ones
to have done so with any real success. As a symptom of this
general failure, one may point to the astonishing paucity in
England of novels or plays which strive to digest the experiences of the Second World War and its aftermath from the
standpoint of those who lived through them. The general
impression left by much writing of the late nineteen-forties
(and of the early nineteen-fifties for that matter) is of a turning away from urgent and living contemporary issues, almost
as though their challenge were too difficult or too appalling
to face—a turning away into cloudy or tenuous rhetoric on
the part of the poets, into triviality or unreality on the part
of the novelists and dramatists. In these circumstances, it
looked, for a brief time, as though the future was to lie with
that alternative tradition which, even in the thirties, had pinned
its hopes to a revival of religious belief and a re-establishment
of the principle of authority. It was this intellectual eddy which
finally conferred social prestige and academic respectability
on T. S. Eliot (formerly the *enfant terrible* of the literary
world) and brought him a host of new admirers who possibly
did not understand his poetry, but who could at least feel
themselves in sympathy with his opinions. But this movement, too, failed to gather real momentum, and, in literature
at least, T. S. Eliot's play *The Cocktail Party* seems likely
to prove its sole enduring monument. Evidently, in the atomic
age it was to be no easier to believe in the ultimate truth
of religious experience than in the possibility and value of
material progress. In retrospect, the intellectual activity of
the immediate post-war years (whether worldly or unworldly
in its concerns) has the air of a rootless survival from an

earlier period—a belated response to a challenge which had already ceased to exist.

In general, then, we can say that after 1945 the writers who had first established themselves in the thirties failed to develop or to adjust themselves to new issues; while those who were approaching early middle age at the end of the war flowered but meagerly in the new environment. This left a vacuum which was bound to be filled eventually by younger writers; but it also made for a gap in continuity, a hiatus in the transmission of experience from one generation to the next, which accounts for much that seems most character- istic of the sensibility of the nineteen-fifties. It was not, however, until the middle of the decade that anything resembling a "movement" began to be discernible; obvious landmarks were the appearance of *Lucky Jim* in 1954, of *Look Back in Anger* and the poetry anthology *New Lines* in 1956, and of the collection of personal manifestos entitled *Declarations* in 1957. We are dealing now with the group popularly known as the "Angry Young Men"; the journal- istic appellation obscures important differences between indi- viduals, but it does bring out one quality (of rebellion against their elders, impatience with the established order) which these writers have in common.

By contrast with the thirties, the period since 1950 has been one of marked material prosperity. Continued infla- tion may have left pensioners and the salaried middle class with a justifiable sense of grievance; but however one may apportion the credit between the social welfare legislation of 1945-51 and the "free enterprise" policies of subsequent Conservative governments, the fact remains that the majority have been in more comfortable circumstances than for a very long time. There has been work for all, and there has been no really searing poverty; the housing shortage has steadily diminished; in times of sickness, adequate medical care has been guaranteed. Many more families than ever before have been able to afford a motor-car; and most seem to have found in the contemplation of television a satisfying

substitute for the consolations of religion. True, the international scene remains as troubled as ever, but disagreements
at this level have taken on a lunatic unreality that makes their
threat seem remote and unbelievable. Nevertheless, despite
all this, the mood typical of the young writer of to-day is one
of protest and revolt—intolerant of humbug and complacency,
suspicious of the social and literary "establishment", irrever-
ent towards all traditionally-accepted institutions from the
monarchy downwards, often petulant, sometimes self-pitying,
sometimes genuinely indignant. The protest may be directed
against minor irritations (the "precious" atmosphere of a
University madrigal group, the disfigurement of the coast-
line by long-disused military hutments) or against major
scandals (the poisoning of the earth's atmosphere by the continued testing of weapons so atrocious that it seems unthink-
able that any sane statesman could ever sanction their use).
It is, however, of a deliberately *ad hoc* kind, and careful to
avoid entanglement with any ideological system. The savage
farce of Suez and the bitter tragedy of Hungary seem to have
contributed almost equally to form this prevalent mood of
disgust and contempt for all political parties and all politicians.

These attitudes, though they have given rise to a good
deal of writing that is both lively and interesting, have not
so far produced any work of literature which can be said to
have unquestionable permanent significance. They constitute, nevertheless, a force to be reckoned with. The phenomenon we are concerned with here is a specifically English
one, and perhaps owes more than its protagonists realise to
the long and honourable tradition of English radicalism. It
has its counterpart, however, among the young of almost
all Western countries, and also of a number of those beyond
the Iron Curtain. It may not be an adequate response to
the sickness of our time, but it is at least better than no
response at all.

As we turn, with this cursorily-sketched background in
mind, to consider individual writers, it will be convenient to
take them roughly in order of seniority. For a man in his

seventies, our greatest living writer, E. M. Forster, has been amazingly productive, and though we have given up hope of any successor to *A Passage to India*, we have reason to be grateful, nevertheless, for the less ambitious volumes of his Indian summer. In 1951 a miscellaneous collection of essays was published under the characteristic, half-ironical title *Two Cheers for Democracy*. Then, in 1953, came *The Hill of Devi*; this gave a fascinating account of Forster's two visits (in 1912-13 and 1921) to the tiny Indian State of Dewas Senior, and at the same time threw interesting light on the genesis of *A Passage to India*. *Marianne Thornton, 1797-1887: A Domestic Biography* (1956) has less of E. M. Forster himself in it, since it consists mainly of family letters and diaries. As a portrayal of the family life of members of the famous Clapham Sect it has considerable charm and an unquestionable historical value; while for the student of literature it has the further interest (since Marianne Thornton was Mr Forster's great-aunt) of providing some illuminating background information about the milieu within which the novelist grew up.

Our greatest living poet, T. S. Eliot, has published only a single short poem, "The Cultivation of Christmas Trees"; but his two new plays deserve extended attention, even though they must be judged, finally, to represent a falling-away from his earlier level of achievement as a dramatist. *The Confidential Clerk*, first produced at the Edinburgh Festival of 1953, is a comedy concerned with questions of identity. The plot is almost wilfully complicated. Colby Simpkins, the confidential clerk of the title, is believed by both to be the illegitimate son of his employer, Sir Claude Mulhammer; while Lucasta Angel is (unknown to Colby) Sir Claude's illegitimate daughter. Sir Claude's wife, Lady Elizabeth, becomes convinced that Colby must be her own long-lost son, but eventually the cross-examination of Colby's "aunt", Mrs Guzzard, reveals that his true parents are Mrs Guzzard herself and the unsuccessful organist who was her husband. And it turns out that Lady Elizabeth's son is none other than B. Kaghan, Lucasta's vulgarian fiancé.

On the surface, this suggests a successful West End comedy, amusing in an artificial, almost Wildean, way. In the stage production (which may have been at fault in this respect) the verse form of the dialogue went almost unnoticed, while some of the witticisms seemed a wholly irrelevant angling for laughs. (One remembers, for instance, Lady Elizabeth's mirth-provoking line:

> He was run over. By a rhinoceros
> In Tanganyika.)

We may, indeed, feel that on this level the play has been almost too successful, since the deeper significance which Mr Eliot seems to be hinting at cannot really be grasped during performance, and could easily be completely overlooked. At the opening of the play Colby has begun to accept his role of future financier, and is about to abandon his dream of becoming an organist, or else keep it only as make-believe. In this he is following the example of Sir Claude who, as a young man, had dreamed of becoming a potter. The point being made here is that one becomes the role one plays. As Sir Claude puts it:

> The life changed me, as it is changing you.
> It begins as a kind of make-believe,
> And the make-believing makes it true.

Yet, as Colby questions:

> If we all have to live in a world of make-believe,
> Is that good for us?

In the event, Colby's discovery of his true parentage frees him to resolve the conflict between his two worlds, private and public, and he determines to become an unsuccessful organist like his father before him. It is also hinted (a shade inconsistently, perhaps) that his is in some way a religious vocation, and that he will end by taking holy orders. The trouble is that there appears to be a disjunction between the dramatist's symbolic intention and the stage-vehicle in which he has chosen to clothe it. Whereas *The Cocktail Party* was powerful enough in its own way to be found distinctly unpleasant by those who disliked its message, *The Confidential Clerk* is in danger of seeming merely null.

In *The Elder Statesman* (first performed at the Edinburgh
Festival in 1958) the central character is Lord Claverton, an
elderly and ailing public figure who is pursued in his retirement by two ghosts from his early life.   These are Mrs
Carghill (formerly Maisie Montjoy), who once sued him for
breach of promise but settled out of court, and Fred Culver-
well (now known as Federico Gomez) whom he led into
extravagant ways at Oxford and who later emigrated after
serving a prison sentence for forgery.   In the course of the
play he is led to face his own past for the first time, and
to recognise and repudiate the element of "pretence" in his
own public role.   He confesses his youthful "sins" to his
daughter and her fiancé ("It is harder to confess the sin
that no one believes in/Than the crime that everyone can
appreciate"); and as a result finds peace.

> I've been freed from the self that pretends to be someone;
> And in becoming no one, I begin to live.
> It is worth while dying, to find out what life is.

Or as Monica, his daughter, puts it:

> In becoming no one, he has become himself.

One cannot fail to notice the continuity between this theme
and that of *The Confidential Clerk*; but the main impression
left by the new play is of a surprising thinness.   The texture
of both the plot and the verse is slack and uncertain, and
one detects at times a note which verges on the sentimental.
Nevertheless, if a failure, it is not an unsympathetic one;
Mr Eliot has become more human in his old age, and in
consequence seems rather more likeable, even if in the process he has lost something of his former artistic stature.
Neither of these plays is negligible (Eliot has written
nothing which is that); but between them they do seem to
mark the final collapse of the high hopes which were once
entertained for the "poetic drama" revival.   If T. S. Eliot has
been unable to prevail against the habits and expectations of
the theatre-going public, it is unlikely that others can succeed
where he, in the end, failed.

It is when we turn to the next generation of established
writers that we have a sense of stasis, the impression of a

working-over once again of ground that hardly repays further cultivation. Aldous Huxley, for instance, has published a collection of essays *Adonis and the Alphabet* (1956), a short novel *The Genius and the Goddess* (1955), and in *Brave New World Re-visited* (1959) a re-examination and attempted vindication of the ideas expounded in his earlier satire. Readable as they undoubtedly are, none of these volumes contains any notable fresh perception or exhibits any significant development of the position he had already made his own. Again, Elizabeth's Bowen's output has been limited to a single, not very satisfactory, novel, *A World of Love* (1955). Graham Greene, it is true, has ventured an assault upon the stage with his two plays, *The Living Room* (1953) and *The Potting Shed* (1958); but though well received at the time these cannot be said to represent more than a transference to a new medium of themes which had already been worked out more convincingly in his fiction. His recent novels, again, only confirm the impression of an almost obsessive preoccupation with a severely limited group of issues, so that the whole of his oeuvre appears in the end little more than a set of variations on what is virtually a single theme. *The End of the Affair* (1951) is perhaps the most threadbare and implausible of the many versions. *The Quiet American* (1955) has all the technical virtuosity which makes this novelist so compelling as a narrator, and the Indo-Chinese setting is presented with vividness and economy. At the same time one is left with the feeling that Greene's moral vision is somehow at odds with his novelist's perception, so that the reader hardly finds it possible in the end to accept the writer's valuation (admittedly a little ambivalent) of his markedly repugnant American, Howard Pyle. *Our Man in Havana* (1958) is a lighter affair altogether, and on its own level both skilful and amusing.

Of the four poets who had appeared so compact a group in the thirties as to invite the composite sobriquet "Macspaunday", only W. H. Auden showed any real development in the fifties. C. Day Lewis and Stephen Spender published

little that could advance their reputations, while Louis Mac-
niece's two volumes, *Autumn Sequel* (1954) and *Visitations*
(1957), displayed only technical accomplishment, without
any compelling pressure of experience behind the professional
fluency. Auden, after withdrawing to the United States during
the war and taking out American citizenship shortly after it,
has moved steadily further away from both his near-Freudian
approach to individual psychology and his near-Marxist concern with social issues, turning instead to an exploration of
inner spiritual experience in which an increasingly orthodox
Christianity is buttressed by a free use of Jung's conception
of archetypes. A recent textual study by an American professor, Joseph Warren Beach, has demonstrated the extent
to which Auden has taken trouble to cover up his tracks in
the process, by re-writing, re-titling, or suppressing, in successive collected editions of his poems, those items which conflict
awkwardly with his later beliefs. He even went so far, in one
case, as to present, under a new title and ostensibly as an
expression of his own standpoint, a "Vicar's Sermon" written
in 1935 which, in its original context in *The Dog Beneath the
Skin*, had clearly been intended as an ironic parody of
Christian ideas. Auden's changed views have naturally made
themselves felt in his poetry, though at first their influence
hardly seemed to be for the better. In *Nones* (1952), the
journalistic liveliness which formerly showed itself in apt
contemporary comment, has almost entirely vanished.
Instead, we are offered large gestures towards universal
understanding, couched in language that is generalised and
often vague in its reference, while the rhythms of the verse
are tired, devitalised, and nerveless. Among a good deal of
rather grandiose "topographical" verse, there can be found
occasional successes of a less ambitious kind; but all too
often the unity imposed on the individual poem suggests either
a facile saintliness or a slickly-conceived worldliness. *The
Shield of Achilles* (1955) contains a further set of "Landscape" poems in which the offered profundity never quite
materialises; but there is also a sequence "Horae Canonica"

in which Auden comes much nearer to forging a new style to express his new Christian preoccupations. Intricate yet austere, self-conscious but with a pressure of felt experience behind them, these poems show that Auden's talent is still alive, even though its vicissitudes have often been both disconcerting and disappointing.

At a time when established writers fail to satisfy, it is natural for readers and critics to look around for others, hitherto unnoticed, who may be capable of filling the gap. This, at any rate, seems to be the likeliest explanation for the increasing respect which has accrued, since 1950, to three novelists (Joyce Cary, C. P. Snow, and Anthony Powell) whose work attracted little attention when they first came on the scene in the thirties. Each of these very different writers has his own distinct, if limited, interest; but it is difficult to see how any of them can justify the rather exaggerated homage which they have lately received. Joyce Cary continued to be active as a novelist up to his death in 1958, but his work (as opposed to his reputation) does not really belong to the period under review. His early novels about African life (*Mr Johnson* and *Aissa Saved*) were competent but in no way remarkable. His later work is both more varied and more ambitious, yet even at its best it leaves the reader with a sense of dissatisfaction not altogether easy to account for. His most popular novel, *The Horse's Mouth* (1944), extracts some exuberant farcical comedy from the antics of the eccentric ageing painter, Gulley Jimson, but this seems to have obscured, for many readers, an underlying intention which is wholly serious, even tragic. The author has evidently aimed to convey the inexorableness with which life bears down, ultimately, on us all, together with a sense of the uselessness and presumptuousness of trying to do anything but put a brave face on it. ("For it saves a lot of trouble between friends to swear that life is good, brother.") The fact is, perhaps, that despite the thoughtfulness and humanity of the larger design which Cary has sought to impose on his later novels, the elements (characterisation, dialogue, incident) which he uses to make up his pattern are inescapably secondhand—stereotypes which are incapable of successfully communicating his best perceptions.

C. P. Snow's ambitious sequence of novels *Strangers and Brothers* started to appear in 1940, and is still "in progress" twenty years later. The first two volumes in the series (*Strangers and Brothers* itself and *The Light and the Dark*) have an uncertainty of touch, which suggests that the writer was still engaged in finding his own characteristic tone of voice as a novelist. What he found, in the end, is a surprisingly old-fashioned, almost Trollopian, naturalism, which resolutely turns its back on not only all "stream of consciousness" experimentation, but also on any of the complexity of narrative technique which can be learnt from Conrad and Henry James. *The Masters* (1951), with its setting in a Cambridge college, and *The New Men* (1954), concerned with a government research establishment, show what the method is capable of; in each the interest lies in the almost documentary sense of time and place, the way in which a restricted community is convincingly portrayed as if from the inside. And while there is no sense of any spontaneous creativity at work, the reader feels himself in contact with an intelligent mind, which is deliberately making the most of its advantages and sensibly concealing its deficiencies. Elsewhere in the series, however, Snow's attempts to render more intimate aspects of personal experience show a wooden insensitivity and, at times, an almost embarrassing lack of psychological insight.

Anthony Powell achieved a very modest success in the thirties with a number of satirical novels rather in the vein of Evelyn Waugh and the early Huxley. Since the war he has made a fresh start with a novel-sequence whose over-all title, *The Music of Time*, presumably indicates a conscious indebtedness to Marcel Proust. The world he portrays here is a curiously limited one, confined almost exclusively to Old Etonians and their female relatives. Up to the present, four volumes have appeared (*A Question of Upbringing* in 1951, *A Buyer's Market* in 1952, *The Acceptance World* in 1955, and *At Lady Molly's* in 1957); but the individual books are not separate, self-contained entities (the plan contrasts in this respect with C. P. Snow's series), so that one will clearly have to wait until the sequence is complete in order to judge it fairly. While the total effect so far is diffuse and at times confusing, much of the detail is keenly observed, and in Widmerpool Mr Powell has certainly created a memorable comic character.

We come next to four writers (two playwrights and two novelists) who belong to an older generation than that of the Angry Young Men, but whose output belongs essentially to the fifties. Each highly individual, they exemplify no recognisable tendency and have little in common beyond the date of their first appearance on the literary scene. Nevertheless, it seems possible that their work will prove, in the end, to possess more enduring merit than anything else produced in the period. John Whiting's three plays were published in a single volume in 1957; but it must be emphasised that to read them in book form can give scant impression of their true quality. Whiting has a marked talent for finding and establishing the strong dramatic situation which will embody and, in the theatre, communicate immediately the themes with which he is concerned. His first play, *Saint's Day*, won the prize in the play competition held by the Arts Theatre to mark the Festival of Britain; when produced in September 1951 it was savagely attacked by all the critics, and championed only by leading actors and producers of the day. There was some excuse for the critics' incomprehension, for in this case the dramatic situations are too powerful, too melodramatic, almost, indeed, "stagy". One can sense the intention to use them for serious artistic communication, but what is to be communicated remains inchoate. Dramatic effects are piled one on top of the other, without being integrated together organically; and in the end the drama sinks under an excess of symbolic purposes.

John Whiting's second play, *A Penny for a Song*, had already been produced in the West End a few months earlier, though with little commercial success. There is in this nothing of the slightly hysterical note which marred and weakened

Saint's Day; instead we have a wry comedy, ironic in general tone, at times bitter, at times inconsequent, but suffused with poetry and shot with exuberant hilarity at the quirks of human idiosyncrasy. The setting is almost identical with that of Hardy's novel *The Trumpet Major*—rural England in 1804, under threat of Napoleonic invasion. The comedy derives mainly from the local squire, Sir Timothy Bellboys, full of his fantastically elaborate plans for thwarting the invasion, and his brother, Lamprett, who can think only of his fire-brigade. Believing the invasion to have started, Sir Timothy disguises himself as Bonaparte, and after a sequence of extravagant misadventures is taken prisoner by the local defence volunteers. The more serious aspects of the theme are represented by the young, war-blinded soldier, Edward Sterne, who is on his way to London to ask the King to stop the war. His brief love-idyll with Lamprett's daughter, Dorcas, is punctuated by a series of conversations with Hallam Matthews, a fashionable London dandy who finds himself an amused spectator of the local confusions.

> Hallam: Everyone attempts to be other than they are
> . . . It is clowning, you know. A most con-
> sequent factor of life.
>
> Edward: He means, I think, that we find the reality
> unbearable. That factor within us—ah!—the
> infrangible burden to carry: self-knowledge.
> And so we escape, child-like, into the illusion.
> We clown and posture, but not to amuse others
> —no—to comfort ourselves. The laughter is
> incidental to the tragic spectacle of each man
> attempting to hide his intolerable self.

It is left to Hallam, however, to destroy Edward's own illusion, when he explains that "His Majesty will grant any request you may care to put to him", but "it will be no good . . . because—dear, sweet, kindly soul—he is not quite right in the head". In spite of this, Edward continues on his journey, knowing his mission is bound to fail; and herein seems to lie the central message of the play. ". . . Our destination is unimportant, Hallam. We journey forward only to discover the reason for our travelling." This is a singularly attractive play, and it succeeds in conveying, with a complexity which defies paraphrase, an attitude (of muted hope, of persistence in face of disillusionment) whose value is both timely and long-lasting.

Whiting's third play, *Marching Song* (1954), is more concentrated and highly unified than either of the other two; the author himself has described it as having "a single and undeviating line in story and treatment". The drama centres round the dilemma of Rupert Forster, a general and professional soldier who has been imprisoned as a war-criminal ever since the war ended. After seven years' solitary confinement he is now suddenly released and brought to the home of his wealthy ex-mistress, Catherine de Troyes, with the warning that, for reasons of state, he will have to be brought to public trial as a coward and traitor, unless he takes his own life within thirty-six hours. On the surface, Forster is a somewhat ambiguous figure; but it becomes clear by the end of the play that, while understanding him and even commiserating with him, we are intended, finally, to repudiate the values he stands for. His own view of his catastrophe is that he was "trapped" by pity—by a sudden and unexpected awareness of the common human plight. During a carefully-timed advance through a town, his armoured column was surrounded and fatally slowed-up by a crowd of children who swarmed out into the streets around his tanks. To maintain the time-table of his advance he shot one of them, and thus started a ruthless massacre. But immediately, he found himself "trapped" by the memory of the child. "I couldn't free myself from that moment. The moment when I stood alone, sad, lost, childless with the child in my arms. And looking down saw that it was a human being." The "secret" that he had hitherto shut out in order to make his own "prison of pride and ambition" had been forced upon him. As a result he halted, stupified, for twelve crucial hours, and the subsequent attack failed.

In the course of the play we watch him coming to his decision—at first willing to die, later forming with a post-war waif of the streets, Dido Morgan, a relationship which gives him a renewed desire to live, finally having this desire to live destroyed by a realisation of the universality of illusion. (The crowning blow comes when the goatherd's songs, which in prison had kept alive his will to exist, turn out to have been not a form of prayer, but "obscene—just filth".) Before he dies, he urges on Dido: "Don't stay caught in the memory of this past day. Escape. Get out". Nevertheless, at the final curtain Dido returns, herself trapped by pity, in order that she may help Catherine to re-learn the desire to live which she has now lost. It may be that here, too, the drama carries a burden of significance greater than it can readily bear; even so, this play must be accounted a powerful and impressive achievement of a distinctly original kind.

Samuel Beckett is an Irishman who was for some years secretary to James Joyce, and who has lived in Paris ever since 1938. His plays and novels have all been written in French, and subsequently translated into English by the author himself. In spite of this, his work has certain qualities (not easy to define) which seem to justify the claim that he belongs, primarily, to English rather than continental literature. His major work, *Waiting for Godot*, was first performed in Paris in 1952, and later produced, with outstanding success, at London's Arts Theatre in 1955. In this tragicomedy in two acts the action (if such it can be called) takes place on two successive evenings on a deserted country road, whose only article of scenery is a stunted tree. Two down-and-outs, Estragon and Vladimir, occupy the time revealing, through their talk, misunderstandings, and lamentation, the grotesque hopelessness of the human situation. Each has his own private agonies to contend with (for Vladimir these are his erratic internal workings, for Estragon his sore feet and bad dreams), but both are waiting for Godot, the deliverer who is somehow to relieve them from their torment—a nebulous, deity-like figure whom they don't know much about and don't quite believe in. All that happens is that in each act Pozzo, a wealthy land-owner, passes by with his slave, Lucky.

On the first occasion Pozzo arrogantly displays his wealth, his power over Lucky, his pride in the latter's accomplishments; he also reveals, unconsciously, his own lonely need for an audience. Lucky is shown as a sort of sub-human automaton who performs to order—"dancing" with pathetic incompetence, and "thinking" in a bizarre parody of science and pseudo-scientific jargon. The second time, Pozzo is blind and Lucky is dumb. Each act ends with the appearance of a boy, a messenger from Godot, who assures them that Godot will meet them in the same spot the following evening without fail.

In this extraordinary mélange of sordidness, poetry and music-hall farce, the ingredients have been drawn together into a subtly profound pattern. In the first, the unrelenting misery and pointlessness of life on "this bitch of an earth" is built up piece by piece; even the unattractive figure of Pozzo has its function in representing the nothingness of worldly success. At this stage we (like the protagonists) still believe that Godot exists, and may yet come. As the second act starts, we wonder how on earth the author can contrive to vary the pattern, to give any dramatic development. In fact, by a further turn of the screw we are led to realise now that in their talk Estragon and Vladimir are merely trying desperately to fill a void—to pass the time somehow. As Estragon says about their farcical efforts to try on a pair of old boots, "We always find something, eh, Didi, to give us the impression that we exist?" The now-miserable Pozzo is for them no more than a diversion; and when he falls down and appeals to them for help, their response is hopelessly and ludicrously bungled. The point is that this time we know that there will be no deliverance—ever; and we suspect that they know it too.

Beckett has created in this play a vague disembodied world peopled by extraordinary characters, who are simple, indeed almost lunatic, yet somehow recognisably human in their distortion of human traits. We sympathise and feel with Estragon and Vladimir; and despite the thoroughgoing way in which the play presents despair, futility, and sordid nothingness, it is saved from unrelieved nihilism by a muted sense of human comradeship which emerges from the relationship between the two protagonists. It is impossible, however, to give in summary any adequate impression of the texture of this remarkable work; one can only record the conviction that, unlikely as it may sound, this is the one indisputable masterpiece which the decade has produced.

Beckett's subsequent plays, *End Game* and *Krapp's Last Tape*, seem to have missed the peculiar and elusive balance which constitutes the real success of *Waiting for Godot*. In the same way, it is impossible to feel satisfied with the radio play, *All That Fall*, which Beckett wrote for the B.B.C.'s Third Programme in 1957; interesting and arresting though this was to listen to, one had the feeling that the author's technique had dissolved into an incoherence which failed to communicate.

Angus Wilson had reached the age of thirty-five when he published his first volume of fiction, a collection of short stories entitled *The Wrong Set* (1949). Here—as in the stories in *Such Darling Dodos* (1950) and *A Bit off the Map* (1957)— the characters are sharply observed and skilfully delineated, but the writer's approach to them is hard, external, even a shade cruel. They give almost the impression of botanists' specimens impaled and held up for unsympathetic examination. A similar technique is used to people the background of Wilson's novels, where there sometimes results a disharmony between the fully-rounded portrayal of the main protagonists and the slightly malicious caricature which serves for the minor characters. Indeed, there is perhaps an element of self-indulgence in the sharp contrast which is drawn, in the world of these novels, between the "us" (the sensitive and intelligent few with whom the author clearly identifies himself) and the unattractive "them" who make up the unregenerate majority.

For all that, *Hemlock and After* (1952) is a remarkably accomplished piece of work which displays none of the weaknesses one expects to find in a first novel. Bernard Sands, a distinguished novelist and Grand Old Man of letters, has fathered a scheme to use Vardon Hall as a democratically-run retreat for young writers. He, himself, is a liberal humanist, his intellectual attitude marked by a "habitual irony" which has led him to an "eternal questioning of their best-loved 'truths'". Latterly, nevertheless, a "growing apprehension of evil" has begun to "disrupt his comprehension of the world". In the novel, this evil is symbolised above all by Mrs Curry, a repulsive procuress and black-mailer, and Sherman Winters, a bullying theatrical "queer". Bernie falls foul of both, and, ultimately, after his death, thwarts both. The novel is, in fact, an assertion, qualified, half-apologetic, but determined, of liberal humanist values (rational, sceptical, disinterested, founded in a belief in the value of the individual) against a fashionable neo-authoritarianism ("the imposition of dogmatic spiritual values").

Yet the story of Sands himself up to his death is one of increasing uncertainty, self-distrust, and disillusionment. At the outset we are told that "Bernard's humanism was not the less violently held because he had lately begun to doubt whether it was a totally adequate answer". His self-doubt grows as a result of an uncomfortable conversation with his daughter Elizabeth about his own homosexual proclivities; he feels no real guilt, yet is aware of inadequacy in his self-justification. Later, when he sees a man arrested in Leicester Square for importuning, he becomes conscious of a violent sadistic excitement within himself. This unexpected experience gives him a new and intense awareness of motive—"the dual nature of all human action"—so that he makes a disastrous speech at the opening of the Vardon Hall project. Only Ella, his withdrawn and melancholic wife, understands what he is getting at in his repeated circling round the theme that "motives were so difficult, so double"; she sees that in the upbringing of their own children they have been wrong "only in motive" ("we did the right thing for the wrong reason"), and after the speech she makes a slow and agonised return from mental illness to the real world. Despite his growing self-distrust, Bernie continues his struggle against the evil which he now sees all around him; but he is ill, and his efforts are feeble and unavailing. Nevertheless, after his death his influence lives on, not because of what he has done but because of what he was.

> "My dear," Ella replied, "doing doesn't last, even if one knows what one's doing, which one usually doesn't. But Bernard *was* something to people—lots of people—me, for example—and that has its effect in the end, I think."

The central scene of the garden party at Vardon Hall is brilliantly realised; and the novel as a whole achieves a mature complexity in the orchestration of its themes. The humanism that is reaffirmed in the course of it is modified and cautious (as Ella puts it, "Such a lot of wicked things get mixed up with any good one does"), but its courage and honesty command unqualified respect.

The tone of *Anglo-Saxon Attitudes* (1956) is more aggressively self-confident, almost at times jaunty. Gerald Middleton, Emeritus Professor of Medieval History, is "a man of mildly but persistent depressive temperament" who has never faced up to the facts about his own life. In particular, he has always repressed his suspicion that the discovery of Bishop Eorpwald's tomb, in which he was remotely involved as a young man, may have been a malicious fake. Led now to investigate and search for evidence, he is brought face to face with various aspects of his earlier life—particularly his relationship with his neurotic wife, his worthless children, and his former mistress, Dollie. Dollie had at one time been the wife of Gilbert Stokesay, a fascist-minded associate of Wyndham Lewis and T. E Hulme, who is proved in the end to have perpetrated the archaeological hoax as a heartless practical joke against his historian father. The scandalous truth publicly established at last, Middleton comes to terms with himself, and at the close of the novel is embarked (in manic mood by now) on a further phase in his life-work, editing the new medieval history and writing his long-deferred masterpiece on Edward the Confessor. In this entertaining and engaging novel, Angus Wilson handles his crowded canvas with great skill, though one might perhaps object to a certain over-ingenuity about the way in which the generous supply of incident is contrived and knit together (a lack of the art which conceals art). But the full-length characterisation of Middleton himself is wholly convincing, while the atmosphere of the academic world has been caught to perfection.

In her first novel, *Under the Net*, Iris Murdoch showed herself at once to have the born novelist's flair for inventing situations and characters which are capable of bodying forth a deeper meaning. In this case, the theme is a young man's discovery of his true vocation as a creative writer; and the setting, in the rootless bohemianism of London intellectual life, enables the writer to exploit a marked gift for bizarre comedy. After this singularly promising beginning, Iris Murdoch's next two novels were somewhat disappointing. *The Flight from the Enchanter*, though it contained some striking episodes, seemed, as a whole, bafflingly overcharged with a confused and heavy symbolism; while *The Sandcastle*, for all its interest and accomplishment, had a disturbing unreality which made it impossible to believe sufficiently in either the characters themselves or in the minor public school where the action took place. Far more impressive was *The Bell* (1958), which is essentially a study, penetrating yet compassionately sympathetic, of opposed types of moral and religious conviction. The setting of this novel is a lay religious community which has made its home in a country house adjacent to an Anglican convent. A complicated but persuasive plot has been constructed round the installation of a new bell in the Abbey, and the discovery of its long-lost medieval predecessor in the mud of the lake. Here, too, the action is tinged with a certain element of fantasy, at times grotesque, at times almost poetic; but as the events unfold with an inner logic of their own, we find ourselves prepared to accept them on their own level of reality—a level which has been deliberately distanced and set apart from the everyday world. In this book, the novelist has again found a satisfying embodiment for her themes, enabling her to express in fictional terms moral perceptions which could not be stated in any other way.

We turn, finally, to the group of younger writers who obviously constitute the characteristic "movement" of the decade. What they have in common is mainly an outraged sense of rebellion against the establishment in all its forms, a repudiation of the literary aims and values of their immediate predecessors, and a conscious intention to forge new means of expression which shall be more honest, unpretentious, and true to the real facts of contemporary experience. Inevitably, the poets, novelists, and dramatists each envisage this new beginning a little differently, according to the problems of their own medium. It is, perhaps, among the dramatists that one can most easily trace a homogeneity of aim, even though (or perhaps because) the movement emerged slightly later in the theatre than in fiction and poetry. In his essay "Theatre and Living" (included in the volume *Declarations*, published in 1957), Kenneth Tynan castigated the West End stage for its continued acceptance of outmoded, comfortably-smug assumptions which consistently insulated its audience from any contact with living contemporary issues. Claiming that "our stages are still overgrown with petty snobberies and glib acceptances", he went on to charge that ". . . the really big belligerent international problems—poverty, ignorance, oppression, and the rest—are theatrically shunned . . . The job of the new playwrights is to remove the rubble, to sweep the floor; to make room in a theatre which is, as Arthur Miller said, 'hermetically sealed off from life' for the real causes of contemporary human pain. This means that a number of simple platitudes must be reasserted . . ." This complaint against the shallowness, complacency, and unreality of the post-war London theatre was in itself by no means new; Terence Rattigan, himself a successful playwright who had worked within the conventions trying piecemeal to enlarge them, had already expressed his own frustrations in terms of the image of Aunt Edna—the typical middle-class theatre-goer whose expectations must always be satisfied and whose sense of the proprieties must on no account be outraged. Tynan went on, however, to contend that certain "younger

adherents" of the Left (he clearly had John Osborne principally in mind) were already "recalling the writer to the
writer's basic job, which is never to lose sight of the ways
in which ordinary people think and feel and eat and earn
and work". In John Osborne's highly-successful first play,
Look Back in Anger (1956), it is perhaps easier to recognise
the "simple platitudes" than the "ordinary people". The
central character, Jimmy Porter, is an ex-student who earns
his living by keeping a sweet-stall in the market-place of a
provincial town, and has taken his revenge upon society by
marrying a conventional upper-class girl named Alison; they
live in a curious but perfectly innocent three-cornered ménage
with Jimmy's friend Cliff Lewis. The plot, such as it is, is
banal in the extreme (though perhaps it should be admitted
that this does not necessarily disqualify it from being "true
to life"). Alison is expecting a baby, though she has not
told Jimmy of this. Her friend, Helena, who, unlike the
rest of the characters, believes in churchgoing, the existence
of sin, and the importance of right and wrong, persuades
Alison to leave her intolerable life with Jimmy and return
home. From Jimmy's point of view, however, his wife's
crowning betrayal is her refusal to accompany him to the
deathbed of Mrs Tanner, the "common" mother of his closest
friend. Immediately Alison has left, Helena falls into
Jimmy's arms and steps into her friend's place. Some
months later, Alison returns, having lost her baby through
a miscarriage, and Helena leaves. The final curtain shows a
reconciliation between husband and wife, the point being,
apparently, that Alison's new-found experience of suffering
will now enable her to understand and commiserate with
Jimmy's discontents, whereas previously she tried to maintain
a detached neutrality.

The emotional centre of the play is to be found not in
these events, but in the angry tirades from Jimmy for which
they provide a pretext. What makes the play so difficult
to accept is that this anger seems insufficiently explained.
Much of the time it looks like mere selfish petulance, but it
is alleged to have deep social roots and to represent an

important protest against the gutless, hypocritical world of to-day. We are told that it started when, as a mere boy, he watched his father die of wounds received in the Spanish Civil War.

> "You see, I learnt at an early age what it was to be angry and helpless. And I can never forget it . . . I knew more about—love . . . betrayal . . . and death, when I was ten years old than you will probably ever know all your life."

This personal distress is merged somewhat inconsequently with a more generalised indictment:

> "There aren't any good brave causes left. If the big bang does come, and we all get killed off, it won't be in aid of the old-fashioned grand design. It'll just be for the Brave-New-nothing-very-much-thank you. About as pointless and inglorious as stepping in front of a bus."

What gave the play its pull in the theatre was no doubt this forceful expression of a disgruntlement which is widely felt, but is seldom uttered in public. It would be hard to deny that *Look Back in Anger* is callow, confused, and at times embarrassingly sentimental. Nevertheless, there is an awkward sincerity about the self-pity which makes its way through the dramatist's technical ineptitude, giving the effect of a genuine outburst of strong feeling that is rare in the theatre. It can scarcely be claimed that the result is a work of art, but it remains difficult to shrug off.

In his next play, *The Entertainer* (1957), John Osborne, though still concerned with the "big belligerent international problems", has abandoned naturalism in favour of an expressionistic use of music-hall techniques. Scenes in which we see Archie Rice, the seedy music-hall comedian, dispensing his tired patter and mechanical songs alternate with others showing his shiftless, disorganised family life. Here Osborne's talent is more unmistakable, even if it shows itself mainly in the local details; he has, for instance, a marked ability to create dialogue that catches the tone of ordinary conversation, while at the same time conveying a criticism of the valuations which underlie such conversation. Yet the larger structure remains singularly incoherent; and the story-element can only get by because it takes places largely off-stage and is marginal to the main interest, which is that of defining an attitude or feeling. Archie Rice seems intended to typify not only the dying English music-hall, but also the decadence of England itself—an England conscious of its own decay, but capable only of continuing to go through the same old meaningless gestures. At times, particularly in the character of Jean Rice, Archie's daughter, the disgust-reactions do succeed in generating a slightly more positive energy.

> "Here we are, we're alone in the universe, there's no God, it just seems that it all began by something as simple as sunlight striking on a piece of rock. And here we are. We've only got ourselves. Somehow, we've just got to make a go of it. We've only ourselves."

More generally, however, the only value asserted seems to be that of protest—protest for its own sake, however unorganised or ineffective. As Jean says of her brother:

> "Poor Frank! . . . he went and said no [to the call-up] and what's more, he went to jail for it. Oh, he gave in eventually, but he said no for six months of his poor protected life—he said no! I think that's something."

One certainly hopes that Mr Osborne will eventually acquire the self-discipline which would enable him to make fuller use of his evident gifts—though the easy success of these two plays may be thought to make this less rather than more likely. (In 1959, his satirical "musical", *The World of Paul Slickey*, had an unfavourable reception and only a brief run.) On the other hand, his talent, even in its present raw state, can be seen to make a considerable impact. The young enthuse over his work; the middle-aged and elderly are enraged by it. If getting people's backs up was part of Mr Osborne's aim, he can be said to have had a success which is more than merely commercial. The commercial success itself, moreover, has had the beneficial effect of letting loose, in London and elsewhere, a flood of theatrical activity of a new kind. For the first time for many years, young writers have been able to get plays produced dealing, not with the plush lives of members of the upper-income brackets, but with such diverse subjects as national servicemen in Malaya, working-class family life, capital punishment, workers on a building-site, and so on. Much of the credit for these enlarged opportunities belongs to George Devine's English Stage Company (operating at the Royal Court Theatre, where John Osborne's plays were first performed) and to Joan Greenwood's Theatre Workshop, which has its home at Stratford, in East London. Among the more promising authors to be brought to light so far may be mentioned Brendan Behan (*The Quare Fellow* and *The Hostage*), Shelagh Delaney (*A Taste of Honey*), and Arnold Wesker (*Chicken Soup with Barley* and *Roots*). Even though the general level of achievement (and even of competence) characteristic of this new drama may not be particularly high, it can at least be said that the atmosphere to-day is a good deal more favourable to the recognition and development of fresh talent than it was half-a-dozen years ago.

It may be suspected that the intellectual cachet which has accrued to expressions of anger during the current decade owes a good deal to the influence of George Orwell, a markedly uneven writer with a puzzlingly inflated reputation among the current younger generation. Overtly, what is valued in Orwell is his "frankness"—his insistent claim to tell the truth just as he sees it, in detail and without distortion by any preconceived set of ideas. It cannot be said that Orwell lived up at all consistently to his own ideal; he was far too committed a writer for that—committed even in the nature and strength of his own violent reaction against all political thinking and all political action. What is left behind, however, from a reading of his essays and fiction, seems to be above all a hatred of cant, a distaste for all constructive social effort, and an overpowering bitterness. Alongside these attitudes (considerably watered down) we may trace in the work of such younger novelists as Kingsley Amis and John Braine the influence, surprising but demonstrable, of so very different a writer as C. P. Snow. The influence has come not so much from Snow's own example as from his precept—his expressed demand that the novel should abandon, as a fruitless dead-end, all poetic or stream-of-consciousness pretensions and return, instead, to a straightforward naturalism which concentrates on plausibility of surface, recognisable characters, and an accurate sense of period and locality. An almost unnoticed precursor of the *Lucky Jim* school was William Cooper, himself a close associate, professionally, of C. P. Snow, and a convinced adherent of the older novelist's views about the future of fiction. His first two novels, *Scenes from Provincial Life* (1950) and *The Struggles of Albert Woods* (1952), share between them almost all the ingredients that were later to bring resounding success to Kingsley Amis's first novel: a flat narrative style, a certain amount of broad comedy, a strong feeling for local colour, some calculated impropriety, an exposure of the manoeuvring and chicanery which is necessary for success in the university world, a preoccupation with what the sociologists call "upward social mobility", and a hard unscrupulousness of attitude towards the wiles of a designing young woman. In their cheerful unpretentiousness, these two novels are, in fact, more consistently lively and entertaining than *Lucky Jim* itself; and it is a pity that in his subsequent novels Cooper has lapsed into either a cheap cynicism (as in *The Ever-Interesting Topic*) or a dull portentousness (as in *Young People*).

Though more derivative than it may have at first appeared, *Lucky Jim* (1954) is amusing enough in its own way. Jim Dixon, temporary assistant-lecturer at a Redbrick university, is presented as an "average man" caught up among a bunch of pretentious phonies and finding, in the end, that he is too honest to be able to play the academic racket successfully. There is some telling satire at the expense of university professors, and a good deal of energetic slapstick, culminating in the public lecture, in the course of which Dixon, hopelessly drunk, inadvertently mimics professors and Principal in turn.

Perhaps it is in keeping with the unambitious spirit of all this that the issues raised should be naively evaded in the end by the introduction of an unlikely millionaire, who rescues Lucky Jim from the corrupt university world by offering him an "honest" job in commerce. A more serious weakness is the somewhat equivocal attitude towards Dixon himself; presumably he is intended to represent, in his own person, an indictment of the failure of provincial universities to exert any educative influence on even their most examination-proud products, but it is doubtful if the author thinks his hero quite such an uncouth boor as we do.

Kingsley Amis's next novel, *That Uncertain Feeling* (1955), is rather more serious in intent, and also has a more organised structure and a more consistent tone. His hero this time is a public library assistant in a Welsh town; married and hard-up, he is taken up by the nymphomaniac wife of a local bigwig, who both seduces him and arranges a better job for him. Much of the local detail is both convincing and highly amusing; the account of the interview for the post of deputy-librarian, for instance, is a brilliant piece of sustained comedy. Once again there comes a point at which the hero rebels against the tortuous dishonesty which is necessary if one is to get ahead in the middle-class rat-race. ("I don't like fiddles.") He refuses the offered promotion with a defiant gesture, and takes himself off to a minor clerical job with the National Coal Board in his father's mining village, the happy ending this time being presented as a commendable return to decent, unpretentious working-class standards and values. This book does at least suggest that Mr Amis's talents might be capable of reaching more ambitious targets than any he has so far attempted. His third novel appeared, in part, in *Punch*, and is best forgotten.

Lucky Jim has had its host of imitators, but the only one that calls for attention here is *Room at the Top* (1957). In this highly accomplished first novel, John Braine has given his own distinctive imprint to similar material, at the same time shaping it into a far more telling pattern. The setting is a North Country town whose life and physical presence is

realised with convincing solidity. The narrator and central
character is a scholarship boy who has worked his way up to
a comfortable position in the treasurer's department at the
Town Hall; concurrently with an unexpectedly serious emotional entanglement with a married woman older than himself, he achieves his ambitions by seducing the attractive
young daughter of a local industrialist and ultimately marrying her. The point which is hammered home is the price
which has to be paid, in terms of lost integrity and joy in
living, for worldly success—"the muck one's forced to wade
through to get what one wants". At times, Mr Braine finds
it necessary to fill in the gaps by falling back on a tight-lipped,
sub-Hemingway idiom; but where the subject-matter comes
within the scope of his first-hand experience he renders his
themes with authenticity and power.

As far as the younger poets are concerned, a representative
statement of their aims is to be found in Robert Conquest's
introduction to the anthology, *New Lines* (1956). Conquest claims explicitly that "a general tendency has once
again set in, and a genuine and healthy poetry of the new
period has established itself". The new school is differentiated from the typical poetry of the thirties in that it "sub-
mits to no great systems of theoretical constructs", and from
that of the forties in that it is not at the mercy of the unconscious demands of the Id. Instead, the new poetry is characterised by an "empirical attitude to all that comes" and a
"reverence for the real person or event", accompanied on
the technical side by a "refusal to abandon a rational structure and comprehensible language, even when the verse is
most highly charged with sensuous or emotional intent". In
reality, it seems clear that the *New Lines* group is in a more
direct line of descent from the poetry of the thirties than this
account would imply. Thus, echoes of Auden and Empson
are not uncommon in the work of Kingsley Amis, John Wain,
and even Robert Conquest himself; while it is noticeable that
the verse of the rather older poet Roy Fuller, who derives
more directly from the early Auden, often takes on a surface
appearance very similar to that of the *New Lines* poets. It

is evident that what these writers are reacting against, principally, is the tangled rhetoric of Edith Sitwell, Dylan Thomas, and the "Apocalypse" movement. Indeed, it often seems to be Dylan Thomas who has been cast for the role of villain-in-chief. Thus Kingsley Amis, in reviewing Thomas's volume of stories, *A Prospect of the Sea*, dismissed them peremptorily as the work of "ranting, canting Thomas the Rhymer", and castigated those readers who "hanker after something sublimer than thinking". "That something," he contended, "Thomas wasted his talent and integrity in trying to provide."

The dust has not yet settled on Dylan Thomas's reputation, so that any estimate at present must be a personal one. My own view is that Thomas had a genuine minor talent, which was steadily dissipated in his later work by a persistent striving after grandiose and largely meaningless verbal effects and by a habit of playing to the gallery, which was bound, in the end, to undermine his artistic integrity. The cheapness of effect with which he came finally to be satisfied can be studied in his radio play, *Under Milk Wood* (1954); this has had immense popular success, and has acquired immense prestige, but its real quality seems to me sufficiently characterised by the critic who described it as "the best vaudeville show of a generation". By contrast, one feels compelled to applaud the determination of these younger poets to achieve an uninflated precision of statement, unclouded by pseudo-poetic verbiage, and the verse that results is usually both respectable and interesting, even though it may at times seem a trifle dry, flat, and earthbound. Kingsley Amis's *A Case of Samples* (1956) is ironic in tone (often uneasily or defensively so), and strikes a note of slightly self-conscious cleverness; nevertheless, he is capable at times of achieving distinct successes of a rather limited kind. A more distinctive voice is that of Philip Larkin, whose volume *The Less Deceived* (1955) suggests the presence of a considerable, if still nascent, talent. His poems are quiet, unemphatic, almost self-deprecatory; but they have a sincerity of feeling and a careful exactness of texture which repays repeated re-reading.

Mention should also be made of D. J. Enright, whose casual colloquial idiom owes a good deal to the free verse of D. H. Lawrence. Many of the poems in his *Bread Rather Than Blossoms* (1956) have an ironic poise which enables him to approach (as in his "Monuments of Hiroshima") the larger and more serious topics which other members of the group are inclined to shy away from.

In general, then, we can say that at the end of the decade the younger writers, whether poets, novelists, or dramatists, are pursuing unexceptionable aims, and pursuing them with what we may admit to be (in Robert Conquest's phrase) a commendable "determination to avoid bad principles". If they have produced little as yet that seems destined to last, at least the atmosphere they have created is a healthier one than we have seen for a long time. One noticeable feature of their work, however, is a tendency to address themselves not to the common reader, but more exclusively to members of their own generation—the under-thirties or the under-thirty-fives. One wonders whether this foreshadows a permanent stratification of the serious reading-public along age-division lines, to match the parallel division which has already developed in the commercial "culture" of the cinema, popular music, and television. And will this habit of mind make it more difficult for the younger writers to move towards full artistic maturity as they, in their turn, grow older? But the answers to these questions must be left to the nineteen-sixties.

FOR FURTHER READING

Chapter I

(a) General

E. BATHO and BONAMY DOBRÉE. *The Victorians and After,* 1830-1914. 1938.

DAVID DAICHES. *The Present Age after 1920.* 1958.

B. IFOR EVANS. *English Literature Between the Wars.* 1948.

J. ISAACS. *An Assessment of Twentieth-Century Literature.* 1951.

EDWIN MUIR. *The Present Age from 1914.* 1939.

A. R. READE. *Main Currents in Modern Literature.* 1935.

H. V. ROUTH. *English Literature and Ideas in the Twentieth Century.* 1946.

ROBERT SPEIGHT and others. *Since 1939.* 1949.

STEPHEN SPENDER. *The Destructive Element. A Study of Modern Writers and Beliefs.* 1935.

FRANK SWINNERTON. *The Georgian Literary Scene.* 1935.

SHERARD VINES. *A Hundred Years of English Literature,* 1830-1930. 1950.

(b) Poetry

KENNETH ALLOTT. *Contemporary Verse.* (The Penguin Poets.) 1950. Introductory and other Notes.

CLEANTH BROOKS. *Modern Poetry and the Tradition.* 1948.

G. BULLOUGH. *The Trend of Modern Poetry.* 1934.

D. DAICHES. *Poetry and the Modern World.* 1939.

B. DEUTSCH. *This Modern Poetry.* 1936.

G. R. HAMILTON. *The Tell-Tale Article. A Critical approach to Modern Poetry.* 1949.

J. HEATH-STUBBS and D. WRIGHT. *The Faber Book of Twentieth Century Verse.* 1953.

F. R. LEAVIS. *New Bearings in English Poetry.* 1932. 2nd ed. 1950.

C. DAY LEWIS. *A Hope for Poetry.* 1934.

L. MACNEICE. *Modern Poetry.* 1938.

R. L. MEGROZ. *Modern English Poetry, 1882-1932.* 1933.
HERBERT PALMER. *Post-Victorian Poetry.* 1938.
V. DE SOLA PINTO. *Crisis in English Poetry, 1880-1940.* 1951.
MICHAEL ROBERTS (editor). *The Faber Book of Modern Verse.* 2nd ed., with supplement of poems chosen by Anne Ridler. 1951.
D. S. SAVAGE. *The Personal Principle. Studies in Modern Poetry.* 1944.
EDITH SITWELL. *Aspects of Modern Poetry.* 1934.
ANTHONY THWAITE. *Contemporary English Poetry.* 1959.
W. B. YEATS. *The Oxford Book of Modern Verse.* 1936. Introduction.

CHAPTER II

C. M. BOWRA. *The Heritage of Symbolism.* 1943. Chap. VI.
R. ELLMANN. *Yeats: the Man and the Masks.* 1949.
The Identity of Yeats. 1954.
T. R. HENN. *The Lonely Tower.* 1951.
J. M. HONE. *W. B. Yeats, 1865-1939.* 1942.
NORMAN JEFFARES. *W. B. Yeats. Man and Poet.* 1949.
L. MACNEICE. *The Poetry of W. B. Yeats.* 1941.
V. K. N. MENON. *The Development of Yeats.* 1942.
STEPHEN SPENDER. *The Destructive Element.* 1935. Chap. VI.
EDMUND WILSON. *Axel's Castle.* 1936.
W. B. YEATS. *Autobiographies.* 1955.

CHAPTER III

Kipling. HILTON BROWN. *Rudyard Kipling.* 1945.
CHARLES CARRINGTON. *Rudyard Kipling. His Life and and Works.* 1955.
T. S. ELIOT. *A Choice of Kipling's Verse . . . with an Essay.* 1941.
C. S. LEWIS. "Kipling's World": in *Literature and Life, Addresses to the English Association.* 1948.
GEORGE ORWELL. *Critical Essays.* 1946.
E. SHANKS. *Rudyard Kipling.* 1940.
EDMUND WILSON. *The Wound and the Bow.* 1941.

De la Mare. *A Tribute to Walter de la Mare on his 75th Birthday.* 1948.

    H. C. DUFFIN. *Walter de la Mare: a Study of his Poetry.* 1949.

    FORREST REID. *Walter de la Mare.* 1929.

GLENN HUGHES. *Imagism and the Imagists.* 1931.

T. E. HULME. *Speculations.* 1924.

W. JERROLD. *Alfred Noyes.* 1931.

MICHAEL ROBERTS. *T. E. Hulme.* 1938.

MURIEL SPARK. *John Masefield.* 1953.

EDWARD THOMPSON. *Robert Bridges.* 1944.

CHARLES WILLIAMS. "Robert Bridges": *Critical Essays, XX Century.* (World's Classics.)

<h2 style="text-align:center">CHAPTER IV</h2>

Wilfred Owen. EDMUND BLUNDEN (editor). *The Poems of Wilfred Owen.* 1933. Memoir and Notes.

    D. DAICHES. *New Literary Values.* 1936.

    SIR OSBERT SITWELL. "Wilfred Owen": *Penguin New Writing,* No. 27. 1946.

Edward Thomas. *Collected Poems.* 1936. Foreword by Walter de la Mare.

    ALDOUS HUXLEY. *On the Margin.* 1923.

    JOHN MOORE. *The Life and Letters of Edward Thomas.* 1939.

    HELEN THOMAS. *As It Was.* 1926.

    World Without End. 1931.

CHARLES MORGAN. *Reflections in a Mirror.* Second Series. 1946. Essay on Robert Nichols.

ROBERT NICHOLS (editor). *Anthology of War Poetry,* 1914–1918. 1943. With long preface.

<h2 style="text-align:center">CHAPTER V</h2>

Hopkins. *Poems.* 2nd ed. 1930. Introduction by Charles Williams.

    C. C. ABBOTT (editor). *Letters, mainly to Robert Bridges and R. W. Dixon.* 1935.

W. H. GARDNER. *Gerard Manley Hopkins, 1844-1889.*
2 vols. 1944, 1949.

HUMPHRY HOUSE (editor). *The Notebooks and Papers of Gerard Manley Hopkins.* 1937.

F. R. LEAVIS. *New Bearings in English Poetry.* 1932.

E. E. PHARE. *The Poetry of Gerard Manley Hopkins.* 1933.

JOHN PICK. *Gerard Manley Hopkins, Priest and Poet.* 1942.

HERBERT READ. *Collected Essays.* 1938.

ELEANOR RUGGLES. *Gerard Manley Hopkins. A Life.* 1947.

J. G. SOUTHWORTH. *Sowing the Spring.* 1940.

T. S. Eliot. C. M. BOWRA. *The Creative Experiment.* 1949.

ELIZABETH DREW. *T. S. Eliot: the design of his poetry.* 1950.

HELEN GARDNER. *The Art of T. S. Eliot.* 1949.

D. W. HARDING. Review of *Collected Poems, 1909-1935* in *Scrutiny,* Sept. 1936.

F. R. LEAVIS. *New Bearings in English Poetry.* 1932.

F. O. MATTHIESSEN. *The Achievement of T. S. Eliot.* 1935. 2nd ed. 1947.

D. E. S. MAXWELL. *The Poetry of T. S. Eliot.* 1952.

K. NOTT. *The Emperor's Clothes.* (On T. S. Eliot, Graham Greene, and others.) 1953.

RAYMOND PRESTON. *"Four Quartets" Rehearsed.* 1946.

B. RAJAN (editor). *T. S. Eliot, A Study of his Writings by Several Hands.* 1948.

STEPHEN SPENDER. *The Destructive Element.* 1935. Chaps. VII and VIII.

EDMUND WILSON. *Axel's Castle.* 1936.

CHAPTER VI

ROY CAMPBELL. *Light on a Dark Horse.* 1951. Autobiography.

RICHARD CHURCH. *Eight for Immortality.* 1941. Essays on W. H. Davies, De la Mare, Robert Frost, Yeats, Blunden, V. Sackville-West, T. S. Eliot, and Robert Graves.

CHARLES MORGAN. *Reflections in a Mirror.* Second Series. "Edmund Blunden's 'Thomasine'."

Edith Sitwell. DENYS VAL BAKER (editor). *Writers of Today.* 1946. Essay by Henry Reed.

C. M. BOWRA. *Edith Sitwell.* 1947.

MARTIN GILKES. *A Key to Modern English Poetry.* 1937.

R. L. MEGROZ. *The Three Sitwells.* 1926.

EDITH SITWELL. *Selected Poems. With an Essay on her Own Poetry.* 1936.

Preface to *The Collected Poems of Sacheverell Sitwell.* 1936.

CHAPTER VII

RUTH BAILEY. *A Dialogue on Modern Poetry.* 1939.

JOSEPH WARREN BEACH. *The Making of the Auden Canon.* 1957.

DAVID DAICHES. *Poetry and the Modern World.* 1939.

RICHARD HOGGART. *Auden. An Introductory Essay.* 1951.

C. ISHERWOOD. *Lions and Shadows.* 1938. Semi-autobiographical.

C. DAY LEWIS. *A Hope for Poetry.* 1934.

D. S. SAVAGE. *The Personal Principle.* 1944.

F. SCARFE. *Auden and After.* 1942.
W. H. Auden. 1948.

J. G. SOUTHWORTH. *Sowing the Spring.* 1940.

STEPHEN SPENDER. *World Within World.* 1951. Autobiography.

HENRY TREECE. *How I Saw Apocalypse.* 1946.
Dylan Thomas. 1949.

CHAPTER VIII

GEOFFREY GRIGSON. *Poetry of the Present.* 1949. Anthology with Introduction.

C. DAY LEWIS. *Collected Poems.* 1954.

MICHAEL MEYER (editor). *The Collected Poems of Sidney Keyes.* 1945. Memoir and Notes.

E. OLSON. *The Poetry of Dylan Thomas.* 1954.

ALAN ROSS. *Poetry, 1945-1950.* 1951.

STEPHEN SPENDER. *Life and the Poet.* 1942.
> *Poetry since* 1939. 1946. See Speight in List to
> Chapter I (*a*).
DEREK STANFORD. *Dylan Thomas.* 1954.

CHAPTER IX

DENYS VAL BAKER (editor). *Writers of Today.* 1946.
> Essays on Aldous Huxley, Graham Greene, James Joyce,
> J. B. Priestley, Dorothy Sayers, and E. M. Forster.
PHYLLIS BENTLEY. *The English Regional Novel.* 1941.
CLEMENCE DANE. *Tradition and Hugh Walpole.* 1930.
ELIZABETH DREW. *The Modern Novel.* 1926.
G. U. ELLIS. *Twilight on Parnassus.* 1939.
Hardy. DAVID CECIL. *Hardy the Novelist.* 1943.
> W. R. RUTLAND. *Thomas Hardy. A Study of his
> Writings and their Background.* 1938.
D. M. HOARE. *Some Studies in the Modern Novel.* 1938.
> Chapters on E. M. Forster, Virginia Woolf, Hardy and
> Conrad, George Moore and Joyce.
HUGH KENNER. *Wyndham Lewis.* 1954.
ARNOLD KETTLE. *An Introduction to the English Novel.
Vol. II, Henry James to the Present Day.* 1953.
F. O. MATTHIESSEN. *Henry James. The Major Phase.* 1946.
NORMAN NICHOLSON. *Man and Literature.* 1943. Contains
> discussion of Bennett, Wells, D. H. Lawrence, Aldous
> Huxley, James Joyce.
H. C. PORTEOUS. *Wyndham Lewis.* 1932.
V. S. PRITCHETT. *The Living Novel.* 1946. Essays on
> Wells, Bennett, D. H. Lawrence, Conrad, and "The
> Russians".
HENRY REED. *The Novel since* 1939. 1946. See Speight
> in List to Chapter I (*a*).
SIEGFRIED SASSOON. *George Meredith.* 1949.
MICHAEL SWAN. *Henry James.* 1953.

CHAPTER X

GEORGES LAFOURCADE. *Arnold Bennett. A Study.* 1939.
REGINALD POUND. *Arnold Bennett. A Biography.* 1952.

Chapter XI

NORMAN NICHOLSON. *H. G. Wells.* 1950.
A. VALLENTIN. *H. G. Wells: prophet of our day.* 1950.
H. G. WELLS. *An Experiment in Autobiography.* 1934.

Chapter XII

H. OULD. *Galsworthy.* 1934.

Chapter XIII

M. C. BRADBROOK. *Joseph Conrad.* 1941.
D. HEWITT. *Conrad: a reassessment.* 1952.
F. R. LEAVIS. *The Great Tradition.* 1948.
V. S. PRITCHETT. *The Living Novel.* 1946.
HUGH WALPOLE. *Joseph Conrad.* 1916.
VIRGINIA WOOLF. *The Common Reader.* 1925.

Chapter XIV

E. M. Forster. F. R. LEAVIS. *The Common Pursuit.* 1951.
ROSE MACAULAY. *The Writings of E. M. Forster.* 1938.
LIONEL TRILLING. *E. M. Forster.* 1944.
VIRGINIA WOOLF. *The Death of the Moth.* 1942.
See under Denys Val Baker and D. M. Hoare in List for
Chapter IX.

D. H. Lawrence. R. ALDINGTON. *Portrait of a Genius,
But . . .* 1950.
ANTHONY BEAL (editor). *D. H. Lawrence. Selected
Literary Criticism.* 1956.
FRIEDA LAWRENCE. *"Not I, but the Wind."* 1934.
F. R. LEAVIS. *The Common Pursuit.* 1951.
D. H. Lawrence. Novelist. 1955.
HARRY T. MOORE. *The Intelligent Heart: The Story of
D. H. Lawrence.* 1956.
J. MIDDLETON MURRY. *Son of Woman.* 1931.
ANTHONY WEST. *D. H. Lawrence.* 1951.
See G. U. Ellis, Norman Nicholson, and V. S. Pritchett in
List for Chapter IX.

Chapter XV

James Joyce. J. CAMPBELL and H. M. ROBINSON. *A Skeleton Key to Finnegans Wake.* 1947.

STUART GILBERT. *James Joyce's Ulysses.* 1930.

HERBERT GORMAN. *James Joyce: a definitive biography.* 1941.

R. M. KAIN. *Fabulous Voyager. James Joyce's Ulysses.* 1947.

HARRY LEVIN. *James Joyce.* 1944.

L. A. G. STRONG. *The Sacred River.* 1949.

W. Y. TINDALL. *James Joyce.* 1950.

J. A. WALDOCK. *James Joyce and Others.* 1937.

Virginia Woolf. JOAN BENNETT. *Virginia Woolf.* 1946.

BERNARD BLACKSTONE. *Virginia Woolf.* 1949.

DAVID DAICHES. *Virginia Woolf.* 1945.

E. M. FORSTER. *Virginia Woolf.* 1942.

D. M. HOARE. *Some Studies in the Modern Novel.* 1938.

LEONARD WOOLF (editor). *A Writer's Diary.* 1953.

Chapter XVI

Aldous Huxley. See Denys Val Baker, G. U. Ellis, and Norman Nicholson in the List for Chapter IX.

J. A. ATKINS. *Aldous Huxley.* 1956.

JOHN COWPER POWYS. *Autobiography.* 1934.

Porius. 1951. His latest novel.

Chapter XVII

K. ALLOTT and M. FARRIS. *Graham Greene.* 1951.

See Denys Val Baker, List to Chapter IX.

JOCELYN BROOKE. *Elizabeth Bowen.* 1952.

MARIE BÉATRICE MESNET. *Graham Greene and the Heart of the Matter.* 1954.

J. A. ATKINS. *Graham Greene.* 1957.

Chapter XVIII

ANTHONY ALPERS. *Katherine Mansfield.* 1954.

H. E. BATES. *The Modern Short Story.* 1940.

SYLVIA BERKMAN. *Katherine Mansfield. A Critical Study.*
     1952.
D. M. HOARE. *Some Studies in the Modern Novel.* 1938.
     "A Note on Katherine Mansfield."
J. MIDDLETON MURRY. *The Life of Katherine Mansfield.* 1933.
The Journal (1927) and *The Letters of Katherine Mansfield*
     (1928), edited by J. MIDDLETON MURRY.

CHAPTER XIX

WINIFRED BANNISTER. *James Bridie and his Theatre.* 1955.
H. GRANVILLE-BARKER. *On Poetry in Drama.* 1937.
GORDON BOTTOMLEY. *Plays and Poems.* With an Intro-
     duction by Claude Colleer Abbott. 1953.
E. A. BOYD. *Contemporary Drama of Ireland.* 1928.
W. A. DARLINGTON. *J. M. Barrie.* 1938.
T. H. DICKINSON. *Contemporary Drama of England.* 1931.
T. S. ELIOT. *Poetry and Drama.* 1951.
UNA ELLIS-FERMOR. *The Irish Dramatic Movement.* 2nd
     ed. 1954.
ST JOHN ERVINE. *Oscar Wilde: a Present Time Appraisal.*
     1951.
FREDERICK LUMLEY. *Trends in Twentieth Century Drama.*
     1956.
A. E. MORGAN. *Tendencies of Modern English Drama.* 1924.
MIDDLETON MURRY. *Unprofessional Essays.* (Chapter on
     the plays of T. S. Eliot.) 1956.
ALLARDYCE NICOLL. *British Drama.* 4th ed. 1947.
NORMAN NICHOLSON. *Man and Literature.* 1943. For Gals-
     worthy and Shaw.
RONALD PEACOCK. *The Poet in the Theatre.* 1946.
C. B. PURDOM. *Harley Granville Barker.* 1955.
ERNEST REYNOLDS. *Modern English Drama.* 1949.
PRISCILLA THOULESS. *Modern Poetic Drama.* 1938.
J. C. TREWIN. *The Theatre since* 1900. 1951.
     Dramatists of To-day. 1953.
ROBERT SPEIGHT. *Drama Since* 1939. See List, Chapter I (*a*).
J. M. SYNGE. *Plays, Poems and Prose.* Everyman Library.

The Player's Library (Faber) is a complete catalogue of the British Drama League Library.

CHAPTER XX

G. K. CHESTERTON. *George Bernard Shaw.* 1909.

J. S. COLLIS. *Shaw.* 1925.

ST JOHN ERVINE. *Bernard Shaw: His Life, Work and Friends.* 1956.

S. C. SEN GUPTA. *The Art of Bernard Shaw.* 1936.

SIR DESMOND MACCARTHY. *Shaw.* 1951.

HESKETH PEARSON. *G.B.S. A Postscript.* 1951.

R. F. RATTRAY. *Bernard Shaw: A Chronicle and an Introduction.* 1934.

G. B. SHAW. *Selected Prose.* Edited by D. Russell. 1953.

STEPHEN WINSTEN. *Salt and his Circle.* 1951. (Prefaced by the last writings of G.B.S.)

CHAPTER XXI

Admirable selections from the writings of Hilaire Belloc, G. K. Chesterton, and Robert Lynd are available in Dent's Everyman Library.

DAVID GARNETT. *The Essential T. E. Lawrence.* 1951.

R. HAMILTON. *W. H. Hudson: The Vision of Earth.* 1946.

JOHN HAYWARD. *Prose Literature since* 1939. See Speight in List to Chapter I (*a*).

MAISIE WARD. *Gilbert Keith Chesterton.* 1944.

POSTSCRIPT

KENNETH ALLSOP. *The Angry Decade.* 1958.

ROBERT CONQUEST (editor). *New Lines.* 1956.

Poems by Elizabeth Jennings, John Holloway, Philip Larkin, Thom Gunn, Kingsley Amis, D. J. Enright, Robert Conquest, Donald Davie, John Wain.

TOM MASCHLER (editor). *Declarations.* 1957.

Essays by Doris Lessing, Colin Wilson, John Osborne, John Wain, Kenneth Tynan, Bill Hopkins, Lindsay Anderson, Stuart Holroyd.

GENERAL

WRITERS AND THEIR WORK. This series published for the British Council and the National Book League, includes pamphlets on Elizabeth Bowen, Joyce Cary, I. Compton-Burnett, Conrad, De la Mare, E. M. Forster, Kipling, George Orwell, Bertrand Russell, Edith Sitwell, Osbert Sitwell, Evelyn Waugh, and Virginia Woolf.

INDEX

Main references are shown by clarendon type.